I, CONFEDERATE

~◎ THE LOCHLAINN SEABROOK COLLECTION ☜~

AMERICAN CIVIL WAR
Abraham Lincoln Was a Liberal, Jefferson Davis Was a Conservative: The Missing Key to Understanding the American Civil War
Confederacy 101: Amazing Facts You Never Knew About America's Oldest Political Tradition
Confederate Blood and Treasure: An Interview With Lochlainn Seabrook
Everything You Were Taught About African-Americans and the Civil War is Wrong, Ask a Southerner!
Everything You Were Taught About the Civil War is Wrong, Ask a Southerner!
Give This Book to a Yankee! A Southern Guide to the Civil War For Northerners
Heroes of the Southern Confederacy: The Illustrated Book of Confederate Officials, Soldiers, and Civilians
Lincoln's War: The Real Cause, the Real Winner, the Real Loser
The Great Yankee Coverup: What the North Doesn't Want You to Know About Lincoln's War!
The Ultimate Civil War Quiz Book: How Much Do You Really Know About America's Most Misunderstood Conflict?
Women in Gray: A Tribute to the Ladies Who Supported the Southern Confederacy

CONFEDERATE MONUMENTS
Confederate Monuments: Why Every American Should Honor Confederate Soldiers and Their Memorials

CONFEDERATE FLAG
Confederate Flag Facts: What Every American Should Know About Dixie's Southern Cross
What the Confederate Flag Means to Me: Americans Speak Out in Defense of Southern Honor, Heritage, and History

SECESSION
All We Ask Is To Be Let Alone: The Southern Secession Fact Book

SLAVERY
Everything You Were Taught About American Slavery is Wrong, Ask a Southerner!
Slavery 101: Amazing Facts You Never Knew About America's "Peculiar Institution"
The Bittersweet Bond: Race Relations in the Old South as Described by White and Black Southerners

CHILDREN
Honest Jeff and Dishonest Abe: A Southern Children's Guide to the Civil War
Saddle, Sword, and Gun: A Biography of Nathan Bedford Forrest For Teens

NATHAN BEDFORD FORREST
A Rebel Born: A Defense of Nathan Bedford Forrest - Confederate General, American Legend (winner of the 2011 Jefferson Davis Historical Gold Medal)
A Rebel Born: The Screenplay (film about N. B. Forrest)
Forrest! 99 Reasons to Love Nathan Bedford Forrest
Give 'Em Hell Boys! The Complete Military Correspondence of Nathan Bedford Forrest
I Rode With Forrest! Confederate Soldiers Who Served With the World's Greatest Cavalry Leader
Nathan Bedford Forrest and African-Americans: Yankee Myth, Confederate Fact
Nathan Bedford Forrest and the Battle of Fort Pillow: Yankee Myth, Confederate Fact
Nathan Bedford Forrest and the Ku Klux Klan: Yankee Myth, Confederate Fact
Nathan Bedford Forrest: Southern Hero, American Patriot - Honoring a Confederate Icon and the Old South
Saddle, Sword, and Gun: A Biography of Nathan Bedford Forrest For Teens
The God of War: Nathan Bedford Forrest As He Was Seen By His Contemporaries
The Quotable Nathan Bedford Forrest: Selections From the Writings and Speeches of the Confederacy's Most Brilliant Cavalryman

QUOTABLE SERIES
The Alexander H. Stephens Reader: Excerpts From the Works of a Confederate Founding Father
The Quotable Alexander H. Stephens: Selections From the Writings and Speeches of the Confederacy's First Vice President
The Quotable Jefferson Davis: Selections From the Writings and Speeches of the Confederacy's First President
The Quotable Nathan Bedford Forrest: Selections From the Writings and Speeches of the Confederacy's Most Brilliant Cavalryman
The Quotable Robert E. Lee: Selections From the Writings and Speeches of the South's Most Beloved Civil War General
The Quotable Stonewall Jackson: Selections From the Writings and Speeches of the South's Most Famous General
The Unquotable Abraham Lincoln: The President's Quotes They Don't Want You To Know!

CIVIL WAR BATTLES
Encyclopedia of the Battle of Franklin - A Comprehensive Guide to the Conflict that Changed the Civil War
Nathan Bedford Forrest and the Battle of Fort Pillow: Yankee Myth, Confederate Fact
The Battle of Franklin: Recollections of Confederate and Union Soldiers
The Battle of Nashville: Recollections of Confederate and Union Soldiers
The Battle of Spring Hill: Recollections of Confederate and Union Soldiers

CONSTITUTIONAL HISTORY
America's Three Constitutions: Complete Texts of the Articles of Confederation, Constitution of the United States of America, and Constitution of the Confederate States of America
The Articles of Confederation Explained: A Clause-by-Clause Study of America's First Constitution
The Constitution of the Confederate States of America Explained: A Clause-by-Clause Study of the South's Magna Carta

VICTORIAN CONFEDERATE LITERATURE
I, Confederate: Why Dixie Seceded and Fought in the Words of Southern Soldiers
Rise Up and Call Them Blessed: Victorian Tributes to the Confederate Soldier, 1861-1901
Support Your Local Confederate: Wit and Humor in the Southern Confederacy
The Bittersweet Bond: Race Relations in the Old South as Described by White and Black Southerners
The God of War: Nathan Bedford Forrest As He Was Seen By His Contemporaries
The Old Rebel: Robert E. Lee As He Was Seen By His Contemporaries
Victorian Confederate Poetry: The Southern Cause in Verse, 1861-1901

ABRAHAM LINCOLN
Abraham Lincoln: The Southern View - Demythologizing America's Sixteenth President
Lincolnology: The Real Abraham Lincoln Revealed in His Own Words - A Study of Lincoln's Suppressed, Misinterpreted, and Forgotten Writings and Speeches
Lincoln's War: The Real Cause, the Real Winner, the Real Loser
The Great Impersonator! 99 Reasons to Dislike Abraham Lincoln
The Unholy Crusade: Lincoln's Legacy of Destruction in the American South
The Unquotable Abraham Lincoln: The President's Quotes They Don't Want You To Know!

NATURAL HISTORY
North America's Amazing Mammals: An Encyclopedia for the Whole Family
The Concise Book of Owls: A Guide to Nature's Most Mysterious Birds
The Concise Book of Tigers: A Guide to Nature's Most Remarkable Cats

PARANORMAL
Carnton Plantation Ghost Stories: True Tales of the Unexplained from Tennessee's Most Haunted Civil War House!
UFOs and Aliens: The Complete Guidebook

FAMILY HISTORIES
The Blakeneys: An Etymological, Ethnological, and Genealogical Study - Uncovering the Mysterious Origins of the Blakeney Family and Name
The Caudills: An Etymological, Ethnological, and Genealogical Study - Exploring the Name and National Origins of a European-American Family
The McGavocks of Carnton Plantation: A Southern History - Celebrating One of Dixie's Most Noble Confederate Families and Their Tennessee Home

MIND, BODY, SPIRIT
Autobiography of a Non-Yogi: A Scientist's Journey From Hinduism to Christianity (Dr. Amitava Dasgupta, with Lochlainn Seabrook)
Britannia Rules: Goddess-Worship in Ancient Anglo-Celtic Society - An Academic Look at the United Kingdom's Matricentric Spiritual Past
Christ Is All and In All: Rediscovering Your Divine Nature and the Kingdom Within
Christmas Before Christianity: How the Birthday of the "Sun" Became the Birthday of the "Son"
Jesus and the Gospel of Q: Christ's Pre-Christian Teachings As Recorded in the New Testament
Jesus and the Law of Attraction: The Bible-Based Guide to Creating Perfect Health, Wealth, and Happiness Following Christ's Simple Formula
Seabrook's Bible Dictionary of Traditional and Mystical Christian Doctrines
Sea Raven Press Blank Page Journal: For Reflections, Notes, and Sketches
The Bible and the Law of Attraction: 99 Teachings of Jesus, the Apostles, and the Prophets
The Book of Kelle: An Introduction to Goddess-Worship and the Great Celtic Mother-Goddess Kelle, Original Blessed Lady of Ireland
The Goddess Dictionary of Words and Phrases: Introducing a New Core Vocabulary for the Women's Spirituality Movement
The Martian Anomalies: A Photographic Search for Intelligent Life on Mars
Victorian Hernia Cures: Nonsurgical Self-Treatment of Inguinal Hernia
Vintage Southern Cookbook: 2,000 Delicious Dishes From Dixie

WOMEN
Aphrodite's Trade: The Hidden History of Prostitution Unveiled
Princess Diana: Modern Day Moon-Goddess - A Psychoanalytical and Mythological Look at Diana Spencer's Life, Marriage, and Death (with Dr. Jane Goldberg)
Women in Gray: A Tribute to the Ladies Who Supported the Southern Confederacy

REPRINTS
A Short History of the Confederate States of America (author Jefferson Davis; editor Lochlainn Seabrook)
Prison Life of Jefferson Davis (author John J. Craven; editor Lochlainn Seabrook)
Life of Beethoven (author Ludwig Nohl; editor Lochlainn Seabrook)
The New Revelation (author Arthur Conan Doyle; editor Lochlainn Seabrook)
The Rise and Fall of the Confederate Government (author Jefferson Davis; editor Lochlainn Seabrook)

Lochlainn Seabrook does not author books for fame and glory, but for the love of writing and sharing his knowledge.

SeaRavenPress.com

I, CONFEDERATE

Why Dixie Seceded & Fought in the Words of Southern Soldiers

CONCEIVED, COLLECTED, EDITED, & ARRANGED, WITH AN INTRODUCTION BY THE AUTHOR, "THE VOICE OF THE TRADITIONAL SOUTH," COLONEL

LOCHLAINN SEABROOK
JEFFERSON DAVIS HISTORICAL GOLD MEDAL WINNER

Diligently Researched and Generously Illustrated by the Author for the Elucidation of the Reader

2023

Sea Raven Press, Nashville, Tennessee, USA

I, CONFEDERATE

Published by
Sea Raven Press, Cassidy Ravensdale, President
Nashville, Tennessee, USA
SeaRavenPress.com

Copyright © text and illustrations Lochlainn Seabrook 2023
in accordance with U.S. and international copyright laws and regulations, as stated and protected under the Berne Union for the Protection of Literary and Artistic Property (Berne Convention), and the Universal Copyright Convention (the UCC). All rights reserved under the Pan-American and International Copyright Conventions.

PRINTING HISTORY
1st SRP paperback edition, 1st printing, January 2023 • ISBN: 978-1-955351-26-3
1st SRP hardcover edition, 1st printing, January 2023 • ISBN: 978-1-955351-27-0

ISBN: 978-1-955351-26-3 (paperback)
Library of Congress Control Number: 2023930061

This work is the copyrighted intellectual property of Lochlainn Seabrook and has been registered with the Copyright Office at the Library of Congress in Washington, D.C., USA. No part of this work (including text, covers, drawings, photos, illustrations, maps, images, diagrams, etc.), in whole or in part, may be used, reproduced, stored in a retrieval system, or transmitted, in any form or by any means now known or hereafter invented, without written permission from the publisher. The sale, duplication, hire, lending, copying, digitalization, or reproduction of this material, in any manner or form whatsoever, is also prohibited, and is a violation of federal, civil, and digital copyright law, which provides severe civil and criminal penalties for any violations.

I, Confederate: Why Dixie Seceded and Fought in the Words of Southern Soldiers, by Lochlainn Seabrook. Includes a preface, introduction, illustrations, index, endnotes, and bibliography.

ARTWORK
Front and back cover design and art, book design, layout, font selection, and interior art by Lochlainn Seabrook
All images, image captions, graphic design, and graphic art copyright © Lochlainn Seabrook
All images selected, placed, manipulated, cleaned, colored, tinted, and/or created by Lochlainn Seabrook
Title page soldier image from Lochlainn Seabrook's book, 'Heroes of the Southern Confederacy'
Cover photo: C.S. Col. John S. Mosby and 16 of his soldiers, 43rd Virginia Cavalry Battalion, Richmond, VA, c. 1860s, William W. Davies

All persons who approve of the authority and principles of Colonel Lochlainn Seabrook's literary work, and realize its benefits as a means of reeducating the world about facts left out of mainstream books, are hereby requested to avidly recommend his titles to others and to vigorously cooperate in extending their reach, scope, and influence around the globe.

The views documented in this book concerning the War for Southern Independence are those of the publisher.
WRITTEN, DESIGNED, PUBLISHED, PRINTED, & MANUFACTURED IN THE UNITED STATES OF AMERICA

Dedication

To my noble Conservative Southern ancestors: You sacrificed everything in the heroic effort to protect hearth and home, defend personal honor, secure political justice, maintain sectional equality, achieve national independence, perpetuate the original Constitution, maintain the inviolable sovereign rights of the states, and most importantly, preserve our personal, inalienable, God-given natural rights: life, liberty, and happiness; all while enduring 16 fiery years (1861-1877) of violent, unconstitutional, Left-wing mob-rule, authoritarianism, sadism, cruelty, harassment, crime, imprisonment, slander, hatred, coercion, persecution, incendiarism, humiliation, anarchy, terrorism, rapine, and bloodshed.

States' Rights Forever

Epigraph

"Had I known all that was to come to pass, had I known what was to be inflicted upon me, all that my country was to suffer, all that our posterity was to endure, I would do it all over again."

Jefferson Davis
MISSISSIPPI CONGRESSMAN
SECRETARY OF WAR UNDER U.S. PRESIDENT FRANKLIN PIERCE
PRESIDENT OF THE CONFEDERATE STATES OF AMERICA

CONTENTS

Notes to the Reader ❧ page 11
Preface ❧ page 19
Introduction, by Lochlainn Seabrook ❧ page 21

CHAPTER 1 ❧ page 31
CHAPTER 2 ❧ page 53
CHAPTER 3 ❧ page 75
CHAPTER 4 ❧ page 97
CHAPTER 5 ❧ page 119
CHAPTER 6 ❧ page 141
CHAPTER 7 ❧ page 163
CHAPTER 8 ❧ page 183
CHAPTER 9 ❧ page 205
CHAPTER 10 ❧ page 229
CHAPTER 11 ❧ page 251
CHAPTER 12 ❧ page 277
CHAPTER 13 ❧ page 301
CHAPTER 14 ❧ page 323

A Confederate Prayer ❧ page 341
Notes ❧ page 343
Bibliography ❧ page 353
Index ❧ page 363
Quotable Quotes Related to the Southern Cause ❧ page 371
Meet the Author-Editor ❧ page 373
Learn More ❧ page 375

NOTES TO THE READER

"NOTHING IN THE PAST IS DEAD TO THE MAN WHO WOULD
LEARN HOW THE PRESENT CAME TO BE WHAT IT IS."

WILLIAM STUBBS, VICTORIAN ENGLISH HISTORIAN

THE TWO MAIN POLITICAL PARTIES IN 1860
☞ In any study of America's antebellum, bellum, and postbellum periods, it is vitally important to understand that in 1860 the two major political parties—the Democrats and the newly formed Republicans—were the opposite of what they are today. In other words, the Democrats of the mid 19th Century (formed by what we now call "right-wingers" or "traditionalists")[1] were Conservatives, akin to the Republican Party of today, while the Republicans of the mid 19th Century (formed by what we now call "left-wingers" or "progressives")[2] were Liberals, akin to the Democratic Party of today.[3]

Thus the Confederacy's Democratic president, Jefferson Davis, was a Conservative (with libertarian leanings); the Union's Republican president, Abraham Lincoln, was a Liberal (with socialistic leanings).[4] This is why, in the mid 1800s, the conservative wing of the Democratic Party was known as "the States' Rights Party,"[5] as opposed to the Republican Party, which was widely known to have been founded in 1854 by "progressive elements."[6]

Hence, the Democrats of the Civil War period referred to themselves as "conservatives," "confederates," "anti-centralists," or "constitutionalists" (the latter because they favored strict adherence to the original Constitution—which tacitly guaranteed states' rights—as created by the Founding Fathers), while the Civil War Republicans called themselves "liberals," "nationalists," "centralists," or "consolidationists" (the latter three because they wanted to nationalize the central government and consolidate political power in Washington, D.C.).[7] More evidence comes from a common

The author's cousin, Confederate Vice President and Democrat Alexander H. Stephens: a Southern Conservative.

phrase used at the time, "states' rights Democrats," a term that could have only applied to Conservatives, since then, as today, Liberals are squarely against states' rights (unless they find that states' rights benefit their agenda in some way).[8]

In 1889 President Davis, who referred to the 1860 Democrats as "the conservative power of the country,"[9] himself explained the political situation at the time this way:

> . . . the names adopted by political parties in the United States have not always been strictly significant of their principles. In general terms it may be said that the old Federal party [Liberal] inclined to nationalism [then a term for big government], or consolidation [that is, consolidation of power in the Federal government], and that the Whig party [liberalistic], which succeeded it, although not identical with it, was favorable, in the main, to a strong Central Government [liberalism and socialism]. On the other hand, its opponent, the Republican [Conservative], afterward known as the Democratic party [until the election of 1896, when the two parties reversed, becoming the parties we know today], was dominated by the idea of the sovereignty of the States and the federal or confederate character of the Union [Americanism or conservatism]. Although other elements have entered into its organization at different periods, this has been its vital, cardinal, and abiding principle.[10]

Since this idea is new to most of my readers, let us further demystify it by viewing it from the perspective of the American Revolutionary War. If Davis and his conservative Southern constituents (the Democrats of 1861) had been alive in 1775, they would have sided with George Washington and the American colonists, who sought to secede from the tyrannical government of Great Britain; if Lincoln and his Liberal Northern constituents (the Republicans of 1861) had been alive at that time, they would have sided with King George III and the English monarchy, who sought

The War for Southern Independence pitted Northern Liberals (then the Republican Party) against Southern Conservatives (then the Democratic Party).

to maintain the American colonies as possessions of the British Empire. It is due to this very comparison that we Southerners often refer to our secession from the U.S. as the Second Declaration of Independence and the "Civil War" as the Second American Revolutionary War.

Without a basic understanding of these facts, the American "Civil War" will forever remain incomprehensible. For a full discussion of this topic see my book, *Abraham Lincoln Was a Liberal, Jefferson Davis Was a Conservative: The Missing Key to Understanding the American Civil War*.

THE TERM "CIVIL WAR"

☛ As I heartily dislike the phrase "Civil War," its use throughout this book (as well as in my other works) is worthy of explanation.

Our entire modern literary system refers to the conflict of 1861 using the Northern term the "Civil War," whether we in the South like it or not. Of course, this is purposeful, for America's book industry, which determines everything from how books are categorized and designed to how they are marketed and sold, is almost solely controlled by Liberals, socialists, globalists, collectivists, and communists, individuals who will do anything to prevent the truth about Lincoln's War from coming out. An important aspect of this wholesale revisionism of American history is the use of the phrase "Civil War," which Yankee Liberals thrust into the public forum even as big government Left-winger Lincoln was diabolically tricking the Conservative South into firing the first shot at the Battle of Fort Sumter in April 1861.[11]

The American "Civil War" was not a true civil war as Webster defines it: "A conflict between opposing groups of citizens of the *same* country." It was a fight between two individual countries; or to be more specific, two separate and constitutionally formed confederacies: the U.S.A. and the C.S.A.

The progressives' blatant American "Civil War" coverup continues to this day, one of the more overt results which pertains to how books are coded, indexed, and identified.[12] Thus, as all book searches by readers, libraries, and retail outlets are now performed online, and as all bookstores categorize works from or about this period under the heading "Civil War," honest book publishers and authors who deal with this particular topic have little choice but to use this deceptive term. If I were to refuse to use it, as some of my Southern colleagues have suggested, few people would ever find or read my books.

Add to this the fact that scarcely any non-Southerners have ever heard of the names we in the South use for the conflict, such as "the War for Southern Independence," "the War Against Northern Aggression," "Lincoln's War," or my personal preference, "the War for the Constitution." It only makes sense then to use the term "Civil War" in most commercial situations, historically inaccurate though it is.

We should also bear in mind that while today educated persons, particularly educated Southerners, all share an abhorrence for the phrase "Civil War," it was not always so. Confederates who lived through and even fought in the conflict regularly used the term throughout the 1860s, and even long after. Among them were Confederate generals such as Nathan Bedford Forrest, Richard Taylor, and Joseph E. Johnston, not to mention the Confederacy's vice president, Alexander H. Stephens.

Confederate General Nathan Bedford Forrest, just one of many Southern officials who referred to the conflict of 1861 as the "Civil War."

In 1895 Confederate General James Longstreet wrote about his military experiences in a work subtitled, *Memoirs of the Civil War in America*, while in 1903 Confederate General John Brown Gordon, the first commander-in-chief of the United Confederate Veterans, entitled his autobiography, *Reminiscences of the Civil War*. Even the Confederacy's highest leader, President Jefferson Davis, used the term "Civil War,"[13] and in one case at least, as late as 1881—the year he wrote his brilliant exposition, *The Rise and Fall of the Confederate Government* (see the Sea Raven Press reprint of this book, of which I am the editor).[14] Authors writing for *Confederate Veteran* magazine sometimes used the phrase well into the early 1900s,[15] and in 1898, at the Eighth Annual Meeting and Reunion of the United Confederate Veterans (the forerunner of today's Sons of Confederate Veterans), the following resolution was proposed: that from then on the Great War of 1861 was to be designated "the Civil War Between the States."[16]

A WORD ON EARLY AMERICAN MATERIAL

☛ In order to preserve the authentic historicity of the antebellum, bellum, and postbellum periods, I have retained the original spellings, formatting, and punctuation of the early Americans I quote. These include such items as British-English spellings, long-running paragraphs, obsolete words, and various literary devices peculiar to the time. However, I have corrected misspelled names to prevent confusion, and also *where possible*, inaccurate dates and locations (the inevitable result of old faulty memories). Bracketed words are my additions and clarifications (added mainly for my new, foreign, and young readers), while italicized words are (where indicated) my emphasis.

19TH-CENTURY CODE WORDS

☛ An early American *Southern* abolitionist was someone who simply desired the end of slavery. *Northern* abolitionists, however, were something quite different altogether: they identified themselves with socialism and communism. Also, our modern political party names have different meanings than those of the mid 1800s. Hence, one must bear the following in mind when reading 19th-Century literature:

Union General August von Willich: Typically labeled a "radical" in mainstream history books, Willich was actually a card-carrying communist who led a revolutionary workers' party, studiously followed the teachings of Karl Marx, and participated in the failed European socialist revolution of 1848—all before joining Lincoln's army in 1861.

1. "Abolitionist" (Northern): A 19th-Century Left-wing euphemism for a socialist or communist.
2. "Radical" (Northern): Also a 19th-Century Left-wing euphemism for a socialist or communist.
3. "Republican": Between 1854 and 1896 the Republicans were the major Left-wing or Liberal party of that era.
4. "Democrat": Between 1828 and 1896, the Democrats were the major Right-wing or Conservative party of that era.

For more information on items 1 and 2 above, see my introduction in my book *The Bittersweet Bond: Race Relations in the Old South As Described by White and Black Southerners*.

For more information on items 3 and 4 above, see my books *Abraham Lincoln Was a Liberal, Jefferson Davis Was a Conservative: The Missing Key to Understanding the American Civil War*, and *Lincoln's War: The Real Cause, the Real Winner, the Real Loser*.

WHITE RACISM IN THE OLD SOUTH

☛ Anywhere there are human beings, there is racism. Color, region, nationality, age, gender, ethnicity, none have any bearing whatsoever. And just as America has had (and still has) its share of, for example, black supremacist individuals, groups, and organizations, we have also been the home of white supremacist individuals, groups, and organizations.

While, as I have shown in many of my other writings, white racism is, was, and has always been, strongest in the Northern states, Caucasian supremacy has long existed in the Southern states as well, and a few of the 19th- and 20th-Century individuals I have cited in the following pages espoused this doctrine.

Confederate soldier, identity unknown, circa 1862.

As I have gone into great detail discussing the primary reasons for Victorian white superiority in some of my previous books (these reasons are *never* discussed in conventional history books), I have purposefully glossed over this topic in the present volume, *I, Confederate*, as it is not germane to the book's primary theme: the true causes behind Southern secession and warfare.

For more on the topic of white (and black) racism in the Old South, see, for instance, my books *The Bittersweet Bond*; *Everything You Were Taught About American Slavery is Wrong, Ask a Southerner!*; *Everything You Were Taught About African Americans and the Civil War is Wrong, Ask a Southerner!*; and *Nathan Bedford Forrest and African Americans: Yankee Myth, Confederate Fact*.

PRESENTISM

☛ As a historian I view *presentism* (judging the past according to present day mores and customs) as the enemy of authentic history. And this is precisely why the Left employs it in its ongoing war against traditional American, conservative, and Christian values. By looking at history through the lens of modern day beliefs—and, just as heinous, fabricating obviously fake history based on emotion, opinion, and political ideology—they are able to distort, revise, and reshape the past into a false narrative that fits their ideological agenda: the liberalization *and* Northernization of America, the enlargement and further centralization of the national government, and total control of American political, economic, and social power, the same plan that Lincoln championed.[17]

Judging our ancestors by our own standards is dishonest, unfair, unjust, duplicitous, and unethical.

This book rejects presentism and replaces it with what I call *historicalism*: judging our ancestors based on the values of their own time. To get the most from this work the reader is invited to reject presentism as well. In this way—along with casting aside preconceived notions and the fake history churned out by our left-wing education system—the truth in this work will be most readily ascertained and absorbed; truth that has been rigorously researched and forensically uncovered by myself using the scientific method. In 1901 Confederate Colonel Bennett H. Young noted:

> History is valuable only as it is true. Opinions concerning acts are not history; acts themselves alone are historic.[18]

CONTINUE YOUR SOUTHERN HISTORY EDUCATION
☛ Lincoln's War on the Constitution and the American people can never be fully understood without a thorough knowledge of the South's perspective. As this book is only meant to be a brief introductory guide to these topics, one cannot hope to learn the complete story here. For those who are interested in additional material from Dixie's viewpoint, please see my comprehensive histories listed on pages 2 and 3. — L.S.

Keep Your Body, Mind, & Spirit Vibrating at Their Highest Level
YOU CAN DO SO BY READING THE BOOKS OF

SEA RAVEN PRESS

There is nothing that will so perfectly keep your body, mind, and spirit in a healthy condition as to think wisely and positively. Hence you should not only read this book, but also the other books that we offer. They will quicken your physical, mental, and spiritual vibrations, enabling you to maintain a position in society as a healthy erudite person.

KEEP YOURSELF WELL-INFORMED!

The well-informed person is always at the head of the procession, while the ignorant, the lazy, and the unthoughtful hang onto the rear. If you are a Spiritual man or woman, do yourself a great favor: read Sea Raven Press books and stay well posted on the Truth. It is almost criminal for one to remain in ignorance while the opportunity to gain knowledge is open to all at a nominal price.

We invite you to visit our Webstore for a wide selection of wholesome, family-friendly, well-researched, educational books for all ages. You will be glad you did!

Unique Books & Gifts for the Whole Family!

SeaRavenPress.com

LochlainnSeabrook.com
TheBestCivilWarBookEver.com
NathanBedfordForrestBooks.com

PREFACE

I HAVE DEVOTED MANY YEARS OF my life to writing books about the cause of the Great American War of 1861; among them, *Everything You Were Taught About the Civil War is Wrong, Ask a Southerner!*; *Lincoln's War: The Real Cause, the Real Winner, the Real Loser*; and *All We Ask is to be Let Alone: The Southern Secession Fact Book*.

The present volume is also dedicated to this topic. However, rather than being a distillation of my own opinions and research, *I, Confederate* is devoted primarily to the views of Victorian, Southern, military men. As a means of preserving authentic Southern history, this is all important, as perceptive readers will immediately grasp.

MY SOURCES
Though for a century and a half, these voices, those of Victorian Confederates, have been misinterpreted, suppressed, redacted, and censored by the ignorant, the indoctrinated, the wicked, and the malicious, miraculously many of them have been preserved down to the present day, primarily in letters, books, and magazines, all which were my chief sources for *I, Confederate*.

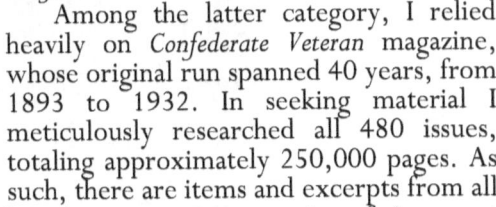

Among the latter category, I relied heavily on *Confederate Veteran* magazine, whose original run spanned 40 years, from 1893 to 1932. In seeking material I meticulously researched all 480 issues, totaling approximately 250,000 pages. As such, there are items and excerpts from all 40 volumes, providing a wide and accurate representation of views; not only from men, but also from women; and not only from Confederate veterans and Southern civilians, but from Union veterans and Northern civilians as well.

THE TITLE
I derived the inspiration for the title of my book *I, Confederate*, from the 1934 novel *I, Claudius*, by my English cousin Robert Graves.[19] Though Graves' work is a fictitious rendition of a slice of ancient Roman history, my book is quite the opposite. Because the material I have collected is taken directly from the writings, speeches, letters, and poems of 19th-Century and early 20th-Century Confederate veterans, *I, Confederate* possesses the highest level of historical accuracy possible on this subject. In essence, there are plenty of lower authorities—but none higher.

L.S.

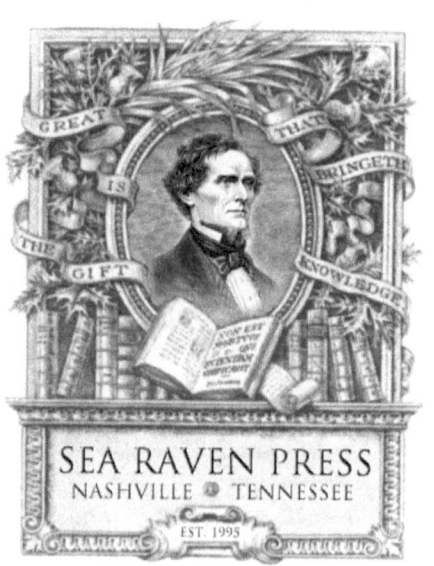

"Books invite all; they constrain none."
Hartley Burr Alexander (1873-1939)

INTRODUCTION

"THE RIGHTS OF THE MANY AGAINST THE EXACTIONS OF THE FEW."
Southern Battle Cry

THIS WORK CAME ABOUT IN part as my attempt to answer an age-old question, one I have been asked hundreds of times over the years: What did the South fight for? What prompted the majority of Southern males over 18 to unhesitatingly enlist in the Confederate military and take up arms against their American cousins to the North? Why were millions of white, black, and brown Southern men and women willing to risk everything, including their very lives? What could possibly have been so important to so many people, that they would sacrifice their families and friends, not to mention their homes, businesses, and towns?

The answer is hinted at in the many terms we Southerners use to express it. Among the countless variations there are:

"The cause."[20]
"The holy cause."[21]
"The just cause."[22]
"The great cause."[23]
"The fallen cause."[24]
"The sacred cause."[25]
"The noble cause."[26]
"The worthy cause."[27]
"The blessed cause."[28]
"The dearest cause."[29]
"The glorious cause."[30]
"The righteous cause."[31]
"The common cause."[32]
"The Southern Cause."[33]
"The cause we all love."[34]
"The ever-sacred cause."[35]
"The cause of the South."[36]
"The Confederate Cause."[37]
"The cause of the Confederacy."[38]
"The cause of our beloved Southland."[39]
"The cause of the Southern Confederacy."[40]
"The cause that is very dear to every true Southerner."[41]

This same Southern campaign is what Confederate General Joseph E. Johnston called "the noblest of human causes,"[42] what Dr. R. H. McKim named "the bedrock of the Southern Confederacy,"[43] and what the women of the U.D.C. referred to as "a cause made dear and sacred by the blood of the South's brave sons and the tears of her loving daughters."[44] Confederate veteran and clergyman James H. McNeilly called it the "great war of principles,"[45] while Matthew Page Andrews knew it, along with numerous closely associated concepts, as "the sacred principles of Revolutionary heritage."[46]

Just what did Victorian Southerners mean when they used such language? What were they referring to when they made mention of "the highest cause on the earth save only that of the Christian religion"?[47] What was this "cause so dear and a principle so worthy,"[48] "the cause that was dearer than life"[49] to the Confederate soldier, his loved ones, and his descendants?

THE SACRED DOCTRINE
It was none other than the sacred doctrine of states' rights[50] and local government;[51] what the Conservative South specifically called the "sacred reserved rights of the sovereign States"[52]—or more broadly, "the principles of constitutional liberty."[53]

I am speaking here of *conservatism*, a word that appears over and over in the writings and speeches of Confederate veterans. Thus, they often referred to the conflict as "the war for Southern rights,"[54] "the War for States' Rights,"[55] or more correctly, as 19th-Century Conservative Congressman James Brooks labeled it in 1862, "the War for the Constitution."[56]

VICTORIAN POLITICS BEHIND THE WAR FOR THE CONSTITUTION
The South being the birthplace of the American abolition movement and the North being the birthplace of American slavery, it is obvious then that the "Civil War" was not fought over the desire to either preserve or destroy slavery, as conventional history books absurdly claim. While some Victorian Southerners believed that the institution was a contributing element, as Jefferson Davis and many others have continuously and strenuously pointed out, if it was, it was entirely peripheral in its influence.[57]

Consider that I have been writing books on the conflict for many decades, and currently have authored and edited some 60 Civil War-related titles. Additionally, my personal home library contains some 20,000 books on the subject, nearly all which I have read or at least reviewed. In my many years of study and research, not once have I come across a single 19th-Century Conservative Southerner who believed or claimed that the War Between the States was directly, or even indirectly, caused by slavery.

The truth, as all knowledgeable individuals are today aware, is that it was a *political conflict*, one that involved sectional and cultural differences, economics, social issues, pride, and honor. But most importantly it revolved around political power and the U.S. Constitution, with the South interpreting the document *strictly*, the North interpreting it *loosely*. Here is the spark that ignited the fuse.

In 1913 Raleigh C. Minor, professor of law at the University of Virginia, gave the following accurate description of the two opposing political camps, which he labeled respectively the "States' Rights School" and the "Nationalist School":

> Since, in the belief of the States Rights school [Conservative], the States retain their sovereignty and all powers and rights not clearly delegated to the United States or prohibited to the States, the disciple of that school will tend to view his State government with the same respect on the one hand as he accords to the federal government on the other. His love for the State to whose sovereignty he owes allegiance will be as great as his regard for the Union. *He will favor a strict construction of the Constitution* [my emphasis, L.S.] and the holding of the federal government closely to its delegated powers, because he believes that any other course would be a usurpation of power by the federal government, harmful alike, in the end, to the Union and to the States; and because he believes in local self-government, and in the principle that the further removed the rulers are from the people they are to govern the less likely is their action to be wise and just.
>
> On the other hand, the Nationalist [Liberal], believing that the Constitution has been ordained by the people at large, and that the collective people of the United States have, through that instrument, distributed certain governmental powers between the United States and the States, and that the ultimate sovereignty rests in the Nation, will tend to pay his homage to that which he regards as the source of sovereignty. He will lay the emphasis on the national power, and will be inclined to disregard or minimize the rights and powers of the States, if it appears to him that the matter in hand may be better controlled by the general government. He will feel few qualms over the usurpation of State powers by the general government; and *will incline to a loose interpretation of the Constitution* [my emphasis, L.S.] and of the powers delegated to the United States—a construction in large measure controlled by the exigencies of the moment, or what would seem to him to be exigencies.

His tendency will be toward any construction that he believes will strengthen and glorify the nation in his eyes, and in the eyes of others, at the expense of the States and of the great principle of local self-government.[58]

These two completely opposing views of America's most important document were bound to create conflict, and they did; and this was noticeable as early as the 16th Century, when Europeans first began to settle in the American South and the American North.

A few centuries later, as friction between the two sections continued to escalate, "the Southern Cause" first fully manifested in the secession of the Southern states, which in turn culminated in all out war, with the Confederates (Southern Conservatives, members of what was then America's major Right-wing party, the Democratic Party), fighting against the Yankees (Northern Liberals, members of what was then America's major Left-wing party, the Republican Party).

THE COMMUNIST FACTOR

The primary enemy of the doctrine of states' rights and self-government is, and always has been, the Left, with its most venomous constitution-hating members being socialists and communists. One from the former group was national socialist leader Adolf Hitler, who, in his autobiography *Mein Kampf*, enthusiastically praised Lincoln's attempt to destroy states' rights.[59]

Anti-states' rights individuals, of course, existed long before *der Führer*. In fact, they were fervently promoting their progressive message even before the War for Southern Independence. Known deceptively in conventional history books by the code words "radicals" and "abolitionists," socialists and communists played a large role in the conflict, naturally siding with, and joining, what was the main Liberal party of the day, the Republican Party, where they used their influence to push their communist agenda on big government Liberal, "the

German atheist, white racist, white supremacist, advocate of violent revolution (Marxism), and founder of modern communism, Karl Marx. Many of Marx's students, friends, and business associates campaigned for Lincoln in 1860, joined the Republican Party (then Left-wing), and later worked in the Lincoln administration and military, where they eagerly advanced their anti-American, pro-communist ideologies.

Great Gaslighter," Abraham Lincoln, and his Left-wing cabinet.[60]

As with modern socialists and communists, the ultimate goal of Civil War era socialists and communists was to seize and maintain absolute control of society (government, education, the media, etc.). This was to be accomplished by destroying traditional Christian America, and replacing it with a heavily taxed, classless, stateless society that would include the elimination of capitalism, religion, monogamous marriage, the nuclear family, and private property (among other things).

Confederate soldier, identity unknown, circa 1862.

Consequently, Karl Marx, the founder of the most far-left and aggressive form of communism, one known as Marxism,[61] called for a "permanent revolution,"[62] one whose "ends can be attained only by the forcible overthrow of all existing social conditions."[63] It was his followers, many of them who were also personal friends of Marx, who infiltrated the U.S. government via the then Left-wing Republican Party, beginning with its formation by "progressive elements" in 1854.[64]

Two, for example, who ended up in the Lincoln administration were socialist Charles A. Dana (Assistant Secretary of War)[65] and Reinhold Solger (U.S. Treasury Dept.), who participated in the disastrous socialist European Revolution in 1848.[66] Lincoln's military was packed with far-left radicals as well, including socialist Friedrich K. F. Hecker (a Union colonel) and communist August von Willich (a Union general).[67] Countless more could be named.

Being political Conservatives, Confederate soldiers were well aware of the insidious presence of socialists and communists on the opposite side of the battlefield, and understood the danger these nihilistic, revolutionary ideologues presented to America. More particularly they realized what Lincoln's communists meant for the South, where the Constitution, self-government, and states' rights were held sacred by every man, woman, and child. One of these was Confederate veteran and clergyman Frank Page, who, at a U.C.V. reunion in 1894, makes reference to the Confederate soldier's Conservative political stance, saying:

"With our faces firmly set, fellow-soldiers, against the aggressions of government, against the aggressions of anarchy, against the aggressions of communism in every shape, come from whatever quarter it may, standing true to the Constitution and the flag of our country, in defense of the rights and liberties of this people . . ."[68]

PRESERVING THE TRUTH ABOUT THE SOUTHERN CAUSE

Such plain facts have been carefully concealed from the public for over 150 years, replaced with malevolent myths, lies, and outright disinformation masquerading as "facts." Tragically, the Left continues to censor the Truth to this day, with the result that the historical facts behind the Southern Cause have all but disappeared from the public forum and hence from general knowledge. There is the old saying: "A lie will travel half way around the world while the truth is putting on its boots."

My book, *I, Confederate*, aims to help fill in this gargantuan hole in the pages of history with both eyewitness testimony and the sagacious words of Confederate descendants concerning the facts about the Southern Cause. For those who are not aware of when and where the Southern Cause began, let me introduce the rest of my book with a selection from Virginian Thomas Jefferson's 1776 masterpiece, the Declaration of Independence. It shows, for all the world to see, that the U.S.A. was founded on the doctrine of self-government and established on the act of secession:

"We hold these truths to be self-evident: That all men are created equal; that they are endowed by their Creator with certain unalienable rights; that among these are life, liberty and the pursuit of happiness; that to secure these rights, governments are instituted among men, deriving their just powers from the consent of the governed; that whenever any form of government becomes destructive of these ends, it is the right of the people to alter or to abolish it, and to institute new government, laying its foundation on such principles and organizing its powers in such form, as to them shall seem most likely to effect their safety and happiness. Prudence, indeed, will dictate that governments long established should not be changed for light and transient causes; and accordingly all experience hath shown, that mankind are more disposed to suffer, while evils are sufferable, than to right themselves by abolishing the forms to which they are accustomed. But when a long train of abuses and usurpations, pursuing invariably the same object evinces a design to reduce them under absolute despotism, it is their right, it is their duty, to throw off such government, and to provide new guards for their future security."[69]

OUR SACRED HERITAGE IS ETERNAL
These essentially Southern concepts, America's "sacred principles of Revolutionary heritage,"[70] are immortal, timeless, and indestructible, making the anti-South, anti-Constitution slogan "the Lost Cause" both absurd and erroneous. There is no such thing.

Americanism, what we now call conservatism, will live on in perpetuity, and I am honored to revive the Truth about the Southern Cause via the thoughts, views, and opinions of my Confederate ancestors. I trust that you will enjoy reading them as much as I enjoyed collecting and recording them. God bless Dixie.

LOCHLAINN SEABROOK
NASHVILLE, TENNESSEE, USA
JANUARY 2023
In Nobis Regnat Christus

Confederate cavalry soldiers, circa 1862.

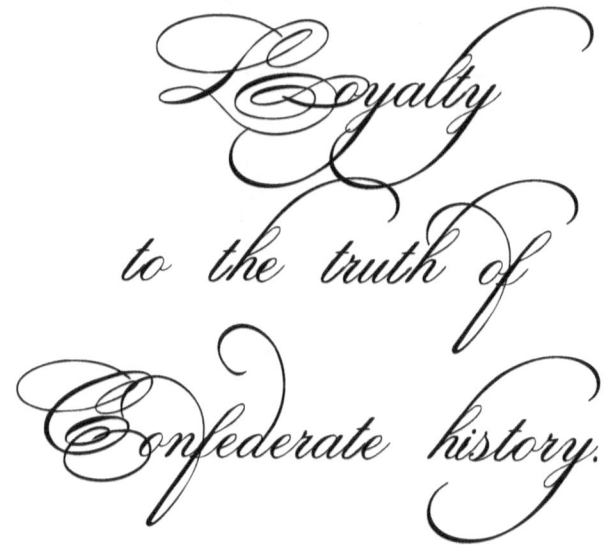

U.D.C. MOTTO, 1921

Confederate lad carrying, not the flag of "hatred, racism, and treason," but the flag of Christian Conservatism and strict constitutionalism.

I, CONFEDERATE

"We had sacred principles to maintain and rights to defend for which we were in duty bound to do our best, even if we perished in the endeavor."

Robert E. Lee

NO ALTERNATIVE
☛ No alternative remained except to seek the security out of the Union which they had vainly tried to obtain within it. The hope of our people may be stated in a sentence. It was to escape from injury and strife in the Union, to find prosperity and peace out of it.[7] — JEFFERSON DAVIS

THE CAUSES OF THE WAR
☛ . . . Twenty-eight years have passed since the close of our civil war. Since then a majority of the adults living in those years have been called home, and almost a new generation has taken their places on the farm and plantation, and in the counting-room, shop and office. Time, I trust, has healed the wounds of war, but with the revolving years the causes and events of that terrible struggle seem to be forgotten, or if not forgotten, considered as unimportant events of history. And even the history of those events, and the causes that led to that struggle, are not set forth fairly and truthfully. It is stated in books and papers that Southern children read and study that all the blood-shedding and destruction of property of that conflict was because the South rebelled without cause against the best government the world ever saw; that although the Southern soldiers were heroes in the skillfully massed and led, they and their leaders were rebels and traitors, who fought to overthrow the Union, and to preserve human slavery, and that their defeat was necessary for free government and the welfare of

the human family.

As a Confederate soldier and as a citizen of Virginia I deny the charge, and denounce it as a calumny. We were not rebels; we did not fight to perpetuate human slavery, but for our rights and privileges under a government established over us by our fathers and in defense of our homes. The South loved the Union. Her interests were identified with it. Her statesmen had aided in its creation and development. Her warriors had fought under its flag, by sea and by land, and shed their blood in its defense. To the South the Union was a temple dedicated to American constitutional liberty—to the principles of a liberty approved by great thinkers and consecrated by the blood of martyrs; a liberty that was designed to protect the individual man in all that was right, and to prohibit him from doing that which was wrong. Not a liberty for one class of people or section of country to prey on any other people or other section. Not a liberty for the majority to invade the rights of the minority, and to use the powers of the government to the aggrandizement of the former and the injury of the latter, but a liberty guaranteeing equality of right and privileges to each section and each State. But when the [Left-wing] priests that ministered at the altars of this temple sought to teach new theories of liberty, such as had not been taught by the [founding] fathers, and which were destructive of the principles of the Constitution, and fatally injurious to the rights of the States, and especially to the Southern States, then the cotton and sugar Southern States determined to abandon the temple and erect one, where they could worship according to what they understood to be the faith delivered by the fathers, who in the belief of man's capacity for self-government, and in prayer to God, had built our political temple.

Confederate Colonel John Singleton Mosby, Richmond, Virginia, circa 1863; a close cousin of the author-editor (L.S.), who descends from the Mosby family.

In determining to separate, those States thought they were sustained by the teachings of the Declaration of Independence, which declared in immortal words that "all governments derive their just powers from the consent of the governed," that when any form of government becomes destructive of these ends it is the right of the people to alter or abolish it, and to institute a new government, laying its foundations on such principles, and organizing its powers as to them shall seem most likely to effect their safety and happiness. They also thought that the powers granted to the general [central] government, by virtue of which it alone controlled the States, were delegated powers, which could be revoked at any time by the party delegating. They read in the resolutions of some of the States adopting the Constitution of the United States an express reservation of this power. Our own State, especially when she adopted the Constitution of the United States, declared that the powers granted to the United States could be resumed when perverted to her injury or oppression.

Those Southern States believed that the powers granted to the federal government had been used to their injury and oppression, and therefore they decided to abandon the Union. In taking this step, slavery was not the cause, but the occasion of the separation. It might as well be said that tea was the cause of our separation from the government of Great Britain in 1776. The government of Great Britain, prior to that date, claimed the power to tax the colonies, although they were not represented in the parliament. That power the colonies denied; they claimed they were British citizens, and as such were entitled to all the rights of every other citizen of that kingdom; that because separated from the island that contained the capital, they were not less citizens of that kingdom; that it was a principle dear to a Briton that no money should be taken from him in the form of taxes except by consent of his representatives, and as they were not represented in parliament England had no right to tax America. Notwithstanding the protest of the people of this country, England taxed America by putting a tax on tea. Hence the Boston tea party, the war of the revolution of 1776 and its results.

The Southern States claimed they had exactly the same right in the Union as the Northern States; that her soldiers had fought in the war for independence, in that of 1812, in the Indian wars and in the Mexican war; that her statesmen had contributed to the adoption of the Constitution of the United States, the development of American institutions and the enlargement of the territory of the Union; that the common government should be administered for the benefit of all the people, and not to develop one section to the injury of the other sections; not to tend the social and moral views of one part of the country to the disadvantage of another part of it. They [the Southern states] claimed that when the Union was formed slavery existed in all of the States; that it was recognized in the Constitution of the United States, and because it had become unprofitable in one portion of a common country [that is, the North], and therefore had ceased to exist in that section, the slaves of the North having been sold South, the powers of the general government should not be used to the injury of the South.

I would not do justice if I did not state just here that there was a section of people at the South and at the North in the early days of the republic and since opposed to slavery on moral and economic grounds. Perhaps at our revolutionary period the anti-slavery sentiment was stronger in Virginia than in New England [this is correct, L.S.].[72] Massachusetts [where both the American slave trade and American slavery got their start] was at that time engaged in the slave trade, deriving profit from the use of her ships in that traffic. It was not until after the great difference of opinion between the statesmen of the country as to the powers of the general government that the sectional differences on the subject of slavery became so decided and marked. With the increase of this difference of sentiment as to governmental powers grew the difference on the subject of slavery. In this State, about 1832, there was a most powerful anti-slavery party, headed by such men as James McDowell, one of the most eloquent and cultured of our Governors, and by Charles J. Faulkner, father of the distinguished United States Senator of that name from West Virginia.

But it was not until the failure of those who claimed large powers for the general government on the subject of a national bank, international improvements and a protective tariff to obtain control of the government, that the anti-slavery party assumed any considerable importance. A combination was made in the North and Northwest by those who claimed the aforementioned powers for the general [that is, central] government with the anti-slavery men. The [primarily Left-wing] combination claimed for the general government, on the subject of slavery:

1. Power to abolish slavery in the District of Columbia.
2. Under the power to regulate commerce, the power to prohibit the carrying of slaves from one slave State to another slave State.
3. The right to prohibit slavery in the territory of the United States.

You will observe, first, that all of these matters related to slavery, but the principle, under all this claim for power, like that in regard to the taxation of tea, was far deeper than appeared on the surface. It involved the integrity of the Constitution of the United States and the equality of the people of the Southern States. The District of Columbia contained the capital of the United States. Southern members of Congress came to Washington to discharge their duties, bringing with them their wives and children, and if by hostile legislation their servants—the maids of their wives and the nurses of their children—were to be liberated by act of Congress as soon as they trod the soil of the District, that city was no place for Southern Senators and Representatives.

2. As to the commerce between the States, as stated before, slaves were recognized as property when the [U.S.] Constitution was adopted. The Constitution of the United States contained a provision for their rendition when they escaped from one State to another; also, for the continuance of the slave trade until 1808. To interdict the selling of slaves from one State to another would have been, in effect, to deprive the citizens of our Southern States of the right to migrate to another. Also to deprive him of the use of what had been considered property from the foundation of the government.

3. To prohibit slavery in the territory of the United States would virtually exclude the Southern citizen of the United States from the common territory. The territory of the United States, about the settlement of which this controversy culminated, was obtained as the result of the war with Mexico, and to exclude the citizen with his slaves was, in fact, to deliver the territory purchased by the money and by the blood of all to one section of the country, to be organized into such political form as to give political power to one section of the country, and thereby give effect in legislation to all the views of the [Liberal] North on the subject of governmental powers. The [Conservative] South claimed an equality of right in all the territories, in the District of Columbia, and in the trade and commerce of the country, and to deny her rights was practically to make her people hewers of wood and drawers of water to the more prosperous and populous section. Notwithstanding the objections and even protests of her statesmen and people, the territory acquired from Mexico was organized so as to exclude slavery, and therefore the South from settlement therein. Not only was this done, but a sectional [Left-wing] President [Lincoln] was elected by a sectional majority [the Republicans, then the Liberal Party] on a national platform of party

principles.

The South then seceded, not in a body, but separately. The Constitution of the United States had been adopted by States, each State acting by itself and for itself. Our own State, Virginia, seceded in April, 1861. I would like to tell about the action of the Gulf States, and of the views of their great thinkers and statesmen, but I have not time to do so. I am sure, however, you will indulge me for a short time, while I recall some things about Virginia, even if I repeat myself, connected with the part she took in the transactions of that period, and in those of our revolutionary days and since, which will present her to you as the grandest figure of any State in the records of time.

In every period of her history Virginia has stood up for the right, as she understood it, against her seeming interest and against power. Settled by English speaking people, she inherited from them the love of truth and liberty, and devotion to right, that has distinguished the inhabitants of Great Britain from the days of her Alfred to our revolution. When the clash of opinion arose as to the rights of the British colonies in America, Virginia, against the seeming interest of her people—certainly against that of her leaders—took the side of the weak in favor of the right, and against the strong and wrong. Her Patrick Henry, by his Demosthenean eloquence, moved the hearts of his countrymen to resistance, as the storm moves the sea. Her George Mason, amid the throes of revolution, gave to his State and the world Virginia's great bill of rights and her first constitution—the first written constitution the world ever saw. Her [Thomas] Jefferson, with his pen, recorded in memorable words the rights of a free people and the wrongs of America. Her [George] Washington led the armies of the rebellious colonies to victory, peace and independence. The war over, the colonies that had been united in defense against Great Britain formed a Union [one that Washington called a "confederate republic"], under what are known as the Articles of Confederation.[73] Then, in order to strengthen that Confederation and promote the common welfare, Virginia ceded to the Confederacy all of her magnificent territory northwest of the Ohio River, now the abode of a great population and the center of wealth and political power.

The Articles of Confederation proving inadequate, a convention of the States was called, and that body gave to the world the Constitution of the United States. That instrument was largely the work of Virginia. The convention that formed it was called chiefly through Washington. Her [James] Madison and Edmund Randolph and [Richard] Henry Lee, its chief defenders in Virginia, against the opposition of such men as Patrick Henry, George Mason, Thomas Nelson, Jr., and Richard Henry Lee, who opposed its adoption by their State without amendment, for reasons which, had they been heeded then, would in all probability have averted our civil war. Some of the writings and utterances of these distinguished objectors, in the light of recent events, seem to be as prophetic as the words of the great Jewish prophet, Isaiah.

The Constitution was adopted, George Washington was made the President of the United States. He put the Federal government in operation, organized the great departments of the government, recommended and approved appropriate legislation, and laid the foundation upon which has been built this great republic. The third President was Thomas Jefferson. Under his administration we obtained from the great Napoleon [Bonaparte] for $15,000,000 [about $360 million in today's currency] title to the territory known as Louisiana, which comprised not only the State of Louisiana, but Missouri, Arkansas, Iowa, and parts of Nebraska, Kansas, Minnesota, and the Indian Territory. Jefferson was succeeded by another Virginian, James Madison. Under his administration war was declared against Great Britain, which brought that power to respect our flag and the rights of our sailors. To another Virginia President, John Tyler, are we chiefly indebted for the State of Texas. Although it was annexed during the administration of James K. Polk, yet the credit of its acquisition is due to John Tyler's administration.

After this came another war, in which our Winfield Scott planted the flag of the United States on the halls of the Montezumas, in the city of Mexico, and thereby obtained peace between this country and Mexico; and as a result of that peace all the territory of the United States, bounded by the Mexican frontier on the south, and the Louisiana purchase on the east and north and northwest, and by the Pacific on the west, was added to this country.

In the Mexican battles Virginia and the South bore their full part. No sooner was the territory acquired than the controversy arose as to its settlement between the sections of our country; one claiming that it should be kept open and free to the people of all the country, whether the North or the South; the other that it should be dedicated to freedom; that the national soil should be like the enchanted ground of an Eastern story, upon which all that entered, no matter how clad, were immediately arrayed in garments of light and beauty—so every slave, as soon as he trod the national soil with his master, should stand clothed in the robes of freedom. Apparently this seemed like the earnest protest of the lovers of freedom against slavery, but in reality it was but a scheme to exclude the South from the occupancy of the newly acquired territory.

The student of the political history of the period will discover that it was not so much opposition, in the decade of 1850-60, to slavery as the desire to get political control of the country, in order that the vast powers of the general government might be yielded to aggrandize one section at the expense of the other. In the furtherance of that scheme it was important to exclude from the newly acquired territory Southern men [that is, Conservatives] and their influence in order that the views of the opposite school [that is, Liberals] might take root and obtain power and control. No more effectual method than the exclusion of slavery, and thereby the Southern slaveholder, could have been devised. The Southerner was accustomed to slavery and slave institutions in his home and on his farm and plantation, and if prevented by law from taking his slaves to the territory of the United States he therefore was virtually excluded. He would either have to forego the advantages of purchasing cheap lands or leave his labor and his domestic habits behind him. Therefore this scheme, however fair to the eye, was in effect a denial to the Southern slaveholder [that is, Conservatives] of any participation in the common territory, and was equal to a deed of cession of all that territory to the Northern States [that is, Liberals].

It was the determination of the Northern States to adhere to that policy, by the election of a President pledged to such views, that caused, as heretofore stated, the separation of the Gulf States from the Union. Virginia, however, did not then secede. Her patriotic Governor, John Letcher, called an extra session of the Legislature to meet January 7th, 1861. That Legislature convened a delegated convention of the people of the State, which assembled at Richmond on the 13th of February, 1861. That convention was composed of some of the most distinguished, conservative and patriotic citizens of Virginia. Among them A. H. H. Stuart, John Janney, Robt. E. Scott, John B. Baldwin, Geo. Y. Summers, and your fellow-citizen, Hugh M. Nelson, whose name graces yon monument—all Union men, as were the majority of that body. That convention chose for its president that eminent citizen of London, John Janney. He belonged to a Quaker family, loved peace and the ways of peace. I doubt not that this had something to do with his selection. It was designed to show that Virginia was for peace, and not for war. Previous to that her Legislature had sent a commission composed of four of Virginia's distinguished sons, viz.: John Tyler, Geo. W. Summers, William C. Rives and James A. Seddon, to Washington to attend what was called a Peace Congress, that convened upon her invitation or suggestion. That Congress failed to accomplish any good results. On the 8th of April, 1861, the Virginia convention sent a commission, consisting of William Ballard Preston, A. H. H. Stuart and Geo. W. Randolph, to see President Lincoln and obtain information as to his views, purposes and policy in regard to the seceded States. The report of that committee was not satisfactory.

After this the affair of Fort Sumter took place. It fired the Northern heart. President Lincoln called for his army of 75,000 men, and on Virginia for her quota. After this Virginia seceded, she did this chiefly because she was called upon to contribute her share of force to coerce the seceding States. As valuable as the Union was to her, as much as she loved it because of her part in its construction and maintenance, she held it was not an end, but the means to an end—personal and political liberty, State equality and sovereignty; that the Union established by the fathers was one of consent, love and affection, and not of force; that whether it was wise on the part of the Gulf States to separate was not a matter for her to determine, because in her judgment they clearly had the right to separate, and those wielding the powers of the government of the United States had not the right to force them back into the Union, and that to force them back into the union, and that to compel them by force to return, would be to trample underfoot the teachings and principles of the fathers, therefore, with sad heart and tearful eyes, she passed, in April, 1861, her ordinance of secession.

I have made this brief reference to the foregoing facts in regard to Virginia's contributions to the cause of American liberty, and to the Union, and to her course in the early days of 1861, to show how dear to her was the Union, how she yearned for peace, and that it was not slavery that induced her to separate from the then government of the United States, but her love for the Constitution and the Union, as established by the [founding] fathers.

. . . Human institutions have their uses and their limitations. They are the scaffolding to the building, a means to an end. Although African slavery was not the cause, it was the occasion of our war. It was useful and valuable in its day. It lifted a people who, in the land of their nativity, were savages, out of barbarism and animalism to such a plane of Christian civilization as to qualify them, in the judgment of the Conquerors of the South, to participate in the government of the great republic. What a tribute to the much abused South! What a monument to Southern Christian men and women! Match me if you can out of the record of missions subsequent to the days of the Apostles and the early teachers of Christianity any work among the heathen that can compare with it in results, when viewed from the standpoint of those who have given the African the ballot.

But in the plan of the Great Ruler, doubtless the time had arrived for African slavery to pass away. So far as we can see, it could not have been gotten rid of in this country except by the means used. Mr. Lincoln did not by his war proclamation intend to destroy slavery in the States. Its destruction was an evolution of the war—a war measure, consequent upon the events and result of war.

Moses, the world's great law-giver, commanded his people to teach the laws he had been directed to give them unto their children, in the house and by the wayside, to bind them as a sign upon their hands, and as frontlets between their eyes. May we not, in imitation of the great law-giver, tell our fathers, mothers, daughters

An extremely rare photo of a black Confederate soldier, one of the estimated 1 million African Americans who fought for the Southern Cause. This former "rebel" appears to have been photographed at Atlanta, Georgia, in 1904.

and teachers to teach the children committed to their care and instruction the principles of American liberty, State and national, not as taught by the precept and example of the multitude [today known as the mainstream media], but as delivered by the fathers of the republic, and for which our comrades died that fell in battle. To tell and teach them that the dead, in honor of whom this monument has been erected, were not traitors, but true citizens, who gave their lives in defense of the truth, as they understood it, and of their altars and their homes; that [Confederate officers] Lee, Jackson, Stuart, Ashby and Hill, and their soldiers, were not rebels, nor traitors, but patriots, loving God and their fellow-men, and that they did their duty to their country [all emphasis, L.S.]. Teach them also to look upward to the Great Ruler of all things, truth and untruth, and forward to the duties in life that may be before them; to do their duty as our brave soldier did; to do it under all circumstances to themselves, to their country and their God—and then come what may, success or failure, they will receive the plaudits of good men, the approval of their own consciences and the approbation of their God.[74] — AN ADDRESS BY COL. RICHARD HENRY LEE, OF VIRGINIA, AT THE DEDICATION OF THE CONFEDERATE MONUMENT AT OLD CHAPEL, IN CLARKE COUNTY

JEFFERSON DAVIS & THE CAUSE OF LIBERTY
☛ Mr. [Jefferson] Davis deserves a monument, as lasting as our native hills, for the splendid record he made in the cause of liberty. As an exemplar his character should be held up to the youth of the country; as an embodiment of everything good in human nature.[75]
— C. A. READ, EDITOR, *TIMES*, LEWISVILLE, TEXAS

JEFFERSON DAVIS: THE EQUAL OF THOMAS JEFFERSON
☛ In a speech at Clarksville, Tenn., Judge Turney said he did not care to make a speech except to keep himself identified with the immortal idea of constitutional government.

This was not altogether an occasion of mourning. The South had much to be thankful for. Her grand leader had lived long, enough to see the intense hatred and slander born of the war pass away, and to know that the divisions among his own people were healed, and all believed that he acted upon conscientious and upright judgment.

He spoke of Mr. [Jefferson] Davis as a comrade as well as a statesman. He had seen him risk his life on two battlefields. He remembered seeing him at the first Manassas, and he felt outraged that the great guiding brain of the Confederacy as he considered Mr. Davis, should take such risks. Again, when the noble [Confederate General Robert Hopkins] Hatton fell Mr. Davis was on the field. He saw Hatton's troops go into the fight, and, noting Hatton at its head, Mr. Davis said: "That brigade moves in handsomely, but it will lose its commander." Mr. Davis thought for others but not for himself.

He thought Mr. Davis the ablest defender of constitutional law in the Union. From his sacrifice he could come to no other conclusion than that Mr. Davis believed in the justice of the South's cause as he believed in the Christian religion. He had absolutely no doubt of the right of a State to go out of the Union when the terms of the Union were violated. His State papers would live as long as [Thomas] Jefferson's. He was the equal of Jefferson, [John C.] Calhoun and [Daniel] Webster, and superior to all who lived when he breathed his last. Mr. Davis was immortal. He would live while manhood lasts.[76] — SUMNER A. CUNNINGHAM, EDITOR, *CONFEDERATE VETERAN* MAGAZINE

IN OUR FATHER'S HOUSE

☛ An experience in the management of the *Confederate Veteran* has revealed certain facts concerning patriotism that it may be will to print. It concerns the Union as well as Confederate soldier elements.

The Grand Army [Union veterans] Posts, in the aggregate led by designing politicians, appear as partisans in politics more to their discredit than is due. *Confederate Veteran* organizations repudiate politics. Your great captain [Union Gen. Ulysses S. Grant], in accepting the resignation of [Confederate] Gen. [Robert E.] Lee, illustrated the sentiment of his best soldiers in refusing that good man's sword, and in telling him that "the [Southern] boys will need their horses to make crops." Grant never had heart in the radical [socialist and communist] measures of the [Republican, then Liberal] administration while Chief Executive. This was given out as a last expression of his life, and kept a secret even from his wife until after he was dead.

True patriots of the two sections are much more in harmony than they think. Unhappily the political victors, by our system of government, wielded so much power that the Union veteran was dashed by the current, and he could not check its tide. Many thousands of the best [Union] soldiers who suffered for the [U.S.] flag but refused to ally themselves with these sectional [Left-wing] partisans, have been refused any benefits of office through all the decades that have followed. Many of them have stood as true to principles, however, as the great body of the Southern people. This element is stronger than it realizes, and the day may yet be predicted when it will he heard.

A letter printed in this *Veteran* commends its "fraternal spirit'" by a Union soldier. Such is its spirit. All honor to the bronzed American [Union] soldier who acted upon the teachings of his fathers and ours, that "the Union must and shall be preserved." The Confederate soldier must not fail to honor such, and he will not. In paying tribute to their courage and manhood we honor ourselves.

Resting upon this declaration the hold assertion is made that the average Southerner is a better patriot than the average Northerner.

American soldiers of the Union should accept this, and they might, with fine grace, admit it. Placing our ancestors on equal footing, and Union veterans will certainly admit as much, they should know that we who suffered greater hardships through the four bitter years of war became more intensely devoted than if we had been paid for our service [as were so many Union soldiers]. We fought for home and the constitutional principle of our fathers, while they can only claim to have fought for the latter and the Union.

So far reference is had only to the American sons [Yankees] who volunteered to battle for the Union, and the premise should be accepted. If positions had been reversed the men of the South would have been less ardent than they are and were. Again, this sentiment will be in greater contrast when we remember that many thousands of foreigners came to America to fight for pay, having not a particle of sentiment. This picture must be depressing to the American soldier who fought for the Union. The ostracism of southern men through all these years has been bad for the spirit of national pride that we all would like to have.

The foreign writer of history who goes about our national capital and sees the bronze dedicated to the Union side only will think of our "reconstructed" rather than our "reunited" country. (These monuments are almost exclusively to officers. In the South the finest monuments are to private soldiers.) If he crosses over to Arlington on the opposite side of the Potomac, he will witness that the magnificent home of Robert E. Lee, which has been converted into sexton's quarters of a national cemetery, has not even a portrait of that eminent man whom the civilized world delights to honor, and a man whose ancestors, back to the formation of the [U.S.] government, were eminent in its establishment and maintenance.

How long, O brothers of American sires, will you keep silent against these unwise and unpatriotic things? "We are," indeed, "in our father's house," and "we love our country's [U.S.] flag." We would not if we could substitute another for it. The "Flag of the Confederacy" is, however, absolutely sacred, and will be forever, yea forever. It is a lost flag, and that should be the term rather than "lost cause." Our cause is not lost. The principles of the [confederated republican] government for which we fought are being maintained, save as to State's rights and slavery [the latter referring to the South's constitutionally sound view that it should be the right of the individual states, not the central government, to allow or ban slavery within its borders].[77] The abolition of the latter is everywhere accepted, and the former is a question of expediency still as much as ever it was.

Constitutional government is the underlying principle for which all good men pray, and for which southern as well as northern men will fight. Do let us all, both North and South, with the issues removed that caused a long "unpleasantness," press forward to our high calling as Americans. Confederate veterans, proud sons of men, you have done and are doing your part well. You will so continue. Nothing can deter you from devotion to the principles impressed by education and grounded in by experience. Continue patient under trial and all will be well in the end.[78] — SUMNER A. CUNNINGHAM, EDITOR, *CONFEDERATE VETERAN* MAGAZINE

OUR UNKNOWN DEAD

☛ . . . [As Lincoln's war progressed, there] . . . was no Confederate Government to collect and care for the remains of the Confederate dead. Along the banks of the Father of Waters [Mississippi River] for more than a thousand miles the inhabitants tread unawares over the unknown graves of those who battled for the South. Along the shores of the Potomac, the Rappahannock and the James, wave the golden harvests on soil enriched by their blood and mouldering dust. From the capes of the Chesapeake adown the stormy Atlantic, and trending around the Gulf, rest thousands of our dead; or go to the heights of Allatoona, to Lookout's lofty peak, or Kennesaw Mountain's top, and you may seek in vain where the dead rest. Time, with the relentless forces of the elements, has obliterated all traces of their graves from human eye; they are known only to Him who can tell where Moses sleeps in "a vale in the land of Moab." So the forgotten are not forgot, the hand that made the thunder's home comes down every spring and paints with bright colors the little wild flowers that grow over their resting places, and they are bright on decoration day. The rosy morn announces first to them that the night is gone, and when the day is past and the landscape veiled with evening's shade, high on the mountain's top the last rays of the setting sun lovingly lingers longest, loth to have the lonely place where the bright-eyed children of the Confederacy rest in death.

And wherefore did they die? They fell in defense of their homes, their families, their country, and those civil rights arising from that liberty God gave man as a heritage in the beginning. They furnished to their country much that will be noble in history, wonderful in story, tender in song, and a large share of that glory which will claim the admiration of mankind. We can to-day place no wreaths of immortelles on their unknown graves, yet we can rest assured the echoes of posterity will render their deeds illustrious. . . .[79] — CONFEDERATE GENERAL SAMUEL G. FRENCH, SPEECH, ORLANDO, FLORIDA, JUNE 3, 1893

DESCRIBING RECONSTRUCTION IN GEORGIA, 1867

☛ Col. C. B. Howard has written of the time [during Reconstruction], in June, 1867, when the State of Georgia was under military rule and the citizens were being annoyed with all sorts of indignities. Judge W. W. Clayton, a prominent citizen, had just been turned out of house and home because his daughters refused to pass under the United States flag, and hid their faces from yankee officers with their parasols. It was a few days before Alexander H. Stephens wrote a letter to Col. R. A. Alston, saying he considered the country in *articula mortis* [at the point of death] that if the South resisted reconstruction [it] would be forced, and if they accepted it they were disgraced, and that it was a choice between martyrdom and suicide, and for himself he preferred martyrdom.

The story of that meeting was told by Mr. S. A. Echols in a letter printed in the *Sunny South* during the summer of 1878, just after the controversy between Mr. [Benjamin W.] Hill and Mr. Stephens over the question, "Who saved the State?" In that article Mr. Echols gives a long interview with Col. Alston, who told how he, Dr. J. P. Hambleton and Mr. Eli Hulsey, in discussing the deplorable situation, decided to call a Democratic [then the Conservative party] meeting. They did so, and wrote a letter to Col. T. C. Howard, at Kirkwood, asking him to attend and preside. The papers refused to print the call and the city hall was secured only by consent of [Union] Gen. [John] Pope [to this day still considered a war criminal in the South]. When the time came for the meeting the house was partly filled with Pope's [U.S.] officers and civil staff, and many of the Democrats present opposed any demonstration.

Col. Howard walked into the room and looked around in astonishment. He had left the plow and walked into town. . . . Charlie called on him soon afterward for a speech. Col. Alston said of it: "I never shall forget the scene and solemn dignity with which he rose. Never shall I forget how he was dressed—an old coat with the lining torn out and hanging in strings, an unbleached homespun shirt, no cravat, a pair of brogan shoes, without socks. His handsome, intelligent face contrasted strongly with his apparel, and even a stranger would not have been surprised to hear something good, even from such a poorly dressed speaker. His first words were:

"'My fellow countrymen, when I am called upon on an occasion like this, surrounded by circumstances like these (pointing to the eager Democrats [Conservatives], and these (pointing to the soldiers), and these (pointing to the scalawags [Southern Union sympathizers]) I feel that deep solemnity which the man of God feels, or at least ought to feel, when he rises in the pulpit to talk to dying sinners about the salvation of their souls.' He then went on to trace the history of this country from the settlement of New England and Virginia down to the breaking out of the Confederate war. He demonstrated that three generations had raised up in these different latitudes two entirely different races of people, that the bloody war which had resulted had been brought on by the love of constitutional freedom on the part of the South, and a love for religion and law battling against a total disregard of all compacts on the part of the North, and an utter disregard of public morality, constitutional law and Bible religion on the part of the North. That while slavery may have embittered the contest it was not the cause, but only one of the incidents of the struggle. That the constant and persevering invasions of our rights had proceeded from envy, hatred and malice. 'Yea,' said he, 'my countrymen, from the day that old John Adams left the white house,' pointing his finger at the portrait of [George] Washington and saying, 'You and your people did this, there began a struggle which never ceased until it left this whole continent with crutches and crape [funerary decorations] in every household, which drew one broad line of charcoal from Dalton to Charlotte, N.C., and brought delicate women to cooking, scrubbing, and scouring, where [Union General William T.] Sherman had left them any thing to cook, to scrub or to scour.' Here he paid a glowing and beautiful tribute to the women of the South, and passing on he said. 'But when I come to speak of the 150,000 dead heroes that lie slumbering in our soil, what shall I say?' Here he burst into tears. . . . Soon rousing himself, with bitter scorn he addressed Pope's people and said: 'And do you call upon me to disgrace the fortitude of women like these? Do you call upon me to desecrate the memory of heroes like these? Never! never! And what for, what to gain—to save what little we have left? No, my friends, this would be to lose our all, to surrender the only jewel that even tyranny cannot wrest from us—our honor. Even [South-hating Yankee socialist] Wendell Phillips says, a few years longer and a change of a few thousand votes will cause the shackles to fall from our limbs. Yes. Wendell Phillips, the worst man who has cursed God's footstool for the last thousand years, always excepting that fiend and scourge of hell, _____.'[80]

"When these words fell from his lips the consternation was painful. We all grasped arms and felt that the supreme moment had arrived. But Col. Howard thundered on and the crisis was passed. Turning to where we were standing he said: 'Go on, my little band of Democrats [Conservatives], bend your backs and take the blows, the anvil will yet wear out the hammer. Recollect that God has said in his word, "One man shall be equal to a thousand, and two shall put ten thousand to flight," armed with the power of truth; then therefore stand firm, and oh, when your hearts grow weary, when you are ready to exclaim, "How long, Lord, how long," faint not, but look back more than 1800 years and behold the most sublime spectacle that assembled creations were ever called upon to witness. See the Son of God condescending to become man to save a sinful world, remembering that when he walked throughout Galilee, armed with the power and majesty of God, distributing his loaves and fishes, whole multitudes followed him. But alas! when the day of his tribulation came, when he had no more loaves to divide, no more fishes to distribute, when we see him swinging upon the cross, whom do we see there then? One poor, lone, weeping woman! Ah, if you yankees had been there then, if you scalawags had been there then, if you timid Democrats had been there then (the scorn dripping from his fingers), you would have gone to her and said: "Get up from here, Mary . . . The majority is against us. Let us yield." And this day you would have been peeping into the quivering guts of birds and animals to learn the will of God [a Pagan practice known as haruspicy], and sacrificing to Jupiter, and we would have lost the Christian religion.'"[81] — *CONFEDERATE VETERAN* MAGAZINE

SPEAKING OF STATES' RIGHTS

☞ . . . But young men will ask, was not slavery so bad that the Constitution, which shielded it, was rightly violated in order to destroy it? That is the question which has been answered by the roar of artillery in the affirmative. But can that answer by force be justified in the forum of morals? If solemn compact may be violated in order to destroy what that compact guaranteed, what value is there in a written Constitution? It only awaits a new fanatical sentiment to justify a new crusade upon its integrity. If the obligation of compact may be impaired or destroyed because of its subject-matter civilization will perish, because it cannot survive the death of good faith or the repudiation of public or private compacts.

But let me present another view. The crusade not only destroyed slavery, but entailed upon the South a social condition for which the crusaders suggest no relief, and a condition which seems to be without the hope of peaceful solution. Those who had no interest in the relation have inoculated the South with a social and political disease for which their statesmen have provided no remedy and can find no panacea. These were the issues upon which the Southern States seceded, and defended their imperiled rights with a valor, constancy and fortitude which has made them immortal.

We cannot be placed in the false position of having fought to hold men in slavery. The South never made a free man a slave, and never took from the dark land one human being to shackle him with servitude. The race of Southern men inherited the institution, which was put on us by the cupidity of [Yankee] slave traders against the protests of our colonial fathers. Eight millions of Caucasians and four millions of Africans—the first masters, the last slaves. That was the problem we inherited. Shall they remain slaves and how long? or be at once emancipated? and then be put into possession of equal power with the white man to direct a common destiny? Shall our constitutional power, our inherent natural right to regulate this special interest, be wrested from us and vested in aliens to that interest, to be exercised by them to create social and political relations never known in the history of civilized man, and for the right regulation of which no prophecy could forecast a law, and our sad experience has been unable to devise a remedy? To put it forensically, the South did not plead to the issue of slavery or no slavery, but to the jurisdiction. To create the jurisdiction was to give up self-government.

If we resisted the government, we defended the Constitution; we supported the sovereignty which ordained the supreme law of the land, though we opposed by force the usurpations of the delegated agent of the sovereignty.

We failed—were defeated—came back to the Union, yes, but to the Union under the Constitution—and though amended—in substance the same old Constitution. The rents in its sacred parchment are healed; the blood-stains are obliterated.

Virginia greets the daughter of North Carolina, a younger sister in this great Union. Let us labor to perpetuate this galaxy of commonwealths, bound by the gravitating forces of commercial, geographical, social and political interests, and of common aspirations, as the inheritors of the free institutions of the

Anglo-American race. Let us co-operate to save the Union from the maelstrom of a centralized paternalism, and to anchor our liberty and right in the safe harbor of ancient constitutional polity. God preserve and perpetuate the union of these States on the solid rock-bed of the Constitution of our fathers!

Let no censorious criticism suggest a doubt of our faithful devotion to the Constitution and Union of to-day because we honor and revere the patriotism of those who died for the lost cause. The heroic purpose failed; our Confederacy sank beneath the political horizon in clouds which could not blacken history. The sun of the Confederacy lighted them with the effulgence of its own transcendent glory. The fame of its heroes, of their genius for leadership, of their constancy, fortitude, martial prowess and devotion to duty, all Americans will one day claim to be the common heritage of the Union.

I come from an historic institution that bears the illustrious names of [George] Washington, the spotless hero in victory, and of [Robert E.] Lee, the no less spotless hero in defeat. I live near the grave of this most splendid type of the Virginia cavaliers, and of that of Stonewall Jackson, the noblest type of the Scotch-Irish race. I come to Tennessee, two of whose sons, the hero of the Hermitage [Andrew Jackson] and the eminent James K. Polk, were elected Presidents by all the States of the Union; the one whose sturdy arm struck down the giant bank monopoly, the other the no less hateful monopoly of tariff spoliation. President Jackson declared the Union must and shall be preserved—the Union under the written Constitution of the fathers. Both of them were of kindred lineage with heroes of the Confederacy, with Stonewall Jackson and [Confederate General] Leonidas Polk, who died as defenders of the lost cause.[82]

Confederate brothers: left, James McHenry Howard, 1st Maryland Infantry; right, David Ridgely Howard, 2nd Maryland Infantry.

Standing reverently near the tombs of your mighty dead, I hesitate not to say that neither would have condemned these Confederate heroes of their blood. The spirits of these Jacksons and these Polks, of [Jefferson] Davis and of Lee, of the two Johnstons [Albert S. and Joseph E.], and of hundreds of others hovering near us, would join in our fervent aspiration that this and coming generations shall be faithful to the Union and the Constitution, upon which, as their best foundation, liberty and right and justice shall ever securely rest. The living and the dead of the lost Confederacy and of the restored Union, by their devotion to truth and right, call upon us, one and all, to uphold and defend this constitutional Union. With patriotic purpose, despite the breakers which threaten our shipwreck, guided by the chart of the Constitution, and with humble trust in the God of our fathers, let us here and now resolve to remit no effort as citizens of a common country to steer this fleet of American commonwealths into the haven of peace and fraternity, with the noble memories of past achievements, and with united aspirations for the heritage of a common glory among the nations of earth.[83] — JOHN RANDOLPH TUCKER, SPEECH, VANDERBILT UNIVERSITY, NASHVILLE, TENNESSEE, JUNE 1893

A STATEMENT OF FACT

☛ . . . let us, our children, and all future generations, see and know who the Confederates were. Let them know that the principles we fought for are fully guaranteed by the Constitution of our country, and that we were patriots willing to offer our all in defense of our homes and rights.[84] — W. F. TRAVIS, TULLAHOMA, TENNESSEE

OUR STRUGGLE

☛ . . . The history of our struggle for constitutional rights has too long been left in the hands of our friends—the enemy. Our children have been taught that we were rebels and traitors, while the reverse is true. It is time this wrong was corrected. . . .[85] — N. B. HOGAN, SPRINGFIELD, MISSOURI

CHIEF EXECUTIVE OF THE C.S.A.

☛ I do not know how any one could have expected me, under the trust which I held from the people of the Confederate States, to propose to surrender, at discretion, the rights and liberties for which the best and bravest of the land were still gallantly struggling, and for which so many had nobly died. The "matter they had at heart" was to maintain the rights their fathers had left them. My heart sympathized with theirs, feeling that duty and honor alike forbade that I should seek peace on conditions which our army, depleted as it was, would have rejected with disdain.

If, while the army defiantly held its position in the field, the sovereign people and their representatives in the Congress of the Confederate States, under the pressure of war and dread of *possible* consequences, had wished to abandon the claims in defense of which the war was waged, and that the battle-torn flags should be furled and cased in humiliation, and the arms so long and so valiantly borne should be stacked for surrender, I should have bowed to their will but would never have executed it. In shame and mortification I would have resigned and left the office to be filled by some one fit for such service as has been indicated.[86] — JEFFERSON DAVIS, PRESIDENT OF THE CONFEDERATE STATES OF AMERICA

Confederate artillery, outside Charleston, South Carolina, 1861.

Left: Confederate private George Hansell, 1st Chickasaw Infantry Regiment ("Hunter's Indian Volunteers"); right: unnamed friend in Confederate uniform with holstered revolvers and two scouting dogs.

GENERAL GORDON TO UNITED CONFEDERATE VETERANS

☛ Comrades, no argument is needed to secure for those objects your enthusiastic indorsement. They have burdened your thoughts for many years; you have cherished them in sorrow, poverty and humiliation. In the face of misconstruction you have held them in your hearts with the strength of religious convictions. No misjudgments can defeat your peaceful purposes for the future. Your aspirations have been lifted by the mere force and urgency of surrounding conditions to a plane far above the paltry consideration of partisan triumphs. The honor of the American government, the just powers of the Federal government, the equal rights of States, the integrity of the constitutional union, the sanctions of law and the enforcement of order have no class of defenders more true and devoted than the ex-soldiers of the South and their worthy descendants. But you realize the great truth that a people without the memories of heroic suffering or sacrifice are a people without a history.

To cherish such memories and recall such a past, whether crowned with success or consecrated in defeat is to idealize principle and strengthen character, intensify love of country and convert defeat and disaster into pillars of support for future manhood and noble womanhood. Whether the Southern people under their changed conditions may ever hope to witness another civilization which shall equal that which began with their [George]

Washington and ended with their [Robert E.] Lee, it is certainly true that devotion to their glorious past is not only the surest guarantee of future progress and the holiest bond of unity, but is also the strongest claim they can present to the confidence and respect of the other sections of the Union.

In conclusion, I beg to repeat, in substance at least, a few thoughts recently expressed by me to the State organization, which apply with equal force to this general brotherhood.

It is political in no sense except so far as the word "political" is a synonym of the word "patriotic." It is a brotherhood over which the genius of philanthropy and patriotism, of truth and of justice will preside; of philanthropy, because it will succor the disabled, help the needy, strengthen the weak and cheer the disconsolate; of patriotism, because it will cherish the past glories of the dead Confederacy and transmute them into living inspirations for future service to the living republic; of truth, because it will seek to gather and preserve as witnesses for history the unimpeachable facts which shall doom falsehood to die that truth may live, of justice, because it will cultivate National as well as Southern fraternity and will condemn narrow-mindedness and prejudice and passion, and cultivate that broader, higher and nobler sentiment, which would write on the grave of every soldier who fell on our side: "Here lies an American hero, a martyr to the right as his conscience conceived it."

A Confederate general named for the Southern Cause: States Rights Gist. He perished at the Battle of Franklin II defending your Constitutional rights.

I rejoice that a general organization too, long neglected, has at last been perfected. It is an organization which all honorable men must approve and which heaven itself will bless. I call upon you, therefore, to organize in every State and community where ex-Confederates may reside, and rally to the support of the high and peaceful objects of the United Confederate Veterans, and move forward until by the power of organization and persistent effort your beneficent and Christian purposes are fully accomplished.[87] —
CONFEDERATE GENERAL JOHN B. GORDON

THE SOUTH IS 100 PERCENT AMERICAN
☞ The war [for Southern independence] ended twenty-eight years ago, but it is still the habit of the North to think of the people of the States which attempted to secede as enemies of the Union and of the Constitution. . . . It is one of the hopeful signs of the times that throughout the South there is a positive and growing interest in historical research. [Let us look at some of that now.]

. . . The white people of the South are almost exclusively the descendants of the Americans of 1775. Upon the other hand, it is safe to say that of the males of voting age in the Northern and Northwestern States, not less than fifty per cent are foreign born, or the sons of foreign born parents.

The white people of the South are not only American, they are, in the main, the descendants of a race which from the days of Tacitus has been known in the world's history as the exemplar and champion of personal purity, personal independence, and political liberty. For them no life but one of freedom is possible, and can never believe that the hybrid population of Russians, Poles, Italians, Hungarians, which fills so many Northern cities and States, has the same love for our country, the same love of liberty, as have the Anglo-Saxon Southerners, whose fathers have always been free. The strongest, most concentrated force of Americanism [that is, conservatism] is in the South, and Americanism is the highest form of Anglo-Saxon civilization. There is no part of the globe, except the kingdom of England, which is so thoroughly Anglo-Saxon as the South.

But it will be said, admitting that the South is American, and has preserved the Anglo-Saxon traits, nevertheless a war was necessary to keep her in the Union. To this matter my own inclinations, no less than limitations of space, require me to refer very briefly.

The excellence of the American Union is in the principles upon which it is established—that is to say in the Constitution. Surely no man will say that it is more important to preserve the physical integrity of the Union than the principles of the Constitution. We claim for the South, in the war between the states, absolute good faith. Whether she was right or wrong, the impartial judgment of the future will fairly determine. I affirm that the South has been, from the first, absolutely faithful to the principles of the Constitution, as she in good faith construed it. Let me indicate briefly the extent of her participation in the formation of the Constitution and the establishment of the Republic. It is correctly said by a Southern statesman that the Constitution was "adopted and promulgated by a convention in which Southern influences predominated." The heading of one of [historian George] Bancroft's chapters is, "Virginia Statesmen Lead Toward a Better Union."

Virginia did lead the movement for the establishment of the Constitution, and the reader who wishes to know the extent of the influence of George Washington, of Virginia, in this movement, is referred to the pages of [historian] John Fiske, of New England. [John] Rutledge and [Charles C.] Pinckney, of South Carolina, were the most important contributors to the form, as to the substance, of the Constitution, with the exception of James Madison, of Virginia, who justly hears the name of "Father of the Constitution." The Bill of Rights is mainly the work of Thomas Jefferson.

During the first century of our national life Southern statesmen held the Presidency and shaped the policy of the Government. They acquired Florida, and extended our domain to the Rio Grande and to the Pacific. The Constitution was first construed by John Marshall, of Virginia. The school of strict constructionists, which made a fetish of the Constitution, was founded and supported by Southern men. When the Southern Confederacy was formed it adopted as its organic law the old Constitution, unchanged in any essential respect.

There is no fact nor logic which can prove that the South ever deviated from her fealty to the Constitution, or ever shed a drop of blood except in defense of its principles as she construed it.

The war construed the Constitution, and the South has in good faith and unreservedly accepted every legitimate result of the war. No man who is honest who is adequately informed will say that her people are not absolutely loyal to the Union and the Constitution. I go further, and affirm that in the troubles which the future is sure to bring, the principles and the institutions of American liberty will find their most loyal and steadfast support in the twelve millions of Southern Anglo-Saxon Americans.[88] — JOSHUA W. CALDWELL, FROM AN ARTICLE IN THE *ARENA*

THE REPUBLIC BEQUEATHED BY OUR FATHERS

☛ I feel that we should educate our children in the true faith while we live, so that when we have bivouacked on the other shore our cause will live. By "our cause" I mean the right of self government and American manhood. Let us teach them to love the Republic our fathers bequeathed to us, the Republic of equal rights for all the States. Teach them that the followers of [Confederate Generals Albert] Sidney and J. E. Johnston, [Nathan Bedford] Forrest, [Joseph] Wheeler and [John B.] Hood, fought for the preservation of civil liberty against centralism [of the national government] and the downfall of American liberty.[89] — W. FORT SMITH, BRAZORIA, TEXAS

CONFEDERATE VETERAN FAN MAIL
☛ Dear Mr. [Sumner A.] Cunningham: The *Confederate Veteran* comes to me full of good things, and I wish to thank you for your faithful work in giving to the Confederate soldiers such an admirable and accurate record of the days that "tried men's souls." . . . The editorials and letters of correspondents are full of interest to one who took part in the struggle to preserve the constitutional rights of the States. I am yours with all good wishes.[90] — BISHOP CHARLES TODD QUINTARD, SEWANEE, TENNESSEE

FIGHTING COMMUNISM DURING & AFTER THE WAR
☛ . . . As I look upon this sea of faces, and hear the [Rebel] yell that is not unfamiliar to my ears, my thoughts, fellow soldiers, go back many, many years. Without bitterness and without malice I stand here to claim the proud honor which belongs to us all—that we were Confederate soldiers.

It is sometimes said that our cause is lost. Some causes are never lost. They may be crushed in defeat, they may go down in seeming ignominy, but in the end, like truth crushed to earth, they rise again. The Confederate soldier is always and under all circumstances true to principle. There was no selfishness in his heart, no thought of the morrow with him. He put all upon his country's altar, and went forth and gave his time and his heart and his life to the cause. What did that cause represent? I said it was not lost, and I repeat the assertion. It could not be lost.

It stood first for the rights of the States. Upon its solid foundation hangs the liberty and prosperity of the whole of America. Inside of eleven years after the surrender of our armies, before the grandest tribunal that ever sat upon earth, it was decided that the States were supreme in this nation. We are not indebted to our friends, soldiers, for this decision, but it came from those who had been our enemies.

They went upon record with the solemn declaration that no matter what might be the action of a State in the selection of a President its action was final. So that part of our cause, instead of being lost, is triumphant throughout the north and the south, the east and the west as the highest law in the land. There was another great principle for which we stood, and that is that we fought against the interference of the government with the rights of the property of the individual. Our contest was broad upon the idea of individual rights of life, liberty and property. The fight is still upon us, fellow-soldiers, the fight for constitutional guarantees in this country, the fight for the enjoyment of our lives, the right of the enjoyment of our liberty and that equal dignity of right to enjoy the fruits of our labor. Tell me not that the cause is lost when hosts of Americans are marshaling in defense of these rights, and that flag [pointing to a Confederate banner], the flag of the old Confederates, typifies the fight. Turn it loose and let them all see it! [The man holding the flag shook it out, and the whole building rang with cheers.] Brave men have followed it, patriots have died under it, lovely woman has blessed it with her prayers and consecrated it with her tears. It stood for the rights of life, liberty and property from 1861 to 1865. It didn't tell a lie then. It speaks no lie to day.

We stand to day with our brethren of the whole country, marshaled now under a different flag [taking hold of the Union (U.S.) banner], and we will be as true to this as we were to that. With our faces firmly set, fellow-soldiers, against the aggressions of government, against the aggressions of anarchy, against the aggressions of communism in every shape, come from whatever quarter it may, standing true to the Constitution and the flag of our country, in defense of the rights and liberties of this people, we would not join any band that would march upon Washington now. We marched upon Washington once before in a manly fight and under the true flag, and the next time we march upon Washington we will take this flag with us [pointing to the United States flag amid cheering] to cover us, and we will raise it against the hosts of communism, let them be led by whom they may. Am I not right when I say it's a misnomer to call our cause lost? It could not be lost. God, in his inscrutable wisdom, if we were untrue to [the] principle for which we contended, and of which we are not ashamed, would raise up another race that would prove better men than we were. The cause is triumphant, and the Confederate soldier will go down into history occupying the proud page he should occupy, and we every year will turn aside one day at least to weep over our dead and talk over the trying times of the past.

We meet in no spirit of malice or of strife, standing as we have ever stood, true to the flag of our country and to the institutions of our government, and I know we will ever stand true to the principles of our cause, which are eternal.

Now, welcome again to Waco; welcome to our homes. Let enjoyment rule all of our hearts; but, comrades, let us not forget in our moment of joy those old heroes who have crossed the river. Let us make it a point, according to our means, to rear to their memories grand monuments, to show to all future eyes the deeds done by them, the cause for which fought and the cause for which they died.[91] — REVEREND FRANK PAGE, SPEECH, REUNION OF UNITED CONFEDERATE VETERANS, WACO, TEXAS, APRIL 1894

WHY A SOUTHERN HISTORY OF THE USA IS NEEDED

☛ One of the pressing needs of our whole country is a history of the United States, for schools and for popular use, written from the Southern standpoint. We do not want a prejudiced, partisan account of our political and social life, and of our civil war, but a clear, vivid story of the difficulties, efforts and growth of our people, in the light of those great ideas and principles which controlled the actions of Southern statesmen from the origin of the Republic.

Hitherto Northern men have written the history, and naturally in the light of Northern ideas and principles. Of course our great civil war has been treated as a "wicked and causeless rebellion," as a war stirred up by a few ambitious spirits for personal ends, and for the maintenance and extension of the institution of slavery. Our children are taught to believe that we were rebels and traitors against "the best government the world ever saw." Now, a movement so widespread, so nearly unanimous, and which called forth the enthusiastic devotion and the heroic efforts of millions of people for four years, is not causeless. But the causes lie far back in our history. The contest was between two different conceptions of the nature of our government. The Southern people made their desperate struggle to maintain the government which they believed its founders established. When they were defeated they accepted in good faith the government as it now is, and are loyal to it, but they do not believe that it is the government according to the idea of the framers of the Constitution. It may turn out to be better. Certainly they have no idea of trying to establish by force their idea of State's rights. But they will always contend that they fought for the Constitutional rights of the people, as originally guaranteed to them.

Now, the histories written by Southern men, as far as I have seen, do not set forth clearly the idea and purpose which animated the South in all the years before 1860, when it controlled the government. Our historians are usually content to give our side of the civil war, with some of the causes that led up to it; but for all the period preceding that fearful contest they differ little from Northern writers.

How few of our children know that Jamestown, Virginia, was settled before the Pilgrim Fathers came to this country, or that the vast domain which forms four-fifths of the United States was won by Southern men, or that slavery was forced upon this country by England, seconded by New England, or that in 1860 one-tenth of the slaves were communicants in churches.

What we need is a history of the country from the beginning, which shall show the wonderful part the South had in its conquest and development, and the patriotic spirit and great sacrifices made by the South for the Union. It can only be written by one in thorough sympathy with the ideas of the South, as with thorough knowledge of the great facts of history.

The history of this country to the close of the civil war is not the "History of the Rise and Fall of the Slave Power,"[92] as Vice President [Henry] Wilson wrote it, but the history of the overthrow of the Constitution as it was originally adopted. While giving hearty devotion to the government as it now is, and while laboring to make it a glory and a blessing to the world, we yet owe it to our ancestors, and to our dead, to show in history that government, as we believe it was intended by its framers, and as it made such wonderful progress under our administration of it until the opposing idea triumphed.

Upon our Confederate veterans lies the duty of securing this vindication of their cause from the facts of all our past history. We owe it to our fathers, to ourselves and to our children that the history of our common country should not he left to be told by those who are out of sympathy with our spirit and principles, and so are unable to do justice to our motives or actions; and who therefore fail to record the glorious part we had in winning and developing the country, and fail to understand the meaning of the heroic struggle we made, not to preserve slavery, but to preserve our rights under the Constitution.[93] — REV. JAMES H. MCNEILLY, D.D., CONFEDERATE VETERAN, NASHVILLE, TENNESSEE

WE FOUGHT FOR WHAT OUR REVOLUTIONARY FOREFATHERS FOUGHT FOR

☛ Loyalty to the past is a duty. Feeling that we were right we staked all on the uncertain chances of battle, and we lost. We were overpowered, and we had to submit to the result, but we cannot be otherwise than proud of the history we [the C.S.A.] made while a nation. We are here to-day not to praise the victorious, but to claim imperishable renown for the vanquished.

When we look backward from the zenith of life we see things with a clearer vision. We see many causes that brought on the struggle. For slavery, the indirect cause of the war, the North is as much responsible as the South. As to the doctrine of "States' rights," the right of a sovereign state to withdraw from the Union, the question is decided forever against us. If we are not convinced we are quieted. We accept the inevitable with such grace as we can, but we cannot blot it from our recollections. We cannot yield the belief in the principles we inherited from our revolutionary forefathers. We fought for what they did, but they had better luck. War was forced on us. Constitutional and sacred guarantees agreed on in one union of sovereign States were trampled under foot under the theory promulgated by Mr. [William H.] Seward and accepted by the North, of a "higher law than the Constitution." We were invaded. We were forced to defend our hearthstones and our property and the inherited rights of local self-government bequeathed us by our forefathers. We need no justification for our conduct. It is a universal law that a man should defend his own. We did that and that only. We would have deserved to be trampled on if we had not resisted. See how gloriously we did it. Look at our record. Never did a nation contend against such odds. I defy contradiction. Read for yourselves the war records now being honestly published by our government.

My young fellow-countrymen, young gentlemen, young ladies, listen to me—you who have lived since the war and have only heard of it from others. Learn now what this monument, the corner-stone of which is now to be laid, is intended to commemorate. Look at these gray-haired veterans. Who are they? I will tell you. They are some of the survivors of an army of 600,000 men who fought and kept back from our Southern soil an invading army of 2,864,272 men not including three and six months volunteers, or with the odds of 2,264,272 men more than they had to confront them. To this great odds must be added 600 vessels of war [unlawfully] blockading our coasts and occupying our rivers, manned by 35,000 [Union] sailors, preventing our getting supplies of arms, provisions, clothing, medicines, and necessaries of all kinds. In this unequal contest the Confederate Army did not lay down its arms until it was completely overpowered, and it had only 100,000 effective fighting men for duty in the field left of that army of 600,000, while the Federals had over 1,000,000 men for duty, or ten men for every Confederate soldier, and all our arsenals, munitions of war and supplies were exhausted or captured.

Before the end of the conflict the Confederate army had lost over one-half of the 600,000 men, or 325,000 men on the death roll. It had fought over our beloved Southland almost foot by foot, on nearly 2,000 battlefields. It had inflicted a death roll on the enemy of 359,528 men, 275,000 of whom lie buried beneath our Southern soil. Comrades of the gray, we made a record unsurpassed in the annals of war or history.[94] — CONFEDERATE GENERAL STEPHEN DILL LEE, SPEECH, CONFEDERATE MONUMENT, BIRMINGHAM, ALABAMA

REBEL: A WORD OF HONOR & COURAGE

☛ The history of the English people is a history of rebels struggling to maintain their rights and liberties against the tyranny and oppression of the governing powers. To the American citizen who has carefully read the history of the race from which we sprang, the term rebel conveys no suspicion of dishonor or reproach. It is a term which tyrannical governments have all times applied to people who have the courage to resist their oppression, and while tyrannical governments may intend to use the term, rebel, as one of reproach, every true lover of liberty who knows his history must regard it as a title of honor; history proves that it is a title of liberty which is older and more honorable than the king's prerogative; it is a title which was originally won by the sword, it has been maintained by the sword, and unless it be defended by the sword, liberty will perish from the face of the earth. All the rights, privileges, and immunities now enjoyed by the American people were acquired for them by rebels and will be bequeathed to them by rebels. There cannot be found to-day in all this world a man in whose veins does not flow the blood of a rebel, whether of English descent or not. Allow me to add that any man

William McBlair Jr., acting master's mate, Confederate States navy, circa 1864.

deserves this honorable title who is ready to fight, regardless of doubts or consequences for the rights of life, liberty, and property. These are the things for which we fought, and we counted not the cost when we bade defiance to the enemy's forces that undertook to despoil us of them.[95] — HONORABLE ED BAXTER, TENNESSEE U.C.V. REUNION

THE CAUSE OF THE WAR

☞ This presence [Confederate veterans] revives many hallowed memories of the past. It calls up the memory of the days when husbands separated from wives and children; when sons separated from fathers and mothers, brothers and sisters; when loving and loved ones left their homes to enter the armies of the Confederacy, with hearts proudly responding to the calls of patriotism, and aching for those who were left at home. It calls to mind the forming of military organizations, and their march to the seat of war, buoyant with hope under bright new banners, in the presence of smiles which came through tears, the waving of handkerchiefs, the silent prayer of hope and love, and the soulful good-bye—God bless you. It calls to mind the long marches, the scenes around the camp fires, and anxious preparations for battle. It brings before the mind anew the panorama of battle. It calls up the memories of first Manassas, of Seven Pines, of the seven days in front of Richmond, of Fredericksburg, of Second Manassas, of Sharpsburg, of Gettysburg. It reminds us of Fort Donelson, of Shiloh and Corinth, of Chickamauga, of Lookout Mountain, of Elkhorn, of Vicksburg, of Stone's River, of Atlanta, of Murfreesboro, of Franklin, where [Confederate General] Pat Cleburne and other heroes fell, and of a hundred other fields on which Confederate skill and courage and constancy were displayed. It causes a renewal of our admiration and love for such great Captains as Robert E. Lee, Stonewall Jackson, [Albert] Sidney Johnston, Joseph E. Johnston, [Pierre G. T.] Beauregard, [Braxton] Bragg, [James] Longstreet, [John Bell] Hood, [Edmund] Kirby Smith, [John Brown] Gordon, [Patrick R.] Cleburne, [Leonidas] Polk, [Sterling] Price, [John C.] Breckinridge, [Hiram B.] Granbury, [Horace] Randall [that is, Randal], [William R.] Scurry, [Matthew D.] Ector, [William L.] Cabell, [Lawrence S.] Ross, [Thomas N.] Waul, Ben McCulloch, John Gregg, Tom Green, W. H. F. [Lee] and Fitzhugh Lee, J. E. B. Stuart, [Nathan Bedford] Forrest, [Joseph] Wheeler, and a hundred other heroic leaders in the lost cause.

Great as was the ability and courage and purity of our Generals, who deservedly achieved a world-wide fame, and proud as we were and are of their characters and virtues, we turn with still greater pride and holier reverence, if such a thing be possible, to the memory of the subaltern officers and private soldiers who, for four weary years of privation, suffering, carnage and death, carried the banners of the Confederacy and offered their lives on the altar of their country's liberty; because they served and suffered without the incentive of office and rank, animated solely by their love of home, country and liberty, and their devotion to a cause dearer to them than life. There were features in the struggle of the Confederacy which must hold their place in history as long as the admiration of genius and courage and virtue shall survive.

Of late years we frequently hear the inquiries as to what caused this great war, with all its sacrifices of life and property? Sometimes this inquiry is doubtless made by those seeking information, but others make that inquiry in order to belittle the war and those who were engaged in it. A struggle which cost hundreds of thousands of valuable lives, and by which many billions of money was spent and property sacrificed, could hardly have been engaged in without sufficient cause.

. . . During colonial times in this country the political authorities of Great Britain, Spain, and France, and the Dutch merchants planted African slavery in all the North American colonies. At the time of the declaration of American independence, 1776, African slavery existed in all of the thirteen colonies. At the date of the adoption of the Federal Constitution, 1787, African slavery existed in all of the States except one. The commercial reason for the planting of African slavery in this country was no doubt stimulated by the hope of ease and gain. It was at the same time justified by the Church on the ground that the negroes were taken from a condition of heathenish barbarism and cannibalism and brought to where they could be taught the arts of civilization and industry, and where they could be instructed in the doctrines and practices of the Christian religion. I am not discussing the question now as to whether this practice and these views were correct; I am only telling you what was done and thought to be right by our ancestors and by the great governments of the world. When the Constitution of the United States, the compact of union, was adopted it recognized the right of property in African slaves. The African slave trade was then still being carried on, and the Constitution of the United States provided that it should not be prohibited by Congress prior to the year 1808, twenty years after the adoption of the Constitution. It also provided that slaves escaping from one State into another should not be discharged from service or labor, but should be delivered up to the owner. There were differences of opinion as to the rightfulness of slavery among the men who formed the Constitution. Subsequently, and before 1861, a number of the Northern States, [the birthplace of American slavery, and] where slave labor was not thought to be profitable, abolished that institution, and by degrees a strong prejudice grew up against slavery, first among philanthropists and religionists, and then in a number of states it became a political question [further provoked by radicals and abolitionists, or what would come to be called socialists and communists]. The agitation of this question was not at first entirely sectional, but it became so subsequently. Its agitation, as early as 1820, threatened the perpetuity of the Union. The agitation went on until it resulted in civil war and bloodshed in Kansas. This was followed by the invasion of Virginia by [murderous socialistic madman] John Brown and his deluded followers for the purpose of inaugurating civil and servile war in that State. And when he was executed for his crimes Northern churches were draped in mourning, and their bells tolled in token of their sympathy with him and sorrow for his fate. In the Thirty-fifth Congress, when the agitation was threatening the peace of the country, thirty-odd propositions of compromise were made for the purpose of averting the danger of disunion: all of these, without exception, were made either by Southern members or Northern Democratic [then Conservative] members. And every such proposition which was presented in the House of Representatives was received by the Republican [then Liberal] members with hooting and expressions of derision, and the Southern members were often told that they had to submit to the will of the majority. The Constitution was denounced by some of the agitators as a league with hell and a covenant with death, and the agitators claimed that there was a higher law than the Constitution. In the campaign of 1860 the Republicans [Liberals] nominated as their anti-slavery ticket both their candidates for President and Vice President from the Northern States, a thing which had not occurred before that time, except in the election of Gen. [Andrew] Jackson as President and Mr. [John C.] Calhoun as Vice President, both from Southern States, in 1828, when there was no sectional issue.

In 1832 the peace of the country, if not the integrity of the Union, was threatened on the question of the revenue policy of the government, which led to the steps taken by South Carolina to nullify the acts of Congress by which duties on imports and for the protection of home industries were levied in a way which, it was believed, did not bear equally on the different parts of the country, and which was believed to involve a violation of the Constitution. Both these were questions which came up under the broader and greater question of the proper construction of the Constitution of the United States. In the Federal [Philadelphia] Convention of 1787, which framed the Constitution of the United States [replacing the Articles of Confederation],[96] the question as to the character of the government we were to have, and of the powers which were to be conferred on it, and in the conventions of the States which ratified the Constitution, were very ably discussed, some of the members in each preferring a strong Federal Government, and others, jealous of the rights of the States, and more solicitous for the liberties of the people, preferring a government with limited powers.

The States represented in the Federal Convention were each free, sovereign and independent. The Constitution formed by that Convention and ratified by the States conferred on the government so formed certain specified and limited powers necessary to enable it to conduct our foreign and federal relations, reserving to the states respectively and to the people all the powers not so delegated. The question was discussed in the Convention as to what should be done in case of disagreement between the Federal Government and one or more of the States. A proposition was made by [Left-wing] Alexander Hamilton to confer on the Federal Government power to coerce refractory states, and it was voted down. So this power was not expressly given by the Constitution, and was not embraced in the powers which were given.

During President [George] Washington's administration, being the first under the [U.S.] Constitution [note: there had been at least ten earlier presidents under the Articles of Confederation],[97] the question as to whether the Constitution should be strictly construed so as to preserve the reserved rights of the states, or should receives latitudinous construction, looking to strengthening the government beyond the powers delegated by it, was sharply made between Thomas Jefferson, the Secretary of State, contending for its strict construction, and Alexander Hamilton, contending for a broader construction.

During the administration of the elder [John] Adams in Congress, with the approval of the President, passed what is known in the history of the times as the alien and sedition laws. The strict constructionists, under the lead of Mr. Jefferson, denied the constitutionality of these laws, and charged that they endangered the liberty of the citizens. Under this issue the American people agreed with Mr. Jefferson, and elected him President in the year

1800, and again in 1804.

In the year 1798 the Legislature of Kentucky, and in the year 1799, the Legislature of Virginia, passed resolutions denouncing the alien and sedition laws as violative of the Constitution and dangerous to liberty, and asserted the right of the States to protect themselves against unconstitutional laws and acts of the Federal Government. And in these resolutions they led the right of the States to protect the people against the unconstitutional acts and arbitrary power of the Federal Government, and that they were the judges of their rights and remedies, but that this power was not to be exercised by them except in extreme cases, when there was no other remedy. Under this issue what was known as the Federal party went out of power and out of existence. And under this the doctrine of the then Republican party [then Conservative], which afterward became the Democratic party [then Conservative], Mr. Jefferson, Mr. [James] Madison and Mr. [James] Monroe, successively held the office of President of the United States for twenty-four successive years. It was always the doctrine of the Democratic party [then Conservative] down to 1860, and was specifically indorsed by its national [Conservative] conventions in several canvasses for President and Vice President preceding the war.

I am not saying whether this is or is not the doctrine of the Democratic party now [at this time, 1894, still Conservative].[98] I am only reciting facts to show the opinions which prevailed before the war between the States, and in a large measure guided the people of the Southern States, when they passed their ordinances of secession. They believed a public opinion had been created in the Northern States which threatened the peace of the country and the rights of the people. They believed the Constitution of the United States had ceased to be a shield for their protection, and that their safety and welfare made it necessary for them to withdraw from the Union and form a government friendly to their people, and under which their rights would he secured to them. They were in part led to this conclusion by the facts I have stated, and by the additional facts that the people of the Northern States had repudiated the provisions of the Constitution and of the acts of Congress, which were intended to protect them in the enjoyment of their local, social, and domestic institutions, and which were intended to protect $3,000,000,000 of property in slaves; that they had repudiated a decision of the Supreme Court of the United States which affirmed the doctrine of the Constitution and laws of Congress on this subject; that some of the Northern States had passed laws forbidding their authorities and people from aiding to execute the provisions of the Constitution and laws requiring the rendition of fugitive slaves.

These things and others of like character caused the Southern States to attempt to withdraw from the Union. And the principles I have called to view and the facts I have referred to led to the great war which cost so much blood and treasure. And these principles and facts are the answer to the new generation as to why their fathers gave their services, their property, and their lives in that war; and why brave men fought and died, and why holy men, pure and noble women prayed for their success. Why Senators and Representatives in Congress, and officers of the army and navy surrendered their offices and emoluments, and abandoned a condition of peace and security and offered their fortunes and their lives in so unequal a contest; and why the people at large in these States, with remarkable unanimity, staked every earthly thing which was precious and dear to them in so unequal a war, rather than submit to the degradation of living under a violated Constitution and laws, and being compelled to accept only such rights in the Union as might be accorded to them by the grace of a hostile popular majority....[99] — JOHN H. REAGAN (FORMER CONFEDERATE POSTMASTER GENERAL UNDER PRESIDENT JEFFERSON DAVIS), SPEECH, U.C.V. REUNION, WACO, TEXAS, APRIL 1894

TWO DIFFERENT CIVILIZATIONS

☛ ... Appomattox was a triumph of the physically stronger in a conflict between the representatives of two essentially different civilizations, and antagonistic ideas of government. On one side in that conflict was the [Conservative] South, led by the descendants of the Cavaliers who, with all their faults, had inherited from a long line of ancestors a manly contempt for moral littleness, a high sense of honor, a lofty regard for plighted faith, a strong tendency to conservatism, a profound respect for law and order, and an unfaltering loyalty to constitutional government.

But, it was not to perpetuate slavery that they fought. The impartial student of the events leading up to the civil war cannot fail to perceive that, in the words of Mr. [Jefferson] Davis, "to whatever extent the question of slavery may have served as an occasion, it was far from being the cause of the conflict." That conflict was the bloody culmination of a controversy which had been raging for more than a generation, and the true issue in which, as far as it pertained to slavery, was sharply stated by the Hon.

Samuel A. Foot, of Connecticut, when, referring to the debate of the admission of Missouri to the sisterhood of States, he said:

> "The Missouri question did not involve the question of freedom or slavery, but merely whether slaves now in the country may be permitted to reside in the proposed new State, and whether Congress or Missouri possessed the power to decide."

And from that day down to 1861, when the war-clouds burst in fury upon our land, the real question in regard to slavery was not whether it should continue in the South, but whether the Southern man should be permitted to take his slaves, originally purchased almost exclusively from Northern slave-traders, into the territory, which was the common property of the country, and there, without interference from the general Government, have an equal voice with his Northern brother in determining the domestic policy of the new State. The question was not whether the negro should be freed or held in servitude, but whether the white man of the South should have the same privileges enjoyed by the white man of the North. It was not the desire to hold others in bondage, but the desire to maintain their own rights that actuated the Southern people throughout the conflict.

That Union was dear to the Southern people, but the Union which the men of the South loved, and which they were willing to make concessions and sacrifices to perpetuate, was that formed by the fathers, "to establish justice, insure domestic tranquillity, provide for the common defense, promote the general welfare, and secure the blessings of liberty." It was a fraternal federation [that is, confederation] of sovereign States, guaranteeing equal rights to all, and leaving each free to regulate its domestic affairs in its own way. It was a Union in which, in reference to questions of foreign policy, every citizen would echo the sentiment expressed by Patrick Henry, when, after Concord and Lexington, in a message to Massachusetts, he said: "I am not a Virginian, I am an American"; and yet it was a Union in which, in reference to questions of domestic policy, every citizen, like that same great orator and patriot, would recognize the right of his own State to his highest allegiance. It was a Union in which the people of each State would enjoy the blessings of local self-government, and find in home rule a safeguard against any possible attempt of the Federal power to interfere with their peculiar interests. . . .[100] — REVEREND R. C. CAVE, SPEECH, RICHMOND, VIRGINIA

SOUTHERNERS: THE GREATEST PATRIOTS
☛ Argument is effective, upon the review of history, that the most loyal friends of the Union, until the actual outbreak in 1861, were the Southern people.

No greater claim is made than for the proportion the South bore in the [American] Revolution. It is but natural that foreigners could not become as loyal as those whose ancestors fought under [George] Washington. Remember the words of Andrew Jackson: "The Union, it must and shall be preserved." Kentucky stood by her motto "United we stand, divided we fall," in remaining neutral. This theme was taught by the firesides and in the schools of those who espoused the cause of the South in our great war. Now and then expressions are given by those who suffered for the principle of State Rights, that must, seem strange to those whose training has been since the war, but the theme of their ancestors was that the Union of the States be maintained. It was argued as policy, however, rather than principle. The right to withdraw from the compact had never been questioned, hence the greater fear that the Sovereign States would do it. The plea of the South during the childhood of those who made the best Confederate soldiers was that the Union be perpetuated, so when they actually went to war under a different flag, the provocation was such as to make them desperate. Confederates honor the memory of ancestors who fought under Washington, whether they went from New Jersey, Vermont or South Carolina.[101] — SUMNER A. CUNNINGHAM, EDITOR, *CONFEDERATE VETERAN* MAGAZINE

THE FIGHT FOR CONSTITUTIONAL RIGHTS
☛ The *Confederate Veteran* [magazine] is a bond that links together the scattered remnant of a type of manhood that the world never saw before and will never know again.

Stripped of all coloring, all prejudice, the question involved in the "Lost Cause" was a struggle, a death grapple, over the construction of constitutional rights as established, vindicated and bequeathed by the [U.S. founding] fathers. Viewed from this standpoint, what an immortality Appomattox becomes!

Richmond abandoned, the executive officers of the Confederacy on the retreat, and left without one solitary adviser, the great commander [Confederate General Robert E. Lee] balanced the odds and alone in the night watches formed his plans only in view of his responsibility to his people, to his conscience and his God.

To look upon him was a vision; to touch his hand was a

sacrament; to hear him was a benediction.

On that sad morning he surrendered his army with all of its munitions of war. The great questions involved in the struggle were the integrity of his people and the honor of his soldiers. Behind that grand old warrior stood the small remnant of weather-beaten survivors of the Army of Northern Virginia, which had so long confronted [Union General Ulysses S.] Grant's large army, "clamoring" for [the South's] extermination, and behind all that the adverse sentiment and active prejudice of the outside world. "Few and faint, yet fearless still" they stood, ready at the word to charge on to slaughter and to death.

Never before was there presented such overwhelming odds. Never before did balance hold such tremendous issues. Solitary and alone, anomalous, majestic, immortal, unrivalled in all the past, unapproachable in all the future, that occasion stands pre-eminent. sublime, the cynosure of all generations.

Tattered and torn, broken and barefoot, despairing of success, yet resolute and defiant in conviction, powerless in strength yet invincible in principle and conscience, that little remnant gathered round its matchless idol as he stood presenting to the universe the concluding act in the splendid pageant of the "Lost Cause," the vanquished dictating terms to the victor: the "old guard," surrounded on all sides, beleaguered beyond all escape, demanding and achieving honorable recognition and triumphant vindication for the living and the dead for whom it stood sponsor.

Alas! tho' coming generations will not again look upon the like, because the world in all coming time will never again behold such a contest for principle by men who, "holding their consciences unmixed with guile, stood amid all conjunctures true to themselves, their country and their God." To us is left the heritage of unsullied and impregnable honor.

Their's no Judas kiss, their's no traitor's promise, and the pledge so given and so vouched, albeit wrung from them in their weakness, has been fulfilled in the gross and in the detail, to the last syllable and the last letter. Immortal, immaculate, the memory! *Esto perpetua* the sentiment![102] — ANONYMOUS, EAST TENNESSEE

LET US TEACH OUR CHILDREN THE TRUTH

☛ . . . Has the old time sentiment of the South departed from its people? Has the old time patriotism and love of truth that characterized the old South given place to business expediency in the New? One would surely think so from the carelessness, not to say indifference, with which it accepts the school histories filled with misleading and false statements concerning the civil war.

Why should not a true history of that war be written thirty years after its ending?

Confederate Lieutenant Colonel William Miller Owen, 13th Virginia Light Artillery Battalion, New Orleans, Louisiana, circa 1863.

Why should the South be charged at this day with going to war in defense of slavery? This institution was a mere incident of a sectional animosity. Measures for the gradual emancipation of the slaves were being considered in the South before the war began. Gen. Lee suggested the freeing of them and the enrollment of the men as soldiers. The character of the two peoples of the North and the South, the habits and customs, the adverse interests, the belief that the legislative power would be used by the North to foster that section at the expense of the South, produced a desire to leave a union which was no longer considered desirable.

The Southern people believed they had both a moral and a constitutional right to withdraw from a union into which they had voluntarily gone. In defense of this abstract principle of right they freely gave their lives and fortunes, and for four years resisted the overwhelming forces of the North.

Who shall say they were wrong?

Mr. [Daniel] Webster said our forefathers of a hundred and twenty years ago "went to war against a preamble." The South withdrew from the Union for a sentiment. Our ancestors rebelled against the king of Great Britain. We rebelled against nobody—we had no masters. We attempted but to dissolve a union which we ourselves had helped to form. The agreement made among the States to concede certain rights to the general government—to reserve forever other rights to themselves—being broken by encroachment on those reserved rights, why should not the States withdraw?

Why should we teach our children that we were wrong, when we know we were right?

... By all means should the true story of the mighty conflict be written. There is nothing so good as truth. The heroic struggle of the South, and the Southern veteran will be a theme of inspiration to the youth of future generations; and shall we of the present for one moment, in our upbuilding of the New South, forget the glorious memories of the Old? . . .[103] — DANIEL BOND, NASHVILLE, TENNESSEE

WHY WE FOUGHT
☛ Who could doubt our loyalty to the conviction that we were defending our constitutional rights, our homes and liberties?[104] — JUDGE L. P. HALL, DIXON, KENTUCKY

Steel engraving entitled: "Prayer in 'Stonewall' Jackson's camp." Confederate General Jackson is standing upper left; Confederate General Ambrose Powell Hill is seated bottom left; Confederate General Richard Stoddert Ewell is standing to Jackson's left (beneath the flag). Artist: Peter Kramer; engraver: John Chester Buttre; published 1866.

Confederate Sergeant William Crawford Smith, Co. B, 12th Virginia Infantry Regiment, Richmond, Virginia, circa 1864.

WE MUST RECORD A TRUTHFUL ACCOUNT
☛ . . . A conquered people seldom have the heart to write the history of their humiliation and defeat, and it is generally left to the victors; and if we consider the abuse and slanders that were heaped on us by northern writers, with accompanying degrading illustrations, it cannot be reasonably expected that they will hereafter, assign the true causes that led to the war, nor give their real motives in carrying it on, nor acknowledge the overwhelming power that eventually gave them success—even in the pleasing language of fiction or much less in the plain language of truth.

History is the life of a nation. We find yet existing monuments of races that have perished and passed into oblivion because, they left neither written nor legendary history. That the Confederate States may for all time live as a nation, born of, and battling for, constitutional rights won by so many revolutions against personal government, it is necessary to collect the testimony scattered over the country and place it in a Repository, ready for the historian to obtain evidence of the facts he may publish, in vindication of justice of the southern people.

No nation ever rose so high, and passed through battle and blood, and came forth from the ordeal so free from disparagement and guiltless of crime. Will you permit those four years of battle, your labor, your toils, your sufferings, your sacrifices, your homes destroyed, your land laid waste, divided into forty acre lots; desolation everywhere far and wide; comrades in unknown graves;

yourself penniless and family in rags, labor disorganized, slaves free [that is, loss of financial investment], sitting idle in the sun waiting for the promised mule; no work animals, no implements of agriculture, no law, no anything save the lone chimneys where your house once stood, with wild animals around grown tame; crows sitting on your gateposts and a raven on a chimney top—that and nothing more? I repeat, will you let all this pass for naught, and take no steps to preserve a record of it in a truthful account of the struggle you made to protect your homes? I am sure you will not. . . .[105] — CONFEDERATE GENERAL SAMUEL G. FRENCH, CIRCA 1896

TO THE CONFEDERATE DEAD
☛ "Go tell the Southrons we lie here for the rights of their States; they never fail who die in a great cause."[106] — INSCRIPTION ON A CONFEDERATE MONUMENT, WARRENTON, VIRGINIA

A CONFEDERATE ICON ADDRESSES HIS TROOPS
☛ Soldiers . . . If your course has been marked by the graves of patriotic heroes who have fallen by your side, it has at the same time been more plainly marked by the blood of the invader. While you sympathize with the friends of the fallen, your sorrows should be appeased by the knowledge that they fell as brave men, battling for all that makes life worth living. Soldiers, you now rest for a short time from your labors. During the respite prepare for action. Your commanding general is ready to lead you again to the defense of the common cause, and appeals to you by a remembrance of the past career, your desolated homes, your insulted women, and suffering children, and, above all, by the memory of your dead comrades, to yield obedience to discipline, and to buckle on your armor anew for the fight.

Confederate Lieutenant Colonel John Nicholas Galleher, Buckner's Corps, Kentucky, Army of Tennessee, New Orleans, Louisiana, 1865.

Bring with you the soldier's safest armor: a determination to fight while the enemy pollutes your soil, to fight as long as he denies your rights, to fight until independence shall have been achieved, to fight for home, children, liberty, and all you hold dear. Show to the world the superhuman and sublime spirit with which a people may be inspired when fighting for the inestimable boon of liberty. Be not allured by the siren song of peace, for there can be no peace save upon your separate, independent nationality. You can never again unite with those who have murdered your sons, outraged your helpless families, and with demoniac malice wantonly destroyed your property and now seek to make slaves of you. A proposition of reunion with a people who have avowed their purpose to appropriate the property and to subjugate and annihilate the freemen of the South would stamp with infamy the names of your gallant dead and the living heroes of this war. Be patient, obedient, and earnest, and the day is not far distant when you can return to your homes and live in the full fruition of freedom around the old family altar.[107] — CONFEDERATE GENERAL NATHAN BEDFORD FORREST, EARLY 1865

THREE SOUTHERN CHAMPIONS OF LIBERTY

☛ . . . It is history that in the beginning North Carolina defied kings, lords, and commons, always self-reliant. Her troops were armed and sent to both Virginia and South Carolina and food sent to sufferers in Boston. In May, 1775, she was the first to declare her independence in the celebrated Mecklenburg Declaration. . . . And then came 1861; and, knowing her rights, she dared maintain them, and embarked her all.

[George] Washington typified the essence of truth; [Robert E.] Lee, integrity and duty; and [Jefferson] Davis was the type of honor.

Washington came in simple guise, forest born and bred. His character was of his own fashioning, his accomplishments self-acquired. No college learning enriched his mind. He was left to his own resources for discipline and culture, fortitude, self-reliance, and endurance. In the vast, solitary depth of the wildwoods he drank in the spirit of independence, the inspirations of freedom, and learned from nature the lesson that obedience to law is the necessary condition of all wholesome growth and development.

Robert F. Lee's name will be monumental, and will be placed by the side of the great captains of history; and as long as the fame of the Southern struggle shall linger in tradition or in song will his memory be cherished by the descendants of the Southern race; while on the scroll of fame no name will shine with a purer, serener, or a more resplendent light than that of Robert F. Lee.

> No braver sword led braver band,
> Nor braver bled for a better land;
> Or better band had cause so grand,
> Or cause a chief like Lee.

Jefferson Davis lives in my memory as one who, dying without a nation or name, stands as grand a man as ever lived in the tide of times. Great in victory, but greater in defeat; great as described through the red haze of war, but greater as contemplated through the clear air of peace; great as a general, but greater as a man—behold him! a character which, if not perfect, conceals its imperfections by the effulgence of its virtues, even as the sun conceals the spots upon his dazzling disk....[108] — MAJOR W. E. BREESE, ASHEVILLE, NORTH CAROLINA

STATES' RIGHTS IN PERPETUITY

☛ ... The world is surely coming to the conclusion that the cause of the Confederacy was right. Every lover of constitutional liberty, liberty controlled by law, all over the world begins to understand that the war was not a war waged by the South in defense of slavery, but was a war to protect liberty won and bequeathed by free ancestors. They now know that the fundamental basic principle of the Revolution of 1775, upon which the governments of the states united were all founded— Massachusetts and Virginia, Rhode Island and North Carolina—was that "all government of right rests upon the consent of the governed," and that they, therefore, at all times must have the right to change and alter their form of government whenever changed circumstances require changed laws.

They now know that the English settlements in America were made in separate communities, at different times, by different societies; that they grew and prospered until an attempt was made to deprive them of an infinitely small portion of their property without their consent. The whole tea tax would not have produced £1,500, less than $7,500. They know that they resisted this attack on their rights as distinct colonies; that as separate states they made treaties with France and the Continental powers in 1778; that their independence as separate states, by name, was acknowledged by Great Britain in 1785; that Maryland fought through that whole [American Revolutionary] war until 1781 as an independent and separate state, and never joined the confederation [a name for the original U.S.A.][109] until the last-named year; that North Carolina and Rhode Island refused to enter the Union created by the constitution of 1789, after the dissolution of the confederation, and for two years remained as independent of the states united and of each other as France and England are to-day—and therefore they know that these independent states, when they entered into the compact of the constitution of 1789, never did (for a state never can, by the very nature of its being, commit suicide) consent and agree to give up forever the right of self-government and of the people of a state to make a government to suit themselves.

There can be no such thing as irrepealable law in free society. Society is immortal. Its atoms arrange and crystallize themselves from generation to generation according to their necessities, but society grows and expands, and constant changes are required in its organization. Therefore a state never can abandon its right to change. It is the law of nature, which neither compacts nor treaties, constitutions nor Congresses, can change. . . .[110] — GENERAL BRADLEY T. JOHNSON, BALTIMORE, MARYLAND

A CONFEDERATE GENERAL'S FAREWELL TO HIS TROOPS
☛ Soldiers: Our last march is about ended. To-morrow we shall lay down the arms which for four years we have borne to defend our rights, to win our liberties. We know and the world knows and history will record that we have borne them with honor. We now surrender to the overwhelming power of the enemy, which has rendered further resistance by us hopeless and murderous to our own people and our own cause. We can never forget the noble comrades who have stood shoulder to shoulder to this moment, the noble dead who have been martyred, the noble Southern women who have been wronged and are unavenged, or the noble principles for which we have fought. Conscious that we have played our part like men confident of the righteousness of our cause, without regret for our action in the past, and without despair of the future, let us to-morrow with the dignity of veterans who are the last to surrender perform the duty which has been assigned to us.[111] — CONFEDERATE GENERAL DABNEY H. MAURY, MERIDIAN, MISSISSIPPI, MAY 7, 1865

PRESERVING THE SANCTITY OF SOUTHERN WOMANHOOD
☛ . . . Through four fateful years of strife we contended not only for political rights, but also for social ideals. We fought not only for the sovereignty of the States, but also to conserve a society in which our highest interests and our deepest affections, our most precious

memories, and our most sacred duties were bound up together. It was a social life which had developed some of the grandest characters in the history of our race.

That old life of the South, not faultless indeed, was yet far truer, purer, sweeter, and kinder than much that now sneers at it and seeks to take its place under the name of progress. It was an agricultural community, dependent on the kindliness of mother earth and recognizing the beneficent providence of God. Living much in the open air, they were familiar with forest and field, with valley and hill. The blue sky above them, with glowing sun and gleaming stars, and floating clouds and changing seasons, poured their benedictions upon them. They were influenced by sighing breeze and flowing brook and songs of birds and all the manifold voices of Nature, until, in communion with her, they drank in her free spirit and were made wise by her home teachings. It was a life of patriarchal simplicity, of large leisure, free from bustle and hurry. There were grave responsibility for dependents, generous hospitality, keen enjoyment of outdoor exercises. The life, moving on quietly, thrilled with quick sense of honor, abounded in kindly charities, in gentle amenities, in stately courtesies.

The center of that old-time social life was the home. Whether that home was lofty or lowly, about it revolved all interests and pleasures. From it went forth sweetest influences, in it were gathered tenderest memories, to it turned the heart's warmest affections. Every true man's soul sought satisfaction not in store nor bank nor shop nor school nor legislative hall, but in the home.

The center of the home was woman. She was its queen, and her presence and ministry gave beauty and attraction. She was to bind together all its multiplied activities into a gracious harmony. To her were turned the eyes of husband and children and servants. She was to rule by love.

This, then, was the ideal life which we tried to realize as the crown of our social system, a happy home with a loving woman as the center of it. The chivalry of the South was careful of the home and jealous for woman's honor and respect.

The term chivalry has in latter days been applied to us with sarcasm as a reproach, but we glory in it. True chivalry means the protecting of the weak by the strong. It meant in those days that woman was to be shielded from the world's rude strife. She was to be defended not only against violence and oppression, but also from the sharp competitions of business and the eager rivalries of politics. Our civilization guarded her not only as the "weaker vessel," but as the one who must not be cast down from her high place of widest and noblest influence, molding character and purifying life. Surely no higher social ideal could inspire and encourage human effort.

Those who in this day seek to make woman a competitor of man in the struggle of life [modern feminists], in the business, are lowering the ideal as much as those who regard her only as the drudge for service or the minister of animal pleasures.

In all those weary, testing years of war our women were true to this ideal. By all womanly ways and encouragements did they inspire men to duty. The memory of their teachings or the hope of their approval has given renewed energy to many a fainting spirit, to many a despondent soldier in tented camp or on stricken field of strife. In the home, by their hospitality, and in the hospital, by their soothing ministries, they wrought mightily for our cause. No historian can ever write nor language ever tell the sacrifices of the daughters of the Confederacy to sustain those who fought to keep that order which God designed, in which man is the home winner and woman the home keeper. And those sacrifices were not in vain. The war ended in the defeat of our armies. Our political idea we surrendered, and we accepted the supremacy of the general government as a nation not to be dissolved. But our social ideal we did not surrender. The conduct of our women during the war glorified and sanctified that ideal. To-day we are ready to vindicate the purity of the home, the social supremacy of womanhood. It is true that many forces of this commercial and material age would degrade our ideal and contemn it as mere sentiment. It is true that we have to maintain it under altered conditions of life. It is true that the framework of the old social order has passed away. And yet it is true that these changed conditions find men and women who cherish the same spirit as "in the brave days of old." The true social ideal must direct our efforts to have homes where woman sways by love the coming age, "to keep the lamp of chivalry alight in hearts of gold."[112] — REV. JAMES H. MCNEILLY, D.D., CONFEDERATE VETERAN, SPEECH, MEMORIAL TO MISS VARINA ANNE "WINNIE" DAVIS, NASHVILLE, TENNESSEE

KEEP IT ALIVE

☛ It is not too late to show the world that the longer the Southern people live the stronger grows their love for those who willingly gave their all for the great cause of Southern rights. So let us continue to honor their heroism and patriotism as long as the old Confederates live, and instill into the hearts and minds of our children to keep the old sentiment alive in their hearts to be transmitted to the next generation.[113] — R. H. RODGERS, PLANTERSVILLE, MISSISSIPPI

WE WERE ONE PEOPLE

☞ Whatever may be the difference about the war and its causes, no brave or generous person can deny that it was made up of deeds of desperate valor, great military strategy, unparalleled endurance of hardship, and patriotic heroism on either side. You, my friends [to the Union veterans in the audience], felt that republican [then Liberal] government and liberty itself were gone if the Union of the States was dissolved. The Southern soldier believed in the sovereign rights of the States and the Union with only certain delegated powers and guaranteed rights, and defended his home and his property from invasion. The ardor with which both sides rallied around their respective flags and followed them through sacrifices, through danger and death, was equal, and proves their conscientious patriotism. Each soldier who laid down his life on either side for his country thought that he died for a holy cause. Both sides believed they were right. Self sacrifice unto death for what a man believes is heroism, and heroism that deserves immortality—yes, more than deserves it; carries immortality in his breast. It is given us now to see that high motives were not all ranged under one banner; that that sublime devotion that leads a man to leave wife and home and mother for the hardships of battle and the crown of death was displayed on both sides. To underrate the courage, the endurance, and the heroism of the men who wore the gray is to dim the luster and tarnish the tune of the men who wore the blue. The heart of every lover of his country swells with just pride at the thought that the men of 1861-1865 of the North and of the South, who displayed such skill and such bravery in battle, such endurance and patience through years of privations and sufferings, such manhood in defeat, and such magnanimity in victory, were one people.[114] — CONFEDERATE VETERAN & SURGEON MAJOR ALEXANDER BEAR OF NORFOLK, NEBRASKA, SPEECH BEFORE A GROUP OF UNION VETERANS, FEBRUARY 1899

A CONFEDERATE PRAYER

☞ Thou, O God, didst not give victory to our arms, and we bow in absolute submission to thy will. Thou knowest what is best. But we praise and bless thee for the characters which were purified by the war, and for the example of those who didst not measure duty by success, who preferred death to dishonor, and who showed to all the world how they valued the rights and liberties thou didst give their land.

We beseech thee, O God, that we and our children may ever be true to the memory of these men; that we may know the principles for which they contended; that we may vindicate their motives and defend their characters from aspersion. Grant that their example may inspire the coming generations with noble enthusiasm, with patriotic devotion, with unyielding courage to dare, to do, to die for God and native land.

We humbly entreat thy blessing on those of us who were once their comrades in the strife or who ministered to them in the weary struggle. Remember in mercy the men and women, now grown old, who shared the hardships of those we commemorate. As the time of our departure draws near may we realize more and more our Father's love and see his wisdom in all the way he has led us; and when the night falls about us may our sleep be sweet, and may we wake to an eternal day.

Father, look in mercy upon our children who come after us. May they in every time of need respond to duty's call, and prove themselves worthy of the heritage thou hast given them. May they seek not in glorious ease, but may they give themselves to do thy will and to benefit the world at every cost.

Especially do we ask thy favor upon those who have served their country against a foreign foe—who are now in the field or who are just returning to their homes. Grant them security against the dangers to body and soul which assail them. May their service, with its hardships, be a means of strengthening and confirming their devotion to duty and love of country.

And we ask thy richest blessings on our country. On this day of thanksgiving we would remember all the benefits, temporal and spiritual, which thou hast given us during this year. May we use thy gifts aright. Make us messengers of liberty and peace to those who have come under our sway. Enable us to fear thee and work righteousness. Give us righteous rulers and righteous laws. Save us from pestilence and famine, from fraud and violence and oppression. Hasten the time when wars shall cease to the ends of the earth, and peace shall rule the world. May our government maintain justice as its only sure foundation.

And now, O God of our fathers, God of battles. King of nations, as we solemnly dedicate this monument to the memory of a glorious past, as it testifies of patriotism, of courage, of devotion to principle, of faithfulness to duty, we implore thee to make it an inspiration to the coming generations, urging them to be true to whatever work thou givest them to do, encouraging them to peace, truth, and righteousness above all earthly considerations.

Now we ask thee to forgive our failures and transgressions, cleanse our hearts, strengthen us for service, and finally receive us to thyself in glory, for the sake of Jesus Christ our Lord. Amen.[115]
— REV. JAMES H. MCNEILLY, D.D., CONFEDERATE VETERAN, OPENING PRAYER, UNVEILING OF THE CONFEDERATE MONUMENT, FRANKLIN, TENNESSEE

A YANKEE GENERAL'S VIEW OF THE WAR

☛ Dear Sir: The public have seen no official announcement of the fact, though it is no doubt by this time very generally known, that I have resigned my commission in the army. I have several times since been assured that my personal friends, and many who without any claim of personal acquaintance have taken an interest in my official career, feel that some explanation of the circumstances and motives of my action is due to them.

It is perhaps unnecessary to enter into an exposition of the circumstances of my supersedure in Tennessee in the fall of 1862, since the particulars, though not without a certain value, involve interests of my own with which it is not my wish to weary you. As far as the facts are concerned, it will suffice for the present to say that after the adjournment, about the 1st of May, 1863, of the "commission" which investigated my campaign, my correspondence with the department was confined to a monthly report made to the Adjutant General that I was waiting the action of the [U.S.] War Department on the proceedings of that commission; that about the first week of April last I was offered command under [Union] Gen. [William T.] Sherman, my junior, which I declined; that a month later I was again offered command under [Union] Gen. [Edward R. S.] Canby,

Confederate Colonel Thomas G. Y. Woodward, 1st Kentucky Cavalry Regiment, Clarksville, Tennessee, circa 1863.

also my junior, which I declined; that about three weeks later I received notification that I was mustered out of my rank as Major General of Volunteers, and that on the same day I sent in my resignation as Colonel in the Adjutant General's Department of the regular army.

The impulses of most men would approve my course in this matter, if it even rested on no other ground than a determination not to acquiesce in any other measure that would degrade me; but I had a higher motive than that. I believed that the policy and means with which the war was being prosecuted were discreditable to the nation and a stain upon civilization; and that they would not only fail to restore the Union, if indeed they had not already rendered its restoration impossible, but that their tendency was to subvert the institutions under which the country had realized unexampled prosperity and happiness; and to such a work I could not lend my hand.

While there may have been more or less of personal ambition mixed up in the movement of secession, as there must generally be in the management of political affairs, yet I do not doubt that it was mainly determined by an honest conviction in the minds of those who engaged in it, that the control of the government had passed permanently into the hands of a sectional party [the Republican party, then the Liberal party] which would soon trample on the political rights of the South. This apprehension was shared in by a very large portion of the people who did not favor secession, and who were so anxious for the preservation of the Union that even coercive measures, if tempered by justice and mercy, would not have estranged them. Under these circumstances the use of military force to put down armed resistance was not incompatible with a restoration of the Union with its former glories and affections, provided the means were employed in such a manner as to convince the people that their constitutional rights would be respected. Such a policy, therefore, in the use of force, if force must be resorted to, had the manifest advantage of weakening the power of the rebellion and strengthening the government, independently of the moral force which dignity and justice always lend to authority.

A policy which recognized these principles was wisely declared by [the U.S.] Congress in the beginning of the war, and from a fervent desire for the preservation of the Union, in which pride of country and all my interests as a citizen centered, not less than from a natural impulse, I gave that policy my earnest support. Unfortunately it was too often cheated of its due effect by the intrusion of sectional rancor, and the injudicious or unfaithful acts of agents of the [U.S.] government, and when, at the expiration of a year, a system of spoliation and disfranchisement was inaugurated, the cause was robbed of its sanctity, and success rendered more difficult of attainment.

You have in these few lines an explanation of the motives of my conduct while I was in command, as well as of the step which, after twenty-three years of service, has closed my career as a soldier, and broken up the professional habits and associations to which I was educated and in which I have passed the larger portion of my life. I am very far from casting unfavorable reflections upon the thousands who are [still] in the service who, perhaps, with views similar to my own, have not chosen my course. Few of them have been similarly situated, and I rather commend the patience with which they have struggled on in positions which must otherwise have been filled by less scrupulous men, and in which they might mitigate some of the calamities which they yet could not wholly prevent. Very truly yours.[116] — UNION GENERAL DON CARLOS BUELL, LETTER, JULY 10, 1864

AN IMPORTANT MESSAGE FROM *CONFEDERATE VETERAN*
☞ . . . Its owner and director [Sumner A. Cunningham] has thought much about how [*Confederate Veteran*] . . . may be utilized to promote the highest cause on the earth save only that of the Christian religion, and of how it might be perpetuated in the event of his death. He has considered arranging to place it in the hands of committees from the Veterans, Daughters of the Confederacy, and Sons, to act jointly with a committee of our senior surviving generals and their subordinate commanders, in the hope that it be continued until the United States government recognizes that the men and women of the South in the sixties were as patriotic as those of the North, and that by the laws of the land and by inherent rights they were justified in their revolution during the sixties, also that by their sacrifices through those awful years they deserve to be recognized not only by their fellow citizens but by the civilized world to be as worthy of all honor and of all praise for their deeds as any people of any land or any time.

Let anybody refer to the record made in every issue of the *Veteran* for the truth of history. It has never favored one class of its patriots in rank or sex over any other, and it has sought at all times to divide justly the honors between the men and the women of the several States as equally as practicable. It has never for pay given preference to any class or section. Whatever may be the fates of the future, its editor has succeeded upon the highest plane, and he is grateful that he has had the heart and the financial ability to treat all alike, and that he has had the courage to do his duty in these matters, regardless of consequences. And he appeals to every friend of the sacred cause so dear to the [Conservative] Southern people that they stand together, and, as one man, unite in opposition to the hidden hands that may seek the destruction of his abilities to perpetuate these principles through their cooperation. His dependence upon such assistance is absolute.[117] — SUMNER A. CUNNINGHAM, EDITOR, *CONFEDERATE VETERAN MAGAZINE*

WAS THE SOUTH JUSTIFIED?
☛ Comrades: Thirty-five years have elapsed since we surrendered to vastly superior forces and laid down our arms. Many of us were at that time middle-aged men, and consequently are now nearing the bound of life. As we cast a glance at the past, we naturally ask ourselves: "Were we right? Was the South right and justified in the course pursued in 1861-65?"

For myself I wish to say that not an iota of the conviction entertained at that time has been yielded, but those convictions have grown stronger with the lapse of time. Our States seceded from the Union because they were denied plain constitutional rights in the Union. We took up arms to resist invasion and conquest. A more righteous cause never appealed to the spirit of heroism, chivalry, and patriotism in man. The South had always been true to the Union and its laws under the constitution. It has been true to the obligations assumed after the war. My belief is that it was the will of Providence that the Union should continue undivided, at least for a time, until the providential purposes of its creation have been accomplished. What will happen then no man has prescience enough to forecast. So far as the war is concerned we may pass down the declivity of life with conscience at rest.

While we are permitted to remain let us do what we can for the relief of our needy and infirm comrades, and for the proper education and training of the children of veterans who may be in want of our help, that they may be fitted for useful, respectable, and independent lives, and become good citizens of their respective States and of the United States.

Proud of the distinction of having been of your number—a Confederate soldier—as noble and heroic a body of men as any age or country has produced; wishing for each one of you abundant peace and prosperity to the close of life, I am your comrade.[118] —

CONFEDERATE GENERAL ALEXANDER P. STEWART, SPEECH, LOUISVILLE, KENTUCKY, REUNION CONFEDERATE VETERANS

HOW THE U.S. REPUBLIC BECAME A NATION

☞ . . . It is five and thirty years since the Confederate war was closed and about thirty-nine years since it was begun, and it is sometimes asked why we should stir the ashes of that ancient feud, why we should not bury the past in its own grave and turn to the living issues of the present and the future. To this question, comrades, we return the answer, with a voice loud as seven thunders: Because it is history, because it is our history and the history of our dead heroes who shall not go without their fame. As long there are men who wear the gray they will gather the charred embers of their old camp fires, and in the blaze of these reunions tell the story of the martyrs who fell in the defense of country and of truth. Nay, more than this: It is the story of a strife that marks an epoch in the annals of the American people.

It is known to every schoolboy in the land that two parties existed at the formation of our government, who could not agree in locating the paramount sovereignty which should decide upon all issues arising between the States themselves—the Federalists [Editor's note: The meaning of this word has changed many times over the centuries, but at the time indicated here it referred to Liberals. L.S.],[119] as they were termed, demanding a strong government, concentrating power in the national administration; the Republicans [then Conservatives], on the other hand, contending for the distribution of power among the States, claiming their original sovereignty among their reserved rights. Both parties were too strong to allow the question to be determined by arbitration or through forensic discussion. It was therefore permitted to slumber beneath certain ambiguities of expression in the Constitution itself to be settled by the exigencies of the future—not as an abstract principle, but as an accomplished fact. I need not remind you how this issue was raised in 1832, and was postponed through the conciliatory legislation of that period. Such an issue could not, however, sleep forever. The admission of new States into the Union, with their conflicting interests, must reopen the question and compel its decision. Thus it arose in our day, leading to the establishment of the Southern Confederacy and to the civil war that followed.

Fellow-citizens, it is simple folly to suppose that such a spontaneous uprising as that of our people in 1860 and 1861 could be effected through the machinations of politicians alone. A movement so sudden and so vast, instantly swallowing up all minor contentions, would spring only from some great faith deeply planted in the human heart, and for which men were willing to die. Whatever may have been the occasion of the war, the hinge on which it turned was this old question of State sovereignty as against national supremacy. As there could be no compromise between the two the only resort was an appeal to the law of force. The surrender at Appomattox, when the tattered remnant of Lee's great army stood guard for the last time over Southern liberties and rights, drew the equatorial line dividing between the past and the future of American history. When the will of the strongest, instead of "the consent of the governed," became the base of our national structure, a radical transformation took place. The [constitutional] principle of confederation gave way to that of consolidations, and the American nation emerged out of the American republic.

It is not my design, however, to discuss these issues. On the contrary, I have traced the remote origin of the Confederate war for a purpose which is entirely conciliatory, and to explain some things which may appear contradictory. It enables both parties in this struggle to give full credit to each other for patriotic motives, though under a mistaken view of what that patriotism may have required. It shows why no attempt was ventured to bring attainder of treason against the Southern chiefs, which could not afford to be ventilated before any civil court under the terms of the American Constitution. It explains how, through a noble forbearance on both sides—always excepting the infamies of the reconstruction period—the wound has been healed in the complete reconciliation of a divided people. It explains how we of the South, convinced of the rightfulness of our cause, can accept defeat without the blush of shame mantling the cheek of a single Confederate of us all. And, while accepting the issues of the war as a decree of destiny, openly appeal to the verdict of posterity for the final vindication of our career. . . .[120] — REVEREND B. M. PALMER, SPEECH, LOUISVILLE, KENTUCKY, REUNION CONFEDERATE VETERANS

WHY THE OLD SOUTH COULD NOT BE RULED

☛ No man who is not willing to bear and to fight for his rights can give a good reason why he should be entitled to the privilege of living in a free community. The decline of the militant spirit in the Northeast during the first half of this century was much to be regretted. To it is due more than to any other cause the undoubted average individual inferiority of the Northern compared with the Southern troops—at any rate, at the beginning of the great war of the rebellion. The Southerners, by their whole mode of living, their habits, and their love of outdoor sports, kept up their warlike spirit, while in the North the so-called upper classes developed along the lines of a wealthy and timid bourgeoisie type, measuring everything by a mercantile standard (a peculiarly debasing one, if taken purely by itself), and submitting to be ruled in local affairs by low, foreign mobs, and in national matters by their arrogant Southern kinsmen. The militant spirit of these last certainly stood them in good stead in the civil war. The world has never seen better soldiers than those who followed Lee, and their leader will undoubtedly rank, without any exception, as the very greatest of all the great captains that the English-speaking peoples have brought forth; and this although the last and chief of his antagonists may himself claim to stand as the full equal of [the Duke of] Marlborough [John Churchill] or [the Duke of] Wellington [Arthur Wellesley].[21] — FUTURE U.S. PRESIDENT THEODORE ROOSEVELT

UNION VETERAN SUPPORTS CONFEDERATE VETERANS

☛ I heartily approve of the action of your [Confederate] Camp [in inviting U.S. President William McKinley to your reunion in Memphis, Tennessee]. These Confederate reunions, like those of the Grand [Union] Army, are of men who fought for certain principles, and those who opposed them cannot properly join them without indorsing the principles for which their opponents made war. Ever since men were associated together there have been different views of the same subject, and there always will be. The result of our civil war did not change the normal aspect of a single question which caused the conflict, nor did it change the views of a single honest man in relation thereto.

There has been a great deal of foolish talk about the joint reunion of the survivors of the opposing armies of the civil war. They have no business celebrating together the memories of their campaigns. The President and every other man in the nation knows that the late Confederates accepted the result of the war, and resumed their rights and duties as citizens of the United States, and that their loyalty to the Constitution cannot be questioned. And among their rights is the privilege of construing that Constitution. It is true that they were forced back into citizenship in the United States, and because of this fact they are entitled to great credit for so patriotically supporting their government. In war they have not sulked—their sons have carried the national flag around the world, and have died fighting for it, and under at least one of the men who stood with their fathers when they made battle under the Confederate ensign. Those of us who opposed the Confederates can love and respect them as neighbors and citizens, but we cannot rejoice with them over the battles they won, nor weep with them when they recount those which they lost, and the man who was not of them has no place at their reunions.

The time has long since passed that men can be called to account for the side they espoused in the civil war between the States. No brave man, no honorable man has any apology to offer on that score, nor will any honorable man ask such a thing. But there are sacred memories of what each did and suffered that can be talked over only with those who truly sympathize with us—no one outside of the family can enter into this sacred, loved confidence. As properly ask the murderer to attend the funeral of his victim, and fill the place of chief mourner.

I do like to see the mingling of the men who fought the civil war; but I want to see the commingling on public, civic occasions pertaining to the present. The war, with all its horrors, cannot be forgotten by the people of the South, for the South was the battlefield, and all of that awful prophecy of [Confederate Vice President] Alexander Stephens was fulfilled within their very sight. There are horrors in war beside which the killing of men in battle become as trifles, and these things cannot be forgotten by those who endured them; nor would I desire the association of persons who would admit that they deserved the wrongs put upon them by brute force.

Soldiers who were in the opposing armies can befriends and honorable citizens to-day without abasing or stultifying themselves; and while each respects the feelings of the other, he is not bound to accept opposing views or apologies for those he holds.

Many people never knew, and others have forgotten, that the date of [the Confederate] reunion for Richmond was changed in a broadly conservative spirit so as to adjourn in time to participate with the Grand Army of the Republic [U.S. / Union army] in a great parade on the 4th of July in New York City; that the commander of the G. A. R. declined such joint celebration in such emphatic terms that there was no compromise. True he was told there would be no Confederate flags in the procession, but he said he would not permit the "Grand Army" to parade with Confederates if they should wear gray clothes. The promptness with which the arrangement was canceled should indicate the settled purpose of

Confederates to avoid another similar humiliation.[122] — J. H. WOODARD, UNION VETERAN, LETTER IN RESPONSE TO HIS UNION VETERANS' CAMP OPPOSING CONFEDERATE VETERANS INVITING PRESIDENT MCKINLEY TO THEIR MEMPHIS REUNION

THE MEN & WOMEN OF HENRY COUNTY, TENNESSEE

☛ . . . The war between the States was not promoted by the men of Henry County [Tennessee]. They were conservative and peaceful. War to them was terrible to contemplate, but they were not afraid of it or of its sacrifices. "They loved peace as they abhorred pusillanimity, but not peace at any price. There is a peace more destructive of the manhood of living men than war is destructive of his material body. Chains are worse than bayonets." The men of Henry were the sons and grandsons of Virginia and North Carolina. Their ancestors fought at Yorktown and King's Mountain, and were with [Andrew] Jackson at New Orleans. They had heard the stories of these great events from the pioneers, and were familiar with the trials and hardships of the cheerless days of the American revolution. They had learned that in a republic the liberty of the citizen and his rights of property must be asserted in the courts of the country, or at the ballot box, and failing here, a resort to arms was the logical consequence.

Up to the year 1861 secession was more than an open question; few thoughtful Southern men denied the right of the State to withdraw from the Federal Union; the wisdom of its exercise was another question. But this right under the Constitution as understood and construed cannot be gainsaid. So when it was exercised by States south of us without consultation or reference to us, the people of Tennessee condemned the action as hasty and ill-advised, and still no Southern man challenged the act, and not one consented to the doctrine that there was legal warrant for the Federal authorities to compel obedience to them. Tennessee declared at an early day, months before her own formal withdrawal from the Union, that if the rue of force was applied to one State it would be accepted by her people as an act of war. The people of the South are and were a homogeneous race. A common ancestry with customs and institutions alike created a brotherhood stronger than the Union of States. So when President [Abraham] Lincoln called for troops and inaugurated war against South Carolina and other seceding States there was no delay nor hesitation, no postponement for advice from leaders. The men of Henry upon their own motion rushed to arms. This action was a response to the lesson evolved from their education; a sense of duty controlled them; their judgments and hearts approved it, and before God and the tribunal of history we have no apology to offer. We made our history honestly and conscientiously, and we will write it truthfully as we made it, the protest of the Grand Army of the Republic [Union veterans] to the contrary notwithstanding. We want no accommodating committee to compromise our history, or to sugarcoat facts unpalatable to the sensibilities of men who will not accord honesty of purpose to the men of the South. We want posterity to knowhow our history was made; that it was done deliberately and voluntarily, and that we put our lives and fortunes to the touchstone of battle, and thus gave to the world the highest evidence of our sincerity. Henry County furnished a larger number of soldiers for the war, in proportion to white population, than any county in the State. They were earnest, brave men, full of dash and steadiness, responsive to discipline, with wonderful power to overcome fatigue and to resist the rigor of winter and the heat of summer. Meager rations were accepted without complaint; our surroundings were appreciated by all. There was no hope of foreign assistance, and no expectation of success unless it could be won on the battlefield. The Federal [U.S.] government had men, money, and munitions of war, and there was no limit to the supply. The Confederate States did not have a current dollar; when a soldier was killed or disabled there was no one to take his place. When a Federal [Union] soldier met the same fate a dozen recruits were sent forward. The Army of Tennessee [C.S.A.] killed and disabled more men of [Union General William T.] Sherman's army than we had on our muster rolls, yet Sherman was stronger in numbers when he reached Atlanta than when he moved against Rocky Face Ridge one hundred days before that date, after fighting a battle almost every day. No recruits came to the Confederates; there was no nation nor people upon whom we could call for help; ours was the orphan nation of the world, poor, naked, and hungry. As time passed hardships multiplied; the clothing of the men and the rations upon which they were fed were growing lighter in weight; ammunition was no longer abundant; the country was exhausted; pinching cold and hunger and poverty were in every household.

To these conditions we at last succumbed. The men of Henry stood by the flag to the last; they participated in every battle of the Southwest. From Belmont to Bentonville they fell "on the red sand of the battlefield with bloody corpses strewn," and hundreds of them sleep in unmarked graves, but they are not forgotten. The stars may go down, but there is no oblivion for good or brave deeds.

... Ladies of the Monumental Association, I have recited to you the names of some of my comrades whose actions you perpetuate by the erection of this monument. No knightlier soldiers ever went out to battle for their country, no soldier ever had a cause worthier of the supreme effort they made, no cause ever promoted greater enthusiasm, no cause ever demanded greater sacrifices, no cause was ever so loyally sustained. We cannot forget them, we cannot forget the sacrifices or the devotion of the women of the South. They accepted poverty that they might promote the cause for which their fathers, husbands, and sons fought and died. History with its splendid recitals cannot furnish illustrations like the self-denial of our own wives, mothers, daughters, and sisters. We cannot forget them, we cannot forget that in the hour of defeat, when we were crushed by a disaster not to be measured by words, they gave us good cheer and welcome, and, next to the Great Dispenser of every good and perfect gift, they gave us comfort and encouragement, and stimulated acquiescence in the result of the war, and encouraged all to a manly effort in the peaceful walks of life. . . .[23] — FORMER TENNESSEE GOVERNOR & CONFEDERATE OFFICER JAMES D. PORTER, SPEECH, CONFEDERATE MONUMENT DEDICATION, PARIS (HENRY COUNTY), TENNESSEE

Confederate Lieutenant Daniel Giraud Wright, Co. H, 1st Maryland Infantry Regiment, circa 1863.

WHAT JEFFERSON DAVIS SAID ELEVEN YEARS BEFORE LINCOLN'S WAR

☛ Give to each section of the Union justice; give to every citizen of the United States his rights as guaranteed by the constitution; have this Union to rest upon that basis from which arose the fraternal feeling of the people, and I, for one, have no fear of its perpetuity; none that it will survive beyond the limits of human speculation, expanding and hardening with the lapse of time, to extend its blessings to ages unnumbered and a people innumerable; to include within its empire all the useful products of the earth, and exemplify the capacity of a confederacy with general, well-defined powers, to extend inimitably without impairing its harmony or its strength.[124] — MISSISSIPPI SENATOR & FUTURE CONFEDERATE PRESIDENT JEFFERSON DAVIS, SPEECH BEFORE THE SENATE, JULY 31, 1850

Four Confederate sailors serving time at the Yankee prison Fort Warren, Boston, Massachusetts, circa 1864. Names: top left, J. B. Belville; bottom left, Acting Midshipman James A. Peters, CSS *Ellis*, CSS *Seabird*, CSS *Atlanta*, CSS *Virginia*, CSS *Richmond*, and Semmes Naval Brigade; bottom right, William McBlair Jr; top right, sailor's identity unknown.

Confederate soldier, identity unknown, circa 1863.

PATRICK HENRY'S PREDICTION

☛ ... The great conflict of 1861, that shook a continent and made a nation to tremble as the aspen leaf, cast its lengthening shadow almost a century before—back [to 1787] to the very hall in which our Federal Constitution was framed. There the conflicting ideas clashed which continued to grow and be intensified until hostile cannons boomed and gleaming sabers flashed and fraternal blood ran like water. The conflict was over the reserved rights of the States and as to what lights and powers were ceded to the general government upon a State becoming a member of the Federal compact. There was one man in particular in a convention in Virginia, called to ratify the constitution, Patrick Henry, who saw that shadow almost as distinctly as did Stonewall Jackson see the substance when he said at the first Manassas: "Sirs, we will give them the bayonet." Mr. Henry wanted it placed in the constitution of his country in black and white, so that there could be no controversy about it, that all the rights, powers, and prerogatives not expressly ceded to the general government were reserved by the respective States. His argument and contention were met with the statements that of course the powers and prerogatives not expressly granted were reserved. Then it was that the old orator and statesman, the very father of our independence, whose eloquence had electrified the colonies and made liberty certain and the constitution a possibility, stood there upon the floor of the hall with the shadow of inevitable conflict falling full upon his mind and heart, tears coursing down his wrinkled cheeks, his prophetic vision sweeping the span of a coming century, when he said:

> "I see it, I feel it. I see the beings of a higher order anxious concerning our decision. When I see beyond the horizon that bounds human eyes and look at the final consummation of all human things, and see those intelligent beings, which inhabit ethereal mansions, reviewing the political decisions and revolutions, which in the progress of time will happen in America, and the consequent happiness or misery of mankind, I am led to believe that much of the account on one side or the other will happen on what we now decide. Our own happiness alone is not affected by the event; all nations are interested in it."

While Mr. Henry was thus speaking the heavens suddenly blackened with a gathering tempest, which burst with such terrible fury that he could proceed no further, and it was the last speech that he made in the convention.

Southerner, Conservative, constitutionalist, Founding Father: Patrick Henry.

What a prophecy were those words! How significant was the bursting storm, typical of the storm of the great civil war, which gathered for almost a century and burst in its terrible fury on the 12th of April, 1861! Here this statesman and orator seemed to have something of the spirit of the ancient prophets, enabling him to see far into the distant future and to predict with certainty a conflict fiercer than any of modern times, a conflict that drenched the country in its best blood. And thus the question was left unsettled by the constitution. It was left unsettled by the fierce debates in Congress, by the Mason and Dixon line, by the nullification act of South Carolina, by Mr. [Henry] Clay's omnibus bill. It was left unsettled by the Dred Scott decision by the Supreme Court, and it was left unsettled until at Appomattox Courthouse Gen. Robert E. Lee, that grand old leader, grander in defeat than most men in victory, said to [Union] Gen. [Ulysses S.] Grant: "My brave army is destroyed, the remnant is exhausted, I surrender."

Thus it became the unwritten law of our constitution that the rights and prerogatives not expressly reserved by the States are granted upon the State becoming a member of the Federal compact, yet at what a fearful cost in human blood and in human woe did this become an unwritten part of our constitution! In contemplating this cost in human blood and treasure, my mind goes back to the bloody fields of Bull Run, Shiloh, Chickamauga, Antietam, Cold Harbor, Brice's Cross Roads, Kennesaw Mountain, Franklin, and Bentonville, where men fell like leaves in autumn, where the pride and chivalry of the nation rushed willingly into the very jaws of death, yielding up their lives for what each thought to be right; and I thought of how many happy homes were made desolate, how many mothers' hearts were broken, and how many aged fathers trembled as the wind-shaken reed when the reports came from these bloody fields, and then that this and all of this death and human desolation might and doubtless would have been averted had thirteen words contended for by Mr. Henry been added to the Federal Constitution, only one word for each of the thirteen original colonies: "Rights not expressly ceded to the general government are reserved by the States."[125] — HONORABLE W. W. FARABAUGH, PARIS, TENNESSEE

OUR SENSE OF DUTY & DEVOTION TO RIGHT

☞ . . . We have become in great measure like the Chinese, worshipers of our [colonial] ancestors, and through the halo of more than a century they seem to us beyond the tongue of criticism. But many as were their virtues, and marvelous as were their sagacity and statesmanship, they left unsettled a question even then threatening, and which grew apace until there was no arbiter to decide it but the sword. The [Conservative or Right-wing] Jeffersonian [Thomas Jefferson] idea of a Confederacy of sovereign States, wherein all powers not expressly delegated to the Federal government were reserved to the States was inherited by us of the South, while the [Liberal or Left-wing] Hamiltonian [Alexander Hamilton] idea of a centralized power, with the States mere particles of a nation, was bequeathed to the people of the North.

As all know, these variant creeds were most often brought into conflict as applied to the negro; but he was merely the fuse that constantly ignited the magazine of difference, fast ripening into discord and developing into hate between the sections. At last there came what to the South seemed organized warfare on its rights and institutions, and then secession of the several States, and then the deluge of war.

The Union had its well-organized and equipped army and navy as a nucleus, with every branch of government in perfect order and system, with unlimited material resources, and the wide world to draw from. We were denounced to all that world as rebels and traitors, seeking to destroy the government which boasted that it was an asylum for the oppressed of all nations. Call followed call, and from Maine to California the tramp of soldiers responded. Why did they come? Can we not alter all these years accord to them, with few exceptions, the honesty of purpose which actuated us? It was to preserve the Union, which they believed we intended to wreck or destroy. It was for this that the American manhood of the North took up arms, but in a short time "every kindred, every tongue on this terrestrial ball" had its representatives in the ranks of the Union, many with no thought nor comprehension of the principles at stake. To beat back this horde, to defend our homes and firesides, and to preserve the rights for which our fathers had devoted their lives, their fortunes, and their sacred honor, the manhood of the South sprang to arms. Here at the beginning, and prolonged from Sumter to Appomattox, was the disparity that would have appalled all hearts and quenched all ardor not born of principle.

With no army nor navy, with no credit in the world's markets, with no resource except the voluntary personal sacrifice of the men and women of the South, God's very best creation in all the cycles of time, misunderstood by all the world, and without sympathy from any foreign powers, but fully realizing the fearful odds against them, these men hastened to offer themselves, their lives, and their fortunes. What had they to gain and what to lose? Did any dream of conquest or of empire enter their minds? Did any hope of personal fortune or acquisition prompt them? Did an ambition to win the world's applause, or to gratify hate, impel them? Did the money value of every slave in all the Southland weigh as the dust in the balance against the life of one young stripling who kissed his mother a fond farewell, then waved adieu and walked beyond the stars? No, in God's great name, a thousand times no. With naught to gain, with all to lose, they bared their breast to the storm for four long years; they exchanged ease and luxury for toil and starvation. Ragged, unshod, and weak from hunger, they marched and watched and fought with no repining and no weakening of purpose, but with dauntless souls they went into the jaws of death, their only inspiration the sense of duty and devotion to right. . . .[126]
— JUDGE R. H. CUNNINGHAM

"DIED FOR STATES' RIGHTS"
☛ It is meet that on all proper occasions the remnant of Confederate soldiers still left in the land of the living should

assemble themselves together, and in the presence of a new generation discuss the issues of the past, to the end that history may be vindicated and that posterity may not be deceived and taught to believe a lie.

My Comrades, nearly forty-one years ago the tocsin of war was sounded throughout the length and breadth of this once happy land of ours. The ordinary pursuits of life were abandoned, the wheels of commerce for a time ceased to roll, the streets of the towns and cities were crowded with anxious inquirers for the latest news from political centers and official circles. To the forum and the press the people looked for news and for advice. War and rumors of war were almost the only topics of conversation. Secession from the Union on one side was threatened as the only means of preserving constitutional rights. On the other side war seemed to be welcomed, and coercion of sovereign States, for the first time in the history of the government, seemed to be seriously contemplated. The Southern people believed that the constitutional rights of the South were held for naught by a number of the Northern States, while the laws of Congress, passed in strict accordance with a plain provision of the Constitution, were nullified and publicly denounced by the press, pulpit, and statesmen of the North.

The excitement ran high. The military arm of the general government began to move; while in the South military companies, regiments, and brigades rapidly formed, and soon the roar of cannon, the rattle of musketry, and the tread of armies declared that the day of compromise had passed, and that the struggle of the South to maintain its constitutional rights had been transferred from the halls of Congress to the field of carnage, where the sword was to be the only arbiter; and for four long and weary years two of the grandest armies that ever trod the earth marched under their respective flags, and on many fields of blood those mighty men of war fought, bled, and died as only heroes can fight, bleed, and die.

The first hostile gun was fired at the bombardment of Fort Sumter. April 12, 1861, and the last battle was fought at Palmetto Ranch, Tex., May 13, 1865, where the soil of Texas was once again bathed in the blood of her gallant sons in defense of her constitutional rights as a sovereign State, and to drive from her soil a hostile invading foe.

But why, we are asked by the misinformed of this day and time, did the South rebel and bring on that cruel and disastrous war? The story is a long one, and yet the truth, without details, can be told in few words. I would that I had the attentive ear to-day of the sons and daughters of every Confederate soldier in the land, for I have no apologies to make for the South or for the manner in which I shall deal with this subject. No true son of the South should treat the case with sugar-coated pills. History has been so grievously perverted that every true man must, on this subject, dare to speak the truth, "though the heavens fall." We owe it to ourselves, to posterity, to truth, and to justice to "hew to the line, let the chips fall where they may."

A few days ago in the capital city of Texas I stood, with uncovered head, at the base of a splendid monument being erected to the memory of the Confederate dead, and upon its most prominent front I read this inscription:

> "Died, for State Rights, guaranteed under the Constitution. The people of the South, animated by the spirit of 1776 to preserve their rights, withdrew from the Federal compact in 1861. The North resorted to coercion. The South, against overwhelming numbers and resources, fought until exhausted. During the war there were 2,257 engagements. Number of men enlisted: Confederate armies, 700,000; Federal armies, 2,859,132. Losses from all causes: Confederates, 437,000; Federals, 485,216."

That monument, my countrymen, quotes history. No well-informed patriot of this day and time will deny the doctrine of State rights under the constitution of the United States as it was from the foundation of the government down to the close of the war. If this doctrine was not supported by the constitution and laws of the United States, then the people of the South were rebels and traitors to their country; but if, as the South has always contended, the doctrine of State rights was supported by the constitution, the people of the South were true patriots, devoted to the constitution and laws of the land, and to maintain them in 1861, like their patriot fathers of 1776, "pledged to each other their lives, their fortunes, and their sacred honor," and for four long and bloody years they did sustain their cause against overwhelming numbers and boundless resources.

Our armies were made up of resident citizens of the Southland, the best Anglo-Saxon blood that ever traced through human veins. Without a navy and our ports all blockaded, our intercourse with the outside world was meager indeed. For new recruits, army supplies, and munitions of war we had to look, almost entirely, to our own people and territory; while the Federal government, with her free and unrestricted intercourse with every nation on earth, from all of whom she drew supplies, munitions of war, and new recruits for her armies at thirteen dollars [$460 in today's currency] a month, the conflict, indeed, was an unequal one. And again, the policy of the South was to with draw from the Union, peaceably if possible, and stand on the defensive on her own soil with no thought of invading the North, while the policy of the North was to invade and coerce the South. Thus the policy of both governments, from the beginning to the close of the war, was to make of the South the battlegrounds, where the tread of mighty contending armies and booming cannon shook the very earth, and where devastation, rapine, and murder inevitably follow where such vast contending hostile armies march.

. . . Let me remind you in the outset that this question of State rights, over which the war was fought, is no new question. It began at the formation of the government, and upon the adoption of the constitution was, by the then contending parties, considered settled. The great [Liberal] Alexander Hamilton and followers, on one side, opposed the doctrine of State rights and contended for a strong Federal government, centralizing all power in the general government and making the States mere dependencies. He believed that a monarchy such as old England was the best form of government, "the happiest device of human ingenuity."

[Conservative] Thomas Jefferson led the State rights party, and in that conflict the Jeffersonian doctrine of State right prevailed, adopting that form of government, and submitted the constitution, which was in due time adopted by the States, and it thus became the organic law of the United States. Hamilton admitted his defeat in the convention, and advocated the adoption of the constitution by the States, expressing, however, his "doubts as to the success of the experiment," as he called it; and later, in 1791, he said:

> "I own it is my opinion, though I do not publish it in Dan or Beersheba, that the present government is not that which answers the ends of society by giving stability and protection to its rights, and that it will probably be found expedient to go to the British form."

The doctrine of State rights thus recognized of course carried with it the right of each State to regulate its domestic affairs in its own way, and Congress possessed no power not delegated to it by the constitution, or in the language of the constitution itself:

> "The powers not delegated to the United States by the constitution, nor prohibited to the States, are reserved to the

States, respectively, or to the people."

The domestic affairs of a State could not therefore be interfered with by Congress, nor by the act of any other State. To illustrate: It will be admitted by every intelligent, honest man that each State had the constitutional right, for itself, and by its own laws prior to the war, to determine whether or not the institution of slavery should exist within its borders. This has never been denied by any one, except by the fanatic [Leftists] who appealed to a "higher law" doctrine, declaring that the constitution was a "league with hell," and should not be obeyed. A provision of the constitution of the United States, then and still in force, reads as follows:

> "No person held to service or labor in one State, under the laws thereof, escaping into another shall, in consequence of any law or regulation therein, be discharged from such service or labor, but shall be delivered up on claim of the party to whom such service or labor may be due."

Seeking to enforce this plain provision of the constitution of the United States, Congress enacted what is known as the Fugitive Slave law. The State of Pennsylvania, as did fourteen other Northern States, sought to nullify this clause of the constitution and law of Congress, and passed laws forbidding the execution thereof in their respective States, and in the celebrated case of Prigg vs. the Commonwealth of Pennsylvania, the Supreme Court of the United States, by a unanimous opinion, upholding the constitution and laws of Congress, said:

> "Historically it is well known that the object of this clause was to secure to the citizens of the slaveholding States the complete right and title of ownership in their slaves as property in every State of the Union into which they might escape from the State wherein they were held in servitude.. . . The full recognition of this right and title was indispensable to the security of this species of property in all the slaveholding States, and, indeed, was so vital to the preservation of their interest and institutions *that it cannot be doubled that it constituted a fundamental article without the adoption of which the Union would not have been formed.* Its true design was to guard against the doctrines and principles prevalent in the nonslaveholding States by preventing them from interfering with or restricting or abolishing the rights of the owners of the slaves. . . . This clause was therefore of the last importance to the safety and security of the Southern States, and could not be surrendered by them without endangering their whole property in slaves. The clause was

therefore adopted in the convention by the unanimous consent of the framers of it, a proof at once of its intrinsic and practical necessity. . . . The clause manifestly contemplates the existence of a positive, unqualified right on the part of the owner of the slave which no State law or regulation can in any manner regulate, control, qualify, or restrain."

Thus spake the Supreme Court of the United States. Human language could not have more emphatically declared the true intent and meaning of the constitution. Daniel Webster, the greatest lawyer and statesman that Massachusetts or New England ever produced, is quoted as saying:

"I do not hesitate to say and repeat that if the Northern States refuse, willfully and deliberately, to carry into effect that part of the constitution which respects the restoration of fugitive slaves, and Congress provides no remedy, the South would no longer be bound to observe the compact. A bargain broken on one side is broken on all sides."

Again, in 1851, he said:

"In the North the purpose of overturning the government shows itself more clearly in resolutions agreed to in voluntary assemblies of individuals, denouncing the laws of the land, and declaring a fixed intent to disobey them. I notice in one of these meetings held lately in the very heart of New England, and said to have been numerously attended, the members unanimously resolved, 'That as God is our helper, we will not suffer any person charged with being a fugitive from labor to be taken from among us, and to this resolution we pledge our lives, our fortunes, and our sacred honor.'"

And Mr. Webster proceeds:

"These persons do not seem to have been aware that the purpose thus avowed by them is distinctly treasonable. If any law of the land be resisted by force of arms or by force of numbers, with a declared intention to resist the application of that law, in all cases this is levying war against the government within the meaning of the constitution, and is an act of treason drawing after it all the consequences of that offense."

From the foundation of the government down to 1861 the State rights doctrine was recognized by the party in power, by the

Supreme Court of the United States, in fact by statesmen of all parties, as constitutional. The difficulty was not in the construction of the constitution, but whether or not it was binding and should be obeyed or held for naught. It was perfectly natural that every Federalist [Liberal], being opposed to the State rights doctrine and favoring a strong centralized government, should gradually fall into line with the abolition party [later calling themselves "communists"],[127] that claimed the right in Congress and in other States to nullify the constitution and laws that sustained the doctrine, and as that party grew in numbers it became fanatical and more defiant of the constitution and laws of the land.

Mr. Edward Quincey said:

> "For our part we have no particular desire to see the present law repealed or modified. What we preach is not repeal, not modification, but disobedience."

Another said: "The citizens of a government tainted with slave institutions may combine with foreigners to put down the government."

The constitution and laws to which we have referred were denounced by such leaders as [socialists] Wendell Phillips and William Lloyd Garrison as "a covenant with death, an agreement with hell." And as early as 1848 [Liberal] Mr. [William H.] Seward declared that there was an "irrepressible conflict" between the sections on the question of slavery, and that the government could not exist in peace "half slave and half free," an expression so often used by [Liberal] Mr. Lincoln in his memorable canvass with [Conservative] Mr. [Stephen A.] Douglas in the State of Illinois in 1858. And when it became apparent that no honest judge of the Supreme Court could ever be found to declare that the constitution of the United States did not protect the rights of the people of the States in their local and property rights, many of them became so fanatical as to appeal to the higher law doctrine, and Mr. Seward himself is quoted as saying:

> "There is a higher law than the constitution which regulates our authority over the domain. Slavery must be abolished, and we must do it."

Here was one of their political idols, who afterwards became Secretary of State under Mr. Lincoln. He here advocated the abolition of slavery, not by the States where slavery existed, the only constitutional way it could be done, and the way it was finally

Confederate soldiers, identities unknown; St. Louis, Missouri, circa 1862.

done, but in obedience to the higher law—that is, in spite of the constitution and the rights of the States thereunder. And then follows the demands of one of those "more-holy-than thou" creatures [Anson P. Burlingame], who was not satisfied with Almighty God. He said: "The times demand and we must have an antislavery constitution, an antislavery Bible, and an antislavery God."[128] They had neither then, and wanted a change. Such language, if used to-day in denunciation of the government, the constitution and laws, would be justly and vehemently denounced as the utterances of crazy anarchists, and yet at the time used they were the utterances of beloved and honored [Left-wing] leaders in social, political, and religious circles of the North, and whose memory is still cherished throughout that section of the country. As one of the many evil fruits of such teachings the sovereign State of Virginia was invaded in October, 1859, by an armed band of cutthroats, murderers, and conspirators, led by John Brown, a Northern [socialistic] fanatic, against the government of Virginia and the constitutional rights of her people. Such an open and deliberate act of treason, rapine, and murder ought to have received the emphatic and unanimous condemnation of the people of the North as it did in the South. But not so. Appeals were made for the remission of the punishment prescribed by the laws of Virginia, and at the North this ungodly traitor, this foul murderer, has been canonized (declared a saint), and Mr. Curry said that "Hughes, in his 'Manliness of Christ,' places John Brown almost on a level with the Son of God."

Well, the time did come when this nullifying sectional party secured an antislavery candidate [Lincoln] for President,[129] who had himself declared that "this government could not endure half slave and half free," because he said, in substance, that there was an irrepressible conflict between the sections upon this question of slavery; that both slavery and the Union could not exist, and that the Union must be preserved. And it was too true. There was an irrepressible conflict waged by a sectional party against the constitution and laws of the land and the rights guaranteed by the constitution to the people of the South.

I have thus quoted from speeches, letters, utterances, laws, the constitution, and decisions of the court of last resort, not for the purpose of reviving prejudices or sectional bitterness—far be it from me—but for the purpose of recalling to the minds of my hearers the signs of the times immediately preceding the war, showing the provocation to the South, the purity of her motives, and to justify her in the efforts she made to peaceably secede from the Union and form a government that would protect her in her constitutional rights.

And now, my comrades, since more than forty years have passed away since the clash of arms in that cruel war began, when the smoke of battle has cleared away, and when the mental vision is no longer obscured by prejudice, and when reason is once again enthroned, let me say that when we remember the long years of struggle in and out of Congress to uphold the rights of the States, guaranteed under plain and unmistakable provisions of the Constitution; and when we remember that many of the State Legislatures of the North denounced the decisions of the Supreme Court of the United States sustaining the State rights doctrine as an arbitrary power, and therefore null and void; and when we remember that honored leaders of that rapidly growing sectional party, ever opposing State rights, were denouncing the constitution thus upheld by the Supreme Court as a "covenant with death and league with hell"; and when we remember that "the voice of the law was no longer in the land," but that the Federal government, which prior to 1861 had administered the government in accordance with the requirements of the constitution and laws, was now "browbeaten and defeated"; and then when this sectional party, thus pledged to the destruction of the rights of the South and the centralization of the government, was about to seize the reins of government, *what*, I ask, *was the South to do?* She was thoroughly convinced that the constitution and laws of the United States were so despised and denounced by the leaders of the party coming into power that they would no longer be enforced, and knowing that she had the legal and constitutional right to withdraw from the Union when necessary to preserve her rights, no alternative was left her, as a free and sovereign State, but to withdraw from the Union, or to submit to what she believed would be an utter destruction of her rights, and to do so without a struggle was impossible for a brave and noble people through whose veins the blood of patriots and lovers of constitutional liberty flowed. She therefore seceded, and the war of coercion followed.

The last almost of the great statesmen and generals who took active part in that struggle have passed away, and the last of the rank and file of those great armies will have soon crossed over the river to "rest under the shade." The Presidents of both governments and the last of their cabinet officers save one are dead. The Hon. John H. Reagan, of Texas, survives them all. An honest man, a true patriot, a wise counselor, and a great statesman, after an active and most eventful life of more than eighty-three years, he stands erect like a giant oak of the forest which has withstood the storms of a century, firmly rooted in the confidence, love, and affection of a great and noble people.

But, my comrades, the war was not fought in vain. It is true that the sacred cause for which we fought went down in gloom. The flag and government we sought to maintain we lost forever. With the hallowed dust of our patriot heroes, and the sacred memories of the past, we laid them away with an abiding faith that posterity will yet see and admit what we know to be true—that is, that the South sought to secede for no other purpose than to protect her people in the enjoyment of a plain constitutional right, which the [Left-wing Republican] party coming into power had assailed for more than a generation with the avowed purpose of destroying it; that the methods used and threatened to be used up to that time were an open violation of those rights by nullification of the constitution and laws that protected them; that no people up to that time had been more devoted to the constitution and Union than the people of the South; that no people had spent so much blood and treasure for the country's cause as her people; that they had ever been ready to uphold the laws and defend the flag whenever and wherever assailed; that no cause was ever more just than our efforts to peaceably secede from the Union to preserve a constitutional right.

No sacrifices so great, no people ever sustained a cause so long against such overwhelming odds and resources. No country so devastated; the resources of no country so completely exhausted, and no victor ever paid so dear for what he won. The flag of no country or cause ever went down in defeat crowned with such a halo of glory. No cause ever had a more devoted, self-sacrificing people to sustain it; while the bravery, the devotion, the energy, the unselfishness, and heroism of the noble women of the South, throughout the entire struggle, is unparalleled in the history of the world. No armies were ever led to battle by greater generals, and no generals ever commanded better, braver, or more patriotic soldiers. And last, but not least, no brighter intellect or purer statesman, no patriot with clearer conscience, purer heart, or more lofty purposes ever wielded power or guided the ship of State than Jefferson Davis, the gifted and noble President of the Confederate States.

The war being over, the remnant of the Confederate army, the best that ever trod the earth, disarmed and poorly clad, sought the desolated homes of their loved ones, and began anew the battle of life, little dreaming that the horrors of reconstruction were yet to be endured. I pass over this uncalled for and disgraceful period in the history of our country, except to note as one of the results that at the close of the war the aggregate debt of the Southern States was $87,193,933.33 [$1.6 billion in today's currency], and at the close of that period of robbery their aggregated indebtedness had increased to the enormous sum of $380,160,575.13 [$7.2 billion in today's currency]. But finally rid of the oppressors, and her local affairs once again intrusted to her own keeping, she rose from the ashes, Phoenix-like, and is now challenging the admiration of the world. Her climate, her soil, her recuperative powers, her patriotism, her statesmanship, her devotion to justice, and her lofty ambition are forcing her to the front rank of every laudable enterprise, and he is blind indeed who cannot see that the time will come when she will, in the future, as she did prior to 1861, become the ruling power in what will then be recognized as the best government the world has ever seen. And then who can say, judging the future by the past, that New England will not again, as she did on one occasion when she thought the South was gaining in power, threaten to secede from the Union; for, as it has been said by the distinguished Republican [then Liberal] statesman, ex-Senator [John J.] Ingalls, of Kansas, in discussing the late amendments to the constitution, that

> "the right of secession, if it ever existed, exists now, so far as any declaration in our organic law is concerned. It has not been renounced, nor is the supremacy of the nation affirmed in its charter."

And it is true, but God grant that a cause for secession may never again occur....[130] — HONORABLE L. J. STOREY, RAILROAD COMMISSIONER OF TEXAS, SAN ANTONIO INTERNATIONAL FAIR, OCTOBER 23, 1901

WHO WAS THE CONFEDERATE PRIVATE SOLIDER? A WOMAN'S VIEW

☞ He was the enthusiastic cavalier without the fiery zeal of the fanatic. He was the devoted, loving patriot without suspicion of mercenary motive. He was the tender, gentle father who put away his prattling infant as he shouldered his musket and marched away, not with stern gesture of the Puritan stoic, but with the earnest sorrow of the Christian and the gentleman. He was the Chevalier [de] Bayard [Pierre Terrail] of Southern knighthood, who placed the farewell kiss on the pale forehead of his bride, and tried in vain to chase from his own face the emblems of keen anguish and regret as he smiled to her with confidence and with hope. He was the impersonation of that honor from whose shield shone the bright image of the truth. In his heart dwelt with unspeakable fondness the beauty and the loveliness of his own Southland. He loved her with the intense affection of the Irishman for the Green Isle of the Sea. He yearned for her with the deep devotion of the Highlander for his Scottish mountain home. Through generations he had imbibed the spirit of personal and of national honor. To the conquered enemy he was courteous and gentle; to the conquering victor he was dignified and courageous. To women he bore himself with gallant tenderness, and to the sick and imprisoned he was patient and helpful.

> To his loved land he gave, without a stain,
> Courage and faith. Vain faith and courage vain.

The civil war is over. The record is made up, the judgment of history is declared and published. With here and there a discordant note, the voice of history pronounces this eulogism on the Confederate soldier, whose heroic fame yon monument has built in enduring stone. That his cause was just, for he demanded only his rights under the constitution and the law; that his courage was unrivaled, for he battled against overwhelming odds and amidst unspeakable difficulties; that his victories were achieved without cruelty or crime, for the page of his accomplishment shows no spot or blemish on his glory; that he was superb in defeat, for no childish tear of despair wet his cheeks when he looked into the face of the inevitable; that he was unconquerable in surrender, for with the supreme consciousness of the truth and the right appealing to Almighty God and to posterity, he took up the burden of life again and hewed out from a blackened wilderness of wretchedness and ruin the civilization which is to-day the pride and the marvel of the world.[131] — MRS. W. L. DAVIS, SECRETARY OF THE LADIES' MEMORIAL ASSOCIATION OF ALBANY, GEORGIA, UNVEILING OF CONFEDERATE MONUMENT

SOUTH & NORTH HELD DIFFERENT CONSTITUTIONAL VIEWS

☛ We are met here again, as is our custom, to do honor to the memory of our Confederate dead. We are met here on this occasion, not only because it is a sacred duty, but also because it is a labor of love; for deeply enshrined in our hearts is the memory of those who, with heroic devotion, laid down their lives in the cause of the Southern Confederacy.

> There is a divinity that shapes our ends,
> Rough-hew them how we will.

The events of recent years show us that we were destined as a people to play an important part in the affairs of this world; and no, in order that we might go forth in our greatest strength, it was heaven's decree that we should remain one nation, under one flag, and become more firmly united than ever before. Why, then, you may ask, that long and bloody war? Why so much destruction of life and property? Why so great sacrifice and suffering?

The story is long, but it may be briefly told. The thirteen original colonies were separate and distinct, and independent of one another their only bond being their allegiance to the British Crown. A common cause and a common danger united them in their struggle for independence. The war of the Revolution won each colony was, in its individual right and in its own name, acknowledged by Great Britain as a free and independent Stale. The old Confederation [that is, the original U.S.A.] was a creature of the thirteen original States, each acting in its sovereign capacity. The federal Government, formed later, and by a process revolutionary in itself, was also a creature of the thirteen original States, each State acting separately through its own people, and in its sovereign capacity, and not a creature of the people of the United States acting collectively, as some have claimed. In no sense were the States the creatures of the federal Government. The creator must exist before the creature.

At the time of the adoption of the Constitution, and for more than three decades afterwards, national sentiment was very weak; in fact, it hardly existed at all. State sentiment was everywhere predominant. [Left-wing] Alexander Hamilton was the most pronounced nationalist of his time, and yet there was hardly a man from [George] Washington and Hamilton down, who did not regard the new government as an experiment, and believe in the right of a State to secede from the union when it so desired. These are not fancies, but historical facts. The men of that time would have laughed at the idea that the Constitution of 1787 gave birth in 1789 to a national government, such as that which now constitutes an indestructible bond of union for the States.

The national idea had yet to be developed. The Constitution is a flexible document; and, says Woodrow Wilson:

> "It is one of the distinguishing characteristics of the English race whose political habit has been transmitted to us through the sagacious generation by whom the government was erected, that they have never felt themselves bound by the logic of laws, but only by a practical understanding of them based upon slow precedent. For this race the law under which they live is at any particular time what it is then understood to be; and this understanding of it is compounded of the circumstances of the time. Absolute theories of legal consequences they have never cared to follow out to their conclusions. Their laws have always been used as parts of the practical running machinery of their politics, parts to be fitted from time to time, by interpretation, to existing opinion and social conditions."

The North and the South, differing in religion and in public policy, though of the same race, and with different climates, developed along different lines. The North became chiefly commercial, the South agricultural. The North, as its commercial spirit grew, inclined more and more to nationalism. Idle regulation of commerce was one of the powers delegated to Congress. Actuated mostly by its own interests, the North came to believe that one of the main objects of government is to aid private enterprise by bounties, subsidies, and protective tariffs. Naturally, then, it fostered the idea of a strong central government, which it expected to control. And so it adopted a loose-construction view of the Constitution.

The South, on the other hand, clung to the idea, as enunciated in the Declaration of Independence, that government is instituted to protect men in life, liberty, and the pursuit of happiness. It adhered also to the original theory of our government, as understood by the framers of the Constitution, as understood by the people when the Constitution was adopted, and as understood by a majority of the people of both sections for more than a generation afterwards.

The South held to conservative views, and believed, then, in a strict construction of the Constitution. It sought no government aid in private enterprise; it was opposed to class legislation, and all undue restrictions of trade. Above all, the South insisted on limiting the Federal Government to its distinctly delegated powers, for, as it believed, it was only by a strict construction of the Constitution that the rights of the States could be preserved.

Such were the fundamental differences between the two sections. Such were both the cause and the effect of the different lines of development. The North grew move rapidly in wealth and population than the South did. Foreign emigrants settled mostly on Northern soil. Largely ignorant of our institutions, and unimbued with the spirit of government as developed among the early colonies, they were, as a rule, national in sentiment.

Slavery was a pretext, and not really the cause of the Civil War. The causes of that war lay deeper than slavery. But slavery was used to intensify sectional feeling, and to prepare the minds of the people of both sections for the clash of arms that, sooner or later, had to come. For whatever of sin there was in the institution of African slavery in this country New England [the birthplace of both American slavery and the American slave trade] was no less responsible than the Southern States, and old England most of all.[132] But while some of us may be unwilling to admit that slavery, as it existed in the South, was a sin, but few, if any of us, will deny that it was an evil, that it retarded the development of the South, and intensified sectional feeling. We must never forget, however, that, originally, slavery was forced upon the South, until by reason of the large increase in the number of slaves it became a political necessity. It was not so much a question of the abolition of slavery as what to do with the negro if emancipated. Self-preservation is the first law of nature, and the majority of the Southern people believed, as far back as [Thomas] Jefferson's time, that life and property would be unsafe if the negroes, semi-savages as they were then [most being first and second generation Africans], were set free and turned loose in their midst. Nor must one forget that slavery had a legal status, that it existed [legally] in all the thirteen original States, and that its protection was guaranteed by the fundamental law of the land.

Had we all been wise and unselfish, both North and South, and worked along on harmonious lines for the common good, we might, perhaps, though I doubt it, have accomplished peaceably what it took a long and bloody war to bring about. But human nature is very perverse, and

> God moves in a mysterious way
> His wonders to perform.

I am inclined to the belief that there is a deeper meaning than is generally supposed in the words that "without shedding of blood there is no remission of sins." That war had to come, and it had to be fought out, too, to the bitter end. We were destined to be a great nation, one and inseparable for divine purposes. The two sections were drifting farther and farther apart, and there were vital questions that could be settled, and settled permanently in no other way.

This is neither the time nor the place to discuss the question as to who was the aggressor in that war, or as to which side was in the right, from a constitutional point of view. Suffice it to say, the only appeal that the North had was the preservation of the Union; the South fought for the maintenance of her constitutional rights. It was not that the South loved the Union less, but States' rights more. We will admit, however, that vital questions may be settled by might, if not by right, for the good, in the long run, of all concerned.[133] — MAJOR WILLIAM A. OBENCHAIN, SPEECH, DECORATION OF CONFEDERATE GRAVES, FAIRVIEW CEMETERY, BOWLING GREEN, KENTUCKY, JUNE 3, 1902

UNITED DAUGHTERS OF THE CONFEDERACY: ORIGIN & OBJECTS

☞ . . . The United Daughters of the Confederacy have five objects, with either one of which its existence is assured—social, educational, memorial, benevolent, and historical.

It is social in bringing together the women of the South, who have a common heritage, and who are bound together by a bond of love and respect for all the principles involved in the issues of the sixties.

It is educational, as it is teaching the present generation, to be handed down to our descendants, the principles on which the South went to war—not for conquest or booty, but that we might live as freemen, as guaranteed in the bill of rights and the constitution of this country.

It is memorial, in building monuments to perpetuate the memory of the men and women of the South who gave up their properties and many of them their lives to maintain their liberties and freedom. These sacred memories must be preserved, and how better can we do it than in marble and bronze? A people who do not revere and hold sacred the memories of their progenitors will have a posterity who will care little for themselves.

It is benevolent, in caring for the maimed and indigent soldiers of the Confederacy, their widows and children; in burying our indigent dead, and annually strewing their graves with flowers in recognition of their heroism and self-devotion to principle; in assisting in maintaining the Confederate Homes, and in providing the delicacies for their hospitals in order that our decrepit soldiers may answer to the last roll call surrounded by the comforts of life.

It is historical, in preserving the history of the old South, a people with conditions and environments, however worthy, that will never again exist. It is said by some that we are living in the past, but how can the present and the future advance without a knowledge of the past, in its traditions and aspirations?

There has never been a time when the true Southron will blush for the part his section of this great country has played in the upbuilding of the republic. Southern men were foremost in opposition to the tyranny of England, and the Mecklenburg declaration of independence antedates the Philadelphia declaration by several years. The men of the South ruled the government and made its laws from its inception until the beginning of the war between the States. When that war came, the South, with 600,000 men, with no military organization, held at bay 3,000,000 men, with unlimited means, for four long, eventful years.

In all history there has never been excelled the patriotism, devotion, and sacrifice of the women of the South. Many of them, raised in affluence and wealth and surrounded with everything that would make life worth living, yielded all, and with an unsurpassed love and devotion they upheld and administered to the Confederate soldier in all of his trials and hardships. They nursed in the hospitals, made clothing for the soldiers, did their own cooking, tilled the soil, and made menials of themselves, that their fathers, husbands, brothers, and sons might keep to the front and repel the invading foe.

With this record of self-sacrifice for principle, and this devotion to a just cause, why should not the United Daughters of the Confederacy exist? Our cause was constitutional freedom, and should live in sung and story as long as freedom has a devotee.

> Know ye why the cypress tree as freedom's tree is known?
> Know ye why the lily fair as freedom's flower is shown?
> A hundred arms the cypress has, yet never plunder seeks;
> With ten well-developed tongues, the lily never speaks.

Being a subjugated people, we for years kept quiet, and until the bitterness of strife had died away did we again reassert our rights and demand recognition of the justice of the cause we espoused. Time has wrought many changes, and the victors are beginning, though tardily, to acknowledge the valor of our men, the heroism of our women, the justice of our cause, and to give us credit for honesty of purpose.

In May last [Union] General [John M.] Schofield, a commandant of the Federal armies, in testifying before a committee of the Senate, said of the Confederate army:

> "It was the best army ever organized; it elected its own officers, its members had an individuality, and were brave even to daring."

In last June, Hon. Charles Francis Adams, of Massachusetts, said in a speech delivered in Chicago that

> "the States had a right to secede under the constitution; that several States had entered the union reserving that right, that it was impracticable, and would break up one of the strong governments of the world."

He moreover said that

> "General [Robert E.] Lee was one of the purest and best generals the world ever produced, and the [U.S.] government should erect a monument to his memory in Washington City."

This is but one instance of the innumerable recognitions of the right of secession by the learned men of the North.

The history of the South, before and during the war between the States, its people and social conditions, should live in memory and be handed down from generation to generation until time is no more.

The Daughters were organized with this main object in view, and who can teach the youth better than his mother? The mothers of the world rule the world; and if the women the South will but be true to their traditions, the coming generations will rise up and call them blessed. "Be just and fear not: let all the ends thou aim'st at, be thy country's, thy God's, and thy truth's."[134] — PAPER READ BY MRS. JOHN P. HICKMAN BEFORE THE MONTEAGLE, TENNESSEE, ASSEMBLY

The Confederate First Lady, Varina Howell Davis, second wife of Confederate President Jefferson Davis. Photographer: Charles D. Fredricks, New York City, New York, circa 1864.

DAVIS PROVES THE SOUTH WAS RIGHTEOUS, HONORABLE, & CORRECT

☛ ... The present generation, in taking steps to raise a monument to commemorate the services of the women of the Confederacy, seem to have forgotten that our beloved President [Jefferson Davis] in his lifetime erected a memorial to their memory more enduring than tablets of marble or brass. In ever-loving remembrance he has consecrated to their unselfish devotion his great work, *The Rise and Fall of the Confederate Government*,[135] in which, as with the hand of a master, he has traced the constitutional history of this country, gathered together and systematized its scattered fragments, analyzed its principles, and by an argument that has never been answered demonstrated to the world that the Revised Constitution of 1787 saved to the States and the people thereof the same rights they had reserved in the Articles of Confederation of 1777.[136] That our fathers framed a Constitutional Compact which, by its terms, did not create a national consolidated government that derived its powers from the people of the United States in the aggregate, but a Confederated republic composed of several sovereign, free, and independent States, which reserved to the people every power, jurisdiction, and right that were not expressly delegated to the general government which they established. That under its provisions the States in severalty reserved the right to withdraw from a Union into which they had entered as sovereign communities, whenever it proved destructive to the ends for which it was created and endangered their safety and happiness.

That the paramount authority resided with the people of the several sovereign States, and that their allegiance was first due to the States of which they were citizens, and not to the Federal Government, which was a mere agent or trustee of their creation.

That the great fundamental safeguards thus ingrafted upon the written Constitution of this country, and without which the Union of these States could never have been formed, came down from their forefathers as the inalienable rights of the people of the South established the righteousness of the cause for which the Confederate soldiers fought, and justified them in resisting the advance of the Federal armies and in defending their homes from invasion.

Confederate soldier, identity unknown, circa 1864.

It appeals to history, to time for the vindication of the Confederate soldiers; and like a flambeau in the night, held high aloft, a torch of liberty, it goes down to posterity to enlighten and instruct the world. All over the pages of this immortal book, and in its dedication, "To the women of the Confederacy," he has described their burning patriotism, their unfailing devotion and patient suffering in such glowing eloquence of words that their fame is coupled with his own illustrious name, and will live and endure forever.

Glorious dedication! whose imperishable lines are inscribed:

"To the women of the confederacy, whose pious ministrations to our wounded soldiers soothed the last hours of those who died far from the objects of their tenderest love; whose domestic labors contributed much to supply the wants of our defenders in the field; whose zealous faith in our cause shone a guiding star undimmed by the darkest clouds of war; whose fortitude sustained them under all the privations to which they were subjected; whose annual tribute expresses their enduring grief, love and reverence for our sacred dead; and whose patriotism will teach their children to emulate the deeds of our revolutionary sires . . . ."[137]

— MISS EDMONDA AUGUSTA NICKERSON, SPEECH, CONFEDERATE VETERANS REUNION, ST. JOSEPH, MISSOURI, SEPTEMBER 9, 1902

MORE PROOF THAT SLAVERY WAS NOT THE ISSUE: THE AMERICAN ABOLITION MOVEMENT BEGAN IN THE SOUTH

☛ . . . The contest between the North and the South over the extension of slavery to the territories was a contest on the part of the South for equal rights under the Constitution, and it ought to be clearly understood that it did not involve the increase of slavery. Had that right been conceded, not one additional slave would have been added to the number existing in the country.

> "[In the South it] was a question of the distribution or dispersion of the slaves rather than of the extension of slavery. Removal is not extension. Indeed, if emancipation was the end to be desired, the dispersion of the negroes over a wider area, among additional territories eventually to become States, and in climates unfavorable to slave labor, instead of hindering, would have promoted this object by diminishing the difficulties in the way of ultimate emancipation."

This is the language of Jefferson Davis, but the argument is Henry Clay's. In 1820 he argued that the extension of slavery was farseeing humanity, and Mr. [Thomas] Jefferson agreed with him, saying that spreading the slaves over a larger surface "will dilute the evil everywhere and facilitate the means of getting finally rid of it." Mr. [James] Madison took the same view, and these three statesmen were all earnest emancipationists."

In 1822 there were five or six abolition societies in Kentucky. In 1819 the first distinctively emancipation paper in the United States was published in Jonesboro, Eastern Tennessee. There were eighteen emancipation societies in that region organized by the Covenanters, Methodists, and the Quakers.

A Massachusetts writer, George Lunt, says:

> "The States of Virginia, Kentucky, and Tennessee were engaged in practical movements for the gradual emancipation of their slaves. This movement continued until it was arrested by the aggressions of the abolitionists [that is, communists]."[138]

— REVEREND R. H. MCKIM, ADDRESS, CONFEDERATE VETERANS REUNION, NASHVILLE, TENNESSEE

THE TRUTH ABOUT THE CONFEDERATE SOLDIER

☛ . . . the soldier of the South, who passed through the terrible ordeal of the war and the far more terrible ordeal of the reconstruction, with his spirit tested in the fire of defeat and suffering, came through it all as a proud and independent American citizen. He has asked nothing but the rights guaranteed him by the Constitution of his country and the privilege of earning by his own brawn and brain an honest living, faithful to his obligations as a man and his duties as a citizen. He stands to-day as the greatest and noblest product of American citizenship. He came out of the bloody struggle with all lost save his life and his honor, with his home in ashes, with his family in poverty. Pursued and harassed by a cruel and savage policy of radical [that is, socialist/communist] reconstruction, he yet stood with bared breast to the winds of adversity, his trust in God, his hope in the future, and by his energy and his patriotism he has wrought the miracle of the South's restoration from hopelessness and despair to a condition of peace and prosperity.[139] — KENTUCKY GOVERNOR JOHN C. W. BECKHAM

A PENNSYLVANIAN DEFENDS THE SOUTH

☛ . . . My friends, I come before you as a Northern man. In the great conflict between the Confederacy and the Northern States, my State was opposed to you, and all true citizens of Pennsylvania were loyal to the cause it supported. The great questions had failed of peaceful solution, and one of the severest wars of any era of the world had to be fought to a conclusion. When Robert E. Lee, before the Virginia Convention, said: "I will devote myself to the defense and service of my native State, in whose behalf alone would I have ever drawn my sword," he defined clearly the obligation of a citizen to throw his fortunes with his State. Here and there men saw their duties in a different light, and no one should criticise harshly an officer of the old [Union/U.S.] army who held different views.

Their position was complicated by their environment. Their training made them less independent in thought, as well as action, and undoubtedly the decision of [Southerner turned Union General] George H. Thomas to adhere to the North was as truly the act of an honorable man as the course of Robert E. Lee. When, acting in its sovereign capacity a State withdrew from the Union, whether such action was a cause for war or not, and in my opinion it was certainly the right of the States remaining in the Union to so decide, the citizen of such a State was, by that withdrawal, carried with it. It is impossible to conceive of an exclusive allegiance to a government which guarantees none of the natural rights of its citizens. Of course, under the Federal [U.S.] Constitution, as long as a State is included in the Union, there are duties of citizenship to both the State and to the United States, but they are distinct. To his State alone can a citizen appeal to secure him in his home, his domestic relations, and his rights of property. Nor can he divest himself of his obligation to serve his State in the protection of its rights from invasion, from riot, or general obedience to its laws. The subject is too large to enter upon here; but it was an unreasonable view to assert that any one failed in his loyalty who clung to his State, on either side, under the conditions which arose in 1861. It is probable that our form of government is too complicated for the uninstructed citizen to comprehend, and certainly few untrained in the law can define the radical difference between the powers of a State Legislature and those of Congress.

The Constitution of the United States, as originally framed, was a marvelous creation, and to my mind if strictly followed would have met every contingency that has arisen. But from the first, beginning with the insidious efforts of [Liberal] Alexander Hamilton, under his doctrine of "implied powers," a process of distortion of the meaning of its plain language and a subversion of its safeguards has been pursued. The States forming the [Southern as distinct from the U.S.] Confederacy, believing that their rights and interests were no longer protected, under the construction of the powers of the general government which had prevailed, through the sectional preponderance of the North and West, made a heroic effort against tremendous odds to maintain their right to separate from the Union. It was early in the struggle that they secured the recognition of belligerents, and in the main the war was fought on lines consistent with the rules of civilized countries.

. . . Slowly but surely the truth is being recognized and public sentiment is approving the assertion of their powers by the several States over their domestic concerns. It has been a strange anomaly that at a time when the right of local self-government is the cry of every State, this very right has been denied to the States themselves. In the vast growth of this great power among nations it becomes more and more necessary that the Federal Government should exercise full powers in our external affairs and in those specific fields assigned to it by the Constitution; but it is even more vitally necessary that in their internal affairs and in those fields retained by the States there should be no Federal interference.

More than ever before will it be impossible to secure peace and contentment throughout this vast territory, extending from ocean to ocean, with its infinite variety of climate, conditions and the occupations of its peoples, unless these peoples are left to themselves to determine and control their private interests. The language of Thomas Jefferson in his first inaugural, defining the essential principles of our government, it is well to repeat. He expressly declares as of the first importance the

> "support of the State governments in all their rights as the most competent administrations for our domestic concerns and the surest bulwarks against anti-republican [Left-wing] tendencies; . . . the preservation of the general government in its whole constitutional vigor, as the sheet anchor of our peace at home and abroad."

I am conscious that I have touched upon much that is full of controversial feeling, but the day has come when justice should be done to those whose [Conservative Southern] views have been condemned by popular clamor, with no foundation of reason. To treat a contest between the peoples of two sections of a great continent as an internal uprising or revolt against constituted authority is not only puerile but grossly wrong. The honesty of convictions on both sides should be admitted, and the legitimate results of the struggle should alone be recognized. I feel no sympathy with those who would deny a place for this monument on Northern soil, over the graves of those whose memory it records. . . .[140] — HONORABLE JOHN CADWALADER, SPEECH AT THE UNVEILING OF A CONFEDERATE MONUMENT AT PHILADELPHIA, PENNSYLVANIA

THE YANKEES WERE THE REAL REBELS & TRAITORS
☛ . . . During the war, 1861 to 1865, and ever since there has been a studied, systematic effort on the part of those who were our adversaries to pervert and falsify the history of the causes which led to that war, and the conduct of the war, and to educate the public mind to the belief that it was a causeless war, brought about by ambitious Southern leaders. And it is much to be regretted that this policy has had a very large measure of success. This has been brought about largely by the baseless assumptions in acts of Congress and the doings of the Executive Department, in the action of State Legislatures and of political conventions, the declarations of public speakers, and by the writers in newspapers and magazines.

It will be the purpose of what I shall say to-day to show the great wrong and injustice done to those who supported the Confederate cause, by this systematic falsifying of the great facts of history on this subject.

. . . When the American colonies came to be formed into

States, as the result of the Revolutionary war, warned by the oppressions and denial of rights imposed on them by the crown of Great Britain, each of them accompanied their State Constitutions with a "Bill of Rights" in which it was declared that the people possessed certain inalienable rights of which they could not be deprived, which they specified; so when the American people came to form the Constitution of the United States, animated by the same jealousy of the unlimited power of government, they created a government with delegated and strictly limited powers only, and for greater security for their liberty and rights they provided that the powers not therein delegated were reserved to the States and to the people respectively. The Federal government was given jurisdiction over questions of a national and those of an inter-State character, while the States retained jurisdiction over all the local questions and domestic institutions. This is the authority for the doctrine of State rights. Slavery was from the first treated by all the States as a domestic institution, to be controlled or disposed of as each State might choose for itself. And this is the reason why the Northern States abolished slavery without asking the sanction of the Federal [U.S.] government. And when the people of the Northern States commenced their crusade for the abolition of slavery by the numbers and powers of their people where slavery did not exist, and in the States where it did exist without their consent, they commenced a revolution in distinct violation of the Constitution and laws; they made themselves a lawless, revolutionary [Left-wing] party, and became rebels against the Government of the United States. And when they levied war to carry out their policy they became traitors. But the minority could not try and punish the treason of the majority. Their pretense was that they were fighting to save the Union, and they made thousands of honest [Yankee] soldiers believe they were fighting for the Union. Their [Liberal] leaders knew that the Union rested on the Constitution, and that their purpose was to overthrow the Constitution. The Union the soldiers fought for was the Union established by the Constitution. The Union the [Left-wing] leaders sought was only to be attained by the subversion of the Constitution, the annulment of the doctrine of State rights, the making of a consolidated central republic, abolishing the limitations prescribed by the Constitution and substituting a popular majority of the people of the whole Union in their stead, and to open the way for individual and corporate gain through the agency of the government [the main policies still advanced by Liberals, socialists, and communists today].

In the face of these great historic truths that party has habitually and constantly charged that the war was causeless and brought about by ambitious political leaders of the South, and that the Confederates were rebels and traitors. Can any one conceive of a greater departure from truth, or of a more audacious attempt to falsify history? And that, too, in the face of the Constitution and laws, in the face of the imperishable public record of the country and of the public history of their own actions.

I have thus endeavored to give some of the facts and reasons which justified the Southern people in attempting to withdraw their allegiance from a government openly hostile to the rights of their State and people in order to form for themselves a government friendly to those rights. Our people were not responsible for the war; it was forced on them. They were not rebels or traitors. They simply acted as patriots, defending their rights and their homes against the lawless and revolutionary action of a dominant and reckless majority. . . .[141] — JOHN H. REAGAN (FORMER CONFEDERATE POSTMASTER GENERAL UNDER PRESIDENT JEFFERSON DAVIS), SPEECH, R. E. LEE CAMP, FORT WORTH, TEXAS, APRIL 10, 1903

SECESSION WAS LEGAL IN 1861 — & STILL IS

☞ . . . The South is reproached for disunion—secession! It is the basis for the charge of treason; of disrupting the Union; of violating the Constitution; of rebellion; of making war on the United States. It must not be forgotten that there is a wide difference between secession and rebellion. The South made no war on the States remaining in the Union. Secession meant disunion so far as the seceding States were concerned, but it meant neither war nor rebellion. It meant a Union intact so far as all the States were concerned which did not secede, and a Union, too, under the Constitution. As the States entered the Union, each under acts of ratification of its own, so secession meant the resumption by each State of its delegated powers, by repealing the acts under which each seceding State entered the compact; but the repeal of such acts did not and could not affect the acts by which the remaining States entered into the Confederacy. The States of North Carolina and Rhode Island did not ratify the Constitution until long after [George] Washington's administration began, and of course were not members of the Union. But the Union existed nevertheless, and existed under the Constitution, as much as it did after these States became members. So when the Confederate States seceded from the Union, the States remaining under the compact were as much a Union under the Constitution as before.

The whole history of secession shows conclusively that in seceding the South had no intention of assailing their former confederates. To their credit, every step taken in the matter of secession, in view of the deep feeling and intense excitement, was marvelously conservative, marked with statesmanlike conduct, and a decent regard for the United States. Its peace commissions, its diplomacy, its unpreparedness for war, all make clear to those who wish to know that the South sought a peaceful withdrawal from the Union, leaving the remaining States unharmed and undisturbed.

. . . Our children should know that the Confederate States, by the act of secession, made no war on the United States; that the war between the States was not rebellion. It was the result of an effort by the United States to coerce States against their will to remain in the Union, a power not to be found in the Constitution, a power which all the earlier fathers believed did not exist, a power utterly inconsistent with the right of secession, which it is believed all parts of the country recognized when the Constitution was framed and for many years thereafter.

If the Southern States had the power, notwithstanding the Constitution, to withdraw from the Union in 1803, in 1812 and in 1845, as New England statesmen then affirmed, they had the same power in 1861. No change of the Constitution had been made, and the relations of the States to each other were unaltered. If that power existed at all, the expediency of withdrawing was one solely for each State to decide for itself. . . .[142] — HONORABLE J. H. ROGERS

WHY SOUTHERN MEN & WOMEN WENT TO WAR
☛ . . . They fought, suffered, and died for the doctrine of State rights, which they knew the Constitution of the United States guaranteed, and had been sustained by decisions of the Federal courts. . . .[143] — WILLIAM TRUMAN, GUYTON, GEORGIA

WE SOUGHT SECESSION NOT WAR
☛ . . . If our national Constitution had so clearly defined the relations of the several States to the Federal government that no difference of opinion in regard to them could fairly have arisen, then those who took up arms in defense of the doctrines of secession might justly be scorned as rebels undeserving of such honor as we accord to those whose ashes lie in this inclosure. But when we remember that their rights, as they had good reason to understand them, were threatened; that they were honest in

Confederate soldier, identity unknown, New Orleans, Louisiana, circa 1862.

believing that the terms of the Federal compact left them free to withdraw from the Union; that it was not war they sought, but peaceable secession; that when they did take up arms it was not to invade sister States, but to protect their property, their homes, and their firesides; and especially when we remember that through four long years, against fearful odds both in numbers and material resources—even fighting in regard to these against the world—they set an example of endurance, daring, and military prowess which won for them undying fame and compelled an astonished world to adopt a loftier ideal for the emulation of its soldiery—I say when we remember these things we do not hesitate to lay votive offerings where such men sleep and to bless God for land that can produce—aye, and reproduce—such spirits. . . .[144] — REVEREND JOHN HEWITT, SPEECH, MEMORIAL SERVICE, CAMP CHASE, OHIO

WHAT CONFEDERATE GENERAL STERLING PRICE BELIEVED

☛ . . . He believed in the sovereignty of the States; he was acquainted with the difficulties attending the formation of the constitution by the representatives of the thirteen original colonies; he knew that constitutional rights in America were born of revolutionary rights, and he felt that when constitutional doctrine endangered the liberties of a people the right of revolution became imperative. "Rights in the Constitution" was his motto; but if rights were not to be had in it, then create a new constitution. . . .[145] — REVEREND J. R. PERKINS, HUNTSVILLE, MISSOURI

PROTECTION OF PROPERTY & CONSTITUTIONAL RIGHTS

☛ . . . [On April 15, 1861] three days after the [battle] . . . of Fort Sumter [Abraham] Lincoln issued a call for 75,000 troops "to subjugate the seceded States," and was answered in half a week by 100,000 men, who wrangled for places in the ranks. This call was regarded by the South as a declaration of war, and was met by stern defiance. In the South the husband and father left his family and the youth his school to take up arms in defense of their beloved homes and their constitutional rights of life, liberty, and the pursuit of happiness.[146] — MISS JANET SCHURMAN, WARRENSBURG, MISSOURI

DARING, HEROISM, & FAITHFULNESS
☛ . . . The [Confederate] museum [at Richmond] is to stand for all time. Here on file will be the record of the men who fought for constitutional rights, handed down the line from our forefathers, and here forever will be the testimony of the daring, the heroism, and faithfulness of lives which make all lives nobler and better for their having lived. In years to come the story of the South, with its romantic devotion between master and slave, of the fanaticism which strove to drag down its chivalric spirit and noble ideals, of the daring determination and limitless sacrifice, the courage and the beauty of unselfishness of its men and women that sprang to meet the invader, and their almost superhuman strength and endurance, will read like tales of the days of Richard Coeur de Lion.

Who then will not be proud to claim descent from this line of more than kings and conquerors?[147] — MISS CARY DANIEL, CORRESPONDENCE SECRETARY, CONFEDERATE MUSEUM, RICHMOND, VIRGINIA

MAINTAINING LOCAL SELF-GOVERNMENT
☛ . . . No one of those of us who served in the Confederate army suffered more for us, for our cause, to establish and maintain the rights of local self-government for which we fought than he did, yet he was never heard to say aught against those who were in the Federal army. No one was braver or truer to our cause and no one more modest in claiming credit for what he had done and suffered.[148] — FROM A MEMORIAL TRIBUTE TO CONFEDERATE COLONEL E. M. DODSON

OUR RIGHT TO LOCAL SELF-GOVERNMENT
☛ . . . We meet to celebrate the cause and the men of the [eighteen] sixties. What was the cause? Was it secession? Not a whit of it. Secession was merely the remedy which was invoked for the assertion of a right, for the maintenance of a cause. It had been twice before virtually invoked in these United States, though the sword had not been drawn to support its invocation—once by New Englanders, in opposition to what they considered the tyranny of

the Embargo Laws, and once by the South Carolinians in denial of the constitutional right of a government of all the people to levy tribute upon all the people in order to make the capital of a part of the people more profitable, or the labor of a part of the people better compensated. War determined that the remedy should fail, and I think we are all agreed that it is well that the remedy failed. I think we are all ready to go forward, marching shoulder to shoulder, with an eye to the possibilities of the future, rejoicing in the lusty strength of a great and reunited people. What was the cause, then? Was it slavery? Not a whit of it. Slavery was undoubtedly the occasion of the quarrel and of the fight; but had the South been attacked in any of her other property or civil rights, she would have defended them just as readily; in fact, more readily than she did in this case. It was merely upon the side of slavery that our right to local self-government was attacked. . . .[149] — HONORABLE JOHN SHARP WILLIAMS, U.S. REPRESENTATIVE FROM MISSISSIPPI, ADDRESS, U.C.V., MEMPHIS, TENNESSEE

STUDY THE TRUE RECORDS
☞ Mr. [Abraham] Lincoln [a big government Liberal,] taught and promulgated the principle that might made right, and his people [the modern day Left] adhere to that principle yet like a piece of steel to a magnet. The perusal of [the records of the South's actions, however,] . . . will convince all unbiased and thinking people that the [Conservative] South was not responsible or to blame for that four years' cruel war. This section of the Union stood by and on its constitutional rights, but it was crushed into the dust by the might and fanaticism of the other sections.[150] — SUMNER A. CUNNINGHAM, EDITOR, *CONFEDERATE VETERAN* MAGAZINE

WHAT THEY GAVE UP & WHY
☞ . . . [Southern boys and men readily] . . . gave up their families, their homes, and their property and fought for four long years to protect the hearthstones and firesides of strangers who, like themselves, were battling for constitutional rights, which were being denied them. . . .[151] — CAPTAIN ANDREW M. SEA

SOUTHERN WOMEN IN THE 1860S
☞ [We Southern females are] . . . brave, loyal women who love to keep alive the memories of home, and who, though staying at home in the [eighteen] sixties, were protected by the faithful darkies who

loved them and were called members of their household, and who guarded them with their humble love, thus making it a little easier for the brave [men] of that time to go forth and fight for love of home and to maintain State rights.¹⁵² — MRS. FLORENCE TUCKER WINDER

OUR OBJECTS
☞ [When the war call came, Southern males of all ages, from teens to the elderly] at once cast [their] . . . fortunes with the young Confederacy, whose objects were for the supremacy of State rights.¹⁵³ — *CONFEDERATE VETERAN* MAGAZINE

THE UNION WAS FORMED AS A COMPACT, WHICH MAKES SECESSION LEGAL
☞ . . . Washington, Jefferson, and Madison, are on record as declaring that the Constitution was a compact between the States, and that those thirteen States were thirteen independent sovereignties. [Let us delve into this topic more deeply, since it sheds light on the Southern Cause.]
. . . It is . . . not amiss to remind the Southern men of this generation that fourteen years before the *Mayflower* landed her pilgrims at Plymouth Rock three English ships—the *Susan Constant*, the *Godspeed*, and the *Discovery* came to anchor in the James River, Virginia, and that the vine of English civilization and English liberty was first planted, not on Plymouth Rock, in 1620, but at Jamestown Island, Va., on the 13th of May, 1607. What [Daniel] Webster so nobly said of the *Mayflower* may be as truly said of these three ships that bore the first Virginia colony.

> "The stars that guided them were the unobscured constellations of civil and religious liberty. Their decks were the altars of the living God."

Let me also recall the fact that on July 30, 1619, eighteen months before the pilgrims set foot on American soil, the vine of liberty had so deeply taken root in the colony of Virginia that there was assembled in the church at Jamestown a free representative body (the first on American soil)—the House of Burgesses—to deliberate for the welfare of the people. There also, more than a century before the [American] Revolution, when Oliver Cromwell's fleet appeared to whip the rebellious Old Dominion into obedience, Virginia demanded and obtained recognition of the principle, "No taxation without representation"; and there, in

1676, just one hundred years before the revolt of the colonies, that remarkable man, Nathaniel Bacon, "soldier, orator, leader," raised the standard of revolt against the oppressions of the British crown.

But this is not all. That spot on Jamestown Island, marked to-day by a ruined, ivy-clad church tower and a group of moss-covered tombstones, is the sacred ground whence sprang that stream of genius and power which contributed most to the achievement of American independence and to the organization of American liberty. That first colony, planted in Tidewater, Va., was, in the revolutionary period, prolific in men of genius and force and intense devotion to liberty never perhaps equaled in modern times in any region of equal size and of so small a population. This is acknowledged by careful and candid historians to-day, among whom I may mention Senator [Henry Cabot] Lodge, of Massachusetts. It was a Southern orator, Patrick Henry, who gave to the colonists in his matchless eloquence the slogan, "Give me liberty or give me death!" It was a Southerner, Richard Henry Lee, who brought forward in the first Congress the motion that these colonies by right ought to be free and independent! It was a Southerner, Thomas Jefferson, who drafted the immortal Declaration of Independence! It was a Southerner, George Mason, who had earlier drawn the Virginia Bill of Rights, a document of even profounder political statesmanship, and which was taken by Massachusetts as the model of her own Bill of Rights! It was a Southerner, George Washington, who made good the Declaration of Independence by his sword after seven years of war! It was a Southerner, James Madison, who earned the title "Father of the Constitution!" It was a Southerner, John Marshall, who became its most illustrious interpreter!

I ask, then, in view of all this, whether the South was not justified in believing that the views of constitutional interpretation which she had inherited from such a political ancestry were not the true views? Let our Northern friends answer, in all candor, whether the South, with such a heredity as this, with such glorious memories of achievement, with such splendid traditions of the part her philosophers and statesmen and soldiers had taken, both in the winning of independence and in the building of the temple of the Constitution, had not good reason for saying: "We will follow that interpretation of the Constitution which we received from our fathers—from Jefferson, Madison, and Washington—rather than that which can claim no older or greater names than those of [Joseph] Story and [Daniel] Webster." For be it remembered that for forty years after the adoption of the Constitution there was approximate unanimity in its interpretation upon the great issue on which the South took her stand in 1861. In truth Webster and Story apostatized from the New England interpretation of the Constitution. It is a historical fact that the Constitution was regarded as a compact between the States for a long period (not less than forty years after its adoption) by the leaders of opinion in the New England States. Moreover, in the same quarter, the sovereignty of the States was broadly affirmed; and also the right of the States to resume, if need be, the powers granted under the Constitution. Samuel Adams objected to the preamble to the Constitution. "I stumble at the threshold," he said; "I meet a national government instead of a federal [that is, confederate] union of sovereign States." To overcome this, [Massachusetts] Gov. [John] Hancock brought in the tenth amendment as to the reservation to the States of all powers not expressly delegated to the general government. The Websterian dogmas had then no advocates in New England. Hancock, Adams, [Theophilus] Parsons, [James] Bowdoin, and [Fisher] Ames were all for State sovereignty.

These statements will no doubt be received by many with surprise, possibly with incredulity. Permit me, then, briefly to justify them by the unquestionable facts of history. The impartial historian of the future will recall the fact that the first threat of secession did not come from the men of the South, but from the men of New England. Four times before the secession of South Carolina the threat of secession was heard in the North—in 1802-03, in 1811-12, in 1814, and in 1844-45. The first time it came from Col. Timothy Pickering, of Massachusetts, a friend of [George] Washington and a member of his Cabinet; the second time, from Josiah Quincy, another distinguished citizen of Massachusetts; the third time, from the Hartford Convention, in which five States were represented; the fourth time, from the Legislature of Massachusetts. On January 14, 1811, Josiah Quincy, of Massachusetts, in the debate on the admission of Louisiana, declared his

> "deliberate opinion that if the bill passes the bonds of this Union are virtually dissolved; . . . that as it will be the right of all [the States] so it will be the duty of some to prepare definitely for a separation—amicably if they can, violently if they must."

In 1812 "pulpit, press, and rostrum" of New England advocated secession. In 1839 ex-President John Quincy Adams urged publicly that it would be better for the States to "part in friendship from each other than to be held together by constraint," and declared that "the people of each State have the right to secede from the confederated Union." In1842 Mr. Adams presented a petition to Congress from a town in Massachusetts, praying that it would "immediately adopt measures peaceably to dissolve the union of these States." In 1844, and again in 1845, the Legislature of Massachusetts avowed the right of secession, and threatened to secede if Texas was admitted to the Union. Alexander Hamilton threatened [Thomas] Jefferson with the secession of New England "unless the debts of the States were assumed by the general government." February 1, 1850, Mr. [John Parker] Hale offered in the Senate a petition and resolutions, asking that body to devise, "without delay, some plan for the immediate peaceful dissolution of the American Union." [Salmon P.] Chase and [William H.] Seward voted for its reception.

The occasions calling forth these declarations of the purpose of dissolving the Union were the acquisition of Louisiana, the proposed admission of Louisiana as a State into the Union, the dissatisfaction occasioned by the war with Great Britain, and then the proposed annexation of Texas. These measures were all believed by the New England States to be adverse to their interests. The addition of the new States would, it was thought, destroy the equilibrium of power and give the South a preponderance; and therefore these stalwart voices were raised, declaring that there was in the last resort a remedy, and that was the dissolution of the Union. This was the language used by the Legislature of Massachusetts:

> "The commonwealth of Massachusetts, faithful to the compact between the people of the United States, according to the plain meaning and intent in which it was understood by them, is sincerely anxious for its preservation; but it is determined, as it doubts not the other States are, to submit to undelegated powers in no body of men on earth."

This stalwart utterance of Massachusetts expresses exactly the attitude of the seceding States in 1861. They believed that "the compact between the people of the United States" had been violated, that they could no longer enjoy equal rights within the Union, and therefore they refused to submit to the exercise of "undelegated powers" on the part of the national government. Thus the North and the South, at these different epochs, held the same view of the right of withdrawal from the Union.

The South held with great unanimity to the doctrine of State sovereignty, and that that sovereignty was inviolable by the general government. She had good reason to believe it, for it had been the faith of her greatest statesmen from the very foundation of the republic. Mr. [James] Madison, the father of the Constitution, held to that faith; and when Patrick Henry opposed the adoption of the Constitution upon the ground that the words "we, the people," seemed to imply a "consolidated government" and not "a compact between States," he replied that it was not "we, the people," as composing one great body, but the people of thirteen sovereignties.

. . . Alexander Hamilton spoke of the new [U.S.] government as "a Confederate republic," a "Confederacy," and called the Constitution a "compact." Gen. [George] Washington wrote of the Constitution as a compact, and repeatedly uses the terms "accede" and "accession," and once the term "secession." Massachusetts and New Hampshire, when ratifying the Constitution, referred to that instrument as "an explicit and solemn compact."

. . . Mr. [Daniel] Webster, in the very last year of his illustrious life, distinctly recognized the right of secession, for in his speech at Capon Springs, Va., in 1851, he said:

> "If the South were to violate any part of the Constitution intentionally and systematically, and persist in so doing, year after year, and no remedy could be had, would the North be any longer bound by the rest of it? And if the North were deliberately, habitually, and of fixed purpose to disregard one part of it, would the South be bound any longer to observe its other obligations? . . . I have not hesitated to say, and I repeat, that if the Northern States refuse, willfully and deliberately, to carry into effect that part of the Constitution which respects the restoration of fugitive slaves, and Congress provide no remedy, the South would no longer be bound to observe the compact. A bargain cannot be broken on one side and still bind the other side."[154]

— REVEREND R. H. MCKIM, ADDRESS, CONFEDERATE VETERANS REUNION, NASHVILLE, TENNESSEE

DEAR CONFEDERATE VETERANS . . .

☞ . . . You clung to the Declaration of Independence, which declares that government exists for the protection of life, liberty, and happiness. You believed in a strict construction of the constitution, and in the preservation of State rights. So when your State rights were set aside—your sovereignty denied—you were ready to strike for your homes and firesides, and to pour out your blood as a libation; and, if need be, to die upon the altar of your country. You left your happy Southern homes and rushed to the fray where honor called; and through four years of dread war you fought with such bravery, endured such hardships, and won such brilliant victories on the battlefield that you deserved and won the name of the grandest heroes the world has ever known—"the wonder of the ages."[155] — MISS MAUD V. HERMAN, KOSSUTH, MISSISSIPPI

THE SOUTHERN PERSPECTIVE

☛ . . . The South's side of that gigantic struggle— the War between the States and the occurrences leading up to it—has been so little [placed] before the world that we have never had justice done us. One of these days a historian, unprejudiced entirely, is going to write a true history of that epoch in American history. Shall we, the descendants of the South's heroes in that struggle, sit with folded hands now, and so when that time comes have this historian fail to be just to the South because we have not done our duty? We might with a little exertion gather and preserve material which will help him with our side of that question. Shall, your children, going to Northern schools and hearing *one* side only, grow up to he ashamed of the great men and women who waged this war for Southern rights because they have been taught that they—their own ancestors among them—were "Rebels" fighting for the enslaving of human beings while you by sitting with idle hands give your approval to this [fake] history which they are taught? Can you expect them to make patriotic men and women if they are made ashamed of their ancestors? Patriotism does not thrive when placed in the same heart with such degrading thoughts.[156] — *CONFEDERATE VETERAN* MAGAZINE

DEDICATED TO THE WOMEN OF THE SOUTH

☛ [To all those incredible Southern women who] . . . lived, suffered, and prayed during that great but terrible struggle with husband and brothers away from home engaged in the war from 1861 to 1865, and knew the patriotic and immense sacrifices made by the South; knew it was a struggle for liberty, honor, and constitutional rights, and that it was an epoch in the history of America that has received and will receive enduring admiration, as no such chapter in a nation's history can be forgotten.[157] — MRS. VALERIE EDWARD AUSTIN, PRESIDENT, UNITED DAUGHTERS OF THE CONFEDERACY, TEXAS

PURPOSES OF THE UNITED DAUGHTERS OF THE CONFEDERACY

☛ . . . Our organization is not merely a Memorial Association, meeting thus annually to place fresh garlands upon the sleeping defenders of a just cause; it has a wider grasp. It would obtain a true history of that gigantic struggle in which our Southern soldiers bled and died. From these heroes the Daughters of the Confederacy are proud to trace their descent, for the unbroken chain of their illustrious deeds forms a luminous page in the annals of our country. We would not forget their sacrifices.

> "They are poor who have lost nothing; they poorer far who, losing, have forgotten; they most poor of all who lose and wish they might forget."

As a people we would be ungrateful if we did not recall their names with a thrill of emotion and if the deep fountains of our hearts were not stirred when we remember how they spilt their patriot blood and sacrificed their heroic lives upon the altar of their country, for the honor of Alabama, for their homes and for their families, for the rights of the States, and for the principles of the Union as they were handed down to them by the fathers of this republic. The South is rich in legends of their valor and heroism. Be it our labor of love to cherish these hallowed memories and to rescue from oblivion

> "Deeds that should not pass away
> And names that must not wither."[158]

— MRS. L. G. YOUNG, GEORGIA DIVISION, U.D.C.

THE C.S. MILITARY DEFINED

☛ [The Confederate military was] . . . the grandest army ever marshaled in defense of constitutional rights.[159] — CONFEDERATE GENERAL WILLIAM L. CABELL

AN EXAMPLE OF HOW THE NORTH SUPPRESSES AUTHENTIC HISTORY & REWRITES THE PAST TO SUIT ITS RADICAL IDEOLOGIES

☛ A recent writer in the Baltimore *Sun* (March 6, 1906) calls attention to the continued circulation and propagation of falsehoods as to the true character of [big government Liberal] Abraham Lincoln, the man who in 1861-65 was the chief foe of the South and of civil liberty. Brief extracts are quoted by the correspondent of the *Sun* "from the mass of material which Dr. [Charles L. C.] Minor, the author, has with great pains collected from Mr. Lincoln's eulogists to make it possible for future generations to know the truth on this subject." As the writer well says:

> "The adage, 'The truth is mighty and will prevail,' is itself true only when the truth has at its back lovers of truth. Untruth, sedulously inculcated, with none to hinder, all too often prevails over the truth. This is painfully shown in the annual apotheosis of Mr. Lincoln, which takes place afresh at each return of his birthday."

It is satisfactory to know that this book [*The Real Lincoln From the Testimony of His Contemporaries*][160] of the late Dr. Minor's refuting the "apotheosis," now in a second and enlarged edition, is surely if slowly doing its work and making its impress upon thinking people wherever it has found readers. A tribute to its value and importance as a historical monograph is manifest in the effort made by the devotees of "untruth" to "suppress" it. The Boston *Journal*, a partisan Republican sheet, apparently the organ of the G. A. R. [Union/U.S. army] in Massachusetts, undertook last summer to conduct what it called a "crusade" against *The Real Lincoln*. Its editor gave a graphic account of the valiant services of the G. A. R. Posts of Boston in having the pamphlet (for copies of the first edition are the only ones mentioned) removed from the libraries. A veteran called the attention of the Mayor of Somerville to the existence of the book, "and the Mayor ordered it removed from the library and destroyed." Then such pressure was brought by the G. A. R. Posts, aided by the *Journal*, upon the trustees of the Cambridge Public Library that they had the offending volumes removed "for all time." The "crusade," we were told, was likely to continue until the book had been ousted from all other Northern libraries and destroyed, perhaps publicly burned. The *Journal* refused to publish a letter replying to its charge that *The Real Lincoln* "was a vicious and scurrilous attack" by a Southern man upon its idol. And this is enlightened Boston, "the hub of the universe."

An *auto-de-fe* ["act of faith," that is, a public condemnation] may be very effective as a punishment, whether inflicted upon a heretic or a book, still it is not an argument or a refutation. But the real authors of *The Real Lincoln*, as is made evident, are Lincoln's personal friends and fulsome eulogists. The "scurrilities," if they are there, are to be traced to these "friendly" sources. Indeed, it was objected to the first edition of Dr. Minor's compilation that the author said nothing himself, but only gave "what other people have said or written." To this Dr. Minor replied that his purpose was simply to "submit the testimony and to leave the reader to draw his own conclusions."

In order to sustain the Lincoln myth, more than one attempt has been made to suppress the ugly facts related by Lincoln's early biographers. For instance, as Dr. Minor points out, [Ward Hill] Lamon's *The Life of Lincoln*, published in 1872,[161] containing what [William H.] Herndon, another biographer, admits as "revelations" and "ghastly exposures," has been withdrawn from circulation, and in its place appeared in 1895 [Lamon's] . . . expurgated *Recollections of Abraham Lincoln [1847-1865]*, edited by Dorothy Lamon [Teillard],[162] with all the damaging matter left out and no intimation given of the existence of the genuine biography. New England's intolerance of truth was shown some years ago in the case of Percy Greg's *History of the United States*.[163] This admirable and brilliant English writer in his exposition of State rights and the justice of the Confederate cause gave offense to a certain individual from the land of the Puritans, and he bought up every copy he could find in order to suppress the book. An American edition of Percy Greg's history, published in Richmond, through the efforts of prominent Southern men now happily supplies the place of the English edition, and is well known in our schools and libraries. And by a singular chance the American edition is owned by the publishers of *The Real Lincoln*, which has also had the compliment paid it of attempted suppression. Both of these books are indorsed by the U. C. V. and the U. D. C.[164] — MISS KATE MASON ROWLAND

Confederate soldier, identity unknown, circa 1863.

Confederate Soldiers' and Sailors' Monument, Libby Hill Park, Richmond, Virginia, circa 1908.

SECESSION WAS THE SOUTH'S ATTEMPT TO SAVE THE CONSTITUTION

☞ . . . It was in 1861, after the secession of several States, when the Peace Congress assembled in Washington, in which Mr. [Salmon P.] Chase, well known to be the intended Secretary of the Treasury of Mr. [Abraham] Lincoln, then elect, openly declared that the Northern States never would fulfill their obligations under the Constitution of the United States in the matter of the return of fugitives from service [Editor's note: see the Fugitive Slave Clause in the U.S. Constitution, Article 4, Section 2, Clause 3. L.S.]. . . . There were then thirteen States, which had avowedly and openly declared that that clause of the Constitution of the United States without which Judge [Joseph] Story said the Constitution never could have been made, and which Judge [Henry] Baldwin, of the Supreme Court, on a circuit bench, said was "the corner stone of the United States government," should be unconditionally repudiated. [There was thus] but one alternative for patriots, and that was to quit the Union as the only hope of saving the Constitution. . . .[165] — CONFEDERATE VICE PRESIDENT ALEXANDER HAMILTON STEPHENS

WHY PRESIDENT DAVIS WAS NEVER BROUGHT TO TRIAL BY THE U.S. GOVERNMENT

☞ While the question of Jefferson Davis's trial for high treason was pending Mr. William B. Reed, counsel for the defense, was a member of my brother's congregation at Orange Valley, N.J. He told my brother, after it had been decided that the trial was not to take place, that if the case had come to trial the defense would have offered in evidence the text-book on constitutional law [William Rawle's *A View of the Constitution of the United States of America*][166] from which Davis had been instructed at West Point by the authority of the United States government and in which the right of secession is maintained as one of the constitutional rights of a State.[167] — L. W. BACON, PHILADELPHIA, PENNSYLVANIA, MARCH 25, 1884

☛ WAIT FOR THE WAGON
Come, all you sons of Freedom, and join our Southern band;
We are going to fight the enemy and drive them from our land.
Justice is our motto, and Providence our guide;
So jump into the wagon, and we'll all take a ride.

Chorus:
Wait for the wagon.
The dissolution wagon;
The South is our wagon,
And we'll all take a ride.

Secession is our password, and our rights we'll all demand,
And to defend our firesides we pledge our heart and hand.
Jeff Davis is our President, with Stephens by his side;
Brave Beauregard, our general, will join us in the ride.

Our wagon's plenty large enough, our running gears are good;
It's stuffed with cotton round the sides, and made of Southern wood.
South Carolina is the driver, with Georgia by her side;
Virginia will hold our flag up, and we'll all take a ride.

There're Tennessee and Texas also in the ring;
They wouldn't have a government where cotton isn't king.
Alabama, too, and Florida have long ago replied;
Mississippi is in the wagon, anxious for the ride.

Kentucky and Maryland are slow;
They must join ere long, or where will they go?
The Missouri boys are ready to join our noble tide,
So come along, brave Jackson, and join us in the ride.

Our cause is just and holy, our men are brave and true;
To whip the Lincoln invaders is all we have to do.
God bless our noble army! in him we all confide;
So jump into the wagon, and we'll all take a ride.[168] — ANONYMOUS

THE OLD SOUTH
☞ There never was a finer manhood on the earth than that of the Old South. They lived an outdoor life favorable to physical strength and marked individuality. The existing state of things in our country furnishes a vindication of what has been sneered at as characteristic of the old Southern school of statesmanship. The old-time Southern statesmen, it was alleged, wasted their time and their breath in the discussion of abstract constitutional principles. They were accused of too much persistency in their demand for strict construction of constitutional provisions. They were satirized as abstractionists and visionaries, and nicknamed in current politics as the "Chivalry." The old-time Southerners who stood for this principle and acted on it in their representative capacity did a work never to be forgotten in the making of this republic. The Bill of Rights, the Declaration of Independence, and the Federal [U.S.] Constitution are their monuments. In [any] . . . contest . . . in defense of the rights and welfare of the American people the names and the deeds of these men of the Old South will be invoked as examples by an awakened and patriotic people.[169] — BISHOP O. P. FITZGERALD, *CHRISTIAN ADVOCATE*, NASHVILLE, TENNESSEE, APRIL 19, 1907

Confederate Assistant Surgeon William McNeil Whistler, Co. F, 1st South Carolina Infantry Regiment, circa 1863.

SLAVERY WAS NOT THE CAUSE OF THE WAR: ALMOST 90 PERCENT OF SOUTHERN BLACKS SAID THEY WERE WILLING TO FIGHT FOR THE CONFEDERACY

☞ . . . slavery, as it existed in the South, was patriarchal in its character; the slaves (servants, as we called them) were regarded and treated as members of the families to which they severally belonged; with rare exceptions, they were treated with kindness and consideration, and frequently the relations between the slave and his owner were those of real affection and confidence. As Mr. [George] Lunt, the Boston writer . . . says:

> "The negroes were perfectly contented with their lot. In general they were not only happy in their condition, but proud of it."

Their owners trusted them with their families, their farms, and their affairs, and this confidence was rarely betrayed—scarcely ever, unless they were forced to violate their trusts by coming in contact with the Federal [U.S.] armies, or were beguiled and betrayed themselves by mean and designing white men. The truth is, both the white and the black people of the South regarded the Confederate cause alike as their cause, and looked to its success with almost, if not quite, equal anxiety and delight. A most striking illustration of this and of the readiness of the slaves to fight even, if necessary, for the Confederate cause, is furnished by the following incident: In February, 1865, when negro troops had been authorized to be enrolled in the Confederate army, there were employed at Jackson Hospital, near Richmond, seventy-two negro men. The surgeon in charge, the late Dr. F. W. Hancock, of Richmond, had these men formed in lines; and after asking them "if they would be willing to take up arms to protect their masters' families, homes, and their own from an attacking foe, sixty out of seventy-two [83 percent] responded that they would volunteer to go to the trenches and fight the enemy to the bitter end."[170]

At the date here referred to we know that the life of the soldier was one of the greatest hardship and peril, and the fact that five out of every six of these negroes were then ready volunteer and go to the trenches showed conclusively how truly they regarded the Confederate cause as their cause as well as that of the white people of the South. Indeed, we doubt if a larger per cent of the whites in any part of the country would have volunteered to go to the front at that stage of the war. If, then, it were true, as alleged, that the white people of the South were fighting for slavery, does it not necessarily follow that the slaves themselves were ready and willing to fight for it too? One of these propositions is just as true as the other.

. . . even if we admit that slavery was, as falsely charged, the "cause of the war" the South was in no way responsible for the existence of that cause; but it was from a condition forced upon it, one recognized by the supreme law of the land, one which the South dealt with legally and justly as contemplated by that law, and history shows that in every respect, and in every instance, the aggressions and violations of the law were committed by the North. [New Englander] Mr. Lunt says:

> "Of four several compromises between the two sections of the country since the Revolutionary War, each has been kept by the South and violated by the North."

Indeed, we challenge the North to point out one single instance in which the South violated the Constitution or any of the laws made in pursuance thereof; whilst, on the contrary, fourteen of the Northern States passed acts nullifying the fugitive slave law, passed by Congress in obedience to the Constitution, denounced and defied the decisions of the Supreme Court, and Judge [Jeremiah Sullivan] Black, of Pennsylvania, says of the abolitionists [that is, radical Left-wingers, or communists, as we now know them]:

> "They applauded John Brown to the echo for a series of the basest murders on record. They did not conceal their hostility to the Federal and State governments nor deny their enmity to all laws which protected white men. The Constitution stood in their way, and they cursed it bitterly. The Bible was quoted against them, and they reviled God the Almighty himself."[171]

— JUDGE GEORGE L. CHRISTIAN, RICHMOND, VIRGINIA

THE CONFEDERATE FLAG REPRESENTS THE ORIGINAL GOVERNMENT OF THE FOUNDING FATHERS
☛ . . . Like Brutus, "'Twas not because we loved the old flag less, but our country more," that we took up arms and marched to battle under the Confederate flag when the old [U.S.] flag (under whose folds our forefathers had fought) ceased to represent our principles and to guarantee our constitutional rights. . . .[172] — THOMAS A. ELGIN, U.C.V. CAMP, MARSHALL, TEXAS

MORE PROOF SOUTHERN SLAVERY WAS NOT THE CAUSE OF THE WAR: IT WAS ON ITS WAY OUT PRIOR TO THE WAR

☞ . . . It is plain to all thoughtful men that the institution of slavery, mild, benignant, and fraternal as that institution was as it existed in the South prior to the days of [William] Lloyd Garrison and gentlemen of his [radical Left-wing] cult, was already doomed, and would have fallen in a few years anyhow, even if it had not been drowned in the blood of half a million victims in the most momentous struggle of modern times. It has been so in Brazil, in Cuba, in all the South American republics, and that within twenty years after the close of our Civil War. Some one, commenting on our Civil War, has remarked that the South was unlucky; and truly has she been unlucky, before the war, during the war, since the war—before the war in that the inevitable institutional revolution which must have been plainly patent to the thinking men of that day could not have been allowed to progress peacefully instead of eventuating in a fratricidal strife which cost her the lives of thousands of the flower of her young manhood, only to end in a miserable fiasco, for the negro problem, which it sought to solve, is as far from solution now as then. The public opinion of the Christian world as well as the fast-gathering force of a strong and growing and thinking minority in the South itself would have compelled emancipation in a few years, whether or no the War of Secession had ever been fought or whether or no that war had ended in her triumph or defeat. . . .[173] — WATKINS LEIGH, MONROE, LOUISIANA

SLAVERY WAS NOT THE CAUSE: IN 1861 THE U.S. GOVERNMENT CAME OUT AGAINST ABOLITION

☞ The President [Abraham Lincoln] himself, in his Inaugural [Address], March 4, 1861, . . . pledged himself against the Abolitionists in his own party, and against his proclamation of Abolitionism [that is, the Emancipation Proclamation]:

> "I have no purpose, directly or indirectly, to interfere with the institution of slavery in the States where it exists. I believe I have no lawful right to do so, and I have no intention, to do so."

[Furthermore] the [U.S.] House of Representatives, by a nearly unanimous vote, in February, 1861, passed the following resolutions:

"Resolved, That neither the federal government, nor the people or governments of the non-slaveholding states, have a purpose or a constitutional right to legislate upon or interfere with slavery in any of the states of the union.

"Resolved, That those persons in the north who do not subscribe to the foregoing proposition are too insignificant in numbers and influence to excite the serious attention or alarm of any portion of the people of the republic, and that the increase of their numbers and influence does not keep pace with the increase of the aggregate population of the union."[174]

— NEW YORK CONGRESSMAN JAMES BROOKS, SPEECH, UNION DEMOCRATIC [THEN CONSERVATIVE] ASSOCIATION, DECEMBER 30, 1862

THE CONFEDERACY'S HIGHEST AUTHORITY ON THE CAUSE OF THE WAR

☛ I tried all in my power to avert this war. I saw it coming, and for twelve years I worked night and day to prevent it; but I could not. The North was mad and blind; it would not let us govern ourselves, and so the war came, and now it must go on till the last man of this generation falls in his tracks, and his children seize his musket and fight our battle, unless you acknowledge our right to self-government. We are not fighting for slavery. We are fighting for independence, and that, or extermination, we will have.[175] — CONFEDERATE PRESIDENT JEFFERSON DAVIS

IN 1865 THE U.S. SUPREME COURT SIDED WITH THE SOUTH

☛ . . . The South's history is grandly glorious just as it is, and so we, the loving Daughters of the South, intend it shall be given to the world. Our State and us people have no regrets to express relative to 1861-65 except that we lost. We have no apologies to make, no pardons to ask. We knew that the movement of the Southern people in 1861, led by the great Mississippian, Jefferson Davis, was within the Constitution of the United States. The whole country knew it; for while Jefferson Davis, a vicarious sufferer, lay in chains at Fortress Monroe, while the clash of arms was still fresh in the minds of men and the echo of the last "Rebel yell" had scarcely died out in the valley, and while the frantic nation, mad with rage, was rending the overburdened air with wildest imprecations against the doctrine for which the South fought—State rights—the Supreme Court of the United States in

December, 1865, declared in favor of the doctrine: "The national government possesses no powers," it decided, "but such as have been delegated to it. The States have all power but such as they have surrendered."[176] — MRS. LUCY GREEN YERGER, GREENVILLE, MISSISSIPPI

A YANKEE CONSERVATIVE ON THE CAUSE OF LINCOLN'S WAR

☛ . . . State sovereignty: It is the principle upon which the American Revolution was founded. It has been called the Anglo-Saxon principle from the jealous devotion of that people to it. [Francis] Lieber says in his *On Civil Liberty and Self-Government*,[177] that,

> "In England we first see applied the practice and on a grand scale, the idea which came originally from the Netherlands, that liberty must not be a book of the government, but that it must derive its rights from the people."

This local sovereignty, within defined limits, exists in England, in counties, shires, cities, towns, and even in the cottage of the peasant. Lord Chatham [William Pitt, the Elder] expressed it thus:

> "Every man's house is his castle. Why? Because it is surrounded by a moat and defended by a wall? No. It may be a straw-built hut; the wind may whistle around it; the rain may enter it; but the King of England cannot!"

Our [European] fathers brought this principle of government with them [to America], and defended it against king and parliament, who attempted to wrest their local sovereignty from them, and centralize all the control over the colonies in themselves. [Despite the claims of Lincoln and other Northern Liberals, the] Union can never be restored without the recognition of this principle—the promised violation of it was the cause of this war.

. . . The Union to-day exists only in name at the [Liberal] North. It has been destroyed by those to whom its preservation was entrusted. Upon its debris they have erected a gigantic, consolidated government, all its power issuing from a Federal head; despotic and usurped power, the object and result of which must be, unless popular agencies prevent [it], the fate of all free Republics which have preceded it.

I owe a fealty to the Union as represented by the Federal government, but to a Federal administration, which distorts the sacred and ordained purposes of the Union, and which usurps the sovereign rights of the States, I owe no allegiance. . . . [78] — HONORABLE ROBERT C. HUTCHINGS, SPEECH, HOUSE OF THE ASSEMBLY, NEW YORK STATE, FEBRUARY 26, 1863

TERMS DISLIKED BY TRUE SOUTHERNERS
☛ Much is being said by speakers and writers on issues of the [eighteen] sixties as to who was "right." Mr. S. D. Van Pelt, a Union veteran, in a published address at Danville, Ky., on last Memorial Day takes to task those who use the term, "We know we were right," and disclaims such emphatic declaration as to himself; but he states that, while believing he was right, he does not declare it. He "loves and honors" the brave Confederate, than whom "no braver soldier ever lived." In paying such tribute it is assuring that he saw the Confederates tested, and it goes without question that such testimony is proof that the author was a good soldier in his country's service.

It is hardly worth while to discuss whether belief makes a fact. As to the Confederate soldier, however, whatever may have been his faith in the right to secede, enlightenment through study of the history and principles of the government in his maturer years, he is amazed at how fully justified he was in serving the powers over him to maintain the cause for which he enlisted before he really knew what his rights were. Hence the declaration that he knew he was right is emphasized without reserve as an expression that he would not modify if even to perpetuate his own life.

For years the *Veteran* [magazine] has permitted the expression without protest that "we are all Americans." This submission has continued without demurring because it has emanated mainly from Union veterans who sought to influence their fellows that Confederates are of the same blood and were actuated by the same principles for which the Union soldiers fought. But how unjust to truth! Many times Confederates fought [Yankee] regiments in which the English language was not known. It may be claimed that foreigners who had come to the country and enlisted at once in the Union army and had taken the oath of allegiance were therefore "Americans"; but natives to the soil whose homes were devastated by those hired bounty men cannot accept that they were Americans.

It is not so easy [for us Southerners] to enthuse over "Old Glory" [the U.S. national flag], either. True, it is our country's flag; it is the flag of the fathers of Confederates; but it was quit alienated by the inestimable infamies perpetuated under its folds. The flag is all right, but adoration is not increased by excessive comment from those who make so much ado about it The Confederates in all soberness accept it and will ever protect it; but patriotism is not enhanced by the gush of foreigners and those who disgraced its sacred origin under martial law.

The term "New South," started and pressed by those who came South after the war and wanted our successes credited to "Northern brains and energy as well as Northern money," has unwittingly been circulated by some Southerners. This should not have been. The *Veteran* has protested against the use of this term for years, and happily it is not used now except in isolated cases. The editor of the *Veteran* protested vigorously at the time—and that was long before this organ was launched [in 1893].

Another term, the most objectionable of all, is "lost cause." Shame upon it! If any article of questionable availability comes to the *Veteran*, the use of that term seals its doom. Let those who write for the *Veteran* take notice. In his beautiful peroration of his admirable address at the Memphis Reunion the Commander in Chief, Gen. Clement A. Evans, said:

> "We have the divine Word for a saying that you may sow a field with wheat and bury the grain beneath the ground so that the external shell will die, but the wheat is not lost. . . . No! No! Our cause was not lost, because it was not wrong. Our cause is a living constitutional principle inherent in the nature of our wonderful system of free government which shall be employed as a power for peace and for our common national glory. No! No! Our cause was not lost for the reason that it was not wrong! This body of venerable soldiers now speak for their people who have faithfully fulfilled all the obligations of citizenship in every respect during every day of all the years that have come and gone since the armies were disbanded and war ended. The South should have and enjoy its proper share of all the true history, the true glory, with all other advantages of a true Union. The whole South will hail a genuine nonsectionalism in feeling, politics, legislation, and administration of the government."

Please help to stop using these reproachful terms. Comrades could render invaluable aid in protesting to newspapers using them. Such a "campaign of education" should be aided by every Southern man and woman.[179] — SUMNER A. CUNNINGHAM, EDITOR, *CONFEDERATE VETERAN* MAGAZINE

OUR FIGHT

☛ . . . our fight was to maintain our constitutional rights, the same motive that inspired the patriots of 1776 when they faced the armies of England and won our proud independence. . . .[180] — T. E. MOORE, LEXINGTON, KENTUCKY

OUR CONFEDERATE ANCESTORS WERE NOT "REBELS"

☛ . . . Daughters of the Confederacy, Sons of Confederate Veterans, and you who come to join in these acts of loving remembrance, I tell you that we do well to honor and unyieldingly memorialize those noble sires of ours who wore the gray and fought beneath the ensign which bore the stars and bars. As an American citizen I love this Union; my heart pulses and thrills at every added distinction which comes to that already glorious emblem of the stars and stripes. I love it more because it floats over an undivided and, I believe, indissoluble federation [that is, confederation] of States. I would not take one jot or tittle from the praise accorded to those strong, brave men who wore the blue. They have played a splendid part in the past of this the greatest republic of all history. They are worthy to be memorialized on special days, in granite shafts, and to have their figures carved in marble. They fought for a principle which time has perhaps proved to be wise and expedient. Give their leaders the honor, if you please, accorded to the far-seeing statesman; but do not try to honor them by defaming fact, perverting history, and degrading our [Confederate] fathers and mothers by calling the cause of the Confederacy "a rebellion."

Confederate Major Walter Virginius Crouch, 13th Louisiana Infantry Regiment, circa 1863.

If secession was a stroke at the government, then the Constitution needs revision and colonial history is at variance with fact. If that revered and fundamental document were even subject to double construction, no one has a right to insult the memory of our noble fathers by calling them Rebels; nor should one question the real virtues of the Northern soldier by building his pedestal on the unstable and disastrous support of a gross injustice. No! No! These were not Rebels! If ever man fought for sacred vested right, if ever heart revolted against encroachment upon these guaranteed rights of the governed—in short, if life was ever forfeited at the stern call of a liberty-loving conscience—then these so revolted, fought, and gloriously died. . . .[181] — DR. MONTGOMERY GANO BUCKNER, MEMORIAL DAY ADDRESS, OWENSBORO, KENTUCKY

REFUTING THE CHARGE OF SLAVERY AS THE CAUSE

☞ . . . [One of the main charges against . . . Jefferson] Davis and the South, . . . is that the object of the Civil War was not to assert and protect the rights of the States, but to perpetuate the institution of African slavery. That this is not true, you veterans of that day know. Not one in five of the men engaged in that war owned a slave or had any interest in them. You and your comrades, slaveholders as well as nonslaveholders, went out to defend your State against invasion and to protect the assertion of a right reserved when the Union was formed.

The people of this commonwealth [Virginia] from the dawn of its colonial existence down to the fanatical agitation of the slavery question on the part of the North recognized that slavery was an evil, and but for that agitation there is little doubt that there would have been a gradual emancipation of slaves in this State without the shedding of a drop of blood, and in a manner which would have redounded to the interest of both races. This is made clear from her history. . . .[182] — JUDGE JOHN A. BUCHANAN, ABINGDON, VIRGINIA

WHEN POLITICIANS HONORED THE SOUTH & HER CAUSE

☞ . . . This day as Secretary of War I approved a contract for the erection at a cost of eight thousand five hundred dollars by the government of the United States of a white marble shaft eighty-two feet in height in the Confederate section of the Finn's Point National Cemetery, near Salem, N. J., to mark the graves of Confederate soldiers who died as prisoners of war.

I stood on Decoration Day by the Confederate monument erected in Oakwood Cemetery in Chicago largely [erected] by Northern contributions and saw a salute fired over those who fought for the stars and bars like that just fired over those lying nearby who fought for the stars and stripes. On a bronze tablet upon the monument to Tennessee's hero, Sam Davis, a monument evoking memories which bring tears to the eyes of all true Southern people, is an inscription showing that there were contributors to this monument from every State in the Union.

. . . No Southern man is treated with disfavor if he publicly expresses before representative people in the North his convictions as to the righteousness of our cause. On the one hundredth anniversary of the birth of Abraham Lincoln before a Northern audience in Chicago I said that in mind, heart, and soul I was loyal to the traditions of the South; I believed that the South was within its constitutional rights as the Constitution then stood; that her leaders were patriots, that her people showed a devotion to principle without a touch of sordidness, that such action as theirs could only come from a deep conviction that counted not the cost of sacrifice, and that I cherished as a glorious legacy the renown of her armies and leaders whose purity of life and heroism were unsurpassed by those of any people.

I always kept conspicuously displayed in my residence in Illinois portraits of Davis, Lee, and Jackson, and with them the Confederate colors. They were seen there by our President [Taft], the son [Frederick Dent Grant] of [Ulysses S.] Grant and the son [Robert Todd Lincoln] of Lincoln, and by many Union soldiers. It never occurred to me to offer explanation or apology.

Sensible people of the North know that in cherishing these sentiments, in holding these convictions, in caring for the graves of our dead, in erecting monuments to perpetuate their fame, in giving a true history of our contest, and teaching our children to reverence the memory of those who sustained the Southern cause, there is no protest against the government under which we live just as sensible people of the South know that devotion to our reunited country and its flag is no disloyalty to the memories of a cause which is enshrined forever.[183] — JACOB MCGAVOCK DICKINSON (OF NASHVILLE, TENN.), SECRETARY OF WAR UNDER U.S. PRESIDENT WILLIAM HOWARD TAFT, ADDRESS BEFORE THE U.D.C.

A U.S. PRESIDENT WHO RESPECTED THE CONFEDERATE SOLDIER
☛ [U.S.] President [William H.] Taft is traveling in California, and recently he paid noble tribute to Confederate heroism in a speech made to the veterans of the G. A. R. [U.S.] at Los Angeles. He said:

"We feel proud of the brave men of the North that they had

an enemy worthy of their steel and in the history of the world, and in the heroism that was displayed by both sides we can now feel a common interest."

[In other news:] The Blue and Gray to Escort Taft—When President Taft reaches San Antonio, Tex., he will be met by the local [Union veterans'] Post and [Confederate veterans'] Camp, and the soldiers of the blue and gray will continue to serve as his escort during his visit to that city.[184] — SUMNER A. CUNNINGHAM, EDITOR, *CONFEDERATE VETERAN* MAGAZINE

POEM TO A CONFEDERATE STATUE
☛ It is pleasing to see you, brave comrade, up there,
Picketed here on the old Courthouse Square.
Your companions here gathered in the dark days of yore
And nobly went forth to fight and endure—
Went forth for State Rights, went forth for the South,
And undaunted they charged to the cannon's grim mouth.

Yes, when we weigh and consider, we all must declare
'Twas proper to place you on the old Courthouse Square,
For 'twas here that you came at war's first alarms;
You volunteered here at the first call to arms.
Here shall you stand while the years wing their flight,
The Defender of Home and the Champion of Right.

When the rumors of trouble came borne on each breeze,
Here met the fathers, here under the trees.
They met here to ponder, to counsel, debate
O'er the God-given Rights that belong to each State;
And 'twas human, 'twas righteous, that anger arose
When those Rights were invaded by merciless foes.

You were fashioned by Yankees (thrice happy the thought);
They clothed you in bronze, and well have they wrought—
In the dread days of conflict you taught them to "feel"
By daring and doing and the thrust of your steel.
Though fashioned by Yankees, the work was well done;
You inspired the chosen by the glories you won.

Your designer (God bless him), it behooves us to say,
Loves and reveres the old soldier in gray;
For his father was one, old comrade like you.

Who fought for the cause so noble and true,
And for you and for him we exultantly raise
Our voices reverberant in sounding your praise.

And do you know it, old fellow, your presence up there
Is due to our women so brave and so fair?
Though human, they seem to us beings supernal;
Their infinite love makes remembrance eternal—
Those creatures of goodness, those angels of light,
Who nursed you in sickness, who nerved you in fight.

A health to you. comrade, a wreath for your brow;
You stood by us then, we'll stand by you now.
Your cause will aye live in song and in story,
Sublime in its sadness, immortal in glory.[185]

— W. SAM BURNLEY, READ AT THE UNVEILING OF CONFEDERATE STATUE, COURTHOUSE SQUARE, CHARLOTTESVILLE, VIRGINIA, MAY 1909

HOW THE SOUTHERN CAUSE MIGHT HAVE SUCCEEDED
☞ As I am the oldest member of this organization and denominated its chief counselor, it may be proper that I should say something in a general way about the soldiers whom I have asked you of the younger generations to approve. I want to express to you my great love for the true Confederates and tell you how our spirit nation was murdered. . . . [which] calls to mind that some who were false to their colors now wish to pose as honorable veterans of our armies.
 . . . I am proud of the South; I am proud of her flag which is folded; I am proud of her silent statesmen under the sodded earth; I am proud of her soldiers who are dead; I am proud of the veterans of her disbanded armies; I am proud of Mason, and Dixon's line, and want it marked in the hearts of her people as long as the blood of chivalry courses in the veins of generations; I am proud of Robert E. Lee, as I believe the South will always be. . . .
 Let the truth of the fight between the North and South be known; let the abiding love of the cause in the land of Davis, Lee, and Jackson be fearlessly proclaimed, and the songs of the Confederate Choirs shall tell the story of its glory from the Gulf of Mexico to the confines of Canada. . . . The United Confederate Choirs of America are now chroniclers of the achievements of the true and faithful men who wore the gray, and the Confederated

Memorial Associations and the Daughters of the Confederacy declare that the landmarks of our battles must be made of everlasting granite and that the memory of the true soldiers shall be cherished in the ever-blazing altar fires of patriotism.

What caused the failure of such splendid armies in consummating the independence of their country? Was it that implied power in the Constitution which satisfied the conscience of such noble Northmen as Charles Francis Adams to enter the ranks of invasion? Was it the power of the frowning fortifications which the Federals held in the South? Was it the great navy which blockaded our ports and forced starvation in our armies? Was it the 494,900 foreigners who enlisted in the armies of the North, of whom 144,200 of the best soldiers were Irishmen from the Green Isle, which has cried aloud for independence and bewailed the oppression of Britain for seven hundred years? Was it the 83,372 deserters who, after enlisting and swearing allegiance to the Confederate States, turned traitors with their backs upon the flag of the South? No. It was the unification of these events that caused the downfall of our nation and the furling forever of its stainless flag. Although the enemies of the South with fanatical intensity were gathering their clans for years in the North and West, she did not believe that war would come when she demanded separation.

All the great statesmen who advocated the adoption of the Federal [U.S.] Constitution [which replaced our first constitution, the Articles of Confederation][186] denied that it contained power either by direction or by implication to coerce a State. Alexander Hamilton, advocating its adoption by the New York State Convention, said:

> "It has been well observed that to coerce the States is one of the maddest projects that was ever devised."

He could not believe that one State would ever suffer itself to be used as an instrument of coercion. So, agreed upon by [George] Washington, Hamilton, and most of the ablest men of that day as without the remotest intent of any implied power to coerce a State, it was adopted. Had such a construction as the Federal government put upon it in 1861 been possible at that time, it would never have been adopted and there would have been no fight between the sections.

Patrick Henry was the wisest of all when he warned the Virginia Convention of the great powers the State was surrendering to the Federal government by the adoption of the Constitution without a bill of rights.

> "Their garrisons, magazines, and forts would be situated in the strongest places within the States; their ten-mile square, with all the fine ornaments of human life added to their powers and taken from the States, would reduce the powers of the latter to nothing."

He insisted that a bill of rights was indispensably necessary; that a general positive provision should be inserted in the new system securing to the States and the people every right which was not conceded to the general government, and that every implication should be done away with.

Had this been done, the War between the States would have been avoided and the blood and suffering of millions of human beings saved. When Virginia ceded the site of Fortress Monroe, when South Carolina gave [Forts] Moultrie and Sumter to the general government, they planted a death germ of State sovereignty. Had these forts been manned by Virginians and Carolinians, the Southern cross would be flying from their ramparts to-day. Had the navy been distributed between the sections, as rightful ownership would have dictated. Father [Abram Joseph] Ryan's banner would be on the halyards of the battle ships of a nation. Had Europe made her hireling hordes, which swelled the ranks of invasion, cultivate the earth for honest bread, a Confederate soldier would be President of the Confederate States at this hour.

Alas! in shame do I speak it: had the deserters from our ranks stood true to the flag, our spirit nation would now be the proudest republic on the face of the globe. Had these false soldiers stood firm, ten thousand of them in support of the men who charged at Gettysburg would have driven Meade from Cemetery Ridge, and the Army of Northern Virginia would have entered Washington [D.C.] in triumph. Had twenty thousand of them fought with Lee in the Wilderness, [Union Gen.] Grant would never have reached Appomattox. Had fifty thousand of them stood bravely in the ranks of the army of Joseph E. Johnston, [Union Gen.] Sherman's march to the sea would be unknown to history. Had these cowards and perjurers been brave enough to fight with the true hearts of patriotism, the South would be independent, notwithstanding all of the other drawbacks I have mentioned. All of the enemy's ships of war, all of his millions of soldiers, both native and foreign, and all of his bristling fortifications at the gateways of our ports would not have conquered the Confederate States if the deserters had been faithful to their flag. Let the names of these infamous men be published and their tainted blood be a scorn forever in the Southland. The deserters were the assassins of the Confederate States—foremost enemies in evil and infamy—the most abhorrent in the eyes of decency as the scum of degradation; the meanest men on the calendar of crime murdered our nation. As the true soldiers of the Confederacy are highest on the lists of praise, so are the traitors deepest in shame.

Children of the South, I am glad of your recognition of your father's heroism in touching melody. I glory in your reverence of the memory of our battle dead—of the 200,000 soldiers who sacrificed their lives for the Confederate cause! I love your love for their faithful comrades who survive. I invoke God's blessings for you and them. I pray that they shall hereafter live in the companionship of innocence and virtue beautiful as the blooming lilies, and when the hour comes death will be sweet, the parting of the body and soul like the perfume of the fading flowers floating out on boundless space as the spirit of universal love.[187] — COLONEL W. H. STEWART OF PORTSMOUTH, VIRGINIA; SPEECH, MOBILE, ALABAMA, REUNION OF THE UNITED CONFEDERATE CHOIRS OF AMERICA

THE "BOYS OF THE SIXTIES": WHY THEY FOUGHT
☛ . . . These "boys of the sixties" stood in the forefront for the South. Her men and women united in one great effort for the maintenance of individual rights under the Constitution of our Revolutionary forefathers, and in this supreme loyalty crowned the Southland with immortal fame. When outnumbered and overpowered, they accepted the conditions in good faith, giving to the world an example of lofty citizenship in the restoration of their stricken and desolated homes. . . .[188] — MRS. C. B. STONE, CONFEDERATE REUNION, MOBILE, ALABAMA

DAVIS ON THE PROBABLE OUTCOME OF A MCCLELLAN ELECTION
☛ [Suppose the South Had Succeeded? This much discussed idea recently] brought to my mind Mr. [Jefferson] Davis's speech while on a visit to the Army of Tennessee just before its start under [Confederate] General [John Bell] Hood into Tennessee. Our division, [General Henry DeLamar] Clayton's, Lee's Corps, was drawn up in a square around the platform on which the President and Gen. Howell Cobb addressed the division. Mr. Davis's speech was a masterful effort to enthuse the soldiers for future deeds of

valor. What he said that particularly struck me and has stayed in my memory to this day was:

> "They are going to have an election up North. It lies between [George B.] McClellan and Lincoln. You would naturally think that [Union] General McClellan as a Democrat [then a Conservative] would suit us [Southern Conservatives] very well if he could be elected; but I think, however, that if McClellan should be elected there will be a division or another secession between the East and the West. There would be an Eastern and Western as well as Southern Confederacy. The West, on account of the Western rivers which would flow to the sea through our land and those by the highway of commerce, might think it advisable to join hands with us; but we would not accept their offer of a union with them. We would tell them it was impossible; that there had been too much blood spilled between us, but that the rivers would and shall be free for our common commerce."

These words left an impression on my mind that I have not forgotten. They were the very words our President spoke; therefore if the South had succeeded by the secession of the West from the East through McClellan's election, one of the things that would have happened, according to Mr. Davis, would have been the free Mississippi River. The other question, States' rights, would also have been settled for good in the way we believe it was intended it should. The third, slavery and slaveholding aristocracy, would certainly have continued for a time; but Russia's first abolishing the slavery of the serfs, Brazil emancipating slavery, the West India Islands following suit, an anti-slavery movement in the South would have become an immense lever against them, to which they would have had to yield or have the world against them. [Editor's note: writer Hartman seems unaware of the fact that the American abolition movement got its start in the South—in the 1600s. L.S.][189]

There were too many nonslaveholding soldiers (called "white trash" by the slaves) that fought for State rights bravely, but not for the perpetuation of slavery. It was supposed in early days that no white labor could raise cotton, sugar, rice, etc., on extreme Southern plantations; but this idea has long since been exploded by actual facts, which further make the South generally more prosperous than in olden times.[190] — J. C. HARTMAN, SHIPPINGPORT, PENNSYLVANIA

FURTHER JUSTIFICATION FOR SOUTHERN SECESSION

☛ [A careful study of true American history] . . . shows first how each State when colonized become a separate kingdom, even when acknowledging the rights of a common king, each passing the supreme sovereignty of its own deeds and decisions. When the rebellion [the American Revolution] from the authority of this king took place, each State, or small kingdom as each practically was, assumed the full rights of self-government. . . . President [James] Monroe. . . says that the two propositions are beyond dispute; that when the sovereignty was wrested from the king it passed at once directly to the people, and that it then passed to the people of each colony—to thirteen separate and distinct communities and not to any one of them.

Samuel Chase, one of the signers of the Declaration of Independence, said:

> "I consider this a declaration not that the united colonies jointly or in a collective capacity were independent States, but that each was a sovereign and independent State, and that each State had a right to govern by its own authority and its own laws without any control by any other power on earth."

[Hence was established the]. . . autonomy of the States, and through [this] . . . proves the sovereign rights of the States to secession and to the full right of self-control in the dissolving of a union that had ceased to unite. . . .[191] — SUMNER A. CUNNINGHAM, EDITOR, *CONFEDERATE VETERAN* MAGAZINE

YANK QUITS UNION VETERANS' POST OVER ITS ANTI-SOUTH EFFORTS

☛ About a year ago I first saw a copy of the *Confederate Veteran* in our State Library in Indianapolis. I became interested in the magazine and subscribed for it. I now renew. The *Veteran* is to be commended for its success in keeping the present generation correctly informed on the causes that precipitated our Civil War, the enduring loyalty of the Confederate armies, and their splendid achievements. It is good too to read of the effective and successful work being done by the Daughters of the Confederacy, as set forth in the *Veteran*, to erect throughout the Southland memorials and monuments to perpetuate the fame of their Spartan soldiers.

As surely as "truth crushed to earth shall rise again" will those who record historic truths and who perpetuate the memory of heroes in blocks of stone he classed among such immortals as

Jefferson Davis and the great souls who led the armies of the Confederacy to victory on many a stubborn battlefield in defense of the people of the seceding States in the rights that were theirs under the Constitution—rights that would have been denied them had they remained in the Union. Surely it was a cause for which it was a great honor to fight and fail than not to fight at all.

I have been a member of [Union General] George H. Thomas Post, No. 17, G. A. R., of Indianapolis. It is the most prominent Post in Indiana, having a membership of about three hundred. [U.S. President] Benjamin Harrison and many other noted officers of the Union army, now dead, were members. [Union] Capt. William A. Ketcham, a member of the Thomas Post, introduced the resolution in the recent national G. A. R. Encampment at Atlantic City to have [Confederate General Robert E.] Lee's statue removed from the Hall of Fame at Washington and the profile of Jefferson Davis removed from the battle ship *Mississippi*. I rejoice for my country, and especially do I rejoice with the people of the South, that the National Encampment had the patriotism to turn down this measure. It confirms that open rebellion is not treason; it is the right of a free people to war against despotism.

I was present when the Ketcham resolution was acted on in the Post, but became disgusted with a class of G. A. R. comrades who persistently schemed to induce the G. A. R. to indorse measures denouncing the people of the South, all this in face of the fact that during the history of our country our government has never once had occasion to inflict the death penalty for treason. During our great Civil War neither the North nor the South developed a traitor in the sense that Benedict Arnold proved

Confederate First Sergeant Jacob Gochenour, Price's Field and Staff, Danville Virginia Light Artillery Battery, Alexandria, Virginia, circa 1863.

himself a traitor. I applied for and received an honorable discharge from the order. I regretted the necessity that moved me to such action, for I have ever entertained a profound regard and affection for my comrades of the Union army. All who receive the baptism of fire in battle are close akin. . . .[192] — PRIVATE THAYER, 51ST INDIANA VOLUNTEER INFANTRY

Confederate Lieutenant General Stephen Dill Lee (a cousin of Robert E. Lee), 1st South Carolina Light Artillery Regiment, Augusta, Georgia, circa 1863.

7

IN PRAISE OF JEFFERSON DAVIS

☛ . . . Though [Confederate President Jefferson Davis] . . . endured all the pangs of defeat, no conquering hero, fresh from triumph or wearing the laurels of victory, ever won so permanent an abiding place in the hearts and affections of his countrymen.

He was our representative, typical of that magnificent civilization which commenced with [George] Washington and ended with Lee. Brave in battle, with a polish, a culture, a deep learning and honesty of purpose and courage in action, typical of Southern civilization when in its flower, he was justly recognized as one who was born to command.

If we of to-day can but display in all the arts of peace the same courage, devotion to principle, and patient fortitude which Mr. Davis and his compatriots showed during the long years of weary struggle against overwhelming numbers and resources, we will prove ourselves worthy of our descent from a race of men whose blood freely flowed at honor's call and never stained where it fell.

We have no words of apology on our lips for him who bore so patiently and bravely the burdens and sorrows of his people. The day, my countrymen, will come when the name of Jefferson Davis will stand in history alongside that of Washington, side by side with [Confederate Generals Wade] Hampton and Sidney [Albert Sidney Johnston], and the other great names of those who fought for constitutional liberty and human rights.

It has been said that those men who fought the battles of the

South believed that they were right. I answer with the younger Lee that they not only believed but knew they were right. Their theories have been justified and sustained in the forum of reason, argument, and debate, and successfully defended by the greatest constitutional lawyers of our age.

It should be to us to-day a source of congratulation the right of local self-government and the preservation of the rights of the State for which these men struggled and fought are to-day recognized as essential to the perpetuity of free government in this republic. The cause for which they contended did not perish.[193] — ALABAMA GOVERNOR EMMET O'NEAL, ADDRESS, MONTGOMERY, ALABAMA, FEBRUARY 18, 1911

PROTEST BY SOUTHERN WOMEN'S ORGANIZATION AGAINST NORTHERN-BIASED SCHOOL TEXTBOOKS

☛ The following resolution was . . . presented . . . at the April meeting of the Tennessee Woman's Historical Association, Nashville, Tenn.:

> "Whereas it has been brought to our attention through various newspapers and the *Confederate Veteran* [magazine] that there is being used not only in the North, but also in several preparatory schools, colleges, and universities of a number of our Southern States, Tennessee included, a *History of the United States of America* [1904] by H. W. Elson, of Kansas, which contains slanderous falsehoods against the South, her people and institutions; and whereas we have examined this history and found that this statement is correct; and whereas on page 558 he attacks the morality of Southerners in slavery days, also the sacred relations of the home in language which is false; and whereas we know that in no section of this country or in any other country has there ever been a higher standard of morality than in the South, or has the sanctity of the home been more carefully guarded than by the people of the South; and whereas on page 625 he declares that 'slavery, and slavery alone, and not State rights,' was the cause of the War between the States, which he terms the 'slave-holders' war'; and whereas we know that a great majority of the Confederate soldiers never owned a slave, and that Gen. Robert E. Lee, who had the honor of commanding the Confederate forces, also the honor of declining [Lincoln's offer] to be the commander in chief of the Federal

[Union/U.S.] forces, had several years before this war freed his [wife's family's] slaves; therefore be it

"*Resolved*, That the Tennessee Woman's Historical Association make an earnest protest in the name of truth and justice against the use of Elson's *History of the United States of America* in any school of this country, and that this association in order that the girls and boys of this country may know the truth exert itself that no history which misrepresents the South, North, or any other section of this country be taught in our schools, and that a copy of this resolution be sent to the Macmillan Company, of New York, the publishers of this history."[194] — MRS. N. B. DOZIER, NASHVILLE, TENNESSEE

ANOTHER PROTEST AGAINST ELSON & HIS "HISTORY"

☛ . . . We will cite one instance just to show the pernicious influence this book [Elson's *History of the United States of America*] is having on the young people of the South. A young man who had studied this so-called history remarked that he knew it was tough, but believed every word in it. And he was a Southern boy, the son of a Confederate veteran.

Confederate Captain John Hanson McNeill, Co. E, 18th Virginia Cavalry Regiment, circa 1864.

Shall we sit idly by and see the fair name and honor of our fathers and grandfathers impugned in this shameful way? Too many have given their lives for a cause so dear and whose memories we tenderly revere to permit this slander to go unrebuked. Our Confederate soldiers are peerless, and shall we allow these unequivocal misrepresentations and falsehoods to be taught to the present and future generation? No! A thousand times, no!

We beg of you [all Southern heritage organizations] to join us in the crusade against histories of this character. We only want the truth. Will you not investigate and ascertain what histories are being taught in the colleges and schools of your cities and towns? This is urgent; do not delay. The present generation will not be called upon to defend their principles with their lives as their fathers did, yet we have before us a great and noble work, the recording of the story of our civilization—a civilization which produced such men as our Davis, Lee, and Jackson.

The heart cannot but feel that the true story must be told; the song must be sung through the ages that teaches the South the sublime beauty of devotion to duty.[195] — THE SOUTHERN CROSS CHAPTER, SALEM, VIRGINIA, U.D.C.

A YANKEE ON SLAVERY & THE CAUSE OF THE WAR

☞ Abraham Lincoln in his celebrated Gettysburg address spoke of our nation as conceived in liberty and dedicated to the proposition, "All men are created equal." This is the great, vague, central, germinant idea which lies at the very heart of our national institutions. The fathers of our [confederate] republic [the U.S.A.], who propounded this great principle, were neither Utopians nor socialists [that is, radical left-wingers], but men of profound political wisdom acting under a sober sense of political responsibility. They did not mean to obliterate the past nor to abolish human nature. They simply meant to declare that in our nation there should be a fair chance for every man to develop the best that there is in him, irrespective of race, color, or nationality. The idea was new and untried. It was an experiment; it was not something that could be realized at once, but must be the slow growth of ages.

This much must be conceded, that the Northern States were just as responsible for the existence of slavery as were the Southern States, and that slavery ceased to exist in the Northern States because it was for them an economic failure, and it grew stronger in the Southern States after the invention of Eli Whitney's cotton gin, simply because it was enormously profitable, and property and slaves correspondingly valuable. As a result the two sections of the country grew up on two utterly irreconcilable and hopelessly antagonistic economic bases, that of slave and free labor.

The North, with free labor, was in harmony with the most enlightened intelligence of the age as to slavery, and advanced rapidly toward a conception of a national democratic republic in which the individual should be the unit; while the South, holding to the institution of slavery when it had become an anachronism, and the whole enlightened intelligence of the world was armed against it, was put upon the defensive, shut up within itself, and was as hopelessly isolated from the rest of the world as is China to-day.

Now as slaves were property, according to law, any attack upon this form of property was an attack indirectly upon all forms of property, and an attack also upon the Constitution of the United States. In the minds, therefore, of pious, church-going, orthodox slaveholders, and many such there were, the abolitionists of the North were looked upon as we to-day regard the bomb-throwing anarchists of Chicago or the most radical wing of the socialist party—as the enemies of society and the enemies of God and his holy Word, the Bible, in which the pious slaveholder of the South found abundant authority for his beloved institution.

So along these two points the conflict raged, and slavery, when it was attacked, intrenched itself more and more within the doctrine of State rights, so that at the last the two became identical, and to attack one was to attack the other, to defend one was to defend the other. Consequently, when it came to the outbreak of the Civil War, many patriotic Southern men who cared little or nothing about slavery were stirred with the deepest indignation at the suggestion of the national government subduing a sovereign State by force of arms, and said that a Union that could only be held together by bayonets had better be dissolved; and for the principle of State rights and State sovereignty the Southern men fought with a holy ardor and self-denying patriotism that have covered even defeat with imperishable glory.

And let us look at the matter from the Southern standpoint. The [Republican, then Liberal] party that elected Abraham Lincoln was a party avowedly hostile to the institution of slavery, and elected a man to the presidency who also avowed his hostility to the institution of slavery [Editor's note: This statement is not entirely accurate: At the beginning of the war Lincoln was not against slavery itself, but against the spread of slavery outside the South. L.S.],[196] who had been known to say that the Union could not exist both slave and free, was bound ultimately to become all slave or all free, and who in his Cooper Union address said that the anti-slavery sentiment had already caused more than a million votes, which could have seemed to the Southern States nothing more nor less than a danger and a menace. Consequently, when they drew the sword to defend the doctrine of State rights and the institution of slavery [Editor's note: The South, in no way, fought to defend the "institution of slavery." L.S.], they certainly had on their side the Constitution and laws of the land, for a strict interpretation of the national Constitution gave a certain justification to the doctrine of State rights [see the 9th and 10th Amendments]. As to the institution of slavery, even the abolitionists [that is, socialists and communists] had made the discovery that the Constitution legalized it, and consequently they denounced the Constitution of the United States [as] "a league with death and a covenant with hell," and maintained that no moral or Christian man could find or hold office under such an accursed government as ours, and gave all their energies to proving that secession was the duty of the fellow-States.

Is it not perfectly evident that there was a great rebellion, but that the rebels were the Northerners and that those who defended the Constitution as it was were the Southerners, for they defended State rights and slavery, which were distinctly intrenched within the Constitution?

Origin of Civil War: So we can truly say that the underlying, efficient cause of our Civil War was the compromises of the Constitution, utterly irreconcilable principles existing there side by side, covered only by compromises that could in the end satisfy neither party.

Then came the great controversy that ended in the Missouri Compromise. Into that entered also the element of slavery when the free States denied the slave power any part of the Louisiana purchase, which was the purchase of the whole nation. The slaveholders rose up in anger and asked why they, with their peculiar property, should be shut out from territory which had been purchased by the whole nation. Here again there was a compromise, but not a solution.

. . . We can better understand the anti-slavery agitation in its bearings on the development of our national history when we remember that in the formation of the [American] Colonization Society [a white supremacist organization founded in the North, and of which Lincoln was a lifelong member],[197] of which Henry Clay was President, the conscience of antislaverymen, both at the North and South, found a most effective opiate in the doctrine of gradual emancipation and deportation of the slaves to Africa.

So as we look back upon the war it ought to have for us no sting or bitterness, but every angry thought should be stilled in presence of a great sorrow. On both sides were men of the highest principle and the noblest intention, giving themselves up in heroic devotion and self-sacrificing bravery to what they thought was true.

Sometimes the question is asked "Were not the slaves better off under slavery than they are now under freedom?" I think a candid answer to that question demands us to say that some were better off under slavery than they are under freedom. The abolition of slavery acted on the colored race like a wedge, forcing some down and some up. Those who were fit for freedom, prepared to embrace and make the most of the opportunities offered them as free men, rose. But some were not fit for freedom. Now that is no reflection upon the colored race. We have innumerable numbers of men and women that we are compelled to confine in institutions and keep as wards of the State, or they destroy themselves and everybody else.

If slavery was an unutterably evil institution, with no alleviating features, how are we to account for the fact that when the Confederate soldiers were at the front fighting, as thought, for their independence, the negroes on the plantations took care of the [white] women and children and old people, and nothing like an act of violence was ever known among them? I have seen in Charleston, S.C., a monument erected by former slaveholders and their descendants in grateful acknowledgment of the fidelity of those slaves who remained upon the plantations and cared for their women and children while they were at the front, and I understand that the Confederate veterans are also to erect another such monument

Certainly such kindly feeling between master and slave shows that there must have been something good in the institution of slavery. Certainly that is the plain implication of [my mother's book] *Uncle Tom's Cabin*, for the very noblest characters in the book, Mrs. Shelby, Eliza, Uncle Tom, St. Clare, and little Eva, were all the offspring of the institution of slavery and nourished on its breast, and certainly an institution that in itself was essentially wicked and diabolical could not have produced such noble characters. So we should not look back upon slavery as a reign of unalleviated wickedness and horror, but remember that is had within itself, in spite of its many abuses and intolerable horrors, much that was good.

. . . It is an unfortunate thing, to my mind, that the color line has been so drawn as it has been drawn, and that the attention of both the races is of necessity so concentrated upon the fact of color. But that is inevitable. It cannot be otherwise. To my mind the only solution is that your people [African Americans] should develop their own peculiar culture, their own peculiar race pride, and remove prejudice, not by protest, but by doing away with all worthy cause for such prejudice. That comes through thrift, economy, education, intelligence, and work of character. It is a difficult problem that is before you for solution. I believe you are solving it, and upon you educated young men and women who go forth as teachers, leaders, and inspirers of your own people rests a great responsibility, but with that responsibility a mighty opportunity for good.[198] — DR. CHARLES EDWARD STOWE,

SON OF LEFT-WING YANKEE AUTHORESS HARRIET BEECHER STOWE; ADDRESS GIVEN BEFORE A "GREAT GATHERING OF NEGROES" (INCLUDING BOOKER T. WASHINGTON), FISK UNIVERSITY, NASHVILLE, TENNESSEE

SOUTHERN SOLDIERS WERE HEROES & PATRIOTS NOT REBELS & TRAITORS

☛ ... The superb courage of the Southern soldiers upon the field of battle and the consummate skill of the Southern commanders are recognized and admitted by all. Even Colonel [Theodore] Roosevelt [future U.S. president] in his *Life of Thomas H. Benton* has said that General Lee was the greatest military commander that the English-speaking people has ever produced, and that the Army of Northern Virginia [Lee's army] was the greatest fighting machine the world has ever seen.

But the South is to be judged not alone by the courage and efficiency of her armies and the skill of her commanders, but by the righteousness of the cause for which they fought and suffered. The question of paramount magnitude is the justice of that cause; not that there should be a doubt in any candid, well-informed mind, but from the fact that such persistent efforts have been made to fasten upon the South the stigma and to impress posterity with the conviction that the Southern States were in rebellion and the Southern patriots were traitors, and an unjust and partial world is too ready to stamp upon the back of the defeated soldier "Rebel" and "Traitor," however just his cause, and to emblazon upon the shield of the victorious warrior "Hero" and "Patriot," however unjust his cause. Therefore we of this generation are under a high and sacred obligation to the preceding generation to rescue their names and fame from the aspersion of treason and rebellion.

The Southern States were justified in their action in 1861 upon both principle and authority. They had both precept and precedent, and yet the Southern people of 1861-65 have been stigmatized as rebels. If it be rebellion in man to pour out the best blood that flows in his veins upon the battle's bloody plain in freedom's holy sacred cause; if it be rebellion in an American citizen to defend those constitutional rights which are his dearest birthright and greatest inheritance from those great founders of this great republic, then we accept the appellation and feel a pride in saying that we were members of that rebellious body or are the descendants of those rebels.

Still, secession should not have been resorted to for light and trivial causes, but each State was the sole judge. There is no common arbiter. In the words of the Kentucky resolution, of which [Thomas] Jefferson was the author, "each party has the right to judge for itself as of infractions as of the mode and measure of redress." Each State enumerated her grievances; each State insisted that the Northern States had violated their constitutional obligation to "promote domestic tranquillity." The Southern States insisted that no alternative remained except to seek out of the Union [that] which they had vainly tried to obtain within it.

Mr. [Jefferson] Davis in his speech on retiring from the United States Senate voiced the sentiment of every Southern State when he said:

> "A State finding herself in the condition which Mississippi has judged that she is in, in which her safety requires that she should provide for the maintenance of her rights out of the Union, surrenders all the benefits (and they are known to be many), deprives herself of the advantages (and they are known to be great), severs all the ties of affection (and they are close) which have bound her to the Union, and thus divesting herself of every benefit, taking upon herself every burden, she claims to be exempt from any power to execute the laws of the United States within her limits."[199]

— JOHN S. BEARD, ADDRESS AT PITTVILLE NATIONAL CEMETERY, PHILADELPHIA, PENNSYLVANIA—THE FIRST CONFEDERATE MONUMENT ERECTED BY THE U.S. GOVERNMENT

WHY U.S. VICE PRESIDENT BRECKINRIDGE SIDED WITH LEE

☛ . . . For the Confederates this country, known as the Western Department of Virginia, was held by Gen. John Cabell Breckinridge, one of the finest types of the manhood of the Old South. A splendid career in politics had been followed by brilliant success in war. He had been Vice President with [U.S. President] James] Buchanan, and then the Southern candidate for the presidency against Lincoln. When the Civil War began, he entered the service of the South, believing with Lee that the question of State rights was the paramount issue. By 1864 he had taken part in numerous battles and had gained a high reputation for boldness, energy, and dash. He was the idol of his men, who long afterwards remembered his magnificent appearance as he rode past them on horseback. . . .[200] — EDWARD RAYMOND TURNER, HISTORY PROFESSOR, UNIVERSITY OF MICHIGAN

WHY LEE DREW HIS SWORD

☛ Both [George] Washington and [Robert E.] Lee were patriots, but Washington stood before the world an avowed revolutionist. The movement he led was an acknowledged insurrection against established authority. He drew his sword to sever the connection between colonies and their parent country, between subjects and their legitimate sovereign—a connection that rested on historic foundation and undisputed legal rights. But there was not in Lee or his cause one single element of revolution or rebellion. Conservative in his nature and associations, unswerving in his loyalty to the power which was for him paramount to all others, the cause in defense of which he drew his sword was founded upon historic rights, constitutional law, public morality, and the inviolable rights of free and sovereign States, many of whose constitutions were established and in peaceful operation while that of the United States lay unthought of in the far-off years of futurity.[201] — LUCIUS QUINTUS CINCINNATUS LAMAR, FROM A LETTER WRITTEN SHORTLY AFTER THE DEATH OF GENERAL R. E. LEE

OUR SOUTHERN BOYS WERE NOT SOCIALISTS, THEY WERE CONSERVATIVE PATRIOTS!

☛ . . . The well-to-do, including slave-owning, society of the South had no superior. It was an aristocracy that fostered and cultivated the noblest sentiments of humanity—culture, independence, courage, and knightly courtesy among men; grace, beauty, and virtue among its women. Its hospitality was unbounded. The stately homes of the James [River area], the homes and the plantations of the whole South were scenes of elegant hospitality. Roman riches and the Roman villas and gardens of the days of Cicero, Atticus, and Lucullus were not more famed for elegant hospitality. The lives of the young men were but a training in all manly arts, all noble endeavor. . All outdoor sports and manly exercise were theirs. They delighted in horses and rode like centaurs. The ear and eye, accustomed to hunt and chase, could detect the rustle of a leaf and spy ptarmigan in snow. They fished with skill and swam like Leander. These manly exercises, with generous food and genial but hardy climate, resulted in fine physical perfection. They were as a class a handsome race of men. They were graduates of the best schools, and many of them foreign alumni. The first American to graduate in a foreign university was a Virginian. While born and trained as masters, the parental authority of the race taught them obedience and restraint. Their

Lieutenant Colonel William L. Mitchell, Co. F, 22nd North Carolina Infantry Regiment, circa 1863.

belief in the rights of man did not teach them socialism, nor independence of thought and worship in religion, nor skepticism of the great truths of Christianity. They were taught that "valor was the chiefest virtue. . . ." They were near enough to the frontier life of their fathers and to the [American] Revolution to catch at the fireside stories of the endurance, the skill, and the bravery of those who fought Indians, of how [George] Washington commanded and [Francis "Swamp Fox"] Marion rode. King's Mountain and Yorktown were to them places of pilgrimage; the graves of the heroes of the Revolution were around them. They had themselves declaimed in every schoolhouse from Richmond to Austin the fiery and patriotic words of Patrick Henry. It was not wonderful, then, that when the South was to be invaded—by whom they did not care, for what they did not stop to ask—her youth poured out from every schoolhouse, college, and university at the first call. . . .[202] — L. B. MCFARLAND, CONFEDERATE VETERANS REUNION, MACON, GEORGIA

THE PROUDEST DAY OF ALL
☛ You are to-day paroled as prisoners, not as slaves. The love of liberty which led you into this conflict burns as bright in your hearts as ever. Cherish it: teach your children the principles of State rights and the rights of freemen, and teach them ever to maintain these principles. Teach them that the proudest day in all your career was that on which you enlisted to fight for your our beloved Dixie Land, for God and native land. Farewell.[203] — CONFEDERATE GENERAL ROBERT FREDERICK HOKE, SPEECH TO HIS MEN AT SURRENDER, DURHAM, NORTH CAROLINA, MAY 9, 1865

THE IMPORTANCE OF WILLIAM RAWLE
☛ . . . To conduct a campaign against error, those who would lead must know that they know what they know. In our work we must not only love and honor our heroes and learn the true story of their deeds, but we must know how our people arrived at their course of action when the time for the parting of the ways was come.

It is generally known that many leading men of the South were strongly opposed to seceding from the Union, though firmly convinced of our right to do so—a right that had been claimed seven times prior to 1860, once in 1832 by South Carolina and six times in New England. In 1811 Josiah Quincy advocated the withdrawal of Massachusetts, declaring that the admission of Louisiana to the Union guaranteed the right of separation to all the States, to be effected peaceably if they could, forcibly if they must. In 1814 the Hartford Convention withdrew New England from the Union. In 1844 Massachusetts declared that she "would submit her undelegated rights to no body of men on earth." Thus the records repeatedly had shown their assertion in New England of the right to secede from the Union.

The creed of States' rights had been practiced and recognized according to one of the salient features of the now much battered Constitution of our fathers, and had been taught in the Military Academy at West Point from a book . . . [William] Rawles's, *A View of the Constitution of the United States of America*, in use from 1825 to 1840. From this source were acquired the beliefs that prompted the choice of sides on the part of Jefferson Davis, Robert E. Lee, Stonewall Jackson, Albert Sidney Johnston, Joseph E. Johnston, Joseph Wheeler, and others of the gods of war that directed the marvelous military maneuvers of the Southern army.

When asked, O Daughters of the Confederacy, why the War between the States should not be called the War of Rebellion, remember that you are daughters of men who held with Rawles's *A View of the Constitution of the United States of America*:

> "The right of secession must be considered an ingredient in the original Constitution of the general government."

Even while Rawles's "View of the Constitution" was temporarily ignored, a well-known effort to try Jefferson Davis for his life on the charge of treason was abandoned, because it would prove that he but followed the faith learned at the mother knee of the country in her training school at West Point. Thus did the Constitution vindicate the Southern people against the charge of being rebels or traitors. . . .[204] — MRS. W. D. LAMAR, PRESIDENT GEORGIA DIVISION, U.D.C.

WHY KENTUCKIANS TOOK UP ARMS

☞ . . . In the fact that Kentucky for sixty years played such a conspicuous part in the great debates which ushered in the War of the States lies in no small measure the explanation of Confederate Kentucky. Not to perpetuate human slavery did our fathers leave home and fireside to march under the blood-red cross of the Southland, but to maintain those eternal rights of local self-government which ever since Runnymede their forefathers had been gradually wresting from the favored few who had gathered all authority unto themselves. . . . [205] — REVEREND FRANK M. THOMAS, ADDRESS BEFORE THE U.C.V. AND U.D.C., LOUISVILLE, KENTUCKY, OCTOBER 8, 1912

THE CONFEDERATE CAUSE WAS THE PEOPLE'S RIGHTS
☛ . . . We think that Robert E. Lee was the noblest and grandest soldier and man combined that the world has ever produced. Stonewall Jackson, the vigorous and skillful leader, who walked with God in prayer and used his divinely given genius for the defense for the rights and homes of his people, is to us the embodiment of all that was great and sublime in a Christian soldier's life. To our minds the world has not produced his equal. Albert Sidney Johnston, Joseph E. Johnston, Jeb Stuart, John H. Morgan, Joe Wheeler, Nathan Bedford Forrest, Wade Hampton, Hood, Longstreet, and hundreds of thousands of the men who carried the guns are heroes to us that the world can never match.

Of the 600,000 Southern soldiers, one in every eleven died on the battle field under the Confederate flag. Of the 3,000,000 [Union] men who came, as they believed, to save the nation's life, 47 percent died under the Union flag. The issues that demanded these unparalleled sacrifices were settled in 1865. The men of the South yielded when a prolongation of the struggle meant anarchy, ruin, and a useless waste of life. When Robert E. Lee surrendered because he thought it his duty to surrender, the men of the South acquiesced in his judgment. We believe we failed, not because we were wrong, but because you men of the North had more soldiers, better food, longer and better guns, and more resources than the men of the South. The war could not have been avoided. No arbitration could settle the issues that reached a climax in 1860-61. It has been determined that the States are one, that the Union is indissoluble. War settled that, and it is concluded forever.[206]

But admit all this, my countrymen, and yet there is something greater in a country than its armies, mere potent than its battling legions. The heart and conscience of the American people can put armies can put armies to flight, batter down forts, and sink warships. It can arise to the noblest conceptions of what is right, and against this conviction of 100,000,000 of freemen armies are pygmies and battleships little more than children's toys. The American people in the end will settle all questions right and eventually along lines that will promote the noblest ends of liberty and the highest claims of freedom.[207] — GENERAL BENNETT H. YOUNG, COMMANDER-IN-CHIEF UNITED CONFEDERATE VETERANS, ADDRESS, GATHERING OF CONFEDERATE & UNION VETERANS, GETTYSBURG, PENNSYLVANIA, SUMMER 1913

OUR CAUSE WAS NOT "LOST"
☛ Speaking of the "Lost Cause," it was not lost. If the cause meant anything, it meant "States' rights.". . .[208] — DR. H. K. YATES, PASTOR OF THE FIRST PRESBYTERIAN CHURCH, NASHVILLE, TENNESSEE

WHY AT LEAST ONE UNION GENERAL WAS ENTHUSIASTICALLY PRO STATES' RIGHTS
☛ . . . [New Englander] Major General [Erasmus D.] Keyes, U. S. A., a very gracious and a lifelong friend of [Union General George H.] Thomas [of Virginia], replied to my question about him as to whether it was true that the latter was known as one of the most pronounced State's rights men in the army. "Undoubtedly," Keyes replied. "He served under me two years, and was most violent in his denunciations of the North." "Well," quoth I, "to what do you attribute his going over to your side?" Then that wicked, wicked old warrior whispered with a wink: "You see, my dear fellow, 'twas simply another case of the gray mare's [the Union military] being the better horse."

. . . [After] paying a noble tribute to Thomas, [Keyes] says: "His wife [Frances L. Kellogg] was a noble Northern woman and his deference to her was great, and it is my opinion that it was her influence more than any other consideration that determined him to cast his fortunes with us [the Union]. Had he followed his own inclinations, he would have joined the Confederates and fought against the North with the same ability and valor that he displayed in our cause."

. . . Both [of Gen. Thomas'] . . . brothers served in the Confederate army, and so did all his near kinsmen, both on his father's and his mother's side. Neither of his sisters, who were greatly devoted to him, ever spoke to him again after he turned his back on his State, and only one of his brothers. . . .[209] — CAPTAIN W. GORDON MCCABE, U.C.V.

OUR VOLUNTARY COMPACT

☛ . . . As you gather here for this Reunion it might be well for the instruction of those who come after you and in the interest of the truth of history to consider for a few moments the causes which called you into being and provoked the War between the States. Let me say in the beginning that human slavery was not the cause of the four years of war between the sovereign states of this republic. Let me say that I deny with all the emphasis of my soul that the people of the South were actuated throughout that dreadful conflict by no higher motive than that of African slavery. The war was produced by a difference in construction of the organic law of the land. The Southern States insisted in 1861, as they had insisted ever since the formation of the government, that the Federal Union was a government with no power other than such as had been delegated to it by the States through the instrumentality of the Constitution. The Northern States contended that the Federal government was supreme, while the Southern States contended for the sovereignty of the respective States, and this clash of opposing opinion continued until the Southern States sought peaceably to withdraw from the Federal Union. We believed we had the right to peaceably withdraw from a compact into which we had voluntarily entered. We were willing to remain in the Union so long as the original agreement was respected, so long as the sovereignty of the States was preserved, so long as our rights under the Constitution were safe; but when the Federal government passed into the hands of those who openly trampled upon the compact of the Union, denied the sovereignty of the States, and declared the Constitution to be a "compact with the devil and a league with hell," we attempted, as we had the right to do, to peaceably withdraw from the Union of "free and independent" States.

For four long years [the Confederate National Flag] the Stars and Bars floated proudly over the Southland, sustained by the bravest soldiery the world ever saw. Victorious on nearly every field of battle, although usually overwhelmingly outnumbered, the soldiers of the Southern Confederacy gave to the world exhibitions of military prowess and dauntless courage furnished by no other war in all the annals of time. Poorly provided with munitions of war, scantily clothed, and only half fed, the brave and unconquerable sons of the South, inspired with a deathless love of country and nerved with the righteousness of their cause, held at bay for four years not simply the armies of the North, but the legions of hired Hessians [that is, foreigners] from all over the world. At last in the providence of God the star of the Confederacy went down in gloom on the field of Appomattox. Overcome but not conquered, overpowered but not subdued, the Confederate States of America passed from among the nations of the earth without a stain of dishonor upon her fair name. . . .[210] — FLORIDA REPRESENTATIVE FRANK CLARK, ADDRESS, ANNUAL REUNION OF THE UNITED SONS OF CONFEDERATE VETERANS

THE SECESSION OF THE DOMINION STATE
☛ . . . The election of Abraham Lincoln to the presidency in 1860 marked the triumph of a [far Left-wing] party [at the time, the Republican party] pronouncing freedom national and slavery sectional. This election, with its attendant issues, precipitated the passing of ordinances of secession by the States of South Carolina, Georgia, Florida, Alabama, and Mississippi. Louisiana seceded in January, 1861, and Texas in February. The question of a State's right to secede was one of enormous import. The Constitution was not explicit on this point [though it is tacitly implied in the 9th and 10th Amendments],[211] and each section felt the right to construe it in its own way.[212]

In Virginia's ratification of the Constitution these words occur:

> "We, the delegates of the people of Virginia, do declare and make known that the powers granted under the Constitution, being derived from the people of the United States, may be resumed by them whensoever the same shall be perverted to their injury or oppression, and that every power not granted thereby remains with them and at their will."

There was little, if any, question in the minds of Virginians as to their State's right to secede. The question was, had the time come for the exercise of this privilege? . . .[213] — MISS MARY L. VON DER AU, ATHENS, GEORGIA

THE HOMING OF THE GRAY
☛ Through half a century I see more clear than yesterday
That lonely march, that fateful march, the homing of the gray.
Wrecks of former pride, we came to ruin, wastes, and tears;
Nor have we caught the world step through all the cruel years.
And we have paid the blood price. Shall the grave be all our gain?

You owe us, all! you owe us; long and heavy is the score,
Vain all your gold to pay it, all your plaudits vain,

And your boasted song and story leave it as before.
Vain bronze and soaring marble, though it cleave the Southern blue:
    But would you square the tally sheet and even reverse the score?
Stand for the rights we stood for, stand foursquare and true,
And rear your children's children to guard them evermore.[214] — CONFEDERATE MAJOR T. H. BLACKNALL

MIGHT DOES NOT MAKE RIGHT
☛ . . . [The vast majority of Confederate veterans] . . . never believed, and do not now believe, that material success and prosperity are tests of righteousness or that, because unlimited resources of men and munitions of war can triumph over a weaker government, therefore the weaker government was wrong and should have submitted without a conflict. Might does not make right, and our people felt that they fought for the right as it was guaranteed to them in the Constitution of their fathers; and, as Gen. Robert E. Lee expressed himself, they would have been false to duty if they had done otherwise.

Believing thus, that the South fought for the preservation of the original Constitution, I am bound to believe that the triumph of the Union was the overthrow of the Constitution, which was the bond of Union and was the forcing upon us of a government essentially different from the only one that could have been accepted by the States when they entered the Union. And I believe that this new government was in direct violation of the foundation principle of civil liberty, as announced in the Declaration of Independence, that governments "derive their just powers from the consent of the governed."

But the Southern people, having done their utmost to preserve their rights under the original Constitution and having been overpowered by brute force, could only surrender and yield to the arbitrament of war. In accepting the new order they now feel bound in honor to be loyal to the new government. It has become their government by the terms of capitulation, and they are duty bound to strive to make it a benefit and a blessing to all the people. Recognizing the difficulties and the dangers that threaten us under our new conditions, we should endeavor to ward off the evils and to make our government a real promoter of liberty and as far as possible to remedy the ruin by our defeat. . . .[215] — REV. JAMES H. MCNEILLY, D.D., CONFEDERATE VETERAN, NASHVILLE, TENNESSEE

THE CAUSES OF THE WAR BETWEEN THE STATES

☛ Four hundred years ago in that part of "Merrie England" where are situated the counties of Nottingham, Lincoln, and York lived a band of dissenters who, though loyal to the king, were rebels against the authority of the Established Church. They were called Puritans.

In that far day, as some gay Cavalier and Churchman cantered along those winding lanes upon his gayly bedecked steed and was scowled at from the roadside by one of those stern-faced religionists, there were sown the seed which developed into fruit in our War between the States three centuries later.

The causes that led to this war were many. Some were direct, others collateral; but the one deep underlying cause of the war was the difference in temperament and the differing points of view upon all subjects of the people North and South and the jealousy of the North, particularly the New England Puritan element, for the easy-going and luxury-loving Cavalier element of the South.

The Puritan conscience was ever a troublous thing, allowing its possessor no rest and boding ill for those whose views or modes of living were at variance with the stern and harsh tenets which were supposed to govern the lives of the Puritans. Burning of witches and abolitionism may seem far apart, but the same causes operated in both cases. It was fanaticism, a determination to make others believe and live as they did and at any cost; that was the ruling motive in both instances.

It is not a far cry from Cotton Mather, denouncing witchcraft and those who did not believe in witchcraft, with the Indian slave girl Tituba at his side, and sending to horrible deaths or to torture and prison over two hundred innocent people, to Henry Ward Beecher, standing in his pulpit, a Winchester rifle across his Bible and a mulatto slave girl at his side, pouring out his invectives against the slaveholders and arousing to action and bloodshed the passions of the North.

Slavery was not the direct cause of the war; the South would not have fought to preserve slavery. In the adult white male population of the South not one man in every six owned even one slave. Nor was slavery held in the North to be a crime against either God or man until long after the slaves were found to be unprofitable in the North and had been sold South and the profit of this transaction safely stowed away in Northern pockets, where it remains to this good day. Only then was the enormity of slavery brought forward as a public question and abolitionism began to raise its ugly head.

The South protested against slavery; Virginia legislated against slavery thirty-two times; Georgia and the Carolinas legislated against it previous to 1760. The Historian General of the United Daughters of the Confederacy, Miss [Mildred Lewis] Rutherford, says:

> "Thomas Jefferson's original draft of the Declaration of Independence had a protest against the slave trade; and John Adams, of Massachusetts [the birthplace of both the American slave trade and American slavery], advised that it be stricken out."[216]

Georgia was the first slave State to legislate in opposition to the slave trade, while Massachusetts was the first State to legislate in favor of it. Slavery was as surely forced upon the Southern States as was opium upon China and for the same reason—money.

As new territory came into the Union through conquest and purchase, and as much of this territory lay geographically where Southern influence would naturally dominate, the Northern fear of the growth of Southern power grew, and Northern jealousy increased. The Louisiana Purchase in 1803 was viewed with disfavor in the North. The conquest of Mexican territory and the admission of Texas into the Union increased Northern uneasiness and jealousy. The right of States to withdraw from the Union was early brought into play. In the beginning of the nineteenth century, when a Southern man and slaveholder [that is, Thomas Jefferson] was President of the United States and the Louisiana Territory was secured from [French Emperor] Napoleon [Bonaparte] by purchase, Massachusetts threatened to secede, and Josiah Quincy favored it. The South wanted war with England in 1812 to secure the freedom of the seas, but New England was opposed to it and threatened to secede from the Union if war with England was declared. Massachusetts, jealous of Southern power, again in 1820 threatened to secede if Missouri was admitted into the Union as a slave State. The right of these States to threaten secession and to carry these threats into effect was never questioned; it was universally recognized. It was only when the South at a later period sought to exercise the same right that the right was disputed and the cry of "rebellion" raised at the North.

The differences between the sections multiplied with the passage of time. Free labor at the South and paid labor at the North operated to the advantage of the South. Tariff bills were passed by the manufacturing North which were oppressive to the agricultural South. The breach widened.

The attitude of the North before the war was one of dictation; that of the South was resistance to outside dictation and interference. The North waged a war of invasion and coercion; the South one of self-defense and resistance to invasion and coercion. When [big government Liberal Abraham] Lincoln was elected, representing to the Southern mind the rise to supreme power in the Union of those [Left-wing] elements in the North most determined to defy the Constitution, to coerce the South, and to force that section to live by rules of conduct laid down in despised abolition councils, then the South sought safety and peace by withdrawing apart from these disturbing elements.

South Carolina seceded; other Southern States rapidly took the same steps. Virginia, with a love for the Union, which she had been so largely instrumental in creating and fashioning and preserving, made desperate efforts to stay the storm. To make the Union possible she had given from her own body the extensive territory of the Northwest. Her sons, [George] Washington, Jefferson, Patrick Henry, [John] Marshall, and others, had already figured in the formation and preservation of the Union. "Without her," says Thomas Nelson in his book, *R. E. Lee, the Southerner*, "no Union would have been formed, and without her no Union would have been preserved during the early decades of its existence." Only when coercion was used and invasion threatened did Virginia exercise her constitutional rights and secede, drawing the sword in defense and not in attack. South Carolina, standing on her right to withdraw from a compact which she had helped to formulate, a right previously asserted to be theirs by those States which were now denying it to her, demanded of the Northern government that its troops be withdrawn from her territory. Lincoln promised a commission sent to negotiate these subjects that no reinforcements or supplies should be sent to the troops of the North holding Fort Sumter while these questions were being debated.

Violating this pledge, Lincoln secretly started both supplies and reinforcements toward Fort Sumter in a fleet of several vessels. Undoubtedly this was the first blow struck in the war; it was the first act of war. In the face of this treachery South Carolina in self-defense attacked and reduced Fort Sumter before the reinforcements and supplies could arrive. At once throughout the North the cry was raised that the flag had been fired upon, and troops were started South to coerce and punish that section and force it back into the Union. The die was cast, and the contest began.[217] — ARTHUR H. JENNINGS, COMMANDER GARLAND RODES CAMP, S. C. V., LYNCHBURG, VIRGINIA

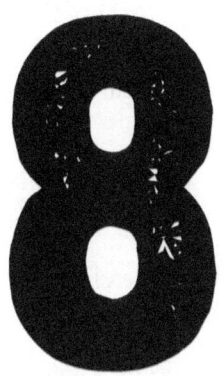

WORLD WAR I SOLDIERS & CONFEDERATE SOLDIERS
☛ With all the machinery, long-range guns, poisonous gases, aeroplanes and air vessels, deep and long ditches, bombproofs, and submarine gunboats of the war now going on in Europe, there has never been displayed any personal chivalry, bravery, and heroism surpassing that of the gallant and heroic boys who wore the gray in the long and strenuous War between the States; for we were actuated by patriotism, lovers of God and native land, fighting for wives, children, and the "girls we left behind us," fighting for a cause we knew was right with all our God-given might, never conquered but overcome by superior numbers and resources, as said our immortal Lee in his farewell address at Appomattox.[218] — REVEREND ARNOLD WRIGHT, BIRMINGHAM, ALABAMA

MORE CONFEDERATE MONUMENTS THAN ANY OTHER
☛ A thrill of pride moves every impulse of our manhood as we proclaim to the world that there are more monuments built to commemorate Confederate history than have ever been erected to any other cause, civil, religious, or political.[219] — GENERAL BENNETT H. YOUNG, DALLAS, TEXAS

A POEM TO THE TRUE CONQUERORS
☛ We live in dreams as well as deeds, in thoughts as well as acts,
And life through things we feel, not know, is realized the most;
The conquered are the conquerors, despite the face of facts,

If they still feel their cause was just who fought for it and lost.[220] — MADISON JULIUS CAWEIN

TIME IS A GENTLEMAN
☛ Time is a gentleman, brave and cool,
Who knows what each State meant
When patriot sires made self-rule
Supreme o'er government.

Having no thought of gain or fear,
Who won or lost the fight,
Time is a gentleman; he'll make clear
Whose cause was just and right.

Time is a gentleman; his decrees
No force can swerve from right.
Unawed, unbought, he calmly sees
And rights the wrongs of might.

Time, a gentleman, thus will accost
The ages in their flight;
A cause that is just is never lost.
Though it may lose the fight.

Time is a gentleman. See how he
Puts in approving light
The cause of gentleman Robert Lee,
The cause of truth and right.[221] — SAM A. GAINES, WASHINGTON, D.C.

A KENTUCKY MOTHER LECTURES HER SON ON THE EVE OF WORLD WAR I
☛ . . . as she takes me tight into her arms [she] exclaims: "But O, my boy, there's another flag you must never, never forget. Look, it's the Stars and Bars." And she draws out the tattered folds from an old chest. "It's the flag of your Kentucky grandfather. He fought for the right of a sovereign State to make its own laws. It's the flag of Lee and of Jackson and Beauregard. Johnny boy, if Uncle Sam [U.S.A.] ever calls you to fight, remember that it will only be in the same old cause of your Armenian ancestors and of your Confederate grandfather, who was made a prisoner twice. It's the cause of the Stars and Bars fought again under the banner of a world's democracy, under our flag, yours and mine, Johnny boy,

the Stars and Stripes. And remember, Johnny boy, if ever Uncle Sam calls you, your Southern mother wants you to go." And Johnny boy is going.²²² — JOHN A. SHISHMANIAN

THE PRINCIPLES OF SELF-GOVERNMENT
☛ We are told by the politicians that the South appealed to war, and the issue has been decided against her, and therefore she must bury the dead issue. Now, I know of no proposition more at variance with the truth in its premises or more illogical in its conclusion. The South did not appeal to war; the North appealed to war and the South to God. War has decided the issue in one way; God perhaps in another. One war bears the same relation to the contest for a principle that one battle does to a war; and the [Battle of] First Manassas no more decided the struggle against the North than has the first war decided the principle of self-government, for which she contended, against the South. I do not say that the principle must of necessity be submitted to the arbitrament of another war, although many indications point in that direction; nor if a second war should occur do I maintain that it must necessarily be upon the same theater or between the same parties; but what I do say is that the question once submitted is still pending before the tribunal of high heaven, and in the end the judgment must be in favor of the right, and therefore the principle of self-government must in the end triumph.

Confederate Second Lieutenant Smith Spangler Turner, Co. B, 17ᵗʰ Virginia Infantry Regiment, circa 1864.

. . . Let it not be supposed that I am ignorant that the war was not waged on account of slavery. The true issue is eliminated by simply placing in juxtaposition two historical utterances. Said Mr. Lincoln in his first inaugural: "We do not fight to abolish slavery, but to restore the Union." Said Jefferson Davis to the semiofficial commission who sounded him as to the amicable adjustment of the controversy: "We do not fight for slavery, but for independence." Here, then, was the issue: the right of each State to govern itself. [Confederate General Stonewall] Jackson thought Virginia had this right, and in vindication of the justice of his view it would only be necessary to place side by side two other historical documents: the one the ratification by the people of Virginia of the Constitution of the United States on the 25th of June, 1788, and the other the repeal and abrogation of the same act by the ordinance of April 17, 1861; the one the delegation of specific powers by an admitted sovereign and such only as a sovereign could delegate, and the other the resumption of those powers in the case contemplated and provided for by the very act of delegation. If these passages from history do not make a platform broad and strong enough to support a man who believed himself right, then Jackson must fall. The intelligence of this present time has decided in his favor, and there is little danger of this verdict's being set aside in the future. Rather shall it be confirmed by posterity and ratified by history; so that Jackson shall not only be spoken of always, but shall be always well spoken of, his name itself a benediction throughout all ages.[223] — JUDGE DANIEL B. LUCAS

HOW THE SOCIALIST & COMMUNIST NORTH PROPAGANDIZED THE WORLD & HELPED LAUNCH LINCOLN'S WAR

☛ Historians have been busy assigning causes for the terrible war of 1861-65, which desolated the southern section of the United States and destroyed an institution which had become a part of its domestic life. The war is attributed to ignorance of each other in the two sections of the Union, to sectional prejudice, to conflict of economic interests, to different interpretations of the Constitution, to ambitious rivalries for supremacy in the government.

No doubt each of these factors contributed to bring about the final outbreak of hostilities and to the bitterness of the struggle. But in reality it was a war of conscience against conscience—a conflict of moral ideals. Each side believed it was contending for righteousness against iniquity. The [Liberal] North thought it was fighting against an order of society unjust and oppressive; the [Conservative] South believed it was fighting for a social order in the main kindly and beneficent. The North fought for a theory of human rights; the South for a condition, the best conserver of actual rights of two races widely different yet forced to live together.

It is frequently said that if the Northern people [Liberals] had known the actual condition of the slaves in the South [Conservatives] and the kind feeling which in general subsisted between master and slave, then all bitterness of feeling would have disappeared and the radical demands of the abolitionists [that is, socialists and communists] would have been so modified that the questions could have been settled without war.

But the chief obstacle to settlement was that these abolitionists, with their active [communist] propaganda, would not accept any fact that would controvert their theory of human rights. Intensely prejudiced and partisan [Left-wing] writers with very limited opportunities to know all the facts went through the South to observe conditions. They reported the exceptional cases of cruelty and oppression, and their statements were accepted as gospel, which no amount of evidence could invalidate as to the terrible condition of the slaves and the tyranny of the masters. Thus the conscience of the Northern people was aroused against a system for which they felt the nation was responsible. At the same time the conscience of the Southern people resented what they felt was an injustice to them and a false judgment of their institutions.

When conscience is involved in any great question, compromises are only temporary. At length it has to be settled by force, the appeal to arms, that *ultima ratio regum*. Although the result of the appeal is not necessarily just and righteous, war never settles the right or wrong of anything. It often only establishes some giant wrong. One of the mightiest agencies of oppression and injustice in this world has been a perverted conscience. Our Saviour warned his disciples that their persecutors would think they did God service. And the horrors of the Inquisition were inflicted by conscientious ecclesiastics. No doubt many of those who accomplished the emancipation of the slaves in the South at such fearful cost of blood and treasure, of life and suffering have the approval of their own consciences, and congratulate themselves on their success as agents of God's righteousness. Yet we of the South, who were the victims of that conscience, believe that it was blinded, perverted, and unjust. And our consciences do not reproach us for having resisted to the utmost of our power.

It was essentially the Puritan [Left-wing] conscience which forced on the war. And inasmuch as the Southern [Conservative] conscience was as firm in its conviction as to the duty of resistance, the war was inevitable. My observation of the Puritan [Yankee Liberal] and my reading of his history leads me to think that when he has made up his mind as to what is right no amount of fact is allowed to interfere with his course. Every one must admire his stern devotion to principle as he sees it, his firmness of purpose, his self-sacrificing zeal, his energy, his independence of thought, and his brave assertion of that independence at any cost.

But on the other hand I have noted an intolerance of opposition, an assumption of infallibility in judgment, a self-confidence which would denounce the Almighty if he differed from the Puritan idea, a willingness to deny or to pervert and misrepresent facts, to sustain a theory which have led to persecution and oppression in order to establish a certain theory or course of conduct. So in the early days of New England Baptists and Quakers were banished because their consciences could not conform to those of the Puritan.

In the course of nearly half a century as a minister of the gospel I have had various illustrations of this peculiarity of the Puritan [Liberal] conscience which will not accept any fact that would contradict its moral ideals. And let it be said that the Puritan has been so masterful in the realm of higher thinking that he has molded and controlled the ideals of the whole northern section of our country. He has claimed liberty to his own opinions, also liberty to force them on others.

Starting my ministerial life with the highest admiration for the Puritan, I fear I shall close it with a feeling of utter revolt against his [Left-leaning] character as an enemy of true liberty of conscience. This feeling applies only to the English Puritan, from [Oliver] Cromwell down, until I sometimes wonder whether to class the great Lord Protector as hypocrite or saint.

But my purpose in this paper is to give some illustrations of that stubborn prejudice in the [Liberal] North which misrepresented and misjudged the [Conservative] South and which refused to listen to any facts that might correct or modify opinions that rested on theory and not fact.

The theory was that all slavery was wrong, a violation of inalienable rights; that it must necessarily oppress and maltreat the slave, and also it must brutalize the master and make him cruel; therefore Southern slavery must be a system of cruel oppression, and that any facts to the contrary were only exceptional. So the system was denounced as "the sum of all villainies," and conscience was invoked and cultivated to destroy it. The abolitionist [socialists and communists] gloried in the war of emancipation as a righteous war. The true Southerners [Conservatives] looked upon it as an unrighteous [Left-wing] attack upon a social order which was forced on them largely by the Puritan [Yankee Liberal] and whose overthrow would bring dire consequences.

The first illustration I shall give was related to me by the late Col. John McGavock, of Franklin, Tenn. [owner of Carnton Plantation].[224] He was a typical gentleman of the old school, brave, gentle, upright, scorning a lie or any hypocrisy with utmost contempt. In his boyhood days he spent a good deal of his time in Washington with his relative, Hon. Felix Grundy, Senator from Tennessee. He heard frequently the discussions in the Senate between the great leaders, Clay, Calhoun, Webster, Benton, and their peers. It was my privilege to enjoy the friendship of Colonel McGavock for a number of years before his death, and his reminiscences of those days were exceedingly interesting. As he sat in his great arm-chair, which had belonged to General [Andrew] Jackson, and talked of those old days of strenuous debate, I felt that his memories ought to be recorded as a valuable contribution to the history of the time.

Among other things, he told me that several years before the war a prominent United States Senator visited Tennessee and was the guest of Gen. W. G. Harding at Belle Meade,[225] the celebrated stock farm near Nashville. He spent several days observing closely the life of the place, and all were pleased with his agreeable manners and his brilliant conversation, revealing the treasures of a wide culture. He asked General Harding if there would be objection to his talking with the negroes on the place, as he wished to know the facts of our Southern life. He was told to make himself perfectly at home and to speak any of them freely on any subject he chose. Of course it was understood that he wished to hear the slave's version of his condition. The guest was a gentleman, and had no such thought as stirring disaffection among the slaves. He went into the quarters and saw them at their meals and on to the farm and saw them at work. He talked with [black] men and women. He was impressed with the intelligence and answers of one especially, who became afterwards the noted "Uncle Bob," in charge of the thoroughbreds. He suspected that Bob knew who he was and that he had been posted as to his answers, so he said after a long talk: "Do you know who I am?" Bob answered promptly [though incorrectly]: "Yes, sir; you are Marse Pony Cheatham"—a man whom Bob had seen at Belle Meade and who bore some resemblance to him.

When his visit ended, Mr. S. was very cordial in his thanks to General Harding for the opportunity of seeing for himself the life of a large Southern plantation. Colonel McGavock, who had it from General Harding, said that the guest remarked in substance: "Well, sir, the institution is entirely different from what I had supposed.

Sir, this is really the old patriarchal system of the family, like that of Abraham."

Yet this man went home and, disregarding his own observations, was induced to listen to the statements of [Left-wing] partisans, and was driven by the exigencies of party to become the most bitter in his denunciations of the South and its institutions. His [largely socialistic and communistic] theory of the wrongs of slavery must be maintained.

Another illustration of this [biased] peculiarity of the [Liberal] New England mind was given to me by one of my teachers in college.

In the years 1854 to 1856 I was a student at Jackson College, in Columbia, Tenn., which was [illegally and unnecessarily] burned by the Federal forces in 1864. I was fifteen years old when I entered. The students were assigned rooms in the college building—four to a room—for study by day; and as the rooms were all occupied, the professor of Latin and Greek took me to room with him. He was an old bachelor, and treated me as a son. He was a native of Maine, a graduate of Bowdoin College, the *Alma Mater* of Longfellow, Hawthorne, and Franklin Pierce. He was a man of broad and liberal culture, who bought and read many books. One day in the late fall, when we had begun to have fire in our room, he came in with a new book and sat down to read. After a while he got up and thrust the book into the grate. Of course I was surprised, and asked why he did it. He said: "That book is Mrs. Harriet Beecher Stowe's Sunny Memories of Foreign Lands. I thought I had a book of travels, which I know Mrs. Stowe could write well. Instead, it is only an abolition document." I afterwards learned his experience of abolitionism, which was in substance that after his graduation he determined to be a teacher. So he looked for a place which would yield him a living. There was a better prospect in the South then than in his own home [state]. Although he was against slavery and was prejudiced against the South, yet for the sake of the salary he swallowed his prejudices and came to Pulaski, in Giles County, Tenn., where he secured a select school of boys, twelve or fifteen sons of the neighboring planters. He thought he could stand it for a few years until he could make enough money to return to God's country, and there spend the rest of his life as a teacher amid congenial [Left-wing] surroundings. After a little while, as he became acquainted, he was invited nearly every week to go home with one or other of the boys to stay from Friday evening until Sunday morning, when the family came to the town to church. At the end of six months he wrote home to his people in Maine, telling them that they were mistaken as to slavery; that it was not the cruel system they imagined it was. They answered that he had not had a chance to see the dark side. At the end of a year he wrote again, urging them to revise their judgment. They replied that the slave holders, knowing that he was from the North, had concealed the cruel features of their treatment of the slaves, and that he did not know the real conditions.

He then concluded to write no more on the subject, but to take utmost pains to inform himself on the general treatment of negroes by white masters. At the end of three years he expected to return to Maine, and then in personal talk with his family and friends he would convince them of their error. But he was sadly disappointed. He went back to spend three months before returning to Tennessee, where he had made up his mind to spend the rest of his life. He had been at home only a short time when the subject of slavery was brought up. He told them simply what he had seen, not concealing the occasional cruelties nor apologizing for the real evil of the system. He told of the contentment of the slaves, their freedom from care, the provision for food and clothing, the attention in sickness, the kind feelings of master and slave for each other. He only asked that they recognize facts and the difficulties in the way of carrying out their theories.

His friends were impatient with his story, and finally intimated in plain terms that he was in the pay for the [slave] holders, hired to make false statements; that they knew that conditions were different from his representations.

At the end of three weeks he had enough of Maine, and he packed his trunk and came back to Tennessee. I understood that he never went back to his old home until after the war, when he married and took his bride to see his people.

He did what he could for the Confederacy, serving in hospitals and in such positions as his strength would permit. His last years were spent in the ministry of the gospel.

Another incident involving two ministers of the gospel will show how thoroughly this prejudice existed in the Churches of the North. It was related to me several years ago by the late Mrs. Mary Thompson, the mother of the Hon. John Thompson, Commissioner of Agriculture of Tennessee, and of Mr. Joseph H. Thompson, a prominent banker of Nashville. She was one of the loveliest and saintliest characters I ever knew, and also most charitable in her judgment of everybody.

The General Assembly of the Presbyterian Church met in the First Presbyterian Church in Nashville, Tenn., in May, 1855. Dr.

Edgar, the pastor, and his committee of entertainment received two letters, one from a minister in New England, the other from a minister in the West. These men were brothers, who had not met for twenty years, being in such widely separated fields. Each was appointed a commissioner to the Assembly. They asked that if possible they be assigned to the same home during the Assembly's meeting.

Mrs Thompson's husband, Mr. John Thompson, was very much interested in these letters, and asked that the brothers be sent to his home. He lived on a large plantation a few miles from the city. He promised to put a comfortable buggy and a gentle horse at their disposal, so that they could go and come at their pleasure.

On the afternoon before the meeting of the Assembly Mrs. Thompson went to meet her guests and brought them to her home. It was a pleasant May day, and they were delighted with the freshness and beauty of the country. While they were sitting in the parlor for a few minutes before going to their room the [black] house maid came in to make some inquiry or announcement, and she and her mistress had some little talk aside. As she left the room the ministers looked after her with evident surprise. At length one of them said to Mrs. Thompson: "She didn't seem to be afraid of you." Her reply was: "Afraid? Why should she be afraid of me?" He said: "Why, we had understood that the black people do not dare to speak to the whites without permission, and they usually get down on their knees." Of course Mrs. Thompson ridiculed his foolish and false ideas.

The work on the plantation interested them very much. It was the season of planting, and everybody was up early and everything was moving from morning until night. The ministers were busy too, seeing as much as they could in the intervals of the Assembly's sessions.

When the Assembly adjourned, Mr. Thompson invited them to remain with him as long as they could, that they might see more of Southern life and the condition of the slaves. They gladly accepted his invitation, and spent several days in going over his place and in visiting the neighboring plantations. They were shown the storerooms with bales and bolts of cloth to make up into clothing for the negroes, with boxes of boots and shoes and hats and caps; the work rooms, where Mrs. Thompson directed the sewing women; the smoke-houses, with the great supply of cured meats; the mills for grinding the corn; the nursery for the babies while the mothers were at work; the cabins in which the negroes lived, each with its garden spot; the barns and stables and tool houses—in a word, all the necessary equipment of a large plantation, with its many slaves forming a village in itself, clustered about the "big house" of the "white folks."

They visited Colonel [John] Overton's and General [William G.] Harding's plantations ["Traveler's Rest" and "Belle Meade" respectively] and several of the farms of the neighborhood. They seemed much surprised at the general air of content and happiness which prevailed among the negroes, to whom they spoke freely, asking many questions.

Mr. Thompson told them that several of these gentlemen owned plantations in Arkansas and Mississippi, where they raised cotton and where the life was much the same as here, under the direction of a trusted overseer and his family. He told them that what they had seen was a fair sample of the treatment of the slaves generally by their owners; that, while there were no doubt cruel masters, they were the exception, and public opinion as well as [the law and] self-interest restrained them from excess of harshness.

The brothers were very thankful for the attentions which they had received, and said to Mr. Thompson: "We have had our eyes opened. Now how can we repay your kindness and show our appreciation?" He replied in substance:

> "Gentlemen, I foresee great trouble for our country in the near future to come from the agitation of this question of slavery. Your people are denouncing us with great bitterness as the oppressors of a helpless race. They do not know the actual condition and treatment of the slaves nor the difficulties that beset their demands. This is with us not a question of a theory of human rights, but of actual facts with which we have to deal, and we are trying to give the negroes all the rights which they are fit to exercise. Surely if your people but knew the truth, they would cease their agitation of a question which they are incompetent to deal with. The Southern people cannot be expected to submit patiently to abuse which they feel to be unjust. Now I ask of you gentlemen that when you go home, one to the East, the other to the West, you tell your people just what you have seen of the treatment of the slaves. Use your position and influence to get facts before them. I do not wish you to apologize for us nor to cover any unfavorable facts which you have noted. You have seen a fair example of the way the large proportion of the negroes are treated. You also can judge of the difficulty in the way of freeing such a mass of an utterly different and inferior [in other words, as yet still largely uneducated] race from the restraints of slavery and having them live among us. And you might at least help to stop this agitation."

Mrs. Thompson heard the whole conversation of which I have given the substance. She said that as her husband ceased speaking both ministers threw up their hands and said:

> "Mr. Thompson, if we were to tell our people exactly what we have seen just as we have seen it, we could not keep our pulpits a month. We would be set down by public opinion as liars, bribed by the slaveholders. Our people are so set in their views of slavery that they would not believe a word we spoke and would refuse to hear us preach."

Mr. Thompson loved the Union with his whole heart. His father was one of the pioneer settlers of Tennessee. He bade his guests "good-bye" with a heavy heart, feeling that if they judged their own people aright there was no escape from a bloody conflict of the sections.

Several years ago I spent some weeks in Edinburgh [Scotland] and Belfast [now Northern Ireland], and met some of the most intelligent and fair-minded Scotchmen and Irishmen. Of course they asked me about the life of the South, and seemed astonished that Christian people could defend the institution of slavery. I became convinced that for years the abolitionists [that is, socialists and communists] of the North had systematically carried on a propaganda of misrepresentation and falsehood for the purpose of prejudicing the minds of the European peoples against us, and to a large extent they had succeeded. I was enabled to correct some of these false impressions. But while some were willing to hear our side, others refused to believe me. These two classes of foreigners were represented directly after the war by two different delegations that visited this country.

The circumstances were given to me by the Rev. Dr. Thomas V. Moore, for many years pastor in Richmond, Va., and afterwards pastor of the First Presbyterian Church in Nashville, where he died, and by the Rev. Dr. E. T. Baird, Presbyterian Secretary of Publication. Two or three years after the close of the war a delegation from the Free Church

Lieutenant General Nathan Bedford Forrest, Forrest's Cavalry, circa 1863.

of Scotland, consisting of the Rev. Drs. Patrick Fairbairn and Edgar, visited this country, to bear greetings to the Presbyterian General Assembly North. Dr. Fairbairn was a distinguished professor and author, and had edited in Scotland a volume which Dr. Moore had issued in this country.

On landing in New York, some days before the meeting of the Assembly, they were cordially welcomed, and in their speeches they were effusive in congratulating the pious North for its glorious work in breaking the fetters of four millions of bondmen. They were equally effusive in condemning the South for her effort to rivet those same fetters more firmly. As there was time to spare, they visited Richmond, as Dr. Fairbairn wished to visit his friend, Dr. Moore. They wished to see something of how the negroes lived in slavery. Drs. Moore, Moses Hoge, and Baird took pains to show them some of the old homes around Richmond and visited several of the old plantations down the James River. They pointed out the negro quarters, with their cabins and gardens, and also the various buildings in which provision was made for their comfort. They told of the life and work not only on the large plantations but on the smaller farms and in the villages and cities and in the homes of the masters. They told of the religious instruction of the slaves, of the buying and selling of them, and of their family life. The whole story was told honestly, not concealing the harsher features.

When the delegation was received by the General Assembly, the effort was made to have them repeat their speeches made on their arrival. But they evaded the subject of slavery and emancipation, and their references to the war were slight and guarded. Dr. Fairbairn intimated that he had found that they did not know enough to talk wisely on the subject.

After his return to Scotland, Dr. Fairbairn wrote letters to Dr. Moore expressing deep sympathy with the Southern people and Churches in the very difficult problems forced upon them by emancipation. Especially did he deplore the giving [of] the ballot to the negro. Dr. Moore gave me two or three of these letters, but in moving my library I have lost them.

Now for the other class of foreign critics. The next year another delegation came from Scotland on a similar mission. It consisted of Dr. James McCosh, afterwards the distinguished and able President of Princeton University, and Dr. William Arnot, a minister and author of great talent and learning. They also went to Richmond, anxious to see for themselves the conditions. They received the same courteous treatment from the same gentlemen, who took them on a steamer running to Norfolk, that they might see something of the old Virginia mansions. But Dr. Baird told me that the response to these courtesies, especially by Dr. Arnot, was so rude as to be positively insulting. Whenever any statement was made indicating that the negroes were well treated and happy, Dr. Arnot would dispute it in the most offensive manner: "No, sir! I know better than that; you can't deceive me. I have investigated this matter, and know that there was not a redeeming feature in the system." This in substance was his reply to anything that did not conform to his opinions, until at last Dr. Hoge, the most courteous of men, lost his patience and said to them: "As you seem to have no confidence in us as Christian gentlemen, we shall leave you to yourselves." So the Richmond gentlemen withdrew into the boat and had no more to do with the visitors. Dr. Baird said that he could not explain such boorishness in men of such unquestioned ability and high position except on the ground of inveterate prejudice with boundless self-conceit. I suppose all who know anything of Dr. McCosh know how profound was his confidence in his own opinions. I was told that when the visitors returned to Richmond they were entertained by a prominent negro family. If it were so, I can't see how any Southern man could attend Princeton under his presidency.

These incidents show how difficult it was to get the facts before the Northern and the British people. In Great Britain the anti-slavery sentiment expressed itself in self-righteous glorification of English freedom in contrast with the slavery-darkened United States. It was their boast that as soon as the foot of a slave touched English soil one breath of English air made him a free man. They sneered at our flag as having stars for the white man, but stripes for the negro. These complacent censors seemed utterly oblivious to the terrible conditions of large sections of their [own] laboring population held in bondage to an oppressive service far more exacting than a Southern slave ever knew. They seemed also to forget that negro slavery was imposed on this country by the British government, which was ably seconded by the traders of New England trading rum to Africa for slaves to be sold in America.[226]

We are told that our Civil War was the result of ignorance of each other in the two sections of our country. But there was no chance to relieve the ignorance when prejudice so intense and inveterate was cultivated in the North by pulpit and press—a prejudice which was founded on conscientious devotion to a theory and which refused to believe anything contrary to the theory.

The abolitionist [socialist/communist] thought he was doing "God's service" by his crusade against an institution which he regarded as the "sum of all villainies." And so he demanded "an anti-slavery constitution, an anti-slavery Bible; and an anti-slavery God." It was not the first time [nor would it be the last] that conscience has trampled on justice in the name of religion.

The war was bound to come. The abolitionist [socialist/communist] won the victory. To-day he boasts of the achievement as a glorious triumph of righteousness. No Southern man would restore the institution of slavery. But the end is not yet. We are confronted by the most difficult problem that ever a nation had to solve. Can the relations, social, political, economic, of two races as widely differing as Caucasian and negro living under the same government be so adjusted as to give justice and proper development to both races? Thus far we have had only an experiment. It remains to be seen whether emancipation has been a blessing to our country, and especially to the negro, or has introduced evils that in the end will be more terrible than slavery.[227] — REV. JAMES H. MCNEILLY, D.D., CONFEDERATE VETERAN, NASHVILLE, TENNESSEE

A POLITICAL ECONOMIST & AMERICAN PATRIOT

☞ [If the truth about the War, as declared by Dr. James H. McNeilly above] . . . could only be given to the calm consideration of every newspaper editor in this country, it might inaugurate a campaign for compulsory education where enlightenment is most sorely needed. We are daily confronted with such ignorance in papers and periodicals as to make us despair of the uses of popular education, but it is consoling to contemplate as we review the pages of history that it has never been the most clamorous tongue and pen that represented the true voice of the people. The clamor of conscienceless politicians must have prevailed to have made possible the destruction of that constitutional government founded by the fathers of our republic. It was a destiny designed by Providence, else the coercion of Americans by Americans could never have been accomplished. One fact generally overlooked is that the whole North cannot be indicted for the crimes of the politicians and abolitionists against the South. As Dr. McNeilly writes:

> A very large element in the North was thoroughly opposed to the theories, purposes, and methods of the [Liberal Republican] party which forced war on the South.

It belongs to us now, after the cause of the Confederacy has been so fully vindicated by the argument of events and results that followed the triumph of the destruction of the Constitution of the United States, to remember and honor that [Conservative] "element" of Northern patriots who ever stood by the principles of republican government. A curious bit of testimony has reached me in a fragment of a publication that was launched, if not established, in Philadelphia in 1833; a fragment marvelously eloquent of the best element of Northern sentiment and intelligence, which was to be finally crushed into subservience by the dark plots and propaganda of the abolitionists [that is, socialists and communists]. So worthy to be memorialized is the noble and pure type of American that this fragment of a past era should be rescued from the oblivion that has engulfed it. I asked an acknowledged authority on United States history if he knew anything of one Condy Raguet, who published this "Journal of Political Economy" in Philadelphia in 1833, and he replied in the negative. Hence I feel justified in bringing a notable but obscure item to light.

Condy Raguet is mentioned in *American Facts*, a book published by G. P. Putnam in 1845, as making useful contribution to the science of political economy. This bare mention and the fragment of his publication are all the present writer has learned about a man whose valiant effort to keep the different sections of his country united in bonds of liberal [a 19th-Century word for what we now refer to as conservative] and mutual understanding is beyond praise. If tardy recognition can avail anything, I should like to accord all possible by sending out a message from the spirit of our countryman, Condy Raguet, as expressed in one copy of his "Journal." Herewith are given the full title, motto, prospectus, and table of contents, with a brief excerpt from editorial comment. The matter in full should be made into a pamphlet and read as a side light on stock histories of the United States; it would likewise prove vastly illuminating in a comparative study of different periods of political development under that constitutional government planned by the convention of 1787. When Condy Raguet labored in the cause of political science, the Madison papers had not [yet] been made public. Copied from the old fragment is the following:

The Examiner and Journal of Political Economy

Devoted to the Advancement of the Cause of State Rights and Free Trade.

The powers not delegated to the United States by

the Constitution, nor prohibited by it to the States, are reserved to the States respectively, or to the people. — Amendment to the Constitution, Article X

"Freedom of industry is as sacred as freedom of speech or the press." — Thomas Jefferson.

Philadelphia, Wednesday September 18, 1833, Vol. 1, No. 4.

Prospectus.

This paper is . . . chiefly political, but partly miscellaneous, its design being to disseminate the great principles of *Constitutional Liberty* and to assist in drawing men's minds from the worship of their fellows to an acquaintance with the nature of their government.

It will be open to the *examination* of all political questions of a general nature and will communicate to the people of the North the political movements of the South and to those of the South the political movements of the North.

It will advocate the Republican doctrines of 1798, as set forth in the Virginia and Kentucky resolutions and as maintained by Jefferson, Madison, . . . and other distinguished champions of *State* . . . and *State Remedies.* It will also record . . . important documents and State Papers connected with the proceedings of South Carolina, so as to preserve a complete history of the times for future reference of politicians and statesmen.

The principles of Free Trade will be illustrated and enforced as useful to reconcile the public mind at the North to the approaching reduction of the Tariff to *a uniform standard of ad valorem duties,* as well as necessary to prevent any future attempts to reestablish the restrictive system.

The impolicy and unconstitutionality of appropriations for works of internal improvement by the *Federal Government* will be maintained, and all attempts to encroach on the rights of the States by that Government will be resisted, *from whatever party they may emanate*; and especially will its interference with the peculiar domestic policy of the Southern States, should any unhappily be attempted, be denounced as a violation of the Federal compact.

It will oppose *monopolies, special privileges,* and *sinecures* of every description as interfering with the *equality of rights* upon which our institutions are founded and will be emphatically the advocate of a *Cheap Government.*

It will also be opposed to *man worship*, the bane of republics, and it will expose corruption and dereliction of principle in public servants, *to whatever party they may profess to belong*. This, however, it will do in a manner which shall not degrade the press, and upon no occasion will the columns of the *Examiner* be the vehicle of scurrility or vulgar personal abuse.

This number of the *Examiner* contains: "Mr. Jefferson, the author of the Kentucky Resolutions," which includes the full "Original Draft, in the Hand-Writing of Mr. Jefferson, of the Kentucky Resolutions of 1798 and 1799."

Editorial.

Pennsylvania Democracy. — A great Democratic meeting was held in Northampton County, Pennsylvania, on the 20th of August, at which a preamble and resolutions were adopted containing the following correct exposition of Pennsylvania Democracy:

> "The principles of government, as inculcated by Jefferson and maintained by General [Andrew] Jackson, may be taken as the broad basis of the Democratic party [then the Conservative party] of the Union. A frequent recurrence to these principles is wholesome and necessary, inasmuch as it enhances our veneration for them and increases our zeal in maintaining them."

We once astonished a Virginian by telling him that the mass of the people of Pennsylvania were as ignorant of the Constitution under which they live as they are of the Calmuc language. In fact, not one man in ten has ever read it, and of those who have read it not one in ten is really conversant with its provisions. The fact may readily be now believed when we see a large meeting of leading men and politicians solemnly sending forth to the world a manifesto in which they express their conviction that General Jackson's political principles are identical with those of Jefferson, thereby proving, if they are honest, as we presume them to be, their entire ignorance of the principles of the government under which they live. The precious paragraph which we have quoted above is precisely on a par with one which should assert that "The principles of political economy, as inculcated by Adam Smith and maintained by Hezekiah Niles, may be taken as the broad basis of the Free Trade Party of the Union."[228] — HOWARD MERIWETHER LOVETT, GIRARD, GEORGIA

SLAVERY & THE TRUE CAUSE OF LINCOLN'S WAR

☞ . . . In nothing has the South suffered so much at the hands of writers of school history as in the treatment of the subjects of State sovereignty, nullification, slavery, and secession. Since the success of the northern resources over southern arms in the Civil War, it has been the practice of northern writers to isolate the period of the war and either uphold the specific acts of the South in withdrawing from the Union as a political crime, using as a term of reproach the term of rebellion, or to infer from the fact that southern independence was not maintained that secession was morally wrong. The facts of American history rob the reproach of its sting when it shows that the foundation of our present government was laid in secession, the states moving in the matter virtually seceding from the perpetual union under the articles of confederation;[229] that the structure of American Independence was upreared in rebellion; that subsequently every section of the country has at some time threatened to secede.

The wife of a Confederate soldier, whose photo she is holding; identities unknown; circa 1863.

In reference to the question of nullification it was not one of the southern states that alone proposed it, but it originated in the North, where many of the states, by legislative enactment, nullified the Constitution of the United States, especially with respect to the fugitive slave law; "that the whole country, and not the South alone was responsible for slavery, the system prevailing in the North as long as it was profitable; that the slave trade was made possible only by New England vessels, manned by New England crews."

The true cause of the war between the states was the dignified withdrawal of the Southern States from the Union to avoid the continued breaches of that domestic tranquility guaranteed, but not consummated by the constitution, and not the high moral purpose of the North to destroy slavery, which followed incidentally as a war measure.

As to the war itself and the result thereof, the children of the future would be astonished that a people fought so hard and so long with so little to fight for, judging from what they gather from histories now in use, prepared by writers from the North, they are utterly destitute of information as to events leading to the war. Their accounts of the numbers engaged, courage displayed, sacrifices endured, hardships encountered, and barbarity practiced upon an almost defenseless people, whose arms-bearing population was in the army, are incorrect in every way.

A people, who for four long years, fought over almost every foot of their territory, on over two thousand battlefields, with the odds of 5,864,272 enlisted men against their 600,000 enlisted men, and their coasts blockaded, and rivers filled with gunboats, with 600 vessels of war, manned by 35,000 sailors, and who protracted the struggle until over one-half of their soldiers were dead from the casualties of war, had something to fight for. They fought for the great principle of local self-government and the privilege of managing their own affairs, and for the protection of their homes and fire-sides.[230] — THE HISTORICAL COMMITTEE ON SOUTHERN SCHOOL HISTORY

THE CAUSE OF EACH SIDE
☛ [Thus ended the War for Southern Independence]—the one great army [C.S.A.] contending for State rights, self-government, and because their country was invaded; the other [U.S.A.] for the Union and centralizing government . . .[231] — JASPER KELSEY, CONFEDERATE VETERAN

EXAMPLES OF CALLS TO ARMS BY CONFEDERATE LEADERS
☛ It is said that the art of oratory died in the [eighteen] sixties, and I must confess that the following extracts from proclamations of Southern leaders are a cut above anything that I have ever heard:

- "Men of Virginia! Men of Kanawha! To arms! The enemy has invaded your soil. Rise and strike for your, firesides and altars. Repel the aggressors and preserve your honor and your rights. Come to the aid of your fathers, brothers, and comrades for the protection of your mothers, wives, and sisters." Good!
- "A reckless and unprincipled tyrant has invaded your soil. Abraham Lincoln has thrown his abolition [communist] hosts among you. Their war cry is 'Beauty and booty.' Your honor and that of your wives and daughters, your fortunes and your lives are involved in this momentous conflict." Better!

- "The North has not openly and according to the usage of civilized nations declared war on us. We make no war on them; but should Virginia soil be polluted by the tread of a single man in arms from north of the Potomac, it will cause open war. Men of the Potomac border, to arms! Your country calls you to her defense. Already you have in spirit responded. You await but the order to march, to rendezvous, to defend your State, your liberty, and your homes. Women of Virginia, cast from your arms all cowards and breathe the pure and holy, the high and glowing inspiration of your nature into the hearts and souls of lover, husband, brother, father, and friend. Almighty God, Author and Governor of the world, thou Source of all life, truth, justice and power, be thou our God, be thou with us, then shall we fear not a world against us." Best![232]
— JOHN C. STILES, BRUNSWICK, GEORGIA

Chromolithograph entitled "Confederate camp during the late American war." Created by M. & N. Hanhart; publisher Louis Zimmer, London, UK, circa 1871.

Confederate Major, identity unknown, Frederick, Maryland, circa 1863.

WAR TITLES & HOW THEY REFLECT THE TRUE CAUSE

☛ The titles given by writers to the war of 1861-65 are altogether confusing. Is there no way by which this confusion can be set to rest? It is the province of history to remove all rubbish and let the bare facts in every case stand out, no matter who is to be touched by them. It is called the war of secession, the war of the rebellion, the war between the States, the war between the sections, the civil war, the war against slavery, the rich man's war, the poor man's fight, etc. Now, all of these cannot be true; it is possible that none of them is true. How, then, are we to arrive at the proper title? Fifty-odd years seems quite long enough for it to be wandering around with a half dozen names or more. Are there no facts to guide the historian back to the origin of this war? He should, it seems to me, be just as able and as willing to give us the right title to it as he is to lead us along the line of its progress. It is not the historian who is to make the facts which determine the name, but it is his business to select from the facts the fact which above all others determines what the title shall be. He should not shrink from this plain duty on account of any personal or political preference or feeling. To do this would disqualify him for the accredited position of historian.

Great as is the need for this, and abundant as have been the opportunities for settling this title, I do not know of a single historian who has set about to fix the right title. It may be that, owing to the character of the facts, a general looseness as to title has been thought to be best. In that way the most unwelcome facts can be easily obscured. But is this a fair way to treat an important matter? I should say not! Forasmuch, then, as more than fifty years have passed and the war of 1861-65 has been under the cover of more than half a dozen loose titles, I venture to throw aside these loose titles and give it the title which the facts of history will maintain. These facts are abundant and are within reach of students of history. Here it is: *The War of the Abolition* [Communist] *Party against the Principles of the Constitution of the United States.* If the facts do not sustain this title, then I ask, What do they show?

Another priceless photo of a black Confederate soldier: right, Silas Chandler; left, Sergeant A. M. Chandler of Co. F, 44th Mississippi Infantry Regiment, circa 1862.

The first gun was fired by [socialist-leaning] John Brown at Harper's Ferry and not by [Pierre G. T.] Beauregard at Fort Sumter. James Gordon Bennett asserted boldly in 1861 in the New York *Herald* that the principles of the Constitution of the United States were rightly interpreted by the Confederate States. When Jefferson Davis was brought before Chief Justice [Salmon P.] Chase, no charge of treason was sustained. In the fall of 1860 the legislative and the executive departments of the United States passed into the hands of the Republican [then the Left-wing] party, and that which had for years been planned was put into operation.

Obstructions had been thrown in the way of these principles for nearly half a century, but now the way was clear for open hostilities against them. [Big government Liberal] Abraham Lincoln fought them with all the energy of his soul; U. S. Grant gnawed at them like a consuming cancer; W. T. Sherman with his torch tried to consume them; but to-day they are alive and vigorous. They are alive to-day because Jefferson Davis lived, because a Confederate host lived, and last, but not least, because the judicial department of the United States government stood firmly by them in it all. It was doubtless for this that Mr. [William E.] Gladstone said: "Jefferson Davis has created a nation."

After the death of Mr. Lincoln, the war being closed, the conduct of the Republican party [Liberal] toward the [Conservative] principles of the Constitution and common rights was such as to drive President [Andrew] Johnson out of that party. They wanted to be self-appointed guardians for the rights and property of the people of the South, using as a pretext therefor that there was "no legal government or adequate protection for life or property . . . in Virginia, North Carolina, South Carolina, Georgia, Alabama, Mississippi, Louisiana, Florida, Texas, and Arkansas." (See Acts of Congress, March 2, 23, and July 19, 1867.) The forming of the five [Reconstruction] military districts out of this territory was foreign to the Constitution. The spirit of madness had to succumb; and when the Republican party [Liberal] had to break its military grip on the South and return to constitutional methods of procedure, it was doubtless wiser, if not better. Mrs. Harriet Beecher Stowe lived long enough to discover that the act she regretted most was the publication of *Uncle Tom's Cabin*. If President Lincoln had lived long enough, he might have discovered that the misuse of the power of the President's office was the act he regretted most. If the Republican party [then Liberal] lives long enough, it may discover that its war against the Constitution and its effort to dethrone the intelligence of the Anglo-Saxons of the sunny South are what it regrets most. When it does this, the South may break its solid ranks and take its erring brother into closer confidence.

I could heartily wish that these facts did not stand at the mileposts of our country's march; but while lamenting that they are facts, there is some comfort in the thought that they lay the responsibility of the war of 1861-65 at the feet of the Republican party [Liberal]. It failed to override the Supreme Court of the United States; it failed to impeach President Johnson; it failed to demolish Anglo-Saxon rule. It controlled Abraham Lincoln; it controlled Congress; it controlled the United States army and navy;

it crushed the Confederate army, but the principles for which that army stood are living to-day, and "Dixie" has more inspiration than ever before, while no one gathers any inspiration from *The Spirit of John Brown Goes Marching On.* The acts of Congress in June, 1866, in relation to the payment for property other than slaves, marked "etc.," is a reflection on good morals and an insult to justice; and all of these things combine to show that history must ultimately say that the war of 1861-65 was a "war of the Republican party [Liberal] against the principles of the Constitution of the United States" or keep the facts in the background. It is impossible to estimate the cost of that party to the United States government.

There was one incident in the life of Judge [John C.] Underwood which doubtless influenced his action in the trial of Jefferson Davis. It was his arrest by order of Mr. Davis. Capt. T. H. Clark, of Company I, 2nd South Carolina Cavalry, made the arrest; he found the Judge hidden away in a wardrobe. This no doubt so humiliated his honor that he wanted some revenge on Mr. Davis. He, like the Republican party [Liberal] at the time, was so blinded by personal feeling against Mr. Davis that he lost sight of constitutional principle and was ready to seek personal revenge.[233]
— JOAB EDWARDS, LEESVILLE, SOUTH CAROLINA

WHY THE SOUTH LOST

☛ "Because she would not pay the price of independence!" The people who for the cause next their heart paid in blood, in treasure, in suffering, in humiliation, in every species of disaster the heaviest price in all history, not willing to pay the price of independence!

The South (and by the South I mean the patriotic [Conservative] element within her borders) was willing to pay and did pay every price but one. But, alas! that was the one without which all the others proved vain. That price was liberty, the temporary subordination of law and personal rights to military necessity. The South could not bring herself to let liberty wait even until independence was won. She could not bow to the maxim of the most practical liberty lovers that the world has ever seen, the ancient Romans. The maxim that amid the clash of arms law must be silent was not for her.

Our civil officers in the discharge of their duty as they saw it hampered and thwarted the Confederate government in the prosecution of the war to a degree hardly to be believed in these iron days. Governor [Zebulon B.] Vance, of North Carolina, Governor [Joseph E.] Brown, of Georgia, and [John G. Shorter] the Governor of Alabama, to mention only the most prominent cases, were patriotic men. For Southern independence they stood ready to sacrifice everything but Southern liberty. No matter how dire the extremity, how urgent the necessity that forced it, every encroachment of the Richmond authorities upon the rights of the States was opposed and more than once to the verge of armed resistance. In the main the State courts backed the Governors and the people, or at least the civil population backed the courts.

Unfortunately, the measures most stoutly opposed and most persistently thwarted were those of conscription and impressment, without which the army could not be recruited or supplied. The result was that the South never fully mobilized her resources in either men or supplies. More than once within a stone's throw of independence, even this small margin of unmobilized resources must have strengthened her to reach the shining goal.

War as we waged it was a grilling thing, testing human nature to its inmost fiber. There has never been a war without its shirkers. The great body of Southern people, steadfast to the bitter end, were willing to lay upon the altar of independence their lives, their fortunes, everything but the rights of the people, even if these rights included the right of the shirker to shirk. Suppose we had commandeered everyman, every dollar, every mouthful of food, and every tongue, or bridled it as, I will not say Germany, but as England and France [1917] are now doing—in short had prodded our dead weight into action, the "thin gray line" would have stiffened and never broken.

Northern historians of the war devote whole chapters to "The Military Despotism" at the South. But what was her true liberty status? Despotism always bridles the tongue before it manacles the hand. Numerous papers were suppressed by the Federal [that is, Union/Northern/USA/Liberal] authorities. If the Confederate authorities [that is, Conservatives] ever suppressed one, I have never found record of it, and I have looked diligently. The Charleston *Mercury* criticized the administration from beginning to end. The Richmond *Examiner* was almost rabid in its assaults on the President [Davis] and his policy. [William W.] Holden, in the Raleigh *Standard*, by encouraging desertion and every possible form of disloyalty to the Confederacy, probably did as much as Grant or Sherman to defeat Southern independence. But he kept within the law as our liberal-minded [then a term meaning conservative-minded] forbears saw it and to the very end was suffered to weaken the cause which our highest and best were dying to uphold.

That the Confederate authorities did not in their desperate straits resort to arbitrary and unlawful measures, no one cold pretend to deny. Impressment, unnecessary at the opulent North, where the wily contractor stood ready to supply with one hand and rake off with the other, worked great hardships and often injustice at the lean South. Nor did the Northern draft ever develop into the keen man hunt that the Southern conscription did, for there were fully five times as many available men within the Federal lines by 1864 as in the Confederate. What I mean is that through all the stress and strain and dire necessity of war, with the enemy, sword and torch in hand, forever thundering at her doors, the South strove valiantly to keep liberty alive and went down to defeat and ruin thereby. "Liberty is a delicate plant," said one of our war editors, beautifully expressing Southern sentiment. "Liberty is a delicate plant. Watered with blood and tears, it will grow; but once uprooted, where upon that soil did it ever thrive again?" As another put it: "Liberty has ever said, the veil of the temple once rent, 'let us depart.'"

On the other hand, the [Left-wing] North from the beginning of the war to the end of Reconstruction destroyed every bar, legal or moral, that stood in the way of working her will with the [Right-wing] South. The Declaration of Independence, at once the creed and gospel of American liberty, proclaimed as its cardinal principle, as its very reason for being, that "governments derive their just powers from the consent of the governed." Thirteen sovereign States, the identical number that made the declaration of American independence, and inhabited by ten million people, nearly three times as many as the original thirteen and under far greater provocation, now made a declaration of Southern independence. These States, all thoroughly organized, fully capable of self-government, solemnly, deliberately, and observing every form of law and of procedure, sought to exercise the "just power" of self-government. But twenty million Northerners were as much benefited by the union as the ten million Southerners were harmed by it. The declaration of independence became a scrap of paper.

The Constitution, the bond of union, the solemn covenant that bound the States together, the destruction of which automatically destroyed the Union, by every possible implication and construction forbade the Federal government to interfere with slavery in the States. Northern military and political expediency called for abolition. The Constitution became a scrap of paper.

Humanity demanded that the cartel empty Northern and Southern prison hells. Northern military expediency required that these hells remain in full blast. The cartel became a scrap of paper.

The *habeas corpus* act, forbidding arrest and imprisonment

without due form of law, hindered the North in subjugating the South. [William H.] Seward touched the little bell at his elbow. The *habeas corpus* act became a scrap of paper.

The time-honored rules of civilized warfare prohibited an invading army from vandalism, from the wanton destruction of private property. These rules had been scrupulously observed by the army that the tyrant [Britain's King] George III sent through the South in the [American] Revolution. Northern military expediency required that Sherman devastate, give over to pillage, torch, and rapine an area three times as large as all Belgium combined. The rules of civilized warfare became a scrip of paper.

"But didn't all this shorten the war?" the unthinking are given to asking. Perhaps it did. But so did Attila's butcheries shorten his job, and Alva's: so did the cruelties of the painted savage shorten his job.

But civilized man has by common consent bound himself to forego such doubtful advantage bought at such fearful cost to the innocent and helpless. Frightfulness, savagery brands the savage, be it veneered with New England Puritanism or German Kultur. To her everlasting honor the South lost not only because she was short in resources, but because she was long in principle. After all, was it not better to have nobly lost than to have basely won?[234] — O. W. BLACKNALL, KITTRELL, NORTH CAROLINA

AN ODE TO JEFFERSON DAVIS

☞ A century and eight years ago to-day, in the little hamlet of Fairview, Christian County, Ky., the light of day for the first time dawned upon the vision of Jefferson Davis. While he was an infant his father and mother moved to Louisiana; but owing to the children suffering from acclimatization, his father sought a more congenial climate and in a short while moved to Woodville, in Wilkerson County, Miss. His father's family consisted of ten children, of whom Jefferson Davis was the youngest. At the age of seven years he was sent on horseback by his father, in company with friends, to St. Thomas College, near Springfield, Ky., where he entered school for a year. He afterwards attended school near his father's home in Mississippi until he was sufficiently advanced and was then sent to Transylvania University, at Lexington, Ky. In November, 1823, he was appointed to the West Point Military Academy by [U.S.] President [James] Monroe; was graduated from this institution in 1828 and was sent to the Jefferson Barracks and afterwards to Fort Crawford, in Wisconsin, and to other forts in the Northwest.

He resigned from the army in 1835 and married Miss [Sarah Knox] Taylor, daughter of Gen. Zachary Taylor, over the protest of her father, and went back to Mississippi to farm. The estrangement between General Taylor and Mr. Davis never was healed. His wife lived only a short time. He was married again in 1845 to Miss Varina Howell.

Jefferson Davis was elected to the Twenty-Ninth Congress in 1845 and in 1847 was appointed United States Senator by the Governor of Mississippi [Albert G. Brown] to fill the vacancy caused by the death of Senator [Jesse] Speight. While United States Senator he resigned to run for Governor of Mississippi, but was defeated. In 1853 he was appointed Secretary of War by President [Franklin] Pierce and served for four years. He went back to the Senate from Mississippi on March 4, 1857. In 1861, when Mississippi seceded from the Union, Mr. Davis, as one of the United States Senators from Mississippi, immediately resigned his office and cast his fortunes with the Southern Confederacy. The speech which he made in the United States Senate at the time he resigned is one of the brightest and most pathetic [that is, poignant] gems of English literature and should be read by every liberty-loving and patriotic American citizen. He was shortly afterwards elected President of the Southern Confederacy.

The war clouds were lowering over the country at this time. The bloody conflict that transpired during the early sixties is well and familiarly known to all. It is not my purpose to-day to pluck one laurel wreath from the brow of any Union soldier, either living or dead. They were loyal and patriotic and bared their breasts to the bayonets in order that this country might still remain an undivided Union. However, it shall be my endeavor to pay a just tribute to the brave and patriotic men of the Southern Confederacy, thousands of whom gave their lives in defense of a constitutional right, which theretofore from the adoption of the Federal Constitution had never been questioned by any one, much less denied to any State. The principle for which they fought is clearly enunciated in the tenth amendment of the Federal Constitution, which reads as follows:

> "The powers not delegated to the United States by the Constitution nor prohibited by it to the States are reserved to the States, respectively, or to the people."

It was agreed by all when the Constitution was adopted that it was a compact between the States, that the Federal government was limited to the authorities granted in the Constitution, and that any State had a right to secede from the Union whenever that State was satisfied that the administration of the government of the Union was oppressive or that its constitutional right had been invaded.

Thomas Jefferson, the greatest of all Democrats [then Conservatives] of his age, in the celebrated Kentucky resolutions expressed this sentiment and placed this interpretation upon the Constitution. In the Virginia convention when this question was raised it was conceded by all that this was the correct interpretation of the Constitution, and Virginia would not have ratified the Constitution nor joined the Union without this understanding. Patrick Henry raised this question in the convention and received the assurance from Mr. [James] Madison, the father of the Constitution, that this was the correct interpretation of it.

In the Constitutional Convention a proposition was made to authorize the employment of force against a delinquent State, on which Mr. Madison remarked:

> "The use of force against a State would look more like a declaration of war than an infliction of punishment and would probably be considered by the party attacked as a dissolution of all previous compacts by which it might have been bound."

The convention expressly refused to confer the power proposed, and the clause was lost. This interpretation of the Constitution was prevalent among the Northern as well as the Southern States. The acquisition of Louisiana in 1803 created much dissatisfaction in the Northern States, and especially in Massachusetts. [New Englander] Col. Timothy Pickering, who had been an officer of the War of the Revolution and afterwards Postmaster-General, Secretary of War, and Secretary of State in the Cabinet of President [George] Washington, and later a representative of the State of Massachusetts in the Senate of the United States, was one of the leading secessionists of his day. Expressing his dissatisfaction at the way Louisiana was acquired, he wrote in December, 1803:

> "I will not yet despair. I will rather anticipate a new confederacy. . . . There will be (and our children at the farthest will see it) a separation." In January, 1804, he further wrote: "The principles of our Revolution point to the remedy—a separation. This can be accomplished and without spilling one drop of blood. I have little doubt. I do not believe in the practicability of a long-continued union. A

> Northern confederacy would unite congenial characters; . . . while the Southern States, having a similarity of habits, might be left to manage their own affairs in their own way. . . . It (the separation) must begin in Massachusetts. The proposition would be welcomed in Connecticut, and could we doubt of New Hampshire? But New York must be associated, and how is her concurrence to be obtained? She must be made the center of the confederacy. Vermont and New Jersey would follow, of course, and Rhode Island of necessity."

I do not show this in any spirit of criticism of this great man, but to show that his interpretation of the Constitution coincided with the views of Thomas Jefferson. James Madison, Patrick Henry, and other great men of his day.

Even as late as 1860, when many men of the North were appealing to passion and inciting the multitudes to support a war waged against the Southern States in the event of their secession, the New York *Tribune*, the organ of the Abolitionists [that is radical Left-wingers, or what we now call socialists and communists] declared:

> "If the cotton States wish to withdraw from the Union, they should be allowed to do so. Any attempt to compel them to remain by force would be contrary to the principles of the Declaration of Independence and to the fundamental ideas upon which human liberty is based. If the Declaration of Independence justified the secession from the British Empire of 3,000,000 subjects in 1770, it is not seen why it would not justify the secession of 5,000,000 Southerners from the Union in 1861."

So we see that the right of a State to secede from the Union was claimed by the North and the South.

At the time of the adoption of the Constitution there were many people in the North and Northeast engaged in the slave traffic, importing slaves from America to this country, and when the fact was ascertained that these slaves were not acclimated to the North they were sold to the planters of the South. The question then came in this constitutional convention whether the right longer to traffic in slaves should be recognized by the Constitution. Some of the greatest leaders of thought in the South in this convention protested against the further legalizing of the slave traffic, while several States of the North and Northeast insisted that this right should be recognized, and thus this baneful institution was fostered by the fundamental law of this republic for twenty years, to be assailed by their descendants in 1856 and 1861.

As a result of this concession in the Constitution, the institution of slavery spread over the South, its climate and soil being favorable to the institution. A great number of the people of the Northern States were just as much in favor of the institution of slavery as were the people of the South.

In December, 1805, a petition of the Legislative Council and House of Representatives of the Indiana Territory, then comprising all the area now occupied by the States of Indiana, Illinois, Michigan, and Wisconsin, was presented to Congress, accompanied by a letter from Governor [William Henry] Harrison, afterwards President of the United States, for a suspension of the sixth article of the ordinance, so as to permit the introduction of slavery into the Territory. These resolutions were submitted to a committee of the House, which reported the resolutions favorably, and this report was sustained by the House, and a resolution to suspend the prohibitory article was adopted. The proposition failed, however, in the Senate. But I cite this merely to show that the people of the Indiana Territory were unanimous in indorsing these resolutions so as to permit the introduction of slaves into their Territory. The African slave trade was carried on largely by New England merchants and Northern ships (not surprisingly, as both the American slave trade and American slavery began in Massachusetts in the early 1600s).[235]

Native American Confederate, Private Lewis Downing, 1st Cherokee Mounted Rifles, circa 1864.

[Conservative] Thomas Jefferson, a Southern man, the founder of the Democratic party [then the Conservative party] and the vindicator of State rights, was a constant enemy to every form of slavery. The Southern States took the lead in prohibiting the slave trade, and the State of Georgia was the first State to incorporate the prohibition in her constitution. These facts of history must be considered when judgment is pronounced by posterity upon the justice of the act of the Southern people in choosing the fearful alternative of war rather than submit to an invasion of their chartered rights under the Constitution.

So in 1860-61 the Southern people stood upon the constitutional rights as interpreted by their statesmen since the government was founded, that a State, in the strictest interpretation of the Constitution, had the power, never surrendered, to withdraw from the Union should it be denied its right.

Eleven States, with South Carolina first, seceded from the Union and formed the Southern Confederacy. The great conflict lasted for four years.

In this great abandonment proceeding between Uncle Sam and eleven of his Southern daughters, which was settled in a court of arms, Kentucky as a State was neither a party plaintiff nor party defendant. She was not even correspondent, but yet she furnished to the North and South her full quota of as brave men as ever went upon the battle field in the history of the world. She did more: she furnished to the Union its President, . . . Abraham Lincoln, and to the Southern Confederacy its President, that brave and patriotic statesman, Jefferson Davis.

The South fought against many odds, but yet she fought for a principle guaranteed to her under the Federal Constitution. Finally, at the end of four years, at the battle of Appomattox, when General Lee surrendered, [and] the sun of the Southern Confederacy set. The hopes of a brave and patriotic people were blighted. These men were not traitors to the government, but were just as patriotic and liberty-loving as the men who fought to maintain the Union.

Jefferson Davis was indicted and imprisoned for treason, but without trial he was acquitted of the charge, and history must accept this result as conclusive of the fact that this great man in standing for the constitutional right of a State to withdraw from the Union and in resisting force to coerce the State into submission was guilty of no treason, but was justified by the law as it then existed. Such will be the verdict if unerring history. Were they guilty of treason? If they were, they were inspired to this act by the teachings of Patrick Henry, James Madison, and Thomas Jefferson in their interpretation of the Constitution.

After Lee's surrender, these soldiers, in their faded gray uniforms, with rusty canteens upon their shoulders, wended their way to the sunny South, only to find burned homes, wrecked farms, and separated families. A great war debt had been contracted; Confederate money was worthless; but notwithstanding the unfavorable circumstances that then existed, they again united for grander and nobler purposes. Amid the ashes, wrecks, and their dead, holding the inspiration of the past for the future, they took their horses from the battle field to the furrow, their cotton, which was hidden, and sold it for the necessaries of life, and went with the same energies to rebuild the South as they had gone upon the battle fields to defend her. And to-day America has no better citizens in peace and would have no braver soldiers in war than those who over fifty-six years ago followed Robert E. Lee as their general, the grand old tune of *Dixie* for their inspiration, and the Bonnie Blue Flag as their banner.

The negroes of the South, as hard as were the conditions of slavery, owe a thousandfold greater debt of gratitude to the Southern people than to any other people on earth. The people of the South tutored the negro in the way of civilization. They found him a savage, fresh from the jungles of Africa. They have taken him by the hand and led him up the hill of progress and civilization and taught him that there is a God and that they may be the recipients of his choicest benedictions. They are giving him an education. And it is to the eternal credit of the South and its people that under the law of practically every Southern State each negro boy and girl draws as much per capita of the school fund as do the white children of the South.

The Southern people have erected negro colleges at the expense of the taxpayers of the South and are maintaining them at such expense in order to better the condition of the negro and to give him an equal chance in life's battles. That the institution of slavery has been abolished and that every man beneath the fold of our country's flag is a freeman is the gratification of every man of this great republic, and the people of the South also rejoice in this fact. Slavery was not the cause of the war, but the institution died as an incident of the war; and the Southern people are exerting their best efforts to uplift and educate the negro, and every good colored citizen in the South will agree to this statement.

The deeds of valor and heroism of Jefferson Davis in his devotion to the South and to the people who had honored him will live in the memory of the posterity of the South so long as she erects an altar to her heroes and so long as men have grateful hearts. Wherever in this broad land of ours the ashes of a Confederate soldier lie, the clay that wraps his remains is the sepulcher of an American patriot who died for a vital principle of government as taught by the fathers of this republic. History, calm, fair, and truthful, will yet record this truth as the final and considered judgment of mankind.

> "Not for fame or reward, not for place or for rank, not lured by ambition or goaded by necessity, but in simple obedience to duty as they understood it, these men suffered all, sacrificed all, dared all—and died."

When the war had ended, soldiers of the North and of the South shook hands across the graves of their comrade dead and said: "We will be friends: we will again have a Union, one and undivided." And when they did this they made a government that will live on united until time shall cease its flight in the centuries to follow.

I rejoice with every patriotic American to-day in the fact that we have a hundred million free, happy, peaceful, united, and patriotic people, with one country, one government, one flag, and one God.[236] — DAVID H. KINCHELOE, KENTUCKY REPRESENTATIVE, IN CONGRESS, JUNE 3, 1916

RESOLUTIONS OF THE MISSISSIPPI DIVISION, UNITED DAUGHTERS OF THE CONFEDERACY

☛ Whereas the United States government is at war with a foreign foe and needs the united efforts of all citizens in every part of every State, and the United Daughters of the Confederacy, of which the Mississippi Division is a component part, feels proud of its descent from patriots, men and women, who gave all they had for the blessed privilege of being governed only by their own consent, the great States' right principle of our government; and whereas these United States have entered this great world war [World War I] that the peoples of the earth may enjoy the privilege of being governed by their own consent, thus making the world safe for democracy; and whereas we believe it right and just that President Woodrow Wilson should be assured that he has the whole of every part of this country [that is, the former Confederate States of America] back of him in these days of stress and trial; therefore be it

Resolved, That the Mississippi Division, U. D. C., in convention assembled, wishes to go on record as approving the course its country has pursued in staying out of the struggle as long as it consistently could and preserve its ideals of peace and democracy and then enters only to preserve those ideals and rights which our "fathers fought for and which it is our duty to transmit to our children"; that the Mississippi Division wishes President Wilson and all others in authority to know that it stands ready to help with influence and work at any time it is needed; that the Mississippi

Division does not think that failure to do a patriot's duty now is worthy of the records made by the fathers and mothers of its members, the men and women of the Confederacy, and therefore urges its members to follow the examples of their fathers and mothers and place themselves and all they have at the service of their country.[237] — OFFERED BY THE J. Z. GEORGE CHAPTER, UDC, AND ADOPTED BY THE MISSISSIPPI DIVISION IN CONVENTION AT GREENWOOD, MISSISSIPPI, MAY 3, 1917

THE RELIGIOUS ASPECT OF PATRIOTISM
☛ . . . Faith was the guiding star of the Confederate cause. . . . [That is,] the cause of the Southern States was rooted and grounded in [religious] faith, in devotion to the unseen. The point at issue was not one of bare political economy, still less of personal property. It was loyalty to principles which sire had handed down to son through countless generations, the very warp and woof of Southern civilization. The election of President Lincoln was not the cause: it was the occasion merely of secession. Secession to many of the Southern people became then a sacred duty, as sacred as the Bill of Rights or the driving out of the Stuart kings, a question of fundamental human right, of the liberty for which the blood of the Anglo-Saxon had been spilled from the days of Magna Carta until their own. They were not playing for power or political dominance. They exercised only what they and their forefathers believed was the inalienable right of every State—the right of secession from a compact which they had entered into voluntarily and from which they believed they had the right to withdraw just as voluntarily whenever it ceased to conserve the highest interests of any of the contracting parties. They were not rebels; they were patriots. They felt that they were not alone. They never doubted for a moment that they were one with the great company of liberators, with [John] Pym and [John] Hampden and [Oliver] Cromwell and the seven bishops and [George] Washington and Patrick Henry. There was no break. The army of the faithful was one, and they were only its latest recruits, righting under the same old flag the same eternal battle of liberty.[238] —FROM A SERMON BY BRITISH REV. H. D. C. MACLACHLAN, MAY 30, 1909, RICHMOND, VIRGINIA

AN EARNEST ENLISTMENT CALL
☛ Fellow Citizens: In June last I was called to the command of a handful of Missourians who nobly gave up home and comfort to

espouse in that gloomy hour the cause of your bleeding country, struggling with the most causeless and cruel despotism known among civilized men. When peace and protection could no longer be enjoyed, your chief magistrate called for fifty thousand men to drive the invader from your soil. To that call less than five thousand responded out of a male population exceeding two million; only one in forty stepped forward to defend the cause of constitutional liberty and human rights. Where are those fifty thousand men? Are Missourians, then, no longer themselves? Are they a timid, time-serving, craven race fit only for subjugation to a despot? Awake, my countrymen, to a sense of what constitutes the dignity and true greatness of a free people! Come to the Army of Missouri, not for a week or a month, but to free your country."

> 'Strike till each armed foe expires!
> Strike for your altars and your fire,
> For the green graves of your sires,
> God and your native land.'

"Do I hear your shouts? Is that your war cry which echoes through the land? Are you coming, fifty thousand men? Missouri shall move to victory with the tread of a giant? Come on, my brave boys! We await your coming."[239] — CONFEDERATE GENERAL STERLING PRICE, PROCLAMATION TO THE CITIZENS OF MISSOURI, NOVEMBER 26, 1861

A U.S. PRESIDENT ADDRESSES CONFEDERATE VETERANS
☛ Mr. Commander, Ladies, and Gentlemen: I esteem it a very great pleasure and a real privilege to extend to the men who are attending this Reunion the very cordial greetings of the government of the United States.

I suppose that as you mix with one another you chiefly find these to be days of memory, when your thoughts go back and recall those days of struggle in which your hearts were strained, in which the whole nation seemed in grapple, and I dare say that you are thrilled as you remember the heroic things that were then done. You are glad to remember that heroic things were done on both sides and that men in those days fought in something like the old spirit of chivalric gallantry.

There are many memories of the Civil War that thrill along the blood and make one proud to have been sprung of a race that could produce such bravery and constancy, and yet the world does not live on memories. The world is constantly making its toilsome way forward into new and different days, and I believe that one of the things that contribute satisfaction to a Reunion like this and a welcome like this is that this is also a day of oblivion. There are some things that we have thankfully buried, and among them are the great passions of division which once threatened to rend this nation in twain.

The passion of admiration we still entertain for the heroic figures of those old days; but the passion of separation, the passion of difference of principle, is gone—gone out of our minds, gone out of our hearts—and one of the things that will thrill this country as it reads of this Reunion is that it will read also of a rededication on the part of all of us to the great nation which we serve in common.

These are days of oblivion as well as of memory, for we are forgetting the things that once held us asunder. Not only that, but they are days of rejoicing, because we now at last see why this great nation was kept united, for we are beginning to see the great world purpose which it was meant to serve.

Many men, I know, particularly of your own generation, have wondered at some of the dealings of Providence; but the wise heart never questions the dealings of Providence, because the great, long plan as it unfolds has a majesty about it and a definiteness of purpose, an elevation of ideal, which we were incapable of conceiving as we tried to work things out with our own short sight and weak strength. And now that we see ourselves part of a nation united, powerful, great in spirit and in purpose, we know the great ends which God in his mysterious providence wrought through our instrumentality, because at the heart of the men of the North and of the South there was the same love of self-government and of liberty, and now we are to be an instrument in the hands of God to see that liberty is made secure for mankind. At the day of our greatest division there was one common passion among us, and that was the passion for human freedom. We did not know that God was working out in his own way the method by which we should best serve human freedom—by making this Union a great united, indivisible, indestructible instrument in his hands for the accomplishment of these great things.

As I came along the streets a few minutes ago my heart was full of the thought that this is registration day. Will you not support me in feeling that there is some significance in this coincidence, that this day, when I come to welcome you to the national capital, is a day when men young as you were in those old days, when you gathered together to fight, are now registering their names as evidence of this great idea, that in a democracy the duty to serve and the privilege to serve fall upon all alike? There is something very fine, my fellow citizens, in the spirit of the volunteer; but deeper than the volunteer spirit is the spirit of obligation.

There is not a man of us who must not hold himself ready to be summoned to the duty of supporting the great government under which we live. No really thoughtful and patriotic man is jealous of that obligation. No man who really understands the privilege and the dignity of being an American citizen quarrels for a moment with the idea that the Congress of the United States has the right to call upon whom it will to serve the nation. These solemn lines of young men going to-day all over the Union to the places of registration ought to be a signal to the world, to those who dare flout the dignity and honor and rights of the United States, that all her manhood will flock to that standard under which we all delight to serve, and that he who challenges the rights and principles of the United States challenges the united strength and devotion of a nation.

There are not many things that one desires about war, my fellow citizens, but you have come through war; you know how you have been chastened by it, and there comes a time when it is good for a nation to know that it must sacrifice, if need be, everything that it has to vindicate the principles which it professes. We have prospered with a sort of heedless and irresponsible prosperity. Now we are going to lay all our wealth, if necessary, and spend all our blood, if need be, to show that we were not accumulating that wealth selfishly, but were accumulating it for the service of mankind.

Men all over the world have thought of the United States as a trading and money-getting people, whereas we who have lived at home know the ideals with which the hearts of this people have thrilled; we know the sober convictions which have lain at the basis of our life all the time, and we know the power and devotion which can be spent heroicwise for the service of those ideals that we have treasured.

We have been allowed to become strong in the providence of God that our strength might be used to prove, not our selfishness, but our greatness; and if there is any ground for thankfulness in a day like this, I am thankful for the privilege of self-sacrifice, which is the only privilege that lends dignity to the human spirit. And so it seems to me that we may regard this as a very happy day, because a day of reunion, a day of noble memories, a day of dedication, a day of the renewal of the spirit which has made America great among the peoples of the world.[240] — PRESIDENT WOODROW

WILSON, CONFEDERATE REUNION, WASHINGTON, D.C., SUMMER 1917

A CONFEDERATE GENERAL ON THE WAR

☞ . . . To be compelled, resisting outrage, to meet our fellow men in deadly shock cannot but be under any circumstances painful to a Christian mind. Especially is the trial grievous when we must be slain by or slay those who so lately were our countrymen, but who, having trampled upon our rights, now seek to desolate our homes, appropriate our soil, kill off our young men, degrade our women, and subdue us into abject submission to their will because we claim under our own government exemption from their insults and control. And it is still more distressing to find requisite toward contributing to avert the ruin threatened by malignant millions, thus to send the sleeping, however unprepared, to their great account.[241] — CONFEDERATE GENERAL WILLIAM NELSON PENDLETON, FIELD REPORT

CONFEDERATE PATRIOTISM DURING WORLD WAR I

☞ [The following is] . . . a letter from a member of the American colony in Brazil which shows their loyalty to this country [U.S.A.] in its time of stress. It will be remembered that after the close of the War between the States [1865] a number of Southern men who had fought for the Confederacy moved their families to South America and established this colony in Brazil rather than live under a government which they felt would not respect their rights. The letter is from Dr. Cicero Jones, son of one of the original members, and he writes from Villa Americana, State of Sao Paulo, Brazil, South America, on June 23 [1917] as follows:

> It may be of interest to some to learn that the week following the declaration of war between the United States and Germany [April 4, 1917] the boys of the American colony, some thirty-odd, met in my office at this place and through me sent to our consul the following resolution:
>
> "We, the undersigned sons and grandsons of Confederate veterans, most respectfully offer through our consul in Sao Paulo our services to the American government, to be used as it may see fit during the war between the United States and Germany, promising the same loyalty to the Stars and Stripes that our fathers gave to the Stars and Bars."[242] — *CONFEDERATE VETERAN* MAGAZINE

WHY DID THE CONFEDERATE STATES FIGHT?

☛ Probably there is no aspect of the war for Southern independence that has been so persistently, not to say maliciously, misrepresented as the motive and purpose of the Southern States in withdrawing from the Union and in defending their action with the sword. These misrepresentations have been industriously propagated from the close of the war to the present day in elaborate histories, in schoolbooks, in magazines and newspapers, by essays, speeches, and sermons. The press, the platform, and the pulpit have been abundantly used to assert that the action of the South was a "wicked and causeless rebellion." All this with a view to lead our own people of the coming generations to think that their fathers were moved by ambition, prejudice, greed, and a spirit of tyranny over a helpless race to precipitate a war against "the best government the world ever saw." It seems to me that a brief statement of the actual issues involved in that war will vindicate the righteousness of the Southern people in seeking to establish an independent government.

1. The South fought for the sacredness of constitutional guarantees, that they might not be treated as "a scrap of paper" to be set aside by the interest or the sentiment of any section of the Union. The Constitution was the compact, or bond, of union to which the States agreed in forming the republic. It defined clearly the rights granted to the Federal government, and all other rights of sovereignty were reserved to the States. The South insisted on a strict construction of the Constitution and the limitation of the general government to the powers granted in that instrument. By a theory of implied powers invented by the Federalists [here used to mean Liberals] the sphere of the general government could be, and was, indefinitely extended. The South held that a persistent and determined violation of the Constitution released her from the compact, and in this she was sustained by Daniel Webster, the great Northern expounder of the Constitution. The attempt of Mr. Lincoln's apologists, some of them Confederate soldiers, to justify his open, confessed, and egregious violations of the Constitution by the assertion that he did it to preserve the Union seems to me silly, as it declares that he destroyed the bond of union to hold the Union together. He overthrew the Constitution that he might under its forms establish a different government, a consolidated nation, rather than a federated republic. The South fought for the form of government established by Washington, Jefferson, Madison, and their compatriots.

2. The South fought for the right of a State, as a member of the

Federal compact, to be the ultimate judge of the violations of the compact and of the mode and measure of redress, and this involved the right of withdrawal from the Union when the State should consider that the best or the only remedy against invasion of her rights. This right has been asserted over and over again by New England statesmen and legislatures in 1803, 1814, and 1845. And Mr. Lincoln in the thirtieth Congress, of which he was a member, asserted the same doctrine in vigorous terms. The South exercised this right only after a [Left-wing] political party [then the Republicans] became dominant in the North whose leaders had denounced the Union under the Constitution as "a covenant with death and a league with hell," a party which had passed in many Northern States personal liberty bills directly annulling the Constitution and had denied the rights of the South in the territories that were largely won by her blood and statesmanship. When that party had elected a [big government Liberal] President pledged to carry out its policies, then she withdrew from the Union and resisted to the death Mr. Lincoln's effort to coerce her into submission to these wrongs. Even Mr. Lincoln confessed that he had no right "to reduce the seceding States to obedience by conquest."

3. The South fought to free herself from a commercial tyranny which used the general government to give special privileges to the Northern and Eastern sections by levying high tariffs on those things which she had to buy abroad, thus exacting heavy tribute for the benefit of "infant industries" that never seemed to grow to maturity. And rivers and harbors of the Northern States, with their extensive opportunities for graft, were improved at immense expense to the comparative neglect of the Mississippi River and the magnificent harbor of Norfolk and other Southern points. The South fought for a government that gave equal opportunities to all the States and sections and special privileges to none.

4. The South fought to free herself from outside interference and fanatical intermeddling with her domestic institutions—the right to manage her own internal affairs in her own way. She had inherited a system of domestic slavery forced upon her originally by the rapacity of England and by the activities of New England slave traders. She had taken the victims of this rapacity, black savages from Africa, and in two centuries had given them a measure of Christianity and civilization, had made them the best-cared-for and most contented body of laborers in the world. Then in New England and other Northern States was organized a propaganda whose object was to free the negroes even at the price of destroying

the Union and arousing the slaves to the butchery of their masters' families. This ruthless purpose showed its real spirit in the John Brown raid of 1859, when a noted thief and murderer tried to arouse the slaves to insurrection and was backed by influential leaders of the abolition [that is, communist] propaganda. When he received the just punishment of his deeds [hanged], he was canonized by large numbers of Northern people as a martyr, and his statue represents the State of Kansas in the National Hall of Fame. When this abolition [communist] fury gained control of a great political party [the Republicans, then the Liberal party] and elected the President of the United States [Lincoln], it was plain that interference and efforts to destroy the kindly relations of the white and black races would continue. It was time for the Southern States to withdraw and defend their homes and their most sacred rights at any cost.

Confederate Major John C. Pelham of Alburtis Light Artillery, circa 1862. General Lee called him "the gallant Pelham."

. . . Of course we know that there was a very large element in the North [Southern sympathizers, or "Copperheads"; that is, Yankee Conservatives] that was thoroughly opposed to the theories, purposes, and methods of the party which forced the war upon the South; but they were held in subjection by the unscrupulous use of force and falsehood as to the purpose of the war. Our contention is that the South was justified in her heroic defense of the principles of constitutional liberty. And that we were right in interpreting the motives and aims of the [Left-wing] party of which Mr. Lincoln was the leader is clearly shown by the [authoritarian and unconstitutional] Reconstruction measures which followed the victory of the North. These measures, the shame of all good men in the North, were the logical outcome of the policy of the abolitionized [that is, communized] Republican party in waging the war, for the effort of the Reconstruction leaders was for a mighty centralized government at Washington, with absolute control of the Southern States as conquered provinces and ultimately of all the States, the central government to determine what rights might be given to the State, the right of unlimited taxation either directly or by tariff exactions, and the supremacy of the negro in politics and in social life. Negro judges, negro legislatures, negro and white social intermingling were no accident; they were the logical result of abolition [communist] sentiment and legislation.

Against these things the South had to fight or be traitor to her traditions, to her blood, and to the true principles of civil and religious liberty. She fought "that government of the people, by the people, and for the people might not perish from the earth." And her defeat leaves it still in doubt whether the present regime of the trust or the labor union is to prevail over liberty, equality, and fraternity. The South is proud of her record. Though defeated, she fought to the death for liberty, justice, and truth.[243] — REV. JAMES H. MCNEILLY, NASHVILLE, TENNESSEE

Confederate breastworks, Petersburg, Virginia, April 3, 1865. Mounds with chimneys (to the right) mark the sites of underground soldiers' quarters.

Confederate Private Austin Augustus Trescott, Co. A, 21st Mississippi Infantry Regiment, circa 1863.

10

SPEECH TO CONFEDERATE VETERANS AT THE CONFEDERATE MONUMENT, ARLINGTON CEMETERY

☞ . . . By those qualified to judge, and that without regard to section, it is now universally admitted that you [Conservative, at the time, Democratic] men of the South did not create the causes of that sad and terrible war, nor were those causes exclusively a Southern product. They were nation-wide, and your generation inherited them, and not from your immediate ancestors. They were in the facts of our national life, the joint contribution of our revolutionary and colonial forefathers, North and South. They were sown in the Constitution itself and were seen and noted, but could not be prevented by the men who wrought out that amazing document. With the makers of the Constitution there was a vague and feeble hope that the division in sentiment, in prejudice, in purpose, in interpretation, which ran deep down into the subsoil of that compact of astonishingly able compromises, might be healed by a slow first intention of our developing Federal union, that our opportunities, our necessities, our dangers might prevent infection of the wound of division and produce a healthy granulation of sound living tissue. Our form of government was an experiment, an acknowledged experiment, the most venturous experiment in the turbulent history of civics. Its framers feared its failure. Some predicted that it would fail, some few foresaw and foretold a bloody conflict, certain, unavoidable. Prior to the Revolution the only sovereignty known and acknowledged in the English speaking colonies of this country was in the crown of England. At the beginning of the Revolution each colony assumed and asserted the sovereignty of its citizens. Except the specifically enumerated powers delegated to the United States by the Constitution or prohibited by it to the States, all others were reserved to the States; and this enumeration of rights, it was declared, could not be construed to deny or to disparage others retained by the people. In the Constitution some fundamentals were untouched or overlooked, others were undeveloped. There was a wide neutral and unexplored, if not unsuspected, territory of rights and powers between the several States and the United States. There was ample room for differences, constant provocation to debate. Through long decades, in every known forum, on every hustings, with an ability never excelled, with a learning as exhaustive as the available records made possible, the greatest and best-trained intellects of the country argued, they discussed, they disputed. Neither section consistently maintained one interpretation. Each shifted its position according to its interests or its necessities. Only just before your birth did the two sections crystallize into diverse opinions.

Confederate Captain Edwin Festus Cowherd of Co. C, 13th Virginia Infantry Regiment, circa 1863.

You were born into the settled belief that at your option you had a right to secede, a right inherent in the undisputed sovereignty of the States, a right proclaimed by the Virginia Constitution when it ratified the Constitution in these words: "The powers granted under this Constitution, being derived from the people of the United States, may be resumed by them whensoever the same shall be perverted to their injury or oppression." And you acted on the conviction that your democracy, your liberty, your honor made secession a necessity. The [Liberal Northern, then Republican] men you fought were born into the honest persuasion that the Constitution did not provide for the disruption of the States; that secession was ruinous and wrong; that, if need be unwillingly, you must be held in the Union, even at the expense of a fratricidal war, and when you seceded they made war. Secession was no sudden expedient. You believed it to be a lamentable and a last necessity. Only with agony did you break the bond your forefathers had given their blood to form. With these honest opposite and firm convictions the war was inevitable. Nothing but the red blood of hearts, precious alike in the North and in the South, could fill the crevice left in the foundation of our government. That blood superabundantly shed completely filled that crevice, and this monument above these honored and ever-beloved heroes of the South, hard by the honored and ever-beloved heroes of the North, Americans all, is the material and sufficient evidence of a country genuinely reunited, of a people once more living harmoniously together in the house which their fathers had builded, with the old controversy forever settled, the old wound forever healed. This monument is not the memorial of a bloody division; it is the seal of a fraternal union.[244] — BISHOP COLLINS DENNY, RICHMOND, VIRGINIA, JUNE 6, 1917

THE OLD SOUTH & MODERN GERMANY

☛ [Introductory note:] I hope that no one who reads this paper [the *William and Mary College Quarterly Historical Magazine*] will suppose that I have any feeling in the matter. I am only correcting errors of Northern [Left-wing] writers, and I trust that, after more than half a century since the War between the States, this may be done without exciting any sectional bias. On the other hand, I have no idea that the authors of the articles noticed below were themselves actuated by any ill feeling. It is just a habit merely that some Northern men have of mistaking the facts of history. So far from all Northern writers and speakers acting any ungenerous part, some of the noblest tributes to the [Conservative] South have come from the North.

The United States has declared war against Germany [World War I] and entered into a world contest of which no one can tell the consequences. It is a just and righteous war waged by this government in vindication of long-violated rights guaranteed by the international law. And yet at a moment when union and cooperation on all lines of action are highly expedient there seems to be a concerted effort by [Liberal] Northern writers and speakers to cast slurs upon the [Conservative] Old South by drawing analogies between it and Germany. This course has been taken without any regard for the feelings of the present generation of

Southern men, who see no reason to be ashamed of the conduct of their ancestors.

Probably the most vicious of these [Left-wing] attacks appeared in the New York *Times* for April 22 [1917]. Under the title of "The Hohenzollerns and the Slave Power," the spirit of the Old South to 1861 is said to have been essentially analogous to that of Germany. The slave power was "arbitrary, aggressive, oppressive." "The slave power proclaimed the war which was immediately begun to be a war of defense in the true Hohenzollern temper." "The South fought to maintain and extend slavery, and slavery was destroyed to the great and lasting gain of the people who fought for it, so that within a score of years from its downfall the Southern people would not have restored it had it been possible to do so."

Here is the old [communist] trick of representing the weaker power as the aggressive factor in history. An earlier instance of it occurs in the history of the *Times's* own State. The early [Left-wing] New England writers in excusing their own aggressiveness represent the rich New England colonies, with their thousands, as in imminent danger of being wiped out and extinguished by the handful of Dutchmen at New York. And so it has been with the Southern question. In one breath the Northern historian has talked like the *Times* of the "arbitrary, aggressive, and oppressive power" of the South, and in the next has exploited figures to show the declining power of the South from the Revolution down to 1861. With its "indefensible institution" the South's attitude was necessarily a purely defensive one, and [John C.] Calhoun never at furthest asked any more than a balance of power to protect its social and economic fabric. The North began the attack in 1785 with a proposition to cede to Spain the free navigation of the Mississippi River. In 1820 it attacked again when Missouri applied for admission as a State with a constitution which permitted slavery. It attacked once more in 1828 and 1832, when, despite the earnest protest of the South, it fastened on the country the protective tariff system; and the attack was continued till both Congress and the Presidency were controlled by them. When in pursuance of the decision of the Supreme Court the Southerners asked for the privilege of temporarily holding slaves in the Western territories until the population was numerous enough in each territory to decide the continuance of slavery for itself, it was denied them by the North. Why can't the *Times* tell the honest truth that in this long contest between the growing [Liberal] North and the weakening [Conservative] South it was the North that was "arbitrary, aggressive, and oppressive," that its design from the first was to exploit the South to its own advantage, and that the South only resisted this exploitation?[245] The permanent exclusion of slavery from all the national territory—a principle for which the North contended in 1860—was clearly a more aggressive force than the so-called "extension of slavery," which meant nothing more than its temporary toleration during the formative period of a new State.

It is certain that if nature had been left to regulate the subject of slavery, not one of the Western territories would have had slavery, the odds, by reason of immigration and unfitness of soil and climate, being so greatly against it. In 1861 the [Liberal] North had obtained complete mastery of the political power in the country, and the [Conservative] South, feeling no satisfaction in a union where the majority was so utterly hostile to it, seceded.

Did the slave power "proclaim the war," as the *Times* asserts? Here it is again the old story of the weak man assaulting the strong, the lamb attacking the wolf. Every sensible man knows that the South would have been very glad to have had independence without war. But Lincoln would not even receive the Confederate commissioners for a parley on the subject. He made the ostensible ground of the war an attack on Fort Sumter when, after vacillating for almost a month, he forced the attack, contrary to the advice of his own cabinet, by sending an armed squadron to reenforce the fort. Not a man was killed, and yet Lincoln, without calling Congress, which had the sole power under the Constitution, suspended the writ of *habeas corpus*, instituted a blockade [unlawful], and set to work to raise and organize an army to subdue the South [also unlawful]. President [Woodrow] Wilson waited for two years, till two hundred American citizens had been killed by the Germans, and even then took no hostile step without the action of Congress. Who had the "Hohenzollern temper," the North or the South, in 1861?

Did the "South fight to maintain and extend slavery"? The South fought for independence and the control of its own actions, but it did not fight to extend slavery. So far from doing this, by secession the South restricted slavery by handing over to the North the Western territory, and its Constitution provided against the importation of slaves from abroad.

Slavery was indeed destroyed by the war, and it is perfectly true that no one in the South would care to restore it. At the same time we see no reason why we should be grateful for the way in which slavery was destroyed. At the beginning of the Union there was a strong sentiment in the Southern States, especially in Maryland,

Virginia, and North Carolina, against the existence of slavery; but the action of three of the New England States in joining with the two extreme Southern States to keep open the slave trade for twenty years through an article in the Constitution and the subsequent activity of New England shipping in bringing thousands of negroes into the South made its abolition a great difficulty. The development of the cotton industry and the subsequent tremendous [communist] propaganda launched against slavery caused the views of many in the South to change, and they came to regard it as a beneficent institution; but this was largely a defensive attitude. It is a fact that the South at no period in its history made any guarantee to the North as to the time of its abolition, and the moral question, or the present unwillingness of the South to reestablish the institution, is a totally different one from the historical or material question. In view of the fact that the example of Germany shows that the highest military and industrial developments are not incompatible with a very limited freedom in the citizen, no one can be certain that slavery of the African race in the South would not be a more productive condition than freedom, especially as long as they remain congested as they are in the South and race distinction and subordination are thereby perpetuated.

And here we may ask the question. Was the decline of the South attributable to slavery? Before the [America] Revolution, Virginia and the South up to about 1720 had much less population and wealth than the North; but from that time to the Revolution, with the great influx of slaves, the South forged ahead and acquired all its opulence and importance. Then came a relative decline and finally by war a change to the abolition of slavery. Has the South improved by the change? Since the war for Southern independence fifty-two years have elapsed, but the South relative to the North is far behind what it was in 1861. The single State of Massachusetts, which in 1860 was about equal in wealth to Virginia, has now more wealth than all the eleven States that went into secession, if we leave out the State of Texas. And how about the fabulous wealth of New York and Pennsylvania? To one step taken by the South since the war the North has taken twenty. Make all the allowance for the impoverishment by the war one chooses, and there is no real reason to suppose that the case will be different fifty years hence.

The primal cause of the decline of the South after the Revolution was not slavery, but the presence of the [illiterate and unassimilated first and second generation] negro under the new conditions created by the Union. The secondary causes, principally dependent upon the primal, were the oppressive sectional legislation by the National Congress, agricultural pursuits as contrasted with manufactures, and failure to receive any share of the vast emigration from Europe. These factors are as much in existence now as before 1861.

. . . A word or two may be said as to the ethics of secession and its possible success and actual defeat. As an original question, union is always better than division. If the united empire of all the English-speaking people had not been broken in 1776, perhaps through this overwhelming power universal peace would now be a fact instead of universal war. Had the American colonies failed in their contest with Great Britain, as at times it appeared they would do, even with the powerful assistance of France, all hope would not have been extinguished. There is no reason to suppose that any English colony would ever have experienced the condition of a Spanish satrapy. Probably after a few years, under a change of party and the growing sense of liberty in England, the rebellion itself would have fallen into disrepute in America. But even union, great as the idea is, is not the only thing to be considered. Certainly if in 1776 the unjust and unconstitutional taxes imposed by the British government created an incompatibility which justified the rupture of the British Union, there was just as much reason for the rupture of the Federal Union when the two sections had an "irrepressible" issue between them.

Some things are assured. Had the [Right-wing] South succeeded, it would have had its own laws suited to its own conditions, and it would have developed along its own lines. As it is, it has been forced to conform itself to the conditions of the [Left-wing] Northern section and to be merely tributary to the interests of that section. Brought in direct relation with the rest of the world, slavery, if it had survived the war, would have felt the general condemnation more acutely, and there is no reason to suppose that the evil would have been perpetuated. As to its relations with the Northern Confederacy, it is reasonable to assume that the South's peace conditions would not have been more disturbed than have been the peace conditions of the United States with Canada, which extends along the whole of our Northern border. Fear of the Northern power would have proved the bond of the Southern States. Above all, success would have saved the South from the extensive demoralization incident to all conquests. No one supposes that the New South compares with the Old South in moral force and vigor; and while in the North since the war there has been a marked rise in the character of its public men, in the South, on the other hand, there has been a marked decline. Many

Southerners, by the allurements of Federal offices, Northern capital, and personal preferments, sold their birthrights for a mess of pottage and deserted the old [Conservative] Southern ideals.

The South after the war had the choice of remaining hostile and sullen and of proving, like Ireland, a thorn in the side of the government; but, eminently practical, it resolved to accept the result in a loyal and genuine spirit. Aided by that vast body of Northern citizens constituting the Democratic party [then the Conservative party], who condemned autocracy and who in the fashion of the times have been stigmatized as "copperheads" [that is, Northern Conservatives who sympathized with the South], they managed to rehabilitate themselves as partners in the restored America, from which they are not to be shaken even by any ill-founded and unjust attacks on their history after the spirit of the *Times* article. Not only did self-interest point the way, but there was a recollection, which proved immensely important, that if the North had preserved the Union the Union itself had been chiefly built up by the wisdom of Southern statesmen.

But to come back to the *Times* article and its Hohenzollern analogy, which section represented German spirit more nearly, the North or the South? As a matter of fact, the North went to school to the South in democracy. In the beginning of the Union the North was the headquarters of the Federalist [that is, Left-wing] party, the party of aristocratic ideas, and the South was the headquarters of the Republican [that is, Right-wing] party, the party of democratic ideas. The leaders of the first were [Left-winger Alexander] Hamilton, of [Liberal] New York, and [Left-winger] John Adams, of [Liberal] Massachusetts, who [like most Liberals then as today] had no confidence in the fitness of the people to rule. The leaders of the second were [Right-winger Thomas] Jefferson and [Right-winger James] Madison [both of Conservative Virginia], who taught the true doctrines of popular rights. Personal independence among the whites was far greater in the South than in the North, for in the latter section the menial duties were discharged by white servants, and there were no white servants in the South.[246] It was a condition peculiar to the South that the poorer the white man, the more jealous he was of his rights and his liberties. Any authority the rich slaveowner possessed over his poorer white neighbors was due to their own free volition and was a mere concession to superior education and refinement. Henry Adams, in his *History of the United States*, gives a description of the poorer classes in Virginia, which was true in the early days and continues true to this day:

"Nowhere in America existed better human material than in the middle and lower classes of Virginia. As explorers, adventurers, fighters, wherever courage, activity, and force were wanted, *they had no equals*; but they had never known discipline and *were beyond measure jealous of restraint*."

On the other hand, the difference between the rich and the poor was always great in the North, and this difference has continued to grow deeper and wider, till in this day [1917] a perfect chasm exists between the multimillionaire and the poor man of the slums. The greatest master of slaves in the Old South was nothing in social and political power compared with the present master of Wall Street.

It is sometimes stated that the majority of the Southern whites, despite personal independence, had little or no influence in political affairs; but this if true, and it is not, is offset by the equal or greater number of poor persons in the North who were similarly without weight in political affairs. These included the vast population of the slums of the cities and the millions of immigrants who were mere tools of the manufacturers, men who spoke English with difficulty and were brought up under servile conditions in the lands of their birth. This condition gave rise in the early days to the Albany regency in New York and the city boss of the Tweed type in more recent times, factors in Northern life whose spirit was thoroughly autocratic [that is, dictatorial].

The fact is, there was never anything in common between the system of [Left-leaning] Germany and the system of the [Conservative] South. The German system represented always civil efficiency, great military establishments, and strict subordination of the citizen to the government. The South had little civic organization, was principled against military armaments, and the governmental power in every Southern State was circumscribed within the narrowest limits. There was no likeness whatever between [John C.] Calhoun and [Jefferson] Davis and [Otto von] Bismarck and [Helmuth] Von Moltke. The two first were typical [Right-wing] Southern gentlemen, plain in their dress and manners and deferential even to negroes, and the other two were haughty [Left-wing] representatives of caste who despised the peasant of their own race and color as a common worm.

No country ever waged a war on principles more different from Germany than did the Southern States. Germany justifies its campaigns of "frightfulness" on the plea of necessity, but in any result its national entity is secure. The South, on the other hand, knew that failure in arms would mean the extinction of its national being, but there were some things it could not do even to preserve this; and so Robert E. Lee commanded her armies on land, and Raphael Semmes roved the sea, but no drop of innocent blood stained the splendor of their achievements.

While I am glad to say that the North did not go to the same extent as Germany, the general policy of its warfare was the same, one of destruction and spoliation, and the campaigns of [Left-wing Union Generals Philip H.] Sheridan and [William T.] Sherman will always stand in history in the catalogue of the cruel and the inhumane. The expulsion of all the inhabitants from Atlanta and the burning of the city was the prototype of the martyrdom of Louvain. Rheims and its ancient cathedral have suffered less from the shells of the Germans than beautiful Columbia and Savannah suffered from the torch and wanton depredation of the Federal [U.S.] soldiers.

So much for the *Times* article, and just a few words in reply to an article of similar though much milder character which appeared in the February number of the *World's Work*, entitled "America in the Battle Line of Democracy." In contrast with the *Times*, the author of this article with commendable fairness admits that the Old South had no Kultur [culture] like Germany's, "designed to drive democracy off the earth," and "no dreams of a slave super-state," imposing its iron will upon the peoples of other nations; but the analogy between a victorious South and a victorious Germany is given in this sentence:

> "Nevertheless, despite its lesser menace, if the Confederacy had won, the greatest experiment in democracy would have been broken in two."

In this sentence there is lack of clearness, if not of logic. If "the greatest experiment in democracy" is intended to mean the United States geographically speaking, "the breaking in two" would have been necessarily true. But if the words are to be understood as meaning the principle of popular rule, then the statement is absurd, for an abstract idea cannot be "broken in two." It is to be assumed, therefore, that the rupture of the Union is what the writer intends, but how does this afford any analogy to a victorious German autocracy? So far as democracy is concerned, the situation would not have been changed from what it was in 1860. There would have been the same States with and without slavery, and the only difference would have been two governments instead of one. Nor would the division of the Union resemble anything like the spirit of Germany, whose aim is not to divide, but to heap up territories and extend its conquering power over the world.

In the same article the writer in pointing the moral to his story quotes Lincoln's Gettysburg address and states that these last words of his speech, "That the nation shall under God have a new birth of freedom and that government of the people, by the people, and for the people shall not perish from the earth," described the great cause for which Lincoln sent armies into the field. Here is the same lack of logic and historic accuracy. The [Liberal] North had been antagonistic to the [Conservative] South from the first days of union, but it was really the jealousy of a rival nation. The chief elements that first entered into the situation were antagonistic interests and different occupations. Manufactures were arrayed against agriculture, a protecting tariff against tariff for revenue. Long before the quickening of the Northern conscience, and while the slave trade was being actively prosecuted by men from New England [the birthplace of American slavery], that section was particularly violent against the South. Its dislike of the great Democrat [that is, Conservative, Thomas] Jefferson went beyond all words, and he was described by the Chief Justice of Massachusetts as "an apostle of atheism and anarchy, bloodshed and plunder."[247]

Confederate Corporal William M. Wright, Co. E, 10th Tennessee Cavalry Regiment, Clarksville, Tennessee, circa 1863.

How much of real opposition to slavery was mixed with this old-time jealousy in the Republican [that is, Liberal] plank against slavery in the territories in 1860, no one can exactly say; but, with the exception of the abolitionists [that is, socialists and communists], all persons, Democrats [Right-wingers] and Republicans [Left-wingers] alike, were unanimous in saying that there was no intention of interfering with slavery in the States. Lincoln was emphatically of this view and so declared in his inaugural address.

In instituting hostilities soon after, had he avowed that he wished to raise armies to fight the South for a "new birth of freedom" and to keep popular government "from perishing from the earth," he would have been laughed at; had he avowed his purpose of raising armies for the abolition of slavery, none but the abolitionists [socialists and communists] would have joined him. He obtained his armies only by repeatedly declaring that he waged war merely for preserving the Union. As a matter of fact, the abolitionists [socialists and communists], the only true friends of immediate emancipation, became so disgusted with his opinions as to the objects of the war that nine months after the Emancipation Proclamation they proposed a deal with the Confederacy on the subject of abolishing slavery.[248] Later, in the latter part of 1864, Mr. [Jefferson] Davis sent Duncan F. Kenner abroad to guarantee to the governments of Great Britain and France the abolition of slavery in return for recognition.[249] He went too late; but suppose independence and emancipation had resulted from either of these two movements, with what grace could the South claim that it had fought the war for abolition? No more really has the North any right to claim that it sent armies into the field for freedom because abolition resulted at the end. In his Gettysburg speech Lincoln talked about popular rule, but this was a kind of oratory in which South and North had both indulged for one hundred years,[250] and we are told that the speech made no particular impression at the time. It was not until long afterwards that its literary merits were recognized, and from praise for its sentiments the Northerners have passed to regarding it as presenting a historical concept of the war. It seems that they have ended in actually assuming to themselves the monopoly of all democratic principles on this continent.

The same indifference to the real facts characterizes an article in the *Literary Digest* for April 21 [1917], entitled the "Moral Climax of the War." It states that the Russian revolution and the entrance of the United States into the war have brought about a thrilling change in the moral aspects of the war "resembling the new impulse that fired the North when the Emancipation Proclamation was issued." Did any "new impulse" fire the North as a result of the Emancipation Proclamation? On the contrary, Lincoln in his "strictly private" letter[251] to [Hannibal] Hamlin, the Vice President, manifested his keen disappointment:

> "While I hope something from the proclamation," he wrote, "my expectations are not so sanguine as are those of some friends. The time for its effect southward has not come, but northward the effect should be instantaneous. It is six days

old; and while commendations in newspapers and by distinguished individuals are all that a vain man could wish, the stocks have declined and troops have come forward more slowly than ever. This, looked soberly in the face, is not very satisfactory."

The Democrats [Conservatives] made extensive gains in the House of Representatives, and the elections came near being what the steadfast Republican [then Left-wing] journal, the *New York Times*, declared them to be, a vote of want of confidence in the President. James Ford Rhodes, the historian, commenting[252] upon this disappointing result, writes as follows:

"No one can doubt that it (the proclamation of emancipation) was a contributory force operating with these other influences: the corruption in the War Department before [Edwin M.] Stanton became Secretary, the suppression of freedom of speech and freedom of the press, arbitrary arrests which had continued to be made by military orders under the authority of the Secretary of War, and the suspension by the same power of the writ of *habeas corpus*. But the dominant cause was the failure of our armies to accomplish decisive results in the field."

It was the subsequent employment of negro troops against their masters[253] and the starvation of the South by the blockade, enabling the North to obtain the desired victories, that brought about the collapse of the Confederacy, not the Emancipation Proclamation. In the face of this plain statement of the facts it is difficult to understand where the analogy suggested by the writer in the *Literary Digest* exists. The "thrills" were conspicuously absent in the matter of the Emancipation Proclamation when issued.

To my mind, the present righteous war with Germany represents far more closely the Old South in 1861 than the Old North at that time. Indeed, no two men ever stood farther apart in principle than [Woodrow] Wilson and Lincoln. What does the war [that is, World War I] stand for as currently [1917] stated in the United States?

1. The war stands for the rights of the "small nations," and it insists that Belgium, Serbia, and Roumania have as much right to exist as Germany. The South in 1861 made a similar claim. The Union really consisted of two distinct nations different in institutions, occupations, and ideals. No stronger witnesses of this fact are to be found than Lincoln and [William H.] Seward, both of whom spoke of the Union as containing the elements of an

"irrepressible conflict" and declared that it could not endure "half slave and half free." Of the two nations [republics], the South was much the weaker, but it had a population greater than Belgium or Serbia or Bulgaria or Romania and a territory more extensive than Germany and Austria combined. By fighting a four years' war on equal terms with the powerful North it gave the best proof of its right to exist in the sun as an independent nation [republic]. After drawing in vain on his own population and that of Europe to suppress the South, Lincoln resorted to forcible enlistments from the South's own population to achieve his victory, confessing that without the negro troops the North "would be compelled to abandon the war in three weeks."[254]

2. The war [World War I] stands for "government based on the consent of the governed." This doctrine was announced by [Thomas] Jefferson in the Declaration of Independence, and France appeals to it in behalf of Alsace and Lorraine, Italy in behalf of Trieste and the Trentino, Romania in behalf of Transylvania, while Poland and Bohemia demand its recognition in behalf of themselves. The sacred character of the principle is affirmed by [Woodrow] Wilson in his inaugural address March 4, 1917, and in his letter to the new Russian government,[255] but Lincoln and the North in 1861 denied its application to the South.

3. The war [World War I] stands for "humanity" as recognized by the international law. It is a solemn protest against the frightfulness of unrestricted submarine warfare, the barbarous destruction of the property of noncombatants, the deportation of the innocent inhabitants of conquered regions, etc. How stands history in regard to the North and South? Here is the testimony of the late Charles Francis Adams, a Federal brigadier general and President of the Massachusetts Historical Society: "Our own methods during the last stages of the war were sufficiently described by [Union] General [Philip H.] Sheridan when, during the Franco-Prussian War as the guest of [Otto von] Bismarck, he declared against humanity in warfare, contending that the correct policy was to treat a hostile population with the utmost rigor, leaving them, as he expressed it, 'nothing but their eyes to weep with over the war.'" The doctrine that there must be no humanity in warfare proclaimed by Sheridan was also voiced by [Union General William T.] Sherman in his letter to [Union] General [Ulysses S.] Grant on March 9, 1864: "Until we can repopulate Georgia, it is useless for us to occupy it; but the utter destruction of its roads, houses, and people will cripple their military resources. . . . I can make the march and make Georgia howl."

[Union] General [Henry W.] Halleck wanted the site of Charleston, thick with the heroic memories of the [American] Revolution, sown with salt, and General Grant in his order to [Union] Gen. David Hunter thought it prudent to notify the crows to carry their provisions with them in future flights across the valley. Nothing need be said of the ferocious spirit of the lesser tribe of Federal [Union/Yankee] commanders. And Lincoln, in spite of the fine, catchy sentiments of his Gettysburg speech, gave his sanction to the same policy when he said[256] in response to a protest against his employment of negro troops:

> "No human power can subdue this rebellion without the use of the emancipation policy and every other policy calculated to weaken the moral and physical forces of the rebellion."

Secretary [Salmon P.] Chase in his diary shows that on July 21, 1862, in a cabinet meeting the President expressed himself as "averse to arming the negroes"; but shortly after, on August 3, 1862, the President said on the same question that "he was pretty well cured of any objections to any measure except want of adaptedness to putting down the rebellion." To the spoliators, Hunter, Sheridan, and Sherman, he wrote his enthusiastic commendations and not a word of censure. Were Lincoln and his supporters humane? By an act of Congress approved July 17, 1862, and published with an approving proclamation by Lincoln, death, imprisonment, and confiscation of property were pronounced on five million white people in the South and all their abettors and aiders in the North. To reduce the South to submission, Lincoln instituted on his own motion a blockade, a means of war so extreme that, despite its legality under the international law, it has evoked from the Germans the most savage retaliation when applied to them. He threatened with hanging as pirates Southern privateersmen [a lawful profession] and as guerrillas regularly commissioned partisans. He suspended the cartel of exchange; and when the Federal prisoners necessarily fared badly for lack of food on account of the blockade and the universal devastation, he retorted their sufferings upon the Confederate prisoners, thousands of whom perished of cold and starvation in the midst of plenty. Medicines were made contraband, and to justify the seizure of neutral goods at sea great enlargement of the principle of the "ultimate destination" was introduced into the international law. The property of noncombatants was seized everywhere without compensation, and within the areas embraced by the Union lines the oath of allegiance was required of both sexes above sixteen years of age under penalty of being driven from their homes. Houses, barns, villages, and towns were destroyed, and the fiercest retaliation was employed by the Federal [U.S.] commanders to strike terror into Southerners. Even the act for which Lincoln has been most applauded in recent days, his Emancipation Proclamation, stood on no real humanitarian ground.

Lincoln vacillated very much before deciding to put it out. At a meeting of the cabinet on July 22, 1862, he announced tentatively his purpose of publishing such a paper; but on September 13, only ten days before his issuance of it, he absolutely ridiculed the thing, though not altogether committing himself against the step, pronouncing it as futile as "the pope's bull against the comet." He asked:

> "Would my word free the slaves when I cannot even enforce the Constitution in the Rebel States? Is there a single court or magistrate or individual that would be influenced by it there?"

The doubtful success of the battle of Antietam raised his spirits and decided him the other way; the Emancipation Proclamation was issued; but instead of taking the high ground of general liberty, he applied it to only that portion of the South over which he had confessed himself powerless, exempting from its application that part where he had real authority by means of Federal [U.S.] occupation.

Issued in this form, it could not have contemplated to any appreciable extent a moral effect in making friends for the government. What then? The Confederates denounced it as an effort to incite the negroes to rise and murder the women and children in the South, living lonely and unprotected while their men folks were at war. In this light it was denounced severely in England and France. When the negroes did not rise, Lincoln denied that such was his purpose; but against this are his own words. After urging, as stated, the futility of the Emancipation Proclamation, he used this language:[257]

> "Understand, I raise no objections against it on legal or constitutional grounds, for as chief of the army and navy in time of war I suppose I may take any measure which may best subdue the enemy. Nor do I urge objections of a moral nature in view of possible consequences of insurrection and massacre in the Southern States. I view this measure as a practical war measure, according to the advantages or

disadvantages it may offer to the suppression of the rebellion."

Here there are a distinct recognition that insurrection and massacre were a possible consequence and a distinct affirmation that objections of every nature, legal, constitutional, or moral, had no weight as against the advantages or disadvantages of the measure as a practical war measure. This much, at least, may be said, that if there was any measure calculated to incite the negroes this was the one, and that if the dreadful consequences did not ensue it can never be credited to the humanity of Lincoln, who realized the peril. All the credit goes to the humanity with which the slaveowners treated their slaves.

As Lincoln said, he "wanted to beat the Rebels," and to win he resorted to the most extreme measures. When he thought that milder action might have a chance of prevailing, he tried that too, but seemingly without any particular preference. He never understood the Southern people, and to him the whole question of secession seemed to be the money value of slaves instead of one of violated rights or self-government, as it undoubtedly was. He is, therefore, much lauded for his humanity by those who take the same view of Southern men's motives as his own for suggesting on February 6, 1865, to his cabinet to pay the Southern people $400,000,000 if they would quit fighting, the money "to be for the extinguishment of slavery or for such purpose as the States were disposed."[258] But his cabinet was opposed to the proposition, and Lincoln did not insist on it. It never got anywhere; but to show the light in which Lincoln regarded his offer it is interesting to notice that he justified it to his cabinet, not on any generous or noble grounds, but on the mercenary one that the sum "would pay the expenses of the war two hundred days." The proposition really contained a gross insult to the Southerners. Their men were not fighting for the money value of slaves, but for a national existence which they deemed menaced in the old Union. There was no other meaning to their taking up arms, and there was no solution to the war except independence or absolute defeat. Their principles were not for sale. Suppose [George] Washington during the American Revolution had received from the British government a pecuniary offer to quit fighting, what would have been his reply?

Contrast with all this the record of President [Jefferson] Davis and his generals on land and admirals at sea. The campaign of [Confederate officers Robert E.] Lee in Pennsylvania and the victorious career of Raphael Semmes on the ocean were a contrast in every respect to the actions of the Federal commanders ([Union General] George B. McClellan always excepted) and were about as far removed from the "frightfulness" of the Germans as anything could be. And President Davis, although greatly blamed for his humanity from some quarters[259] in the South, avoided in every way possible the practice of the doctrine of retaliation, which made the innocent responsible for the guilty. The only regrettable instance of severity by the Confederates was the burning of Chambersburg by [C.S.] General [John A.] McCausland in retaliation for [Union] General [David] Hunter's campaign of fire and sword in the Valley of Virginia. It was not a part of any settled plan of destruction and occurred only after a demand for a moderate indemnity had been made of the inhabitants—an indemnity whose amount would make the Germans smile—and had been refused by them.

4. Finally, the war [World War I] stands for democracy against autocracy. As already stated, the [Conservative] South was the champion of democratic principles when the [Liberal] North was wedded to those of an aristocratic character. The South had its [Thomas] Jefferson and [James] Madison, and the North had its [Alexander] Hamilton and John Adams. The difference between the rich and the poor was always greater in the North than in the South, so far as the whites were concerned.[260] Lincoln adopted absolute autocratic principles during the war, making necessity[261] his plea, just as Germany has done. Despite the rulings of his own chief justice and the plain language of the Constitution, he [illegally] assumed the power of suspending the writ of *habeas corpus* and under the pretense of the so-called war powers set aside any clause of the Constitution interfering with his will. He arrested thirty-eight thousand people in the North at different times and confined them in prison, subjected to great hardships, without any formal charge or trial, and in reply to a protest from a mass meeting at Albany, N. Y., used this extraordinary language: "The suspension of the *habeas corpus* was for the purpose that men may be arrested and held in prison who cannot be proved guilty of any defined crime." After the war the South was held by the North under military government for twelve years, and the most ignorant elements of the population were intrusted with the power under the Reconstruction policy. If this does not signify autocratic rule similar to that which Germany would impose upon the world, what does?

How utterly unlike Lincoln has been the conduct of President [Woodrow] Wilson, who has scrupulously consulted Congress on every important question concerning the war with Germany!

In conclusion, it is proper to state that it affords the writer no pleasure to indulge in recrimination; but as long as Northern writers will insist on misstating facts and rubbing the old sores the wrong way they need not expect absolute silence from the South. The North is to be congratulated upon its conversion to the principles for which the South contended both in the Revolution and the War between the States. The war with Germany should be pushed to a successful conclusion, that the rights of small nations, the right of local self-government, the right of humanity, and the right of democracy be "rendered safe for mankind."[262] — LYON G. TYLER, PRESIDENT WILLIAM & MARY COLLEGE, WILLIAMSBURG, VIRGINIA, JULY 1917

LEE'S ACTIONS PROVE THE RIGHTNESS OF THE C.S.A.
☞ . . . General Lee's services in the United States army were highly creditable and even distinguished before the Mexican War. This war gave him his first opportunity to show his great military talents. [U.S.] General [Winfield] Scott made him his chief of staff, and it is said that he really planned most of the important battles fought by General Scott in the Mexican War. His services were so brilliant that he won more renown in that war than any other officer, except General Scott and [later Confederate] General [Richard] Taylor. General Scott said of him: "He was the very best soldier I ever saw in the field." And after the Mexican War he declared that Captain Lee was the greatest living soldier in America. General Scott further said long before the beginning of the War between the States:

> "If I were on my deathbed tomorrow and the President of the United States were to tell me that a great battle was to be fought for the liberty or slavery of the country and asked my judgment as to the selection of a commander, I would say with my dying breath: 'Let it be Robert E. Lee.'"

It will thus be seen what a reputation General Lee had at the outbreak of the war. He has been greatly censured and condemned by the Northern people and Northern writers for having left the regular army of the United States and joining the Confederacy to fight against his country. His enemies claim that he was guilty of treason in having sworn as an army officer to defend the Constitution of the United States, then having resigned and joined the Confederacy and becoming the chief instrument to aid in destroying the Union. This was one of the charges against General Lee when he was indicted and cited for trial after the war.

That General Lee loved the Union with a great love is unquestioned. He was one of the last to resign of the officers of the [U.S.] army who joined the Confederacy. As you know, Virginia was one of the last of the Southern States to leave the Union, and this was not done until after Mr. Lincoln had called out seventy-five thousand volunteers to put down rebellion in South Carolina and other Southern States which had already left the Union and after Virginia had been called on to furnish her quota of these seventy-five thousand men to fight for the Union.

When Virginia left the Union, Lee, who had been waiting on her action, promptly sent in his resignation and stated to General Scott that, his State having gone out of the Union, he owed his first allegiance to her and that he could remain in the service of the United States no longer.

It was with a heavy and sorrowing heart that General Lee took this action. He saw all the greatness of the North and her inexhaustible resources in men and money, and he knew full well the poverty in materials and money of the South; but he felt that all his traditions, his family, his home, and his dearest sympathies were with the people of Virginia. He realized that, while the South was not without blame, the North was the aggressor, and he felt that his first duty was to Virginia. He believed in States' rights and that a State was a sovereign and could leave the Union at any time the majority of her people determined to do so, and that his first allegiance was to his State. He could not bear to fight against his own people, those dear Virginians whose good opinion and love he considered more precious than life itself.

His father [Henry Lee III], speaking in the Congress of the United States on the Kentucky and Virginia resolutions in the year 1789, had said in debate: "Virginia is my country; her will I obey, however lamentable the fate to which it may subject me."

His father had written Mr. [James] Madison a letter in 1792 in which he said:

> "No consideration on earth could induce me to act a part, however gratifying to me, which could be construed into disregard of or faithlessness to this commonwealth."

And right here is an opportunity to look somewhat more fully into General Lee's character. In refusing to remain in the United States army he had given up the chief command of a great army and the prospects of a great reward. He well knew the great disparity between the resources of the North and of the South. He knew that if the North put forth all of her strength in the struggle the chances were greatly against the South's gaining her independence. He was not deceived as to the relative chances of the sections. In fact, I have always felt that he did not see how the South could be successful. But, notwithstanding that, he was determined to fight for and, if need be, to die with the people of Virginia in any way that the majority of the people of his State decreed. He believed it was his duty, and to do his duty had ever been the paramount object of his life.

The South began the war with a white population of about 5,500,000. Of these, the [white] military population numbered about 1,065,000; and of this military population, 200,000 were inhabitants of the mountain regions, which strongly espoused the Union side.

The North began the war with a white population of 22,000,000. Of these, her fighting men whom she could call into the field numbered about 3,900,000. The North enrolled of this fighting strength 1,700,000, besides enlisting 700,000 foreigners and 186,000 negroes.

The South enlisted not exceeding 900,000 [white] men all told during the war. [Editor's note: Today we recognize the fact that as many as 1,000,000 African Americans served in the Confederate military in one capacity or another—over five times as many as those who served in the Union military. As defined under U.S. military law, these black Confederates are legally considered true soldiers, veterans who fully qualified for postwar pensions. L.S.][263]

The North had a completely organized government—State, War, Navy, Treasury, and Justice. The South had nothing and was compelled to organize everything, and, further, she fought on the principle of States' rights, a principle of such disintegrating influence as to enable any State to neutralize the action of the Confederacy at any time.

The North had $11,000,000 of taxable values against $3,000,000 in the South, outside of the slaves. The North had all the manufactories, all the best means of transportation, and an incalculable superiority in equipment. When war broke out the South could hardly manufacture a tin cup or a frying pan, a railroad iron or a carpenter's tool. The North also possessed great superiority in firearms and munitions of war. The South had no arms, no powder, no munitions. The South had no navy, and this was the most fatal of all her defects. Had the South possessed even ten good ships to prey upon the commerce of the United States and one secure naval base, the result of the war would certainly have been in doubt. The navy of the United States, with its 200,000 men, enabled it to seal up all the harbors of the South and to shut it off from all the supplies from the outside world and finally starve it into submission, and no man was more fully aware of the odds against the South than General Lee.

Confederate Brigadier General Samuel McGowan, 14th South Carolina Infantry Regiment, Richmond, Virginia, circa 1863.

. . . In the first of the Seven Days' Battles around Richmond in June, 1862, Gen. Joseph E. Johnston, who was in command, was seriously wounded, and General Lee was placed in command of the Army of Northern Virginia; and from that time forward he commanded this noble army, the like of which had never been seen in the world before; an army composed of the very flower of the South; an army made up of men who felt that they were fighting for their homes, their firesides, and the sacred rights guaranteed to them under the Constitution which their forefathers had helped to establish; an army whose imperishable deeds will reflect glory on the South to the end of time; an army that never went into battle when it was not confronted by terrible odds, but which knew only victory save on three great occasions—at Sharpsburg, when it was a drawn battle, at Gettysburg, and again when, with numbers reduced to one-fifth of its adversaries and starving, it was compelled to lay down its arms at Appomattox.

The renown and the fame of Robert E. Lee are inseparably connected with this mighty army. He made it, and it made him. It is possible that neither could ever have been so great without the other. Without disparagement to others, I think I can truthfully say that no such general has ever been found on this continent and no such army has ever lived in all the tides of time. These are strong words, but I challenge any man to refute them. . . .[264] — COLONEL L. D. TYSON, SPEECH IN HONOR OF LEE-JACKSON DAY, KNOXVILLE, TENNESSEE, JANUARY 19, 1917

ONE REASON THE CONSERVATIVE SOUTH FOUGHT FOR SELF-GOVERNMENT

☞ . . . There are times in the history of a people when it becomes them to look backward in order to compare their past with their present and forward in order to provide for or against their future, and such a time has come to the people of the Southern States. Looking backward, our past is luminous. It was Thomas Jefferson who wrote the Declaration of Independence, which ranks with the Magna Charta and the Bill of Rights as one of the three greatest and most far-reaching State papers among men. It was George Washington who established that independence. It was James Madison who, as. the constructive thinker, did more than all others to create the Constitution and to secure its ratification. It was John Marshall, that prince of jurists, who as Chief Justice for thirty years settled the relations of the executive, legislative, and judicial branches of the government.

John Fiske, New England historian and Harvard professor, says that these four, Jefferson, Washington, Madison, Marshall, with Alexander Hamilton, "are distinguished above all others, and in an especial sense they deserve to be called the founders of the American Union." Hamilton was foreign-born and -bred. The other four were Virginians.

Of the fifteen Presidents from 1789 to 1861, eight were from the South, and a ninth, William Henry Harrison, was born and educated in Virginia. During the seventy-two years between 1789 to 1861 Southern Presidents occupied the executive chair forty-eight years, or two-thirds of the time, and five of them were reelected. Northern Presidents occupied it but twenty-four years, one-third of the time, and no one of them was reelected.

It was Thomas Jefferson, of Virginia, who inaugurated the Southern Democratic [then Conservative] policy of expansion and added the Mississippi Valley to our, at that time, narrow and most vulnerable domain. It was James K. Polk, of Tennessee, who added Texas and the Pacific Slope to our domain; and, in pursuance of this Southern Democratic policy of expansion, during the incumbency of President [Andrew] Johnson, of Tennessee, Alaska was added; and as Jefferson gave us our oceanic river and Polk made us an interoceanic power with the most impregnable continental position among men, the possession of Alaska and the Aleutian Islands gives us control of the North Pacific, while the possession of the Panama Canal Zone (the thing of the most far-reaching importance in our history since the acquisition of the Mississippi Valley and the Pacific Slope) and the possession of Hawaii, Guam, and Manila, the only insular additions to our domain by a Northern President, Porta Rico excepted, make an attack on our Pacific Coast impossible except by the English; and the United States and England, the mighty mother and her mightier first-born, are natural allies in the Anglo-Saxon's manifest destiny to command all seas and to control the commerce and manufactures of all lands.

Conservative U.S. President Thomas Jefferson of Virginia.

It seems absolutely incredible now that the addition of the Mississippi Valley, of Texas, and of the Pacific Slope was each bitterly opposed by New England with threats of "secession," of a "dissolution of the Union," of a formation of a "Northern Confederacy," "peaceably if we can, forcibly if we must," said Josiah Quincy, of Massachusetts, the contention that the Union was dissoluble having been constantly maintained by the New England States till after the Mexican War. The right of secession was taught at West Point as late as about 1840; and if Jefferson Davis or any others of the West Point cadets had been tried for treason, the textbooks in which they had been taught the right of secession would have been put in evidence. None of them were tried, and if they had been tried they could not have been convicted.

From 1831 to 1860 [radical Left-wing agitator William Lloyd] Garrison's [unpopular progressive newspaper] *Liberator* had proclaimed that the Constitution was a "league with death and a covenant of hell," because it licensed slavery, and that slavery must be abolished, which "could not be done," he reiterated, "except by dissolving the Union." And while the Republican party [then the Liberal party], with such a secession record of its most influential members, suppressed secession in the United States of North America with force of arms between 1860 and 1865, the same Republican party supported secession in the United States of South America by force of arms in 1903 [by then the Conservative party], only forty years later. "O consistency, thou art a jewel!"[265]

It thus appears that the men of the South have been preeminent in statesmanship. They brought the republic forth, they maintained its infancy, they cherished its growth from a narrow strip of territory along the Atlantic Coast to its interoceanic manhood, and they steadily opposed its dismemberment, which dismemberment at every period of its growth to manhood New England steadily and repeatedly proposed up to 1860, while the famous proclamation of the Southern Democrat [then Conservative], Andrew Jackson, of Tennessee, put an end to nullification in South Carolina in 1832, the only time that secession was talked of in the South before 1860, and that was about a tariff tax, as the War of 1776 was about a tea and stamped paper tax. . . .[266] — COLONEL ROBERT BINGHAM, ASHEVILLE, NORTH CAROLINA

IN EARLY AMERICA THE RIGHT OF SECESSION WAS ACKNOWLEDGED BY BOTH THE NORTH & THE SOUTH
☛ In erecting this memorial to the Confederate and Union soldiers in the war of 1861, my motive was to pay just tribute to men whose convictions of right and duty in a great crisis of our country's history led them to devote their lives, their fortunes, and their sacred honor to the cause they each believed to be just and righteous; and in thus honoring them fifty years after the close of that great struggle my earnest hope is, at least in our own little county, to draw together the minds and hearts of our reunited people and to commit to oblivion the unhappy differences which then divided and distracted us. This purpose in this day of peril to our liberties [the onset of World War I] should appeal irresistibly

to every thoughtful and patriotic man and woman in our midst, for the time has come when, however we may have differed in the past, we should feel that we are one nation, with one mind and heart upon the question of the day and hour, and with one fixed and high purpose—that the principles of free government shall not perish from the earth and that the blessings which out fathers bought with their blood we will defend and preserve with our own blood.

From the foundation of the Constitution of the United States to the close of the War between the States there were two distinct schools of constitutional construction in this country—one holding the doctrine of ultimate State sovereignty, embracing the right of withdrawal from the Union whenever the State should deem it essential to the preservation of its reserved rights; the other maintaining the absolute sovereignty of the Union and the denial of the right of withdrawal for any cause. These divergent views were held by men of equally distinguished ability as constitutional statesmen and of undisputed integrity and patriotism. The question was not sectional in its origin or its development. It grew out of honest differences of opinion upon fundamental principles inherent in the science of government and which were speedily brought into sharp conflict by the opposing material interests of the Northern and Southern States, resulting from different climatic and economic conditions and from the wide difference in the prevailing avocations of the sections. But the right to withdraw from the Union was frequently asserted as openly in the North as in the South. In 1803 and 1804 there was an open and wide movement in the New England States for a Northern Confederacy, supported by such men as Timothy Pickering, Theophilus Parsons, and George Cabot.

[New Englander] Josiah Quincy said in Congress in 1811 that the admission of Louisiana as a State would be "tantamount to the dissolution of the Union" and that "in such event it would be the right of all and the duty of some definitely to prepare for separation, amicably if they can, violently if they must."

[New Englander] Senator [Henry Cabot] Lodge, speaking in 1877 of the discussions in the Hartford Convention of 1812 of the dissolution of the Union, says: "It must be remembered that the question of nullification and secession was an open one."

[New Englander] John Quincy Adams, in a discourse on the Constitution delivered in 1830, said: "To the people alone is there reserved as well the dissolving as the constituent powers, . . . and the people of each State . . . have the right to secede from the Confederated Union."

[New Englander] George Lunt, the distinguished editor of the *Boston Courier*, writing in 1866 of certain resolutions of the Massachusetts Legislature in 1845, said: "It is quite clear that they enunciated the assertion of the right of nullification and secession."

[Northerner] William Rawle, of Pennsylvania, one of the most eminent of American lawyers, in his *Commentaries*, written in 1829, described the Union as "an association of the people of republics" and said: "The States may wholly withdraw from the Union. The secession of a State from the Union depends on the will of the people of such State."

St. George Tucker, of Virginia, in his *Commentaries* in 1802, laid down the same explicit doctrine, and these two commentaries on law were used as textbooks in the United States Military Academy at West Point up to 1840 and during the period when Jefferson Davis, Gen. Robert E. Lee, and Gens. Albert Sidney [Johnston] and Joseph E. Johnston were students at West Point.

It will thus be seen that the constitutional right of secession continued to be, in the language of Senator Lodge, an open and disputed question until the Gordian knot was cut by the sword in 1865 and the doctrine of Federal [that is, national] sovereignty was established through constitutional amendments as the unquestioned law of the land. . . .²⁶⁷ — JAMES A. PEARCE, SPEECH AT PRESENTATION OF MONUMENT HONORING CONFEDERATE & UNION SOLDIERS, CHESTERTOWN, MARYLAND, AUGUST 11, 1917

WHAT DID PRESIDENT LINCOLN'S STATESMANSHIP ACCOMPLISH?

☛ It is the habit of Mr. Lincoln's admirers, both in this country and in Great Britain, to claim for him a chief place in the ranks of the greatest statesmen of the world, as the highest example of political wisdom that our country has known. He is proclaimed as the peer of Washington and as having completed and confirmed Washington's work. His utterances are quoted by the newspapers and magazines and works on political science for the guidance of our leaders in the conduct of our government, and his conduct of the war against the South is commended as a wonderful example of successful statesmanship.

A statesman is one who understands the science of government and who can so control and direct the government of his country that amid the varying interests of the people justice shall be maintained and their highest interests be protected and developed. The State is the institute of right, giving to every one what is justly due. And so righteousness is the foundation of enduring government, and the man who disregards righteousness in conducting his government is no true statesman. He is laying up for his country strife and confusion in the time to come.

In free governments, like England and America, where the ideals of liberty and justice are expressed in constitutions, traditional or written, the highest type of constructive statesmanship will observe faithfully the requirements of the Constitution; and if he believes that for the good of the people these requirements should be modified or changed, the change should be made in accordance with the provisions of the fundamental law. If it be done otherwise at the behest of an individual or a party, it becomes tyranny and is dependent for its enforcement, not on justice, but on force of arms. The principle holds, whether the rights of individuals or States are involved.

Tested by these principles, what Mr. Lincoln did was, by overwhelming physical force in war against the South, to overthrow the government which Washington and his compatriots established and to substitute for it a government similar in form, but different in its ideals and purposes. That which Washington founded was a federated republic [which he called a "confederate republic"] of equal sovereign States; the government which Mr. Lincoln substituted for it is a consolidated nation with centralized powers, and of the limits or extension of those powers the nation is the ultimate judge.

Originally the Federal government could exercise only such rights and powers as were granted by the States, and the Southern States always insisted that this grant should be strictly construed; and especially did they urge the equality of the States under the Constitution, so that no special right or privilege should be given to one State or section above the others. Under the new [Lincolnian] form of national government the States can exercise only such rights and powers as the central government may allow. And the Supreme Court of the United States, the final tribunal, not only can set aside any decision of the highest State court, but assumes authority to invalidate any act of Congress, although Congress represents all of the States. The party of which Mr. Lincoln was the head [the Republican party, the Liberal or Left-wing party at the time] was an advocate of a centralized government and of special privileges to certain classes and sections of the country and claimed the right to interfere in the domestic and local institutions of the States.

It is agreed by those who have studied the history of the

formation and adoption of the Constitution that it would never have been adopted by a single State if that State had supposed it was surrendering the right to withdraw from the compact should it believe its highest interests were endangered. Indeed, Virginia and New York made this right of withdrawal a condition of their ratifying the instrument, while North Carolina and Rhode Island refused to ratify it until they were satisfied on this point. And this right of withdrawal was asserted over and again by both the great parties which divided the electorate up to 1845.

It is true that probably a majority of the present generation thinks the change in the nature of our government is a blessing. One very able Northern man has written a book, entitled *The Nation*, in which he contends that the nation is the divinely ordained ideal of government and that a federated [that is, confederated] republic[268] is a rebellion against God's ordinance. But in this case it is not the question whether Mr. Lincoln conscientiously believed that a centralized nation was best for our country, nor is it a question of whether this new order is actually best. But the great fact that calls in question Mr. Lincoln's statesmanship is that by sheer brute force of overwhelming numbers and resources and with ruthless cruelty through his agents he shot to death on a hundred battle fields the doctrine of State sovereignty and enforced his doctrine of the supremacy of the nation by the utter devastation of the Southern States. Thus setting aside the original compact which bound the States in the Union, he set up a government acceptable to himself and his [Left-wing] party. And when force tramples on guaranteed rights, that is not statesmanship, but it is only bald tyranny and bad faith; and no assertion of a purpose to preserve "government of the people, by the people, and for the people" can make it anything else. It set aside in the South the fundamental principle of free governments that "governments derive their just powers from the consent of the governed." While it is claimed that the new order is best, it is well to remember that it has introduced dangers of the conflict of classes and interests which threaten revolution and the destruction of liberty and justice which no statesmanship can avert. Under the new order, by means of tariff legislation, vast accumulations of wealth in the hands of a few men give them a power which is a menace to the government, enabling them to control or to defy it.

On the other hand, the organization of labor against an economic tyranny worse than slavery, while right and proper, yet has given to these organizations a power which can stay the activities of the nation and paralyze its economic life. And in both cases organized wealth and organized labor, armed with irresponsible power, are ruthless in the determination to enforce the demands of their special interests. The Kaiser [German Emperor and King of Prussia Wilhelm II] is not more despotic than the trust or the union. As a consequence a social and industrial revolution imperils.

Again, the bringing of an immense body of an . . . utterly unfit race [that is, the largely illiterate first and second generation African population at the time] into the citizenship of the country, with the inevitable corruption of the electorate, was not true statesmanship. And while [white supremacist and white separatist] Mr. Lincoln personally deprecated such a course,[269] yet it was the legitimate outcome of his policy and of the Emancipation Proclamation. Reconstruction was the logical result of the abolition of State sovereignty.

The war for the Union invited aliens from all nations to join the Federal armies and thus opened the doors for avast influx of foreigners, a flood of immigration that threatens to drown our institutions. These foreigners invested with our citizenship are largely loyal to their native lands, rather than to our country, in this hour of stress and sorest need.

These and other evils as the result of Mr. Lincoln's policy he probably did not and could not have foreseen; but they discount the statesmanship that forced a theory of government repudiated by the founders of the republic and that is in the interests of sections and classes and special privilege.

I believe that if the pleas of the Virginia Convention of 1861 had been heeded and Fort Sumter evacuated, as promised, the war could have been avoided and the Union ultimately restored according to the principles of the Constitution. But one question of Mr. Lincoln's to the Virginia commissioners, "What will become of my tariff?" reveals the quality and aims of his statesmanship—only to maintain the supremacy of his [Left-wing] party and section.[270] — REV. JAMES H. MCNEILLY, NASHVILLE, TENNESSEE

SPEAKING OF AMERICAN STATESMAN ALEXANDER H. STEPHENS

☛ Of his wider usefulness, it may be said that the thanks of all American patriots are due to him as an untiring champion of constitutional government and State rights, as opposed to threatening encroachments of the Federal [nationalized] branch of our dual system.[271] — LOUIS PENDLETON

WHAT THE TWO SIDES STOOD FOR
☛ The Confederacy stood for what we are now blessed with, State sovereignty, the right of the people to rule; [big government Liberal Abraham] Lincoln stood for the consolidation of our Federal system into a nation, which would have destroyed liberty by transferring supreme authority from the people to the general government.[272] — *CONFEDERATE VETERAN* MAGAZINE

TRUE CAUSE OF THE WAR
☛ It has been to a large extent assumed that negro slavery was the cause of that war. This is not strictly true. It was the occasion of the war, but not the principal cause of the war. The real cause of the war was sectional jealousy, the greed of gain, and the lust of political power by the Eastern States [that is, Yankee Liberals]. The changing opinions of civilized nations on the subject of slavery furnished the occasion which enabled [Left-wing] political demagogues to get up a crusade which enabled them in the end to overthrow, in part at least, the Constitution of the United States [a Conservative document], and to change the character of the Federal government [in the direction of socialism] by a successful revolution.[273] — HON. JOHN H. REAGAN (FORMER CONFEDERATE POSTMASTER GENERAL UNDER PRESIDENT JEFFERSON DAVIS), APRIL 19, 1903

SOME INSIGHT INTO HOW THE U.S.A. WAS FORMED
☛ A study of the Constitution, of its formation, and of the writings of those who attended the Federal Convention leads one to a somewhat different conception of history since 1787 and of the present office of the Constitution. It becomes strikingly true that the Constitution is not a theoretical document new in its ideas, provisions, and basic principles, but a document drawing on the experience, both good and bad, of the several States, with their constitutions and with the Articles of Confederation,[274] and of England and other foreign countries. [James] Madison, writing in *The Federalist*, pointed out that in the discussion and formation of the Constitution there were "three sources of vague and incorrect definitions: indistinctness of the object, imperfection of the organ of conception, and inadequateness of the vehicle of ideas." After enumerating the difficulties due to factional interests, he continues:

> "Would it be wonderful if, under the pressure of all these difficulties, the convention should have been forced into some deviations from the artificial structure and regular symmetry which an abstract view of the subject might lead an

ingenious theorist to bestow on a constitution planned in the closet of his imagination?"

The Constitution was not a perfect document, but made to meet immediate needs, especially threatening anarchy and separation and the future only in so far as they could see it, and to mold into workable shape the hopes of a liberty-loving people desirous of a more adequate government, but jealous of their newly won rights. In order to make progress in the framing of a document acceptable to a great variety of conceptions and opposing interests, there was a continual use of compromises.

For the present purpose a compromise may be defined as an agreement reached concerning some impending measure in which sharply contrary opinions are evident and the result gained only through mutual concessions of the opposing factions. In a compromise it is not necessary that each side make equal sacrifices or make them at the same time. Sometimes, especially in the light of our present knowledge, it is difficult to see that the point conceded by one side is of any importance compared with concessions made by the other.

The work of the convention may roughly be divided into five parts:

(1) Organization of the convention and adoption of rules;
(2) consideration by a committee of the whole of a set of resolutions presented by [Edmund] Randolph, of Virginia, and another set drawn up by [William] Patterson, of New Jersey, and others and, as an outgrowth of the discussion, the adoption of nineteen resolutions known as the "Resolutions of the Committee of the Whole";
(3) modification by the convention of these into twenty-three resolutions which serve as a basis for the first draft of the Constitution;
(4) consideration of the draft of the Constitution drawn up from these resolutions by a Committee of Detail;
(5) consideration of the report of a Committee of Revision, or Style, and final adoption of the Constitution.

The Federal Convention was called

> "for the sole and express purpose of revising the Articles of Confederation and reporting to Congress and the several legislatures such alterations and provisions therein as shall, when agreed to in Congress and confirmed by the States,

render the Federal Constitution adequate to the exigencies of government and the preservation of the Union."

The means to be used and the extent to which it should be strengthened was a basic cause for difference of opinion. Should the common government be given simply an extension of power? or should the federation now existing be overthrown and a nation set up in its place? Briefly, should the common government be Federal [that is, confederated, the original intention of the Conservative Founding Fathers—whose focus was states' rights] or national [that is, a nationalized super government, which called for the abolition of or sharp curtailing of states' rights, with all political power consolidated in Washington, D.C.—the intention of the Liberal Founding Fathers]? The question was of prime importance in the early weeks of the convention. General [Charles C.] Pinckney and Mr. [Elbridge] Gerry expressed doubt "whether the act of Congress recommending the convention or the commissions of the deputies to it would authorize a discussion of a system founded on different principles from the Federal Constitution." The term "Federal" means here, as it should mean in all discussions of this question, "federated" or "confederated." [Editor's note: The word federate is a corruption/abbreviation of the word confederate. L.S.][275] In the Committee of the Whole the Nationalists [that is, the Liberals or left-wingers of that day] seemed to get the better of the argument for on May 30 it adopted the first resolution, which declared it to be "the opinion of this committee that a national government ought to be established, consisting of a supreme legislature, executive, and judiciary." This action was nothing less than revolutionary, as is shown by the resolution of the Continental Congress, cited above, in authorizing the convention and pointed out by the Federalists [that is, "Confederalists," the Conservatives or Right-wingers of that day]. But the Nationalists claimed that the federation could not be patched up satisfactorily, "that a union of States merely Federal will not accomplish the objects proposed by the Articles of

Confederate Colonel Thomas Benton Roy, 17th Virginia Infantry Regiment, Nashville, Tennessee, circa 1863.

Confederation," and that "a new government must be made. Our all is depending on it; and if we have but a clause that the people will adopt, there is then a chance for our preservation." Necessity justified overstepping their authority, especially when they "were recommending a system of government, not making one."

After the report had been given to the convention, but before any action had been taken, Mr. Patterson, of New Jersey, introduced a plan "purely Federal and contradistinguished from the reported plan." This, Patterson said, was the work of "several deputations, particularly that of New Jersey," and hence became known as the New Jersey plan. The first resolution stipulated that the Articles of Confederation ought to be so revised, corrected, and enlarged as to render the Federal Constitution adequate to the exigencies of government and the preservation of the Union. The government was still to be Federal, not national. The convention again went into a committee of the whole for a consideration of this plan so essentially different from the former resolutions which they had adopted. After much debate the New Jersey plan was rejected, and Randolph's general scheme was adopted.

In the general controversy of national *versus* Federal government the former had won in the committee, where generalizations only were expressed. But after examining the records of details considered and analyzing the Constitution itself, it is evident that the Nationalists [Liberals] were obliged to concede important points to the Federalists [Conservatives]. These points conceded form the basis of the largest and most important class of compromises made in the Federal Convention. In a study of the Constitution before its adoption, *The Federalist*, described by [historian John] Fiske as "the greatest treatise on government that has ever been written," sets forth the proposed new government as a "compound republic partaking both of national [country-wide government control] and Federal character [states' rights]." Farther on it speaks of "the portion of sovereignty remaining to the individual States and of preserving the residuary sovereignty" of the States. Fiske described our Constitution as providing for "two kinds of government operating at one and the same time upon the same individuals, harmonious with each other, but each supreme in its own sphere. Such is the fundamental conception of our partly Federal [confederated], partly national [centralized, consolidated] government. [George Ticknor] Curtis says that this

> "plan was undoubtedly a novelty in political science.... The individual might owe a double allegiance, and there could be

no confusion of his duties, provided the powers withdrawn from the States and revested in the nation were clearly defined."

In the struggle between State sovereignty and centralized government several powers were not, however, defined—for example, the power of a State to withdraw from the Union and the right of control of slavery. It is probable that the delegates did not recognize the importance of the first question and avoided the second because they had reason to believe that it would die a natural death. The formation of the first political parties was determined by a difference of interpretation of the Constitution on the rights of States and nation. The modern question of State or national decision on woman suffrage and prohibition is a matter on which the Democratic and Republican parties differ. These illustrations reemphasize the influence on the convention of immediate need against anarchy or permanent separation as more important than these future needs and differences. Giving satisfaction to differences of opinion by means of compromise rather than ideal constitutional law was the only hope of the Constitution's general acceptance. For a better understanding each of these concrete questions of State *versus* national control, the election of Congressmen, the powers of Congress, control of the State militia, Federal inferior courts, slave importation and navigation acts must be unraveled from the tangled skein of speeches, motions, amendments, and committee reports and treated separately. Hardly any of these questions were, however, settled solely, or even mainly, on the relative merits of State or national power, but other influences of a determining nature entered in to make the decision. This will be very evident as we proceed.

The first of these compromises between Nationalists [Liberals] and Federalists [Conservatives] was on the question of representation. It involved two subquestions: (1) By whom shall the representatives be elected? (2) Shall their apportionment be according to the proportion of people or wealth or on a basis of equality among the States? The two were closely related. On the second the small States naturally took sides against the large, for with proportionate representation a State with the population of Virginia would have sixteen Congressmen to Georgia's one. The vote on the first question was influenced seriously by the delegates' attitude on the second. The Federalists found it much easier to get Nationalists from small States to give in to their method of electing senators, because that was considered to go hand in hand with equality of representation. We thus find delegates from the small States who strongly opposed proportional representation lining up in favor of election of the second branch by State legislatures.

But, although involved in equality of representation, the question of the method of electing legislators for the national government was an issue of its own. It was clearly stated in the third and fourth resolutions of the Committee of the Whole, while equality of representation came in their seventh and eighth.

Although we to-day can see in the argument little reason, it was held by many delegates that taking power from a State legislature and giving it to the people of the State decreased the power of the State. In so far as the people elected the national officers directly, the States as units were relegated to the background. Patterson flatly declared that "if the sovereignty of the States is to be maintained, the representatives must be drawn immediately from the States." [James] Wilson favored popular election in both houses:

> "In explaining his reasoning it was necessary to understand the twofold relation in which the people would stand—first, as citizens of the general government and, secondly, as citizens of their particular State."

In making the former they ought to make it independent of any control by the latter. [Oliver] Ellsworth opposed him and urged maintaining the "agency of the States" in supporting the national government:

> "Without their cooperation it would be impossible to support a republican government over so great an extent of country."

Much of the argument came on popular election of members to the first branch. Wilson considered that such

> "was not only the corner stone, but the foundation of the fabric, and that the difference between mediate and immediate election was immense"; for "the legislatures are actuated not merely by the sentiment of the people, but have an official sentiment opposed to that of the general government and perhaps to the people themselves."

[Rufus] King "supposed the legislatures would constantly choose men subservient to their own views and contrasted to the general interest," and the recent amendment to the Constitution giving the election of senators to the people suggests that there was ground for his supposition. He noted "several instances in which the views of a State might be at variance with the general government and mentioned particularly a competition between the national and State debts for the most certain and productive funds." General Pinckney proposed a compromise "that the first branch, instead of being elected by the people, should be elected in such a manner as the legislature of each State should direct." This motion was voted down four to six, and popular election carried by a good majority.

Now that the Nationalists [Liberals] had won their big point and the Federalists [Conservatives] had conceded a provision for a nation of individuals rather than simply a union of States, the former were disposed to be more lenient. The pull of equality of representation became stronger. In the debate a speech of one of the delegates, Mr. [Nathaniel] Gorham, showed its influence, for he wandered from the issue and stated that he was inclined to a "rule of proportion." But Wilson directly pulled him back: "The question is, shall members of the second branch be chosen by legislatures of the States?" Madison, who favored popular election in both branches, saw the influence of equality of representation and tried to have consideration of the fourth resolution postponed and the eighth taken first. But the motion was lost, and legislative election of senators went through leaning heavily on equality of representation for support. Thus we have our dual Congress, representing the people as desired by the Nationalists [Liberals] and the States as desired by the Federalists [Conservatives].

The other question on the election of representatives proved to be the biggest stumbling block in the whole convention. Under the Articles of Confederation each State had one vote, no matter how many delegates from the State. The same rule was followed in the convention. If representation based on numbers or wealth were introduced, it meant, as pointed out by delegates from the small States, that Virginia, Pennsylvania, and Massachusetts would have enough votes to overrule those from the other ten States, even should they present a solid front. Naturally the small States were loath to give in to the large, because of actual fear of an overriding dominance of the large States. Likewise the large States claimed proportional representation as the only means to prevent a control by a minority of people. It was the same question of federation [that is, confederation] versus nation [that is, centralization]. Equality of State power in the central government is one of the fundamental principles of federation [confederation].

But the division into factions was naturally not on that basis, but according to the size of the States. [Benjamin] Franklin analyzed the situation, saying that the lesser States were afraid of their liberties and the large States of their money. In the committee of the whole the large States succeeded in pushing through the seventh and eighth resolutions, giving proportionate representation in the first and second branches. The vote on the eighth resolution passed by the narrow margin of six to five.

Franklin, who had noted with consternation the warmth [passionate emotions] of the debate in the committee on this question, interrupted the still more heated discussion in the convention by offering the unsuccessful motion "that henceforth prayers imploring the assistance of heaven and its blessings on our deliberations be held in the assembly every morning before proceeding to business." Several weeks later Luther Martin told the Maryland Legislature that the discussion lasted about a fortnight, "during which we were on the verge of dissolution, scarcely held together by the strength of a hair." He said that the large State delegates

> "were informed in terms the most strong and energetic that could probably be used that we would never agree to a system giving them the undue influence they propose; . . . that slavery was the worst that could ensue, and we considered the system proposed to be the most complete, most abject system of slavery that the wit of man ever devised under the pretense of forming a government of free States!"

The vote on proportionate representation in the lower branch finally passed in the convention, six to four. The details of the seventh resolution were postponed to make room for the eighth. The convention was tense. This dreaded matter had to be settled before relations could again become normal. Ellsworth almost immediately moved "that the rule of suffrage in the second branch be the same with that established by the Articles of Confederation." "He hoped that it would be a ground for compromise" with regard to the first branch. He emphasized the national-federal [dual centralized-confederated] nature of the proposed government, and equality between States was conformable to the Federal principle as proportional representation was to the national. He and Martin were about the only delegates to lay much emphasis on this aspect of the question.

When the vote came, two separate factors aided the small States to make a better showing than in the committee. First,

Luther Martin was the only delegate present from Maryland, and he swung that State's vote from a divided one to an affirmative. This made a five-to-five tie, with Georgia still to vote. Now, Georgia, although scant in population, had a large area and was growing fast, so her delegates had sided with the larger States. One of these was Abraham Baldwin, a recent emigrant from Connecticut. Fearful that the small States would immediately withdraw and end the convention, and possibly influenced by his Connecticut kinsmen, he cast his vote in their favor, thereby splitting the Georgia delegation. Luther Martin has expressed his belief that Baldwin did not change his opinion, but simply conceded to his faith in the cause. "All honor to his memory!" exclaimed Fiske. So the vote on the question was five to five, with Georgia divided.

The convention was "now at a full stop," as [Roger] Sherman expressed it. He thought a committee advisable, because they could more coolly consider concessions. After some debate it was voted to select by ballot one delegate from each State to serve as a Committee of Eleven, to whom were referred the eighth resolution and the remainder of the seventh not already voted upon. In the election of this committee the small States played their best card, for the names of the delegates selected suggested what their report would be. On the list were three radical, small State men ([Robert] Yates, Patterson, and Martin), while three of those representing the large States (Franklin, Gerry, and Baldwin) were of a conciliatory frame of mind on this question.

The arguments in the committee were largely a statement of those previously given. Franklin and the original Henry Clay took the first conciliatory step, and the other large State men consented under certain conditions to fall in line. The report had two important concessions, one from each side: First, that all money bills, either for income or expense, shall be originated in the lower branch and not be amended by the second branch; and, secondly, that in the upper branch "each State shall have an equal vote." The new feature offered by the committee was this provision concerning money bills. The idea was evidently borrowed from the British Constitution. The money comes from the people, and the representatives of the people should control it, claimed [George] Mason.

Considerable speculation took place as to just how important this concession of the small States to the large States would be. Madison declared that he could see no concession in it; "for if seven States in the second branch should want such a bill, their interests in the first branch will prevail to bring it forward. It is nothing more than a nominal privilege." But Gerry, the chairman of the committee, declared it to be "the corner stone of the accommodation." "If any member of the convention had the exclusive privilege of making propositions, would any one say that it would give him no advantage over the other members?" Mr. [Caleb] Strong thought that the small States had made a "considerable concession." Martin declared before the Maryland Legislature some weeks later that "the Senate will be rendered almost useless as a part of the legislature." [Pierce] Butler and [Gouverneur] Morris could see no concession, and the latter strongly appealed for a united country giving justice to the majority. "If persuasion does not unite it, the sword will!" he declared heatedly. Mr. [Hugh] Williamson endeavored to calm matters, but still he thought the report contained the most objectionable propositions of any he had yet heard.

The discussion settled clown to the question of a breaking up of the convention, followed probably by secession and civil strife or giving in to the smaller States. Accommodation, declared Mason, was the only means for progress; and as for a dissolution of the convention, he "would bury his bones in the city rather than expose his country to its consequences." The large States had less to lose, however. They still had their desideratum for the lower house, and the money bill provision made that house somewhat more important. The committee had intended that a vote should be taken on its total report, but there was much opposition. So each provision came up separately, was fought over, and finally passed. Equality of States in the Senate went through by a vote of five to four, with Massachusetts divided. Gerry and Strong conceded the demands of the small States. "It is accordingly," says Fiske, "to Elbridge Gerry and Caleb Strong that posterity are indebted for preventing a tie and thus bringing the vexed question to a happy issue." "Great praise," says Curtis, "is due to the moderation of those who made the concession to the fears and jealousies of the smaller States." Thus was "the great compromise," as Professor [Max] Farrand calls it, a success.

Helpful in the consideration of the details of the seventh resolution of the Committee of the Whole were several small compromises. Between a clamor for annual elections of members to the lower house and the provision of the committee for a three-year term, augmented by the difficulty of traveling long distances and the resulting disadvantage to the distant States, a vote was made for a two-year term.

On a question of making a temporary apportionment of representatives from each State much discussion ensued, necessitating reference to two different committees. The final apportionment, sixty-five in all, was "undoubtedly a matter of compromise" between the States. The numbers were settled upon in the second committee; and as it left no record, no proof can be made of this assumption.

The third provision concerning the election of members to the lower branch is classed by most historians as one of the most important compromises. It is the three-fifths provision, so called. The controversy was between delegates of the North, whose States were fast abolishing slavery, and delegates of the South, who claimed that slaves should be reckoned as people in apportioning the representatives according to population. In 1783 the Continental Congress had adopted, in amending the revenue provision, a proposal that five slaves should be reckoned as three citizens. The idea had proved fairly satisfactory, so its incorporation into the Constitution was now suggested. Farrand declared that this three-fifths compromise, as classed by most historians one of the three most important, "ought to be relegated to the myths of the past." He quotes Rufus King in the Massachusetts State Convention as saying that "this rule . . . was adopted because it was the language of all America." He claims that Curtis, the early historian of the Constitution, was influenced to give undue stress to this slavery issue because, in 1858, when his volumes were published, the subject of slavery was predominant in the public interest and that historians since the time of Curtis have blindly continued to overstress this three-fifths clause.

There seems to be some ground for supporting Farrand's position. The question was complicated by other features which occupied much of the debate. It had not yet been decided on what basis taxation should be apportioned. As it was finally placed on a basis of the number of representatives, the North did not have quite so strong objections to including negroes, and the South was not quite so anxious to have them counted. This provision was an influential factor in the final adoption of the three-fifths clause. The insurmountable difficulty of determining whether slaves were people or property also confused the delegates. Most of them hoped that slavery would gradually die out; some thought that as a moral question it could better be handled by the States. Madison records Gerry, Gorham, Mason, Williamson, and Wilson as speaking for acceptance of the three-fifths clause. The question was put to vote separately, but did not pass. The next day, however, "on the whole proposition as proportioning representation to direct taxation and both to the white and three-fifths of the black inhabitants and requiring a census within six years and within every ten years afterwards," it passed by a vote of six to two, with Massachusetts and South Carolina divided. The fact that this three-fifths clause was allowed to slip through along with other features, when on the day before it had failed to pass as a separate issue, indicates its relative unimportance and the influence of the direct taxation clause. On the other hand, the negative vote of the day before indicates that it was hardly the accepted "language of all America." Wilson speaks of the scheme as justified by the "necessity of compromise." A compromise we must consider it, agreeing with Farrand to the extent of not giving it major importance.

Having shown the indispensable use of compromises in establishing a scheme for the election of our national legislators, the question of powers allotted them and of those still held by the State is a natural one. A "spirit of compromise" is evident in several instances, especially toward the end of the convention, when, the main issues having been decided, the delegates rode roughshod over provisions of less importance.

A restriction on Congress, that legislative appropriation for the support of the army should be for no longer time than two years, seems to have been an agreement between the Nationalists and Federalists. The latter feared giving the President a long-continued use of such a powerful weapon as the army. In defending this provision in *The Federalist*, Madison pointed out the power of the House of Commons, corrupted, as they were, by the crown. They can "make appropriations to the army for an indefinite term without desiring or without daring to extend the term beyond a single year." Then he ridicules the State rights men:

> "Ought not suspicion itself blush in pretending that the representatives of the United States, elected freely by the whole body of the people every second year, cannot be safely intrusted with discretion over such appropriations expressly limited for the short term of two years?"

The question of State versus Congressional control of the elections of national legislators caused some debate. [Alexander] Hamilton feared that placing the election in the hands of the States gave them the power to obliterate the national government. "Every government ought to contain in itself the means of its own preservation." So the Constitution gave the power to regulate elections primarily to the State legislatures, but allowed Congress to "make or alter such regulations, except as to the places of choosing senators." Ultimately, therefore, most of the power rested with Congress.

In determining who should control the State militia a perplexing problem was confronted. The question was considered of much importance for the less control that a State had over its militia, the more dependent it would be on the national government. The report of a committee of eleven on this point, made on the twenty-first of August, contained mutual concessions. It gave Congress the power "to make laws for organizing, arming, and disciplining the militia and for governing such parts of them as may be employed in the service of the United States, reserving to the States, respectively, the appointment of the officers and authority of training the militia according to the discipline described." [Luther] Martin thought that the States would never give up this power over its militia. To Madison and Randolph it seemed to be a question of expediency for effectual discipline. They argued for complete national control. But Gerry saw in it a danger to local rights and sarcastically suggested: "Let us at once destroy the State governments and have an executive for life, or hereditary, and a proper Senate." With four States disagreeing, however, the provision for a division of control of the State militias went through.

A controversy over the judicial department of our national government was settled in a noncommittal manner. There had been general agreement on the necessity of a United States Supreme Court. The question was, Should there be also inferior Federal courts? Their establishment was provided for in the report of the Committee of the Whole; but in the convention [John] Rutledge objected, arguing that such would make unnecessary encroachment on the jurisdiction of the States; for State tribunals could handle all cases, and national rights and uniformity of judgment could be secured by the privilege of appeal to the national tribunal. Again, it was a question of strengthening the national government at the expense of the State. Rutledge's argument carried weight, for the provision for inferior Federal courts was stricken out by the close vote of six to four. But the Nationalists [Liberals] were not satisfied. Madison, Sherman, and Wilson saw danger ahead. So they proposed the compromise of allowing Congress to establish these courts, should it see fit. This suggestion proved acceptable; and the fate of the Federal inferior courts was left to the judgment of Congress, to be determined by expediency. Fiske greatly stresses the importance of this provision:

"But for the system of United States courts extending throughout the States and supreme within its own sphere, the Federal Constitution could never have been put into practical working order."

In the light of subsequent history a most important series of difficulties was adjusted between the Northern and Southern States. Madison had pointed out that this was a division greatly to be feared in the future because of the natural opposing interests. More care must be taken, he thought, to satisfy both parties in this division than on the division between large and small States. The interests of the people in the North demanded that commerce be unhampered by the whims of State legislatures and that necessary commercial relations should be freely handled by the National Congress. They, therefore, strongly opposed the sixth section of Article XII of the report of the Committee on Detail providing that no navigation act could be passed by Congress without a two-thirds vote of each house. The South [Conservative] opposed giving the national government unrestricted power to make laws favorable to Northern [Liberal] commercial interests, because they feared a monopoly of the shipping trade, with resulting exorbitant rates.

Also the agrarian South depended upon slaves and unrestricted opportunity to export their products to foreign countries for their prosperity. Any provision to take from the three most southern States the power to import slaves for their rice and indigo fields or to tax their exports was fought with decided vigor. Many delegates, notably Sherman, Ellsworth, and Gerry, favored letting each State decide the slavery question according to its own judgment. Even C. Pinckney declared that if a vote on prohibition of slave importation came up in his State he would favor it. but he strongly opposed giving the national government the right to interfere. Martin, ordinarily a rank State rights man, showed amazing inconsistency by advocating for the national government power "to make such regulations as should be thought most advantageous for the gradual abolition of slavery." Like not a few of the delegates, he was ready to favor national control in matters not vitally affecting his own State.

The question of taxing exports came up first as a separate issue. The vote was not strictly a part of the compromise, but prohibition of a tax on exports by a vote of seven to four undoubtedly aided the passage of the compromise.

The fourth, fifth, and sixth sections of Article VII of the Committee on Detail, dealing with the importation of slaves and with commercial regulations, were referred to a committee of eleven in the hope that "these things may form a bargain among the Northern and Southern States," as Morris expressed it. The committee made the recommendations that "the migration or importation of such persons as the several States now existing shall think proper to admit shall not be prohibited by the legislature prior to the year 1800, but a tax or duty may be imposed on such migration or importation at a rate not exceeding the average of the duties laid on imports," and that a two-thirds vote of Congress on navigation acts be not required. With exceptional good will the year 1808 was substituted for 1800 and the clause accepted. To avoid later friction the maximum tax which could be imposed was arbitrarily fixed at ten dollars per person.

The navigation problem called for considerable discussion. The "liberal conduct" of the Northern delegates on the slavery question caused General Pinckney and Mr. Butler to oppose any necessity for a two-thirds vote, so the final provision of the compromise went through. Madison, in editing his *Journal*, records in a note that "an understanding on the two subjects of navigation and slavery had taken place between those parts of the Union, which explains the vote on the motion impending, as well as the language of General Pinckney and others."

"Too high an estimate," says Curtis, "cannot well be formed of the importance and value of this final settlement of conflicting sectional interests and demands. . . . Thus was accomplished, so far as depended on the action of the convention, that memorable compromise which gave to the Union its control over the commercial relations of the States with foreign countries and with each other," and provided for the eventual extinction of the foreign slave trade.

So far in our discussion we have considered compromises adopted in establishing the legislative and judicial departments of our government. The executive department gave trouble also. Madison told the Virginia State Convention that "the organization of the general government was in all its parts very difficult," and "there was peculiar difficulty in that of the executive." "In agreeing on a method for electing the President," reported Wilson to the Pennsylvania Convention, "there was more perplexity than in any other part of the Constitution."

Various schemes were proposed and were received with more or less favor, each to be thrown out for a more favored one. For a long time election by the national legislature seemed to be a settled thing. This was finally given up because of the opportunity between the legislature and the president for cabal. A scheme of popular choice of Presidential electors grew in favor. But this would give a candidate from a large State such an advantage that a candidate from a small State would have little possibility of success, claimed the small State delegates. A list of our Presidents, with their home States, is abundant evidence of how just was their contention.

Confederate Private A. P. Safford, Co. B, 1st Alabama Infantry Regiment, circa 1863.

Two modifications of the simple scheme of Presidential electors were made before the small State men would accept the plan. First, the number of electors from any State was made equal to the number of representatives and senators. Since the senators were equal in number, no matter how small the State, this gave some advantage over strict proportionate representation. Secondly, if, out of the total vote cast by the electors, there was not a majority for one candidate, the Senate should choose from the first five candidates one who shall be President. In the Senate the small States obviously have the advantage. The large State men claimed that this would happen in a majority of cases, "nineteen times out of twenty," said Mason. So virtually to the large States would fall the power of nomination and to the small States the power of selection. Sherman and King both definitely speak of this balancing of powers.

The compromise finally passed with seven States in its favor. Because of fear of an aristocracy in the Senate, the choice of the President, on failure of the electors to establish a majority, was later vested in the House of Representatives, the members of each State having one vote. The principle of the compromise, however, remained unchanged. The early advent of political parties curbed any opportunity to prove to what extent the electors would fail to secure a majority and how closely Mason had estimated the proportionate number of times the House would be called upon to select a President.

Now that satisfactory adjustments had been made on a basis of the present size of the country and number of States, some provision must be made for future growth by the addition of new States. The delegates were not unmindful of the new country west of the mountains, and several had a hazy fear of a possible future supremacy of this new agricultural section over the commercial coast section. The advocates of wealth as a basis of representation had a view as an important motive a curtailment of power in the new West and Southwest. Gerry and King, of Massachusetts, endeavored to prevent a supremacy of the Southwest by moving that the total number of representatives from the new States should never exceed those from the original States. It failed to pass. So the Committee on Detail seemed justified in including in their article on the admission of new States the phrase "shall be admitted on the same terms with the original States." Gouverneur Morris, always excessively fearful of the new West, succeeded in getting this mandatory clause stricken out by a vote of nine to two and his own substituted to the effect that new States "may be admitted by the legislature."

Apparently this concession was not estimated as important by most of the delegates as Morris considered it. He evidently had a hidden meaning in the phraseology which was not noticed by the delegates. This is suggested by a sentence in a letter to Henry W. Livingston written in 1803: "Candor obliges me to add my belief that, had it [his motion] been more pointedly expressed, a strong opposition would have been made."

"The phraseology is apparently so artless that it might well obtain the unanimous support of the convention," writes Farrand. It never reached any significant importance; and thus the delegates judged it, although Morris tried to read into it the idea that territory becoming a part of the United Sates must be treated as provincial and not be given a voice in the national councils. "I went so far as circumstances would permit to establish the exclusion," he wrote to Livingston.

It is evident that the delegates gave in to Morris on this matter a very minor change, but that he endeavored to interpret the wording of the change to be more than he dared state in the convention. If this is a compromise, as Farrand claims it is, it is of such little importance as to be worthy of no great consideration.

Of the compromises of the Constitution as described in this essay, there seem to be three which stand out as of great importance: (1) The compromise on the question of equal versus proportionate representation in Congress; (2) the compromise between Northern and Southern interests on a control of commerce and slave importation; (3) the compromise on the method of electing the President. Of these three, the first two were basically questions of federation [confederation] or nation [centralization], of State or national control, although decided largely by outside influences. The first and third compromises were the result of mutual concessions between large and small States. The second was but the beginning of a long series of compromises on the slavery question, each one postponing the decision of State or national supremacy. With the minor compromises the relative power of State and nation was usually an issue, but not often the deciding one. All degrees of minority existed. Students do not and need not agree as to the rank of each in importance. How indispensable they were, no one can realize until he reads from the records the very thoughts of the individual delegates, analyzes the great variety of opinions held, recognizes the strain of opposing factions, and sees how often an advance in the work was possible only through a resort to compromises aimed to conciliate opposing opinions and demands.

Wife (or sister) of a Confederate soldier, identity unknown, circa 1860s.

"Thus at length," says Fiske, "was realized the sublime conception of a nation in which every citizen lives under two complete and well-rounded systems of laws, the State and the Federal law, each with its legislative, its executive, and its judiciary moving one within the other, noiselessly and without friction. It was one of the longest reaches of constructive statesmanship ever known to the world."[276] — HAROLD R. BLAKE, DAYTON, OHIO

REPLY TO YANKEES COMPARING THE CONFEDERACY TO 1917 GERMANY

☛ ... [The Liberal Yankees'] argument is, in brief, first, that in the war of 1861 the very conception of government by the people was on trial and would have gone to everlasting smash if the Confederacy had succeeded in maintaining its independence, and this notwithstanding that both of the contending parties "were true Americans" (how this could be is not so clear); secondly, that nations, more particularly as concerns the great war of 1914, are bound by the same moral code which governs individuals.

It seems unfortunate at this time of common endeavor by South and North in the war [World War I] with Germany that such [statements] ... should be written virtually identifying Lincoln's government of 1861 with the allies of 1814 as the army of liberty and by the same token equally identifying the Confederate States with Germany and her allies as the foes of that liberty. But such [words have] ... been written and published widely. So let us now proceed critically to examine the thesis it embodies [beginning with the opening salvo at the Battle of Fort Sumter]. ...

. . . The Washington government's negotiations with the Confederate commissioners preceding the bombardment of Fort Sumter bore all the earmarks of trickery. "The crooked paths of diplomacy," wrote [Confederate] President [Jefferson] Davis to Congress, "can scarcely furnish an example so wanting in courtesy, in candor, and in directness as was the course of the United States

Confederate soldier Achilles Perrin, Co. D, 3rd Kentucky Cavalry Battalion, wearing Kentucky Military Institute uniform, 1861. Fought at Battle of Cynthiana.

government toward our commissioners in Washington."[277]

The Southern Confederacy's position was pacific in the extreme. "We protest solemnly in the face of mankind," Mr. Davis wrote in his message of April 29, 1861, to Congress, "that we desire peace at any sacrifice save that of honor and independence. We seek no conquest, no aggrandizement, no concession of any kind from the States with which we were lately confederated. All we ask is to be let alone; those who never held power over us shall not now attempt our subjugation by arms." In the winter of 1860-61 Southern leaders in the Congress of the United States, Mr. Davis and Mr. [Robert A.] Toombs among the number, advocated a constitutional amendment validating the "Missouri Compromise" line, excluding negro slavery from the common territories north of thirty-six degrees, thirty minutes north latitude, by which the Northwest would have been left for unrestricted Northern expansion and the Southwest for Southern expansion, to the real benefit of both sections and races. And the plea of the South in the peace congress of the States, which was assembled that winter at Virginia's call, was concession and conciliation.

No fair-minded man can read the diplomatic and official record of those proceedings, especially those centering about the Confederate commission to Washington, without concluding that the Lincoln administration deliberately and successfully blocked the South's earnest efforts at conciliation and did so in order that the South might be driven to some overt act, such as the bombardment of Fort Sumter, which would inflame the still reluctant North into supporting a program of invasion and conquest and the imposition upon free and sovereign States and peoples of the shackles of government from the top.

. . . Mr. Justice [John A.] Campbell, of the Supreme Court of the United States, wrote to Mr. [William H.] Seward, Lincoln's Secretary of State, under date of April 13, 1861:

> "I think no candid man who will read over what I have written and consider for a moment what is going on at Sumter but will agree that the equivocating conduct of the Lincoln administration is the proximate cause of the great calamity."

The Southern States in withdrawing from the old partnership of States had acted only after careful deliberation by the peoples of the several States, each State for itself, and under explicit directions from the people to their servants, the proper public officials of the respective States. The Lincoln administration replied first by the maneuvers above noted relative to Fort Sumter, then by calling for troops to invade the South. Several months later, when war was already actually begun, Congress was assembled. No sovereign conventions of the people were called in the North, as was done in the South by a sort of popular referendum, to pass upon the immediate crisis precipitated upon the country, analogous to those conventions which acted upon the Federal Constitution of 1789 and accepted it, each convention for its own particular State. Those leaders of Lincoln's party, having already taken the awful responsibility in fomenting the "free-soil" and "anti-slavery" agitation of flouting the solemn warnings of Washington and Jefferson against "geographical discriminations"—i.e., aggressive sectionalism—as inimical to continued union, now assumed the further responsibility of rebuffing the advances of the South in the peace congress and then actually inaugurating war by action of the executive department of the government alone.

The triumph of the Confederate States would have been a notable triumph for government by the people and for peaceable adjustment of grave international or intersection disputes. Negro slavery, for which South and North were alike responsible, eventually would have gone and with little or no bloodshed. The United States would have been no more destroyed than was the British Empire by the independence of the revolted colonies; and in the one case, as in the other, the portion remaining under the old government would have been actually stronger from the true democratic standpoint by reason of the lesson learned of the vital necessity of protecting the rights of a minority section. [Lee's surrender at] Appomattox put back the hand of progress fully half a century on the dial plate of political liberty, and the self-governing rights of smaller States or nations (real minority protection) awaited its formal recognition by the allies in the war of 1914.

If the State, simple or confederated, is conceived of as the foundation of rights and its interests are regarded as paramount to those of the constituent units, be those units individuals or commonwealths, it is only a short step to the conclusion that that State is not bound by the moral principles which are binding upon individuals.

. . . The point to which such a State or nation will go in violating moral principles may depend entirely upon what the rulers at the moment in power regard as the self-interest of the State. What that self-interest is conceived at anytime to be depends in turn upon the prevailing view of *national destiny*.

We know to-day what infinite suffering resulted from the Northern invasion of the seceded States. We realize how utterly impossible it always is for the ruthless invader and conqueror to make adequate amends for unspeakable loss. As we view one tragic event that succeeded another—rape following robbery and murder accompanied by devastation and political slavery—we are forcibly reminded that all this is excusable only on the specious plea of self-interest and "necessity" or military need.

. . . Interstate comity and broad humanity would have been violated by the invasion and coercion of the peace-pleading Southern States even if there had been no express guaranty by treaty, Constitution, or other formal compact for the observance of the freedom and sovereignty of those commonwealths. But there was such an express guaranty. At least three of the States—Virginia, New York, and Rhode Island—in ratifying the Federal Constitution formally reserved the right of secession or of "resumption" of the delegated powers. Nor did the Constitution declare that the Union thereunder should be "perpetual," as had the old Articles of Confederation (in their title and also in Article 13)[278] regarding the old Union, from which "perpetual Union" each of the States ratifying the new Constitution of 1789 thereupon seceded or withdrew. Moreover, a proposal to embody in the Constitution a power to coerce a recalcitrant State was opposed in the constitutional convention of 1787 on the ground that this would mean war, and the proposal was voted down. The late Charles Francis Adams, of Massachusetts, a veteran of the Northern armies of 1861-65, has remarked that for the first forty or fifty years or so after the adoption of the Federal Constitution the ultimate right of secession "in case of a final, unavoidable issue" was generally recognized in the North and the South alike.

Now, among individuals it is, of course, elementary law and morals that a settled construction of a contract (let alone an express condition by some of the parties embodying that construction) at the time the contract is made cannot rightfully be changed thereafter when the changing interests of one or some oi the parties invite such a change against the interests of others of the parties to such contract. . . . Again, in law and in morals a contract violated in a vital particular by one or more of the parties to it is no longer binding upon the other party or parties.

We have seen that the compact, or contract, of union between the States in 1789 was entered into in order "to establish justice, insure domestic tranquillity, . . . promote the general welfare." In 1860, by a strictly sectionalist [Left-wing] vote, an administration was elected which was pledged to keep the Southerners, with their negroes, out of the common territories won by the common blood and treasure of South and North alike; and many prominent supporters of this new, now victorious [Liberal] political party had openly sympathized with [radical Left-winger] John Brown in his recent efforts to incite a servile insurrection in the South, thus threatening deliberate and wholesale rapine and devastation. Surely for the South under such an administration and such a party the constitutional contract was violated in most vital and essential particulars and no longer made for justice or for the South's domestic tranquillity or her general welfare.

In the face, then, of these plain, stubborn, indisputable facts of record, and in view of that rule of legal and moral conduct which is equally binding upon individuals and upon nations, there was no possible excuse for what was then perpetrated—the invasion, devastation, and conquest of the Southern States—except *the self-interest of the invaders*, real or imagined: "a process of natural evolution," Charles Francis Adams calls it in his very interesting address to the University of South Carolina, and this is only another way of saying "manifest destiny."

. . . The issue must not be obscured by insisting that in the course of the war of 1861-65 cruelties were practiced on both sides. It is inevitable that this should be so. But the things which individuals or even nations do under provocation and in violation of their own standards are not to be compared with the outworkings of a ruthless system founded upon "manifest destiny" and logically buttressed by "military necessity." Such in the last analysis is the difference between a centralized [that is, a socialist or socialistic] government from the top and decentralized [that is, a confederate or confederated] government by the people under written constitutions or charters of government. When seeking for historical comparisons from American annals to shame German barbarities in the war of 1914, Northern papers turned to

[Confederate General Robert E.] Lee in Pennsylvania and [Raphael] Semmes on the sea; not to [Union General Benjamin F.] Butler in New Orleans with his unspeakable Order No. 28; not to [Union General Philip H.] Sheridan with his torch in the Shenandoah Valley nor to [Union General William T.] Sherman with his torch in Atlanta and Columbia and his deliberate depopulation of Atlanta; not to [Union General Henry W.] Halleck in his official suggestion that Charleston be razed and sown with salt [to prevent the future planting of crops]; not even to the policy adopted by Lincoln's administration by which medicine itself was made contraband of war against the beleaguered South, thus condemning to wasting disease and lingering death not only countless sick or wounded soldiers, including Northern captives in Confederate prisons, but also many women and little children among those "enemies" which Scripture commands that we feed and minister unto in their distress.

Such was the natural result of training in the most insidious ways the great people of a great section of country to conceive of a supposed sectional and national self-interest as of more concern than the faithful observance of weighty contractual obligations and the solemn warnings of the Revolutionary and constitutionalist fathers.

As remarked above, it is regrettable that such issues as these should be thrust upon us in the midst of the common struggle of South and North against a European foe [World War I]. But when the situation is thus taken advantage of to draw an attempted parallel by which the invading hosts of the sixties are made to stand for the cause and underlying principles of our present allies, and the invaded South of the sixties is made to represent our ruthless enemy of to-day, we of the South must insist on being heard in a solemn appeal to the record. God helping us, we can do no other.[279] — LLOYD T. EVERETT, BALLSTON, VIRGINIA

HOLDING FAITHFUL TO THE CONSTITUTION
☛ . . . [By 1860 the] . . . Southern States saw certain rights of theirs under the compact of union, guaranteed by the Constitution and affirmed by the Supreme Court of the United States, violated persistently and defiantly by other members of the compact, the States under abolition [communist] control, and they had no other remedy than to withdraw from the Union on the principle announced by Daniel Webster, that a contract broken by one party releases the other party from its stipulations. By the election of [Liberal candidate] Mr. Lincoln the majority of the Northern States

arrayed themselves against the constitutional rights of the South and so released her from obligation to continue in the Union. But from the very nature of the republic as a federation [that is, confederation] every State must be the ultimate judge of the remedy for wrongs for which there is no common arbiter, a right which Virginia, New York, and Rhode Island expressly asserted in their adoption of the Constitution.

Moreover, it was a right which Mr. Lincoln himself asserted in a speech in Congress in 1848 as belonging to any people who are dissatisfied with the government under which they live.

What the South asserted was the right of self-government for the States—"government of the people, by the people, and for the people." For there can be no doubt that the vast majority of the seceded States desired to set up a separate government. And it is one of the ironies of history that, while the South was defeated and condemned, yet the great world war [I] in which the United States is engaged with her allies against Germany is to vindicate the very principle for which we fought—that is, the right of every distinct people to choose their own government. And as we strive for success in the war against centralized imperialism now, we may look back with pride to our great though unsuccessful conflict and feel that

> "Freedom's battle once begun,
> Though baffled oft, is ever won."

. . . [We Confederate veterans believe] that when any people becomes indifferent to the epic periods of its history and careless of the name and fame of its heroes, that people has lost its highest ideals and has become degenerate, sunk in the slough of mere materialism. Therefore we seek to perpetuate the memory of the pure motives and the heroic sacrifices of the men and women who in the South gave their all in defense of their constitutional rights in a federated [confederated] republic. They were defeated, it is true, and the republic became a nation. They yielded in good faith to overwhelming force. Henceforth it is our duty to strive with all our resources to make the nation a guardian of liberty and justice and to hold it faithful to the Constitution which it has adopted.[280] — REV. JAMES H. MCNEILLY, NASHVILLE, TENNESSEE

THE SOUTHERN LOVE FOR THE CONSTITUTION

☞ . . . Fighting for their constitutional rights, the Southerners who supported their Confederacy offered up their lives and their property without pay, stint, or hesitation for their cause. At the end of the war they faced widespread devastation, wholesale bankruptcy, and slavery for years under the [South-hating] carpetbagger and [violent racist] negro regime. Where can such an enormous and heroic sacrifice of life and property for the sake of constitutional principle be found?

The most distinctive and brilliant characteristic of the English-speaking peoples is their deathless love of constitutional principles and limitations. John Hampden, gentleman, as [English historian Thomas B.] Macaulay calls him, and not that bloody despot and hypocrite, Oliver Cromwell, was the hero of the rebellion against Charles I, for the latter's violation of the English Constitution. Hampden said:

> "I am a rich man and am easily able to pay the shilling tax which Charles Stuart has levied against me; but he has done so in violation of the Constitution of England without an act of Parliament, and I will not pay it, but will take up arms against him."

He did so; and when King Charles I heard of his having been mortally wounded in the battle of Chalgrove Field, he sent his royal surgeon to attend him, but in vain. Few names stand as high in the temple of fame as that of Hampden.

The American people in their war of independence started their revolution to vindicate their constitutional rights. So did the Southern people in their War between the States. In no section of the United States have there existed reverence for and obedience to the Constitution as widespread and potent as in the Southern States.

By the Southern people the Constitution has never been regarded as obsolete nor as "a scrap of paper" [as the Left then called it—and still calls it]. One of the strangest and most significant things in American history is the careful suppression by Northern writers of the assertion by the State of Massachusetts and by many of the leading men in the New England States of their right of secession and of the official declaration of open and unyielding resistance to the Federal government by members of the governments of other leading Northern States. These momentous facts of American history are also carefully excluded from the schools and many of the colleges from Boston to San Francisco. . . .[281] — CORNELIUS H. FAUNTLEROY, ST. LOUIS, MISSOURI

THE SOUTHERN PEOPLE WILL BE VINDICATED
☛ . . . Every true American soldier should go into this war [World War I] resolved to keep untarnished the name and fame of his ancestry by his own worthy deeds. This is especially true of those who are heirs of the traditions of the Confederate soldiers of 1861-65, in whose veins flows the blood of the men and women of that heroic period, and all the more because of the malignant and persistent efforts to misrepresent and dishonor the memory of those who stood for four years of dreadful conflict for their constitutional rights. The cause, origin, and course of that war between the States, when truly recorded, will vindicate the Southern people as standing for liberty and justice. It is ours to see that the history is truly written and falsehoods corrected. And we may be sure that time, with slow, unswerving step, will in the end overtake every falsehood and trample it into the dust of forgetfulness. We may not write the final word as to that great war of principles, but we can gather and record the materials from which the future historian shall make up the authoritative verdict of history. . . .[282] — REV. JAMES H. MCNEILLY, NASHVILLE, TENNESSEE

WHY PRESIDENT DAVIS WAS NEVER BROUGHT TO TRIAL
☛ . . . the secession of the South was due to the inauguration of a sectional and unconstitutional policy hostile to the South and destructive of her peace and safety.

Did the South by seceding violate the Constitution? Had not seventy-three years of history affirmed the right of sovereign States to secede from a compact to which they had acceded? Did not the Philadelphia Convention [1787], in framing the Constitution, declare the right of secession when it explicitly provided for "nine States" to secede from the Union, which was declared to be perpetual?

Did not Virginia, New York, and Rhode Island on entering the Union reserve, in express terms, the right to withdraw from the same whenever they deemed it to their interest? Were they not admitted without question? Was not the declared right of these three States the absolute right of all?

In 1844 the admission of Texas was a question. Did not the Legislature of Massachusetts pass the following resolution, "That the project of the annexation of Texas, unless arrested on the threshold, may drive these States into a dissolution of the Union"? Who then said to the New England States, "You have no such right"?

In 1848 Abraham Lincoln said in the House of Representatives: "Any people anywhere have the right to rise up and throw off the existing government and establish one that suits them better." He did not stop here, but said: "This is a most valuable right, a right which we hope and believe is to liberate the world." Nor did he stop here, but added: "Nor is this right confined to cases in which the whole people of the existing government may choose to exercise it. Any portion of such people that can may revolutionize and make their own so much of the territory as they inhabit." Nor did he even stop here, but added:

> "More than this, a majority of any portion of any people may revolutionize, putting down a minority intermingled with or about them who may oppose their movements."

Candidly, was not Lincoln the secessionist of the nineteenth century? Was not the Constitution of 1848 the same as that of 1861? If you had uttered these identical words instead of Lincoln, could you, or would you, have deliberately inaugurated that terrible war, costing approximately a million lives and billions upon billions of treasure, to forbid States of the Union to do what you had declared in such unlimited terms to be their absolute right, to say nothing of the privations and hardships resulting from the widespread destruction of property and ruined and burnt homes?

But of all the many other witnesses, we shall name now but two others. They are most important and most authoritative. I put now on the stand *the United States Senate*. On the twenty-fourth day of May, 1860, the United States Senate passed a set of resolutions introduced by Jefferson Davis, of Mississippi, strongly indorsing the right of secession by a vote of thirty-six to nineteen. Twenty States voted for the resolutions, one State divided its vote, four voted against it, and eight refused to vote. The States refusing to vote belonged to the number that had nullified the fugitive slave law.

We give next a witness which is of supreme and commanding authority. It is no less than the United States government itself. From 1824 to 1842 the Federal government in its own school at West Point taught as a textbook *A View of the Constitution of the United States of America*, the author of which was [a Yankee named] William Rawle, a distinguished jurist of Pennsylvania. In this book are these words:

> "It depends on the State itself to retain or abolish the principle of representation, because it depends on itself whether it will continue a member of the Union. To deny

this right would be inconsistent with the principles on which all our political systems are founded, which is that the people have, in all cases, a right to determine how they will be governed, a right ingredient in the original composition of the government."

Stand in front of these witnesses, look them all in the face, and tell them, if you can, that they were traitors and rebels against the Constitution. Remember when you dare do it that you charge the Federal government itself with rebelling against itself. Know too that it is a universally admitted fact, which all well-informed men know, that an independent sovereign State has both a right to accede to a compact and an equal right to secede from it.

You will search in vain the records of this great republic, from the framing of the Constitution to Lincoln, for a single instance in which one of the States or one of its sections or the government itself ever denied the right of secession. What President but Lincoln ever denied this right? And does he not stand self-contradicted?

Now let me bring to your notice a few witnesses of importance who have testified since the war, only a few of the many. Forty-six years after the war Charles [Edward] Stowe, son of Harriet Beecher Stowe, author of *Uncle Tom's Cabin*, addressing a negro university in Nashville, Tenn., said: "It is certain there was a rebellion, but the Northerners were the rebels, not the Southerners."

Forty years after the war *The American Crisis* was published. In its preface are these words: "The Civil War will not be treated as a rebellion, but as the great event in the history of the nation, which after forty years it is now recognized to have been."

In the fourth edition of *The Republic of Republics* [by Bernard J. Sage][283] are these words:

> "Another event of great historical interest, in which Judge [Nathan] Clifford participated, was 'a solemn consultation' of a small number of the ablest lawyers of the North in Washington, a few months after the war, upon the momentous question as to whether the Federal government should commence a criminal prosecution against Jefferson Davis for participating in the leadership in the war of secession. In this council, which was surrounded with the utmost secrecy, were Attorney-General [James] Speed, Judge Clifford, William [M.] Evarts, and perhaps a half dozen others who had been selected from the whole Northern profession for their legal ability and acumen; and the result of their deliberations was the sudden abandonment of the idea of prosecution in view of the insurmountable difficulties in the way of getting a final conviction."

Do you not know that Jefferson Davis was then and there acquitted as the result of that "solemn consultation"? You must know that he was never tried. Why not? May it not have been because the Republican party [then the Liberal party] itself would have been put on trial instead?

Davis was arrested at Irwinville, Ga., on the 10th of May,1865, incarcerated in Fortress Monroe on the 19th of May, and released on the 15th of February, 1869. He was therefore a prisoner for three years, nine months, and twenty-six days. During that period his case was repeatedly set for trial and as many times postponed. Why all this mockery? Is it not evidence that Chief Justice [Salmon P.] Chase finally suggested to the counsel of Mr. Davis what motion to make? That motion was made, and Mr. Davis was released.

Confederate Corporal Patrick Henry, Virginia Military Institute cadet, circa 1863. Fought at Battle of New Market.

Jefferson Davis was never tried. That mountain fact lifts its tall testimony to tell the ages that the North waged an unconstitutional war against the constitutional South.

A few other important facts. In 1857 the Supreme Court, in the Dred Scott case, handed down a decision which rendered the Republican [then Liberal] party platform unconstitutional. The party rebelled against the decision; and we have the very high authority of *The Civil War From a Northern Standpoint* [by Francis N. Thorpe],[284] that

> "Lincoln's Cooper Institute speech [February 27, 1860] was an effort to put the Republican party on constitutional ground."

How most absurd!

That speech was most widely advertised in advance, most loudly applauded in its delivery, and was landed far and nearby the Republican [Left-wing] press as "equal to the best effort of the great [Daniel] Webster." Does not this look like a conspiracy?

The very facts declare it nothing less than a bold public

rebellion against a decision of the Supreme Court, the office of which is to settle questions of dispute. Its decision is so authoritative that it will annul an act of either of the other two departments of government. Talk of rebels! Where can you find truer specimens than these? What meant this great exhibition? Was it not to prepare the masses for an unconstitutional [Left-wing] platform to follow?

That party had a score of men far more erudite than Lincoln. Why, then, was Lincoln designated to make that high-court-subverting speech? In his debates with [Conservative Yankee Stephen A.] Douglas had he not shown marked irreverence for the Constitution by utterances like this: "Douglas thinks a decision of the Supreme Court a 'thus saith the Lord'"—meaning, but I don't?

Hear him in that Cooper Institute speech deriding the Supreme Court's decision as "a sort of decision"; "its friends differ among themselves as to its meaning"; "made by a bare majority" (concealing that the majority was seven to two); "an obvious mistake"; adding,

> "When the obvious mistake of the judges is brought to their notice is it not reasonable they will withdraw the mistaken statement and reconsider their conclusion?"

Is it any wonder that Lincoln undertook the task assigned him? In all history no specimen of egotism is comparable to it, unless it be this other expression of his found in that same speech:

> "But we, on the other hand, deny that any such right has existence in the Constitution even by implication."

If Lincoln did not know that when the Constitution is silent it means "powers reserved by the States for the States," it is certain the Supreme Court did.

That absolutely unconstitutional platform was framed, and on it Lincoln was the nominee for President. He was elected by a minority vote, strictly sectional, of less than thirty-eight and one-half per cent of the entire vote cast.

His election was legal because in accordance with law. But who can say it annulled the decision of the Supreme Court against which Lincoln's [Liberal] party rebelled? Who, therefore, can say it absolved the President elect and Congress from enforcing the Constitution unchanged?

No one can deny that a legal act can be repealed only by a legal act; or, in the words of [French military commander Michel] Ney's legal maxim: "Everything is dissolved by the same means it is constituted." A decision of the Supreme Court is supreme law, or a legal act holding the highest place in law. It, therefore, cannot be repealed except by amendment to the Constitution according to Article 5—that is, proposals must first be made either by two-thirds of both houses of Congress or by two-thirds of the States, which, when ratified by three-fourths of the States, become part of the Constitution. How immeasurably different is the constitutional plan from that of the Cooper Institute conspirators! If, therefore, the Constitution was changed, it was not according to the compact, and therefore by revolution. And if done by revolution, [then, as Charles Stowe asserted,] "the Northerners are the true rebels, not the Southerners."[285] — JOHN ANDERSON RICHARDSON, 1919

PROOF OF LEFT-WING SECESSION SENTIMENT IN THE OLD NORTH

☛ [English historian Cecil] Chesterton lays sufficient stress on two incidents which most historians have either ignored or skated delicately over. The first was the attitude of the Federalist [then Left-wing] party toward [Conservative Thomas] Jefferson at the time of the Louisiana Purchase:

> "To injure him . . . they were now ready to tear up the Union and all their principles. One of their ablest spokesmen, Josiah Quincy, made a speech against the purchase, in which he anticipated the most extreme pronouncements of the Nullifiers of 1832 and the Secessionists of 1860, declaring that his country was not America, but Massachusetts, . . . and that if her interests were violated . . . she would repudiate the Union and take her stand upon her rights as an independent sovereign State."

The other and kindred incident is the Hartford Convention [1814-1815]. There are living at this time ardent New Englanders who have never heard of this meeting and down-face one that it never could have occurred. It did occur, however, at the time of the second war with England, while British troops were in possession of Washington [D.C.] and when every American should have rallied to the support of the administration. Instead Massachusetts

> "began a movement which seemed to point straight to the dilemma of surrender to the foreigner or secession and dismemberment from within."

She called a convention of New England.

> "Some of its promoters were certainly prepared, if they did not get their way, to secede and make a separate peace."

When Massachusetts later raised the cry of "traitor" against South Carolina [when the state seceded in 1860], she had entirely forgotten that secession had first been her own "ideear."[286] — CECIL CHESTERTON, 1919

THE BRILLIANCE OF THE AMERICAN FOUNDING FATHERS
☛ Sometimes chided with fogyism for her undimming loyalty to States' rights, the South can now take cheer from the fact that British statesmanship is turning to that very principle as a solvent for certain grave problems of the United Kingdom. Mr. [Henry H.] Asquith, the former Premier [and 1st Earl of Oxford], recently declared that his experience of thirty years as a Scottish member of the House of Commons has taught him how utterly impossible it is for the central government efficiently to administer the affairs of Scotland, and how essential it is for the good of the kingdom as a whole, as well as for that of its several units, that a larger, freer measure of local self-government be provided.

With this judgment there appears to be general concurrence. The tasks of government have grown at once so tremendous and so intricate that Parliament cannot handle them with justice to either imperial or provincial affairs. Hence there has developed in the British Isles in recent years a well-nigh unanimous sentiment for the establishment of some sort of legislative and executive machinery for handling matters of domestic concern in the different parts of the kingdom—Wales, Scotland, and England, as well as Ireland—leaving Parliament free for imperial business.

On this side of the water [U.S.A.] we started out with that method, not so much as a matter of practical necessity as of principle, for each State of the original Union was considered a sovereign with inviolable rights. We have kept the form through a long age and have found it most expedient. But have we kept the spirit as well? If the centralizing tendency continues another fifty years at the pace it has gained during the fifty just passed, will the fathers of the republic, revisiting by chance "these glimpses of the moon," ever recognize their handiwork? Assuredly there must come a reaction, if not to their precise principles, at least away from excesses of federalization [that is, Liberalization]. For as our population, already well above a hundred million, multiplies and multiplies in its continent-wide sweep and almost infinite variety of interests, the point will be reached where governmental efficiency itself, now urged as an argument for centralizing, will demand decentralization.[287] — *ATLANTA JOURNAL*

RUMINATING ABOUT THE SOUTHERN CAUSE
☛ . . . we [Confederate veterans] love to "ruminate" about those days of the [eighteen] sixties when we were fighting for what we believed then, and still believe, were the rights guaranteed to us by the Constitution of our fathers. . . .[288] — W. A. CALLAWAY, ATLANTA, GEORGIA

WARTIME TRIBUTE TO CONFEDERATE GENERAL BENJAMIN FRANKLIN CHEATHAM
☛ General Cheatham: We, a large proportion of the officers and soldiers composing the brigade of Gen. O. F. Strahl, which until recently had the honor of belonging to the immortal division that bears your honored name, take this opportunity and this method of expressing to you our high appreciation of your services as a warrior and a patriot in the great cause of Southern rights and Southern honor and the self-sacrificing spirit you have evinced, which is one of the great characteristics of a Tennessean.

This demonstration, General, is not the result of any preconcerted plan or systematic arrangement; it is not based upon that false system of enthusiasm and public excitement, which is not to be relied upon for a moment; but it is the result of a deep-seated and unchangeable feeling of devotion, of veneration, of honor, of pride we have always felt for you, aptly styled by that great chieftain, General [Leonidas] Polk, the bravest of the brave.

Notwithstanding our old State has been wrested from us by the overwhelming forces of [Left-wing] despotism, separated from the loved ones at home by the stern necessities of war, our towns, villages, and homesteads devastated, our fields laid waste, our wives, mothers, and sisters driven from their homes and basely insulted by the demoniac cruelty of a revengeful foe, yet we can still cry out, in accordance with the principles we know animate your bosom and which by your example has done so much to inculcate the same feelings in ours:

> "We are more determined to fight on and fight ever until the proud banner of freedom shall wave its triumphant folds to the breeze, proclaiming to the world we are a free and independent nation!"

When the history of this war shall be written and the action of its different participants shall be noted, the State of Tennessee will be recorded upon its brightest pages in letters of divine light, and the deeds of its heroic sons upon the bloody battle field will be pointed to for ages to come as examples of patience, perseverance, indomitable courage, and patriotic, self-sacrificing devotion to the great cause of truth and justice. And that name which is the synonym of all that is brave, chivalrous, generous, and high-toned, B. F. Cheatham, will be crowned with a wreath of laurel more to be valued than those of Greece or Rome, because it is the voluntary gift of a free people, of soldiers who have so often followed him to battle and to victory in defense of our common inheritance, and that wreath of honor will be as undying as our affection is for the brave old soldier and patriot from the Volunteer State of Tennessee.[289] — CONFEDERATE LIEUTENANT JOHN B. HOGG, CO. F, 4TH TENNESSEE REGIMENT, NEAR DALTON, GEORGIA, DECEMBER 27, 1863

TEXAS GOVERNOR HONORS SOUTHERN CAUSE
☛ Just and exemplary in citizenship, wise and learned in State, bold as Caesar's legions in battle, and knightly as the ancient cavaliers, the soldiers of the armies of the Confederacy are affectionately enshrined in the hearts of their countrymen forever; and all lovers of the Declaration of Independence and all who kneel at the altar of equal rights and all sons and daughters of freedom everywhere will find in the South's holy cause an inspiration to guide them and strengthen them through all the ages yet to come.[290] — TEXAS GOVERNOR WILLIAM PETTUS HOBBY, CONFEDERATE REUNION, HOUSTON, TEXAS, 1920

THE LEFT IS STILL TRYING TO HIDE THE REAL ISSUE BEHIND LINCOLN'S WAR
☛ . . . The fiction that secession was rebellion was originated for the purpose of obscuring the real issue of State rights. . . .[291] — MRS. A. A. CAMPBELL, HISTORIAN GENERAL, U.D.C., ASHEVILLE CONVENTION

ENGLAND'S WARTIME SALUTE TO THE SOUTHERN PEOPLE
☛ The South is doomed. With the surrender of General Lee ends not indeed the possibility of military defense, still less that of desperate popular resistance, but the hope of final success. After four years of war, sustained with a gallantry and resolution that

have few, if any, precedents in history; after such sacrifices as perhaps no nation ever made in vain; after losses that have drained the lifeblood of the country; after a series of brilliant victories, gained under unequaled disadvantages, courage and skill and devotion have succumbed to brute force; and by sheer power of numbers a race inferior in every quality of soldiership and manhood, has prevailed over the bravest and most united people that ever drew the sword in defense of civil rights and national independence.[292] — *EVENING HERALD*, LONDON, ENGLAND, CIRCA SPRING 1865

THE SOUTHERN CAUSE ACCORDING TO PRESIDENT DAVIS

☞ . . . Actuated solely by the desire to preserve our own rights and promote our own welfare, the separation of the Confederate States has been marked by no aggression upon others and followed by no domestic convulsion. Our industrial pursuits have received no check; the cultivation of our fields has progressed as heretofore; and even should we be involved in war, there would be no considerable diminution in the production of the staples which have constituted our exports and in which the commercial world has an interest scarcely less than our own. This common interest of the producer and consumer can only be interrupted by an exterior force which should obstruct its transmission to foreign markets, a course of conduct which would be as unjust toward us as it would be detrimental to manufacturing and commercial interests abroad. Should reason guide the action of the government from which we have separated, a policy so detrimental to the civilized world, the Northern States included, could not be dictated by even the strongest desire to inflict injury upon us; but if otherwise, a terrible responsibility will rest upon it, and the suffering of millions will bear testimony to the folly and wickedness of our aggressors. . . .[293]
— CONFEDERATE PRESIDENT JEFFERSON DAVIS, INAUGURAL ADDRESS, MONTGOMERY, ALABAMA, FEBRUARY 18, 1861

CHATTANOOGA HONORS CONFEDERATE VETERANS

☞ We honor you for the cause for which you fought—a cause inspired by the great principle of constitutional liberty. God never planted in the breast of man a higher principle than that which prompted the soldiers of the Confederacy. . . . We say with that son of Georgia, Charles Colcock Jones:

"Palsied be the tongue that would speak lightly of a Confederate past, and withered be the arm that refuses to lift itself in praise of the virtue and valor which characterized the actors from highest to lowest, not in a war of rebellion, but for the conservation of home, the maintenance of constitutional government, the supremacy of the law, and the vindication of the natural rights of men."

Some one said: "It is better to have loved and lost than never to have loved at all." It is better to have been brave and beaten than never to have been brave at all. . . .[294] — COMMISSIONER E. D. BASS, ADDRESS, CONFEDERATE VETERANS REUNION, CHATTANOOGA, TENNESSEE, 1920

THE POLITICS BEHIND THE WAR EXPLAINED IN THREE PARAGRAPHS

☛ From the beginning of the War between the States to the present day there has been a persistent effort by Northern writers and speakers on the platform, in the pulpit, and by the press to fix on the South the responsibility for bringing on that war and forcing the United States to take up arms against the Southern Confederacy. The conflict of the South for her inalienable rights is characterized as the foolish and reckless revolt of a minority of our people instigated and led by ambitious political demagogues. Its object has been denounced as an attempt to perpetuate and extend human slavery, as an effort to overthrow the United States government and destroy the Union, and the clergy with peculiar bitterness have spoken of it as "a wicked and causeless rebellion" against "the best government the world ever saw."

These statements are not only repeated with endless iteration in lectures, addresses, essays, editorials, but they are emphasized in published school histories and taught to the coming generations. Surely it is the duty of those who know the facts as to the origin, principles, and conduct of that war to expose the falsehood of this persistent propaganda and let it be known that the Confederate States were contending for sacred rights guaranteed to them by the Constitution and denied and assailed by the North; that it was a conflict between a federated republic of sovereign States [the Conservative C.S.A.] and a centralized nation with imperial powers concentrated in certain individuals or classes [the Liberal U.S.A.]. And to-day the strife of contending interests, the conflict of the various classes, the restless discontent of the masses, all threatening anarchy, are very largely the result of the destruction of State rights and the removal of limitations on the power of the central government.

. . . We should insist that the War between the States was the conflict of two antagonistic theories of government—one that, the government is paternal, to promote material interests [U.S.A.]; the other that the government is an institute of righteousness, to see to it that justice is done between all the varying interests of men [C.S.A.]. One [the U.S.A., the Left-wing one] would make government a kind of universal helper; the other [the C.S.A., the Right-wing one] would make it a protector and defender against all forms of oppression or abuse of power. The one [U.S.A.] stood for privilege; the other [C.S.A.] for justice. To the one [U.S.A.] the Constitution was an indissoluble bond; to the other [C.S.A.] a sacred compact. The determination to withdraw from the Union was no sudden impulse of passion, but the deliberate attempt of a people to free themselves from the dominance of a [progressive] section that was using the general government to promote its own interests at the expense of the [traditional] Southern section, and also to escape the fanatical interference in our domestic institutions contrary to the expressed stipulations of the Constitution. . . .[295] —
REV. JAMES H. MCNEILLY, D.D., CONFEDERATE VETERAN, NASHVILLE, TENNESSEE

HOW THE C.S. CHIEF EXECUTIVE DEFINED THE SOUTHERN CAUSE
☛ [Our cause: The] rights of our sires won in the War of the Revolution, the State sovereignty, freedom and independence bequeathed by them to us, their and our children forever.[296] —
CONFEDERATE PRESIDENT JEFFERSON DAVIS

GENERAL LEE ON STATES' RIGHTS
☛ Sir: Although your letter of the 4th ulto. has been before me some days unanswered, I hope you will not attribute it to a want of interest in the subject, but to my inability to keep pace with my correspondence. As a citizen of the South, I feel deeply indebted to you for the sympathy you have evinced in its cause, and am conscious that I owe your kind consideration of myself to my connection with it.

The influence of current opinion in Europe upon the current politics of America must always be salutary; and the importance of the questions now at issue in the United States, involving not only constitutional freedom and constitutional government in this country, but the progress of universal liberty and civilisation, invests your proposition with peculiar value, and will add to the obligation which every true American must owe you for your efforts to guide that opinion aright. Amid the conflicting statements and sentiments in both countries, it will be no easy task to discover the truth, or to relieve it from the mass of prejudice and passion, with which it has been covered by party spirit.

I am conscious of the compliment conveyed in your request for my opinion as to the light in which American politics should be viewed, and had I the ability, I have not the time to enter upon a discussion, which was commenced by the founders of the constitution and has been continued to the present day. I can only say that while I have considered the preservation of the constitutional power of the General Government to be the foundation of our peace and safety at home and abroad, I yet believe that the [Conservative] maintenance of the rights and authority reserved to the states and to the people, not only essential to the adjustment and balance of the general system, but the safeguard to the continuance of a free government. I consider it as the chief source of stability to our political system, whereas the [Liberal] consolidation of the states into one vast republic, sure to be aggressive abroad and despotic at home, will be the certain precursor of that ruin which has overwhelmed all those that have preceded it. I need not refer one so well acquainted as you are with American history, to the State papers of [George] Washington and [Thomas] Jefferson, the [Conservative] representatives of the federal and democratic parties [then Right-wing], denouncing consolidation and centralisation of power, as tending to the subversion of State Governments, and to despotism. The [Liberal] New England states, whose citizens are the fiercest opponents of the [Conservative] Southern states, did not always avow the opinions they now advocate. Upon the purchase of Louisiana by Mr. Jefferson, they virtually asserted the right of secession through their prominent men; and in the convention which assembled at Hartford in 1814,they threatened the disruption of the Union unless the war [of 1812] should be discontinued. The assertion of this right has been repeatedly made

Confederate Lieutenant Andrew J. Gahagan of Co. D, 1st Tennessee Cavalry Regiment, Nashville, Tennessee, circa 1864.

by their politicians when their party was weak, and Massachusetts, the leading state in hostility to the South, declares in the preamble to her constitution, that the people of that commonwealth

> "have the sole and exclusive right of governing themselves as a free sovereign and independent state, and do, and forever hereafter shall, exercise and enjoy every power, jurisdiction, and right which is not, or may hereafter be by them expressly delegated to the United States of America in congress assembled."

Such has been in substance the language of other State governments, and such the doctrine advocated by the leading men of the country for the last seventy years. Judge [Salmon P.] Chase, the present Chief Justice of the U.S., as late as 1850, is reported to have stated in the Senate, of which he was a member, that he "knew of no remedy in case of the refusal of a state to perform its stipulations," thereby acknowledging the sovereignty and independence of state action.

But I will not weary you with this unprofitable discussion. Unprofitable because the judgment of reason has been displaced by the arbitrament of war, waged for the purpose as avowed [by the Leftist North] of maintaining the union of the states. If, therefore, the result of the war is to be considered as having decided that the union of the states is inviolable and perpetual under the constitution, it naturally follows that it is as incompetent for the general government to impair its integrity by the exclusion of a state, as for the states to do so by secession; and that the existence and rights of a state by the constitution are as indestructible as the union itself. The legitimate consequence then must be the perfect equality of rights of all the states; the exclusive right of each to regulate its internal affairs under rules established by the Constitution, and the right of each state to prescribe for itself the qualifications of suffrage. The South has contended only for the supremacy of the constitution, and the just administration of the laws made in pursuance to it. Virginia to the last made great efforts to save the union, and urged harmony and compromise. [Conservative Yankee] Senator [Stephen A.] Douglas, in his remarks upon the compromise bill recommended by the committee of thirteen in 1861, stated that every member from the South, including Messrs. Toombs and Davis, expressed their willingness to accept the proposition of Senator [John J.] Crittenden from Kentucky, as a final settlement of the controversy, if sustained by the republican [then Liberal] party, and that the only difficulty in the way of an amicable adjustment was with the republican party. Who then is responsible for the war? Although the South would have preferred any honourable compromise to the fratricidal war which has taken place, she now accepts in good faith its constitutional results, and receives without reserve the amendment [Thirteenth] which has already been made to the constitution for the extinction of slavery. That is an event that has been long sought, though in a different way, and by none has it been more earnestly desired than by citizens of Virginia. In other respects I trust that the constitution may undergo no change, but that it may be handed down to succeeding generations in the form we received it from our forefathers.

Black Confederate lad in uniform, identity unknown, circa 1864.

The desire I feel that the Southern states should possess the good opinion of one whom I esteem as highly as yourself, has caused me to extend my remarks farther than I intended, and I fear it has led me to exhaust your patience. If what I have said should serve to give any information as regards American politics, and enable you to enlighten public opinion as to the true interests of this distracted country, I hope you will pardon its prolixity.

In regard to your inquiry as to my being engaged in preparing a narrative of the campaigns in Virginia, I regret to state that I progress slowly in the collection of the necessary documents for its completion. I particularly feel the loss of the official returns showing the small numbers with which the battles were fought. I have not seen the work by the Prussian officer you mention and, therefore, cannot speak for his accuracy in this respect. With sentiments of great respect, I remain your obedient servant, R. E. Lee.[297] — CONFEDERATE GENERAL ROBERT E. LEE, THEN PRESIDENT OF WASHINGTON COLLEGE, LETTER TO BRITAIN'S LORD (JOHN DALBERG) ACTON, LEXINGTON, VIRGINIA, DECEMBER 15, 1866

300 ∞ I, CONFEDERATE

Confederate soldier and state senator, Edmund Ruffin, wearing Palmetto Guards uniform, circa 1863. After Lee's surrender, Ruffin took his own life, preferring death to living under Left-wing Yankee rule.

13

FAKE HISTORY IS A CRIME AGAINST THE SOUTH

☛ Time and history have proven the right of secession until to-day it is generally admitted, except by some who, on account of gross ignorance or profound prejudice, insist that it was illegal. Therefore, my paramount idea in submitting this [article] is to reflect honor upon that principle and perpetuate that spiritual purpose and ideal. History, partially written, infers that the people of the Southland to-day are under disgrace in being descendants of ancestors who so patiently fought for their rights and privileges for fifty years in the halls of Congress to no avail and then unsheathed their swords for four long years against the invasion from the North. This causes me to gather a few historical facts concerning two important questions and, in all sincerity of conviction, present them to the public.

    The founders of the Confederacy and its supporters were not outlaws, rebels, traitors, or moral degenerates, nor did they perpetrate outlawry. They were men of moral and social standing, and the leaders were of sterling character and unquestioned culture. Their strong arms fought valiantly for the preservation of the integrity of the race against the cruelty of base, unjust, and tyrannical legislation and insufferable conditions created by a horde of conscienceless, diabolical, greed- and lust-crazed adventurers that swarmed down from the North to use the negro for their own selfish ends. In simple justice, should their sacred memory be forgotten? Should their patriotic achievements be lost to posterity?

Shall we of this generation allow the cruel calumny, satanic slander, and flagrant falsehoods heaped upon them for the past half century to pass, to be repeated, and go unanswered by an accurate and honest revelation of the whole truth? No real man below the Mason and Dixon line will consent to such a crime against our heroic dead. . . .[298] — REVEREND HARNEY M. MCGEHEE, EDMOND, OKLAHOMA

WHY PRESIDENT DAVIS' PORTRAIT SHOULD HANG ON EVERY SOUTHERN SCHOOL WALL

☞ . . . a short while ago an effort was made by a member of the school board of San Antonio to have [Abraham] Lincoln's picture and the Gettysburg address placed on the walls of the schools in that city, which effort was blocked by another member with the support of the [Confederate] veterans and Daughters [U.D.C.]. Yet few schools show the pictures of great men of the South, whose many Christian acts and utterances deserve to adorn our school walls. She says:

> "We should awake and stage a campaign in every city, town, and hamlet in the South for the vindication of our departed leader, Jefferson Davis, who gave up fortune, health, and eventually life itself in vindicating our cause of constitutional rights. If we had a government functioning as the Confederate States of America, with a grand and noble man as President, should not his portrait adorn our school walls? That is his rightful place, we think."[299] — MRS. W. L. KELLAM, AUSTIN, TEXAS

WHAT THE SOUTH FOUGHT FOR

☞ . . . [Originally our] happy people, whose God was Jehovah, dwelt under a government which derived its fundamentals from Magna Charta and *habeas corpus*, but its motto, *E Pluribus Unum*, signified a new conception, one nation composed of many States. The men who framed the Federal Constitution were not copyists; they were originators. It was chiefly evolved by James Madison, and was declared by [British statesman William E.] Gladstone to be the greatest instrument struck off at a given time by the human intellect.

If you wish to know by what small majorities and by what devious means the Constitution was adopted by the thirteen original States, read *The Life of John Marshall*, by ex-Senator Albert J. Beveridge. Naturally, you will find no eulogies of Thomas Jefferson. You do not expect them any more than you expect something flippant and frivolous from the Prophet Jeremiah. But you do find the lucid and convincing proof that the right of withdrawal from the Union, commonly called secession, was recognized to secure the ratification of the Constitution. You find also which States first threatened secession, and why they desired to form a Northern Confederacy.[300] If we exclude this book from our libraries because we entertain a different opinion of Jefferson, and other sections exclude it because it tells the truth about State rights, both sides are in danger of becoming narrow-minded bigots, incapable of appreciating the viewpoint of the other. Our entire history may be interpreted by the amendments to that Constitution. From 1804 to 1865 we did not modify it by the stroke of a pen, and then come the [Left's anti-South] thirteenth, fourteenth, and fifteenth amendments, which differ so radically with all that precedes that it is evident some mighty cataclysm has swept over our people, and the victors are recording the verdict.

Confederate Sergeant Robert Taylor Knox, Co. B and Co. C, 30th Virginia Infantry Regiment, Fredericksburg, Virginia, circa 1863.

One phase of that conflict must not be overlooked. It may have been inevitable, but the blame for its precipitation rests upon the Democratic convention which met at Charleston in 1860 and failed to agree upon a presidential candidate. The Northern Democrats [then Right-wing] chose [Conservative Yankee] Stephen A. Douglas; the Southern Democrats [also then Right-wing] chose [Conservative Southerner] John C. Breckinridge. They defeated each other, put in power the Republican party [then Left-wing], which was hostile to both, and many of the misfortunes which ensued must be traced to this colossal folly.

What is done is done. Let us not look into the past to discover its subtle treacheries, its brutal cruelties, its needless anguish. Rather let us revere in disaster a heroism unsurpassed by any race, and let us listen to the ancient cry of Faith which rose like incense from a bleeding land: "Though he slay me, yet will I trust him."

The eternal stars, Orion and the glittering Pleiades, which witnessed the desolation and also the triumph of Job, still shine in benediction upon all who make human fortitude equal to human adversity.

The person who seeks to perpetuate sectional hatred is a friend to no one, but we would be traitors to our highest trust and recreant to our holiest duty if we failed to teach future generations that the South fought for its constitutional rights, and, as President Davis said, the fact that secession was impractical did not prove that it was wrong. We can stress principles without attacking personalities.[301] — MRS. A. A. CAMPBELL, HISTORIAN GENERAL, U.D.C., ADDRESS, CONVENTION, BIRMINGHAM, ALABAMA

POLITICAL & RELIGIOUS SYMBOLISM OF THE CONFEDERATE FIRST NATIONAL FLAG
☛ The idea of the flag I took from the Trinity—Three in One. The three bars were State, Church, and Press. Red represented State—legislative, judiciary, and executive; white for Church—Father, Son, and Holy Ghost; red for press—freedom of speech, freedom of conscience, liberty of press, all bound together by a field of blue, the heavens overall, bearing a star for each State in the Confederation. The seven white stars, all the same size, were placed in a circle, showing that each State had equal rights and privileges, irrespective of size and population. The circle, having neither head nor foot, signified: "You defend me and I'll then protect you."[302] — CONFEDERATE MAJOR ORREN RANDOLPH SMITH, ONE OF THE CLAIMANTS AS CREATOR OF THE "STARS & BARS"

UPHOLDING OUR CONSTITUTIONAL CLAIMS
☛ At the Philadelphia convention, convening May 14, 1787, for the purpose of discussing and devising means for a constitutional government of States, each State, in adopting the new government, seceded from the old [original confederate republic that operated under our first Constitution, the Articles of Confederation],[303] and at that time no cry of treason was heard. About nine States agreed to the new government, which were enough to put it into operation, but there were four other States which did not enter the compact. Therefore, each State acted for itself, and the Southern States did the same thing when they formed the [Southern] Confederacy [in 1861]. In this agreement, New York and Virginia reserved the right to secede. History tells us that the little State of

Rhode Island remained out of this government for two years. Several States declared absolutely for State rights, among them Massachusetts, New Hampshire, and Pennsylvania. John Quincy Adams at that time was declared a secessionist. Later, when some one wished to let the Southern States go, Mr. Lincoln objected on the ground that their revenue was wanted. Again, in the Missouri Compromise, the South was not allowed to carry its slaves into northern territory—property bought from New England slave traders.[304] Daniel Webster said that the anti-slave methods of New York, Ohio, and Massachusetts were against the constitutional provisions of 1787 and 1850 for noninterference with the return of fugitive persons held in lawful servitude, and distinctly treasonable. To uphold all our claims and our faith in the Constitution, in 1861 we shouldered our arms, as meager as they were, and marched to the front to drive the enemy off of our soil.[305] — CAPTAIN T. C. HOLLAND, STEEDMAN, MISSOURI

MORE EVIDENCE THAT THE SOUTH WAS NOT SEEKING TO PRESERVE THE "PECULIAR INSTITUTION"

☛ . . . The questions of State Rights and that of slavery should be treated fairly and without bias. The Northern States settled the slave question as they saw fit. Why should not Virginia have done the same? By her laws from colonial times she showed her desire to settle it by emancipation, freedom, and otherwise. [Thomas] Jefferson, a Virginian, suggested Liberia, while others favored a State set apart in the Union. [James] Monroe, a Virginian, had the capital of Liberia named for him, Monrovia. [John] Marshall, another Virginian, had a certain section of Liberia named for him. A study of the emancipation movement will show numbers of Virginians prominent in the movement, and given special credit for the same. Numbers of Virginians gave freedom to their slaves in their wills and otherwise.

Robert E. Lee never owned a slave except those he inherited [through his wife's family], and these he emancipated. Matthew Fontaine Maury, the "Pathfinder of the Seas," owned one woman, who remained as a member of his family. He was not in favor of slavery, considered it a curse, yet both these resigned positions in the service of the United States to stand for State Rights.

Gen. Joseph E. Johnston never owned a slave, neither did Gen. A. P. Hill; Gen. J. E. B. Stuart owned two, inherited one, bought one; he disposed of one for cruelty, the other he gave away. Gen. Fitzhugh Lee never owned a slave.

Stonewall Jackson, born in the now State of West Virginia,

owned two, whom he bought at their own requests. He immediately offered both the privilege of buying their freedom; one accepted, the other refused, preferring to remain with the family.

Dr. Hunter McGuire, of the Stonewall Brigade, stated that in Jackson's Brigade, only one man in thirty owned a slave, nor ever expected to own one. (Dr. McGuire attended Jackson after he was wounded, and later became one of the leading surgeons of the country, and a man otherwise prominent.)

Alexander H. H. Stuart, who was classed as a Union delegate in the Virginia convention, made a report to the convention on the slavery question, bearing also on the John Brown outrages at Harper's Ferry. This report should be read, as it was a part of the proceedings of that body.

He stated that

> "No law can be found on the statute books of any Northern State which confers the boon of freedom on a single slave in being. All who were slaves remained slaves. Freedom was secured only to the children of the slaves, born after the days designated in the laws; and it was secured to them only in the contingency that the owner of the female slave should retain her within the jurisdiction of the State until after the child was born . . ."

. . . etc., too lengthy to quote in full here.[306] — STERLING BOISSEAU, RICHMOND, VIRGINIA

STONEWALL JACKSON'S "FIRST DESIRE"

☞ . . . Jackson's first desire was for the cause of the South, and he trusted in the Lord to aid him. He daily studied his Bible, with the verse of Romans 8:28 to cheer him, and the standard at the door of his tent on Sundays from nine to ten o'clock warned against interruptions, except a special order. In the chapel services he was always present and acted as usher in seating the men, as he was so anxious for them to be present and take part in the services. He refrained from writing or sending letters on the Sabbath as a general rule. It is asked why he fought so many battles on Sunday, and the answer given by his negro servant was that "Marse Jack" watched, as well as prayed, with one eye open and was always ready for the occasion. It was so at Port Republic and other places.

Jackson espoused the cause of the South because of the violation of constitutional rights in the invasion of the States, as did General Lee, and was sincerely in earnest in his opposition, believing that

God was with him and would direct all his efforts in this direction. His successes strengthened this view, and his men so believed in him that when in doubt or perplexity the word that it was Jackson's orders would make all clear. . . .³⁰⁷ — JOHN K. HITNER, HUNTINGTON, WEST VIRGINIA

WHEN THE C.S. FLAG REPLACED THE U.S. FLAG
☞ [The Confederate Battle Flag] . . . was a new banner to their forefathers who had fought under the [U.S.] Stars and Stripes, but the old flag, representing a new sectional [Left-wing] political party then in power [that is, the Republican party], no longer safeguarded State rights under the Constitution, but despised and violated with impunity some of its provisions. Besides, the Star-Spangled Banner [U.S. flag] that they had been taught to honor and defend was then waving over 75,000 men [Yankee soldiers] whose purpose was to coerce and conquer as political subjects the people of the [Conservative] South. And so the new [Confederate] flag was thrown to the breeze with a pledge of zealous, undivided support. As to how well it was fulfilled, let the four years' record of arduous [Confederate] service bear testimony. . . .³⁰⁸ — COLONEL W. A. LOVE, COLUMBUS, MISSISSIPPI

THE RIGHT TO SECEDE
☞ . . . If there is any single contention which arose before or during the sixties upon which the South could claim then and now an absolutely correct stand, whether expedient or not, as you may see fit to believe, that point was the right of a State to secede. The United States taught it to its young officers at its military school of West Point, although they were later called traitors and rebels when they put this governmental teaching into practice. Abraham Lincoln believed in it and publicly announced his belief before the Congress of the United States, holding secession as a "most valuable and most sacred right."³⁰⁹ New England believed in it and threatened it on several occasions, and was only prevented from actually putting it into effect on one occasion by a mere fluke of circumstances. Northern public men openly asserted the right of a State to secede, and the act was proclaimed "rebellion" only when the [Conservative] South asserted herself, realizing that her rights and privileges in the union which then existed were gone, swamped under a flood of [Left-wing] fanaticism and sectionalism. . . .³¹⁰ — ARTHUR H. JENNINGS, HISTORIAN IN CHIEF, SONS OF CONFEDERATE VETERANS

MORE YANKEE MYTHS DEBUNKED

☛ [Let's take a closer look at] . . . those history manufacturers of the country [mainly Liberals and uneducated Conservatives] who weave their little fairy tales around the men and times of our country, some quotations from men like [William T.] Sherman, [William H.] Seward, etc., to show how utterly fantastic [and incorrect] the general conception of matters of that time now are. Speaking of the colored brother, Seward says:

> "The great fact is fully realized that the African race here is a foreign and feeble element, incapable of assimilation—a pitiful exotic."

General Sherman said:

> "All the congresses on earth cannot make the negro anything else than what he is. He must be subject to the white man or he must be destroyed."

Lincoln said:

> "I am in favor of the race to which I belong having the superior position. There is a physical difference between the two (negroes and whites) which would forever forbid their living together upon a footing of perfect equality."

Suppose these sentiments of [Liberal] Northern demigods and heroes were read out in a meeting of that most remarkable aggregation, "The Society for the Advancement of Colored Peoples," whose specialty is abusing the South for lynching negro rape fiends—can we imagine the horror and fury which would prevail!

Of course, later [during so-called "Reconstruction"], the Northern radicals [that is, Yankee socialists and communists], of whom Seward, at least, was a leading spirit, tried their best to make the negro into a white man, tried their best to make the white man into a servile creature, subject, in the South, to a former servile race; but this was done on account of hate for the Southern whites, not love for the negro [as U.S. Chief Justice under Lincoln, Salmon P. Chase, later admitted].[311] — ARTHUR H. JENNINGS, HISTORIAN IN CHIEF, SONS OF CONFEDERATE VETERANS

DAVIS' "UNDYING PRINCIPLES"

☛ President Jefferson Davis needs that his people know him. The malignity and hate of his [Yankee] enemies "over the border," the unfairness of his home critics, have given way at last to a knowledge that here stood a man of integrity and highest character and attainment, who occupied exalted position in this country all of his life, and who, for standing for the undying principles which gave birth to the [Southern] Confederacy, which principles his former foes now proclaim as eternally true and fair, was crucified for his people by a malignant [Left-wing] rabble not worthy to tie the lachets of his shoes.[312] — ARTHUR H. JENNINGS, HISTORIAN IN CHIEF, SONS OF CONFEDERATE VETERANS

A MESSAGE FROM THE DAUGHTERS
☛ . . . We would not stir the embers of settled strife nor reopen the graves of buried issues, but we must insist that the rights of States under the Constitution prior to 1860 be taught our children, so that the purity of purpose of our forefathers and of our great Southern leaders may be understood, and that our great Southern leaders may be understood, and that our children be given a fair and truthful version of the causes of secession, not always, alas! appearing in the histories used in our own Southern schools to-day. . . .[313] — FRANCES GOGGIN MALTBY, PRESIDENT KENTUCKY DIVISION, UNITED DAUGHTERS OF THE CONFEDERACY

WHAT LEFT-WING ABRAHAM LINCOLN ACHIEVED
☛ The world claims now, and rightly, that Lincoln made the United States of America a "government of the people, by the people, and for the people." Lincoln found the United States of America a government of the States, by the States, and for the States. He changed it by force of a four-year war into a nation. Up to 1861, the Federal government was a [confederate] republic of sovereign States of such wisdom and power as to win the respect and love of all true lovers of political liberty, but too wise and not powerful enough to coerce sovereign States. Now, since 1861-65, we are a nation with sovereign States reduced to provinces, State rights gone (for what rights have they who dare not strike for them?); a nation, admired still by the world, but feared and mistrusted as a nation boastful and overbearing, ready and willing to regulate, if not to rule, the world like old Rome. . . .[314] — BERKELEY MINOR, CHARLOTTESVILLE, VIRGINIA

PROOF THAT LINCOLN INTENDED TO USE SOUTHERN BLACKS TO LAUNCH A MAJOR RACIAL UPRISING IN DIXIE
☛ This letter I have in Mr. Lincoln's handwriting. I have copied it

verbatim, but there is one word that I cannot make out. It is clear to me that Mr. Lincoln desired to create a condition in the South more horrible than war.

At the time the letter was written, March 26, 1863, the Confederate armies were victorious at every point. The great victory at Fredericksburg, December 13, 1862, when eighteen thousand men of the Army of Northern Virginia defeated [Union General Ambrose E.] Burnside's army of one hundred and thirty-eight thousand, caused great dissatisfaction in the North, and the Federal authorities were anxious and willing to resort to any and every expedient to quiet that discontent.

The letter shows that Mr. Lincoln approved old Sherman's idea of [total] war, and proves that he was not the humane, tender, sympathetic, forgiving man some people have sought to make him. The letter speaks for itself, thus:

> "Executive Mansion, Washington, D. C., Private. March 26, 1863. Hon. Andrew Johnson. My Dear Sir: I am told that you have at least thought of raising a negro military force. In my opinion, the country now needs no specific thing so much as some man of your ability and position, I mean that of an eminent citizen of a slave State and himself a slaveholder. The colored population is the great available and yet unavailable of forces for restoring the Union. The bare sight of fifty thousand armed and drilled black soldiers on the banks of the Mississippi would end the rebellion at once. And who doubts that we can present that sight if the _____ take hold in earnest? If you have been thinking of it, please do not dismiss the thought. Yours truly, A. Lincoln."[315]

— CONFEDERATE CAPTAIN JAMES DINKINS

WHY DID WAR EXPLODE IN 1861?

☛ There is a wide impression that the North made the war to free the negro slaves and the South fought for slavery. For certain reasons—whether good or bad—seven cotton States seceded, while other Southern States refused to secede.

[The U.S.] Congress was in session. A peace convention was held by the [Northern] States to propose measures that would lead the seceded States to return. Congress proposed an amendment [the Corwin Amendment, named after Ohio statesman Thomas Corwin] to the Constitution which, if adopted, would doubtless have led to their return [more proof that the War was not fought over slavery].[316] When Congress expired, March 4, 1861, a special session of the [U.S.] Senate convened. There was no talk about war. The Senate adjourned March 28. All was peaceful and quiet.

History tells us that up to about March 28, 1861, Mr. Lincoln and his cabinet had [deceptively] agreed to avoid any clashing with the seven seceded States, and, the garrison of Fort Sumter being in need of provisions, to withdraw these troops and abandon the forts at Charleston. That had been published in the newspapers, and the South rejoiced.

Then came a change of purpose. To understand the reason of that change, let us look at the report of the [U.S.] Committee on Commerce and Navigation for the year ending June 30, 1859, but subsequently made:

> Imports (omitting re-exports): $317,863,053
> Exports: Southern origin: $193,399,618
>   Northern origin: $45,305,541
>   Mixed products: $39,686,921
>   Total amount: $278,392,080
>
> Balance against us [the South]: $39,470,973
> Gold and silver exported $57,502,305
>   Our surplus balance: $18,031,332

Now strike off the Southern exports, and how could the Northern imports be paid for?

> The cotton exports were: $161,434,923
> The tobacco in leaf: $21,074,038
>   Total amount: $182,508,961

If the North lost these exports, how could she pay for her imports? Nine [U.S.] governors went to Washington, and war was determined on to save to Northern commerce the exports of the South.

Therefore, the *New York Times*, on March 30, giving expression to this purpose, said:

> "With us it is no longer an abstract question, one of constitutional construction, or reserved or delegated powers of the States to the Federal government, but of material existence and moral position both at home and abroad."

No longer a question of legal constitutional right, but of material existence. The *Times* was close to the administration.

It was in conformity to those ideas that Mr. Lincoln was persuaded to bring on the war and keep the South as an appendage to the North.

Without regard to the Constitution and abstract rights, the North declared itself the master of the South and proposed to maintain her mastery by the heaviest artillery.

When that was made known, the other Southern States cast their fortunes with the seceded States. If they had to fight, they would fight for and with the South, and not against the South. It was a question of independence. The South fought to maintain independence.

Mr. Lincoln said in his Inaugural, March 4, 1865:

> "Neither party expected for the war the magnitude or duration which it has already attained. Each looked for an easier triumph and a result less fundamental and astounding."

While the South had only the purpose to withstand the invaders, Mr. Lincoln perhaps thought that the Southern people would not fight to the bitter end for their independence. And possibly had he realized what he was doing, he might not have started the war.[317] — CAPTAIN SAMUEL A. ASHE, RALEIGH, NORTH CAROLINA

D.A.R.: TRUE PATRIOTS SUPPORTING STATES' RIGHTS

☛ The Daughters of the American Revolution proved themselves to be true descendants of the patriots who won their independence and then established a [confederated] republican union of sovereign States when, in their national congress, just concluded [1927], they demanded the preservation of the rights of those States and sounded a warning to the women of the land to scan critically all proposed legislation which would affect the home and the care and education of children.

"Investigate the origin and object of all legislation. Ascertain whether it is in accordance with the Constitution of the United States," warned the committee on national legislation.

The Daughters of the American Revolution are as awake to their duty as

Confederate Colonel Lawrence Massillon Keitt of 20th South Carolina Infantry Regiment, circa 1864.

were the Minutemen of 1775. They must have recalled that the Tenth Amendment to the Constitution of the United States provides that "the powers not delegated to the United States by the Constitution, nor prohibited to it by the States, are reserved to the States, respectively, or to the people." That is the direct inference to be drawn from the vigorous resolution the congress adopted, which demands that all activities of the Federal government be confined to the effective discharge of the national duties expressly delegated to the Federal government by the Constitution, and that all Federal activities not necessary to the performance of those national duties be discontinued as rapidly as possible, thereby restoring to our nation, our States, and our individual citizens the respective responsibilities imposed by the form of government for which our forefathers fought, worked, and died.[318] — *EXCHANGE*

OUR TRUE HISTORY IS NOT BEING TAUGHT IN SOUTHERN SCHOOLS

☞ . . . I have been both surprised and shocked to seethe way in which the South has allowed the great principles of our forefathers, the history of our glorious war for Right and Liberty, 1861-65, and the lives and deeds of our glorious leaders—Jefferson Davis, Robert E. Lee, Stonewall Jackson, and the hosts of others who fought for the gray—to be almost totally ignored in our schools. I have questioned hundreds of school children and high school graduates here in Florida, and very few know anything about the Confederacy, the war of 1861-65, or the great Southern leaders, the Confederate flags, or even the fact that their State seceded or fought for liberty. It should be seen to that every Southern State has in its schools portraits or busts of these great Southerners, and that they use textbooks which set forth fully and fairly the glorious history of our beloved Southland.[319] — HARRY F. BARRELL, ST. PETERSBURG, FLORIDA

PRESIDENTIAL REMINDER OF THE IMPORTANCE OF STATES' RIGHTS

☞ If the Federal government should go out of existence, the common run of people would not detect the difference in the affairs of their daily life for a considerable length of time. But if the authority of the States were struck down, disorder approaching chaos would be upon us within twenty-four hours.[320] — U.S. PRESIDENT CALVIN COOLIDGE, ADDRESS, WILLIAM & MARY COLLEGE, MAY 15, 1926

WHY CONFEDERATE ADMIRAL SEMMES SIDED WITH THE SOUTH

☞ . . . I have nothing to regret, save only the loss of our independence. My conscience, which is the only earthly tribunal of which a good man should be afraid, bears me witness of the uprightness of my intention in choosing my course, when, with many regrets, I severed my connection with the old [U.S.] government and hastened to the defense of my home and section; and now, upon reviewing the whole of my subsequent career, I can see no act with which I have to reproach myself as unbecoming a man of honor and a gentleman. I approved the secession movement of the Southern States, though I had no agency in it. I thought that the separation of these two sections of our republic, which had been engaged in a deadly mortal conflict for thirty years, would ultimately result to the great advantage of them both. The world was wide enough for them to live apart, and peace, I thought, would be the fruit of their mutual independence of each other. . . . I cared very little about the institution of slavery . . . . I believed that the doctrine of State Rights was the only doctrine which would save our republic from the fate of all other republics that had gone before us in the history of the world. I believed that this doctrine had been violated and that it would never be sufficiently respected by the controlling [Left-wing] masses of the Northern section to prevent them from defacing with sacrilegious hands our national bond of Union wheresoever its letter was meant to guard the peculiar rights of the South. Believing this, there was but one course for a faithful Southern man to pursue and maintain his self-respect. I pursued that course. When the alternative was presented to me of adhering to the allegiance due to my State or to the United States, I chose the former. Having taken my side, I gave it zealous and earnest support. I spent four years in active service, and only ceased to labor for my cause when it was no longer possible. I rendered this service without ever having treated a prisoner otherwise than humanely, and, I may say, often kindly, and without ever having committed an act of war, at any time or in any manner, which was not sanctioned by the laws of war; yet my name will probably go down to posterity in the untruthful histories which will be written by bigoted and venal historians as a sort of "Bluebeard" or "Captain Kidd." But I am content, my brother. My conscience is clear, my self-respect has been preserved, and my sense of manhood remains unimpaired. I think, too, the South will be content, notwithstanding her immense losses and sacrifices. If she had yielded to the intolerant exactions of Northern selfishness and fanaticism without appealing to the arbitrament of war, she would have played a craven and unworthy part.

It is better to lose everything than our honor and manhood. I know you will believe me, my brother, when I tell you that I should feel greatly humbled in my own opinion were I this day entitled to wear an admiral's flag in the old navy and in possession of all the means and appliances of wealth if I thought my honors and rewards had been gained by a sacrifice of creed. The preservation of my own self-respect is infinitely preferable to all such gains. I have come out of the war poor, but, God willing, I shall make a support for my family. The President [Andrew Johnson] treats me as an outlaw, unworthy of amnesty. I have nothing to say. If I am deemed unworthy to be a citizen, I can remain in my native land as an alien. A magnanimous people would have passed an act of general amnesty, it being absurd and ridiculous to talk about rebels and traitors in connection with such a revolution as has swept over the length and breadth of this land, in which States, and not individuals merely, were the actors. But enough of this subject. I am still in Mobile, but it is yet uncertain where I shall go, or what I shall do. If I save five or six thousand dollars out of the wreck of my affairs, it will be fully as much as I expect. I think of retiring into the country, where, upon a small farm, I can live in obscurity and peace the few years that remain to me. My children are all grown, are well educated, and will be able, if the worst comes by the worst, to take care of themselves.

Remember me kindly to your family, my dear brother, and let me hear from you. We have become old men. We have both had our troubles, but the chain of affection which binds me to you remains unaffected by the cares of the world and is as bright now as when we slept in each others' arms. Your affectionate brother, R. Semmes.[321] — CONFEDERATE ADMIRAL RAPHAEL SEMMES, WHILE AWAITING TRIAL FOR "MISDEEDS ON THE HIGH SEAS," FROM A LETTER TO HIS BROTHER SAMUEL M. SEMMES, AUGUST 12, 1865, MOBILE, ALABAMA

THE WAR ACCORDING TO A COMMON SOLDIER
☞ . . . I was a bit of a lad when the War between the States broke out, but I soon enlisted in the Confederate service, in Gen. Sterling Price's army, [Joseph O.] Shelby's Brigade, [Col. David] Shanks's Regiment, Company B, and served until the close of the war, surrendering at Shreveport, La., in June, 1865.

I am writing this communication to the *Confederate Veteran* because it may be the last opportunity that I shall ever have to express my love and admiration to the few remaining gallant and brave soldiers who wore the Confederate gray and fought during that bloody war. I wish also to be remembered by all the people of the South. I am proud of you and love you with all my heart.

I hardly know yet whether I have ever been fully reconstructed or not. I do not believe I have, when I come to think of how hard we tried to keep out of war with the North, to be let alone and to attend to our own affairs; but it was forced upon us. We had to defend our homes, our property, our rights, and the women and children of the South. The Yankee armies, with their millions of blue coats, overran the South, killed, burned, and destroyed everything of value they could find. We had to fight, and I have no apologies to make. I believed we were right in what we did, and I would do the same thing again under the same circumstances. The Confederate soldier is as loyal to this nation as any Northern soldier. That has been proved by the late wars. We worked and made our own living, and we never drew a cent of pension from the government either. A great wrong was done the South during Reconstruction days, and she feels it yet.

For seven years after the war, before I was allowed to cast a vote for anything, although I was qualified by age and citizenship, the registrar held that I was disloyal, and I was denied the right in all those many years just because I was a Confederate soldier.

. . . God will bless the Confederate veteran and the dear people of the Southland. Peacefully, quietly, passing away, remember me as your comrade and true friend.[322] — W. J. COURTNEY, OF LIBERTY, MISSOURI

DEFENDING THE SOUTHERN CAUSE FOR FOUR YEARS
☛ . . . Never shall I forget that black day when we, the shattered, starving survivors of the Army of the Northern Virginia, marched out on a sodden field near Appomattox Courthouse to lay down the arms we had borne for four years in defense of State Rights. The hopes of our youthful hearts were with the torn flags we carried before us that April day. The surrender of our great chieftain [Robert E. Lee] seemed to us the end of days. . . .[323] — GENERAL W. B. FREEMAN, FORMER COMMANDER-IN-CHIEF UNITED CONFEDERATE VETERANS

FREEDOM!
☛ . . . What is self-determination but State Rights under another name? . . .[324] — MISS NANNIE DAVIS SMITH, BATON ROUGE, LOUISIANA

OLD SOUTH FARMERS: THE HEART OF AMERICA
☛ . . . the well-to-do farmers of the South . . . were, and are, the backbone of the commonwealth, the keepers of her covenant to preserve State Rights, individual liberty, and the highest type of democratic government.³²⁵ — *CONFEDERATE VETERAN MAGAZINE*

THE BONNIE BLUE FLAG
☛ "Hurrah! Hurrah! for Southern rights, Hurrah. Hurrah for the Bonnie Blue Flag that bears a Single Star." This is the chorus of the first song in praise of the first flag unfurled of the new-born nation—the Confederate States of America—the storm-cradled nation that fell—fell only for the want of men and means to wage its war against the vast armies with unlimited means and engines of war that invaded and crushed it.

History tells of many nations in ages past which, in their struggle for liberty and self-government, have arisen and flourished and fallen, leaving songs and heroes whose memory must forever live. *The Bonnie Blue Flag* is the song of a nation that is dead, the memory of which must be kept forever green. . . .³²⁶ — HENRY WINTER HARPER, MEMPHIS, TENNESSEE

FROM CONFEDERATE REPUBLIC TO CENTRALIZED NATION
☛ . . . In the fight for State sovereignty, the men of the South were battling for the faith of their fathers. When they lost, the rights of States were submerged in a centralized national government, and a nation unified had its birth.

As a result of the war and of a long series of encroachments, the Federal government has become supreme and the States can exercise only such rights as it may allow them. The South resisted these encroachments and fought for the Constitution as it was originally adopted and for the rights of all the States. She was defeated, and this defeat meant a radical revolution in the nature of our government from a Federal [that is, Confederate] republic to a centralized nation.

Men of the South rejoice in this great nation of ours. None are more loyal to the Stars and Stripes than the soldiers of the Confederacy, their sons, and grandsons. When the armies of the South surrendered, the men in gray accepted in good faith the new government and followed the example of the great chieftain, Robert E. Lee, and taught their children to love and respect the flag of the nation, to labor for its peace and prosperity. . . .³²⁷ —

SAMUEL D. RODGERS, FORMER COMMANDER VIRGINIA SONS OF CONFEDERATE VETERANS, ADDRESS, MEMORIAL DAY, PETERSBURG, VIRGINIA, JUNE 9, 1927

NULLIFICATION & SECESSION
☛ I hope none who hear me will confound this expression of mine with the advocacy of the right of a State to remain in the Union and to disregard its constitutional obligations by the nullification of the law. Such is not my theory. Nullification and secession, so often confounded, are indeed antagonistic principles. Nullification is a remedy which it is sought to apply within the Union, and against the agent of the States. It is only to be justified when the agent has violated his constitutional obligation, and a State, assuming to judge for itself, denies the right of the agent thus to act, and appeals to the other States of the Union for a decision; but when the States themselves, and when the people of the States, have so acted as to convince us that they will not regard our constitutional rights, then, and then for the first time, arises the doctrine of secession in its practical application.[328] — JEFFERSON DAVIS

"TWO GLORIOUS ANGLO-SAXON TRAITS"
☛ . . . Those were stirring times of stress and danger in the early [seventeen] seventies when Great Britain, mistress of the seas, dared trample on the rights of a liberty-loving people [Virginians] and lost an empire. For in the new world the invincible and unbroken vigor and vitality inherent in the Anglo-Saxon race had been multiplied many fold. Here in Virginia were to be found, as a natural heritage evolved to the highest degree, those two glorious Anglo-Saxon traits: Respect for authority and resistance to its abuse. . . .[329] — DR. J. B. STONE, ADDRESS, UNVEILING OF GRAVE MARKER FOR REVOLUTIONARY SOLDIER JOSHUA STONE, NEAR ALTA VISTA, VIRGINIA, AUGUST 15, 1928

SECESSION: WITHDRAWING FROM THE UNION
☛ . . . Senators, we recur to the compact which binds us together; we recur to the principles upon which our government was founded; and when you deny them, and when you deny to us the right to withdraw from a government which, thus perverted, threatens to be destructive of our rights, we but tread in the path of our fathers when we proclaim our independence and take the hazard. This is done not in hostility to others, not to injure any section of the country, not even for our own pecuniary benefit; but from the high and solemn motive of defending and protecting the

rights we inherited, and which it is our sacred duty to transmit unshorn to our children.[330] — JEFFERSON DAVIS, 1861

MORE PROOF THAT THE WAR WAS OVER THE CONSTITUTION

☞ . . . It has been my great privilege to know intimately those who were associated with this great epoch in the history of the United States [the War for Southern Independence], men who loved the old commonwealth of Virginia and bared their breasts and sacrificed all to their convictions of State Rights. No Virginian ever fought for slavery; that was a side issue, of which abolitionists made much; but, just as "Light Horse" Harry Lee and George Washington drew their swords to repel British injustice, history repeated itself in the sixties when invasion and injustice threatened the Southland. Stonewall Jackson said: "If war must come, then draw the sword and throw away the scabbard." Gen. Robert E. Lee was himself proffered the command of the Union Army, for Gen. Winfield Scott, then Commander in Chief, U.S.A., recognized his ability as the greatest American soldier then living; but Lee replied: "Never again will I draw my sword save in the defense of my native State, Virginia."[331] — MRS. WILLIAM LYNE, WASHINGTON, D.C.

WEBSTER PREDICTS SOUTHERN SECESSION

☞ . . . In the Constitution of the United States there is a clause on State Rights [see Amendments Nine and Ten].[332] The North rebelled against this clause, and this is what brought on session. Daniel Webster, the great orator and statesman, known as the expounder of the Constitution—the New Englander to the manner born, and the bitter antagonist of our beloved John C. Calhoun of South Carolina—this same Daniel Webster, in the very zenith of his fame thirty years before secession came, made a stirring speech in old Faneuil Hall in Boston, on State Rights, in which he said: "The time will come when the South will positively have to secede." So bitter was the feeling against him that his own publishers were afraid to publish his speech, and it has been silenced, as has a lot of true history; but perhaps some day it may come into its own.

His prophecy was fulfilled. Secession came. . . .[333] — MRS. MAUDE B. HUNNEBERGER, HISTORIAN MARYLAND DIVISION, U.D.C.

THE SOUTH, NOT THE NORTH, FOLLOWED THE CONSTITUTION

☞ ... There is something unique in the War between the States. While the South was overpowered, they were never conquered. The same spirit that actuated the South to resist oppression is in the people of the South to-day. They held fast to the truth for which they contended — State Rights—and a very strange thing to relate is, the people of the North, the children of the bitterest abolitionists [that is, radical Leftists: socialists and communists], are coming to acknowledge that the South, not they, adhered to the Constitution. [334] — MRS. S. M. FIELDS

LETTER TO *CONFEDERATE VETERAN* MAGAZINE

☞ To the Editor: The recent action of the men of the G. A. R. [that is, the Union or U.S. army] in spurning the idea of a rapprochement with their foes of 1861 is, I think, more of a reflection upon them than upon the men of the South, who proved their manhood and their mettle in one of the most grueling contests of history, and who only succumbed to overwhelming numbers and resources.

Confederate Colonel William W. Ward, 9th Tennessee Cavalry Regiment, 1864.

If the men of the South can forgive those who denied them, at the point of the bayonet and the cannon's mouth, those inherent and inalienable human rights asserted in the Declaration of Independence, rights which Lincoln readily conceded to the barbaric black inhabitants of San Domingo and Haiti, and which to-day are conceded to many half-civilized peoples, and which are, in fact, those rights of self-government in defense of which the Allies allegedly fought the World War [I]; if they can forgive not only that they were denied the rights of men, but that they were brutally and repeatedly struck and trampled upon when they were down, in one of the most appalling chapters of oppression in history, what is to be said of the spiritual caliber of men who need only forgive that their "foes" had the "impatient vanity" to claim for themselves the inherent and inalienable rights of men?

If those rights are inalienable, then how could the generation which ratified the Constitution permanently alienate them? The term "inalienable" knocks the bottom out of all of Webster's and Lincoln's shallow pretensions.

In view of the undeniable historical fact that the armies of Lincoln were not in any real sense volunteer armies, it would be interesting to know just how many of those who are now so bigoted, so implacable, so unsportsmanlike, and so unchristian, were drafted or induced to enlist by the offer of money. Such men eventually become the most bigoted and zealous supporters of a cause.[335] — REVEREND PAUL S. WHITCOMB, PORTLAND, OREGON

Confederate Captain Black Dog (also known as Young Black Dog), Co. B, 1st Osage Battalion, C.S.A. (Note bear claw necklace.) Photographer: William Henry Jackson, 1876,

Confederate General Robert Edward Lee in uniform on his equally famous horse, Traveller. Photographed by Adam H. Plecker's Travelling Gallery, circa 1863.

LEAVING A VOLUNTARY UNION OF INDEPENDENT STATES

☞ . . . Such is the position we are taking in regard to the titanic struggle from 1861 to 1865, when, we maintain, that the conflict was not a "Civil" War, but was a "War between the States." Each Southern State seceded from the Federal government after mature consideration, seceded with all the dignity and weight of their State governments and State; conventions back of them, and formed an independent constitutional government—the Confederate States of America.

The South did not fight to overturn the Federal government. It did not wish to destroy that government and set up a rival administration in its place. The Southern States simply desired to withdraw peaceably from what had hitherto been considered a voluntary union of States, to leave the Northern States intact, with their recognized government untrammeled, and to form an independent government of their own. The South fought to repel

Confederate Private George Addison Cooke of 1st Maryland Artillery Battery, circa 1862.

invasion, to protect its homes and its inalienable rights as free men, and it was between two constitutionally organized governments that the war was waged. . . .[336] — MISS IDA P. POWELL, CHAIRMAN U.D.C. COMMITTEE ON "WAR BETWEEN THE STATES"

YANKEE GENERAL DECRIES THE UNION ARMY'S LACK OF CONSCIENCE, PURPOSE, & NOBILITY IN COMPARISON WITH THE CONFEDERATE ARMY

☛ Our men in the field do not lack food, or clothing, or money, but they do lack noble watchwords and inspiring ideas, such as are worth fighting and dying for.

The Southern soldier has what at least serves him as such; for he believes that he fights in defense of country, home, and rights; and he strikes vehemently, and with a will.

Our men, alas! have no such ideas. The Union is to most of them an abstraction, and not an inspiring watchword. The sad truth should be known—that our army has no conscious, noble purpose; and our soldiers generally have not much stomach for fight.

Look at the opposing armies and you will see two striking truths. First, the Northen men are superior in numbers, virtue, intelligence, bodily strength, and real pluck; and yet on the whole they have been outgeneraled and badly beaten. Second, the Northern army is better equipped, better clad, fed, and lodged; and is in a far more comfortable condition, not only than the Southern army, but than any other in the world; and yet, if the pay were stopped in both, the Northern army would probably mutiny at once, or crumble rapidly; while the Southern army would probably hold together for a long time, in some shape, if their cause seemed to demand it.

The animating spirit of the Southern soldier is rather moral than pecuniary; of the Northern soldier it is rather pecuniary than moral.[337] — UNION GENERAL SAMUEL G. HOWE, BOSTON, MASSACHUSETTS, DISTRIBUTED CIRCULAR, FEBRUARY 20, 1862

THE SACRED CAPITOL CITY OF ALABAMA

☛ . . . Every child in Montgomery has stood on the sacred spot where Jefferson Davis was sworn in as President of the Confederate States. Every girl in Montgomery has trod the sacred steps leading into the First "White House of the Confederacy." Every Montgomery boy has stood where the order was given to fire on Fort Sumter. Our ears still ring and our hearts still leap in memory of those stirring words proclaiming the doctrine of States' Rights and Local Self-Government.

The Confederacy had its birth in the hearts and on the soil of Montgomery. Jefferson Davis knelt in prayer at old St. John's, and asked Divine guidance for the sacred Cause he represented. Time has not dimmed the memory of our people, nor their love of the South. We shall hand down to our children and to our children's children a love that passeth all understanding for that noble band who stood guard to preserve memories no true Southerner can ever forget.[338] — EDITH DRAKE POPE, EDITOR, *CONFEDERATE VETERAN* MAGAZINE

HISTORICAL BASIS FOR NULLIFICATION & SECESSION
☞ . . . According to the peace treaty with Great Britain, signed in Paris in 1783, the independence of each State was recognized. And as a Sovereign State, each had the right to remain independent or to delegate such powers as that state deemed wise incase of a union. And when the Constitution was adopted—after the obvious failure of the Union under the Articles of Confederation[339]—some States held that a State had the right to nullify any and all laws not specifically delegated to the government by the several States. This theory of government was first embodied in the Virginia and Kentucky Resolutions of 1798. These resolutions from the pens of [James] Madison and [Thomas] Jefferson, respectively, declared alien and sedition acts unconstitutional. They set forth the doctrine of States' Rights, according to which it was claimed, first, that when the Constitution was formed, the States by a common agreement united to create the national government and entrusted to it certain powers; second, that the national government so created was authorized to act simply as the agent of the States, which were the real sovereigns, and to do only those things which were specifically granted to it in the compact of the Constitution; and, third, that the right to decide whether the national government did or did not act according to the terms of the compact belonged to the States alone, the creators of the national government. . . .[340] — MISS ANNIE MCCORD, GREENWOOD, SOUTH CAROLINA, 1930

THE SOUTHERN CAUSE CONTINUES
☞ One could render no greater disservice to the country than by going about arousing sectional feeling, reviving antagonisms, and kindling the fires of bitterness generated by the conflict of 1861-65 and the outrages of reconstruction during the eleven years that

followed.

It is true the "bloody shirt" [that is, purposefully inflaming sectional hatred] is still doing a diminishing business in certain regions of the country. It is still the mendacious banner of the demagogue and ambitious office-seeker in those regions. But its effectiveness has greatly waned.

I would avoid even the appearance of a purpose to awaken sectional resentment or animosity while I must refer to certain truths which are matters of record and not subject to dispute.

Keeping in mind the sound rule announced by [Marcus Tullius] Cicero, long ago, that "it is the first and fundamental law of history that it should neither dare to say anything that is false or fear to say anything that is true, nor give any just suspicion of favor or disaffection," I feel disposed, in addressing this body of noble women, one of whose purposes is to see, as far as they can, that the facts in connection with the experiences of those trying years and the truth, the whole truth, and nothing but the truth, shall be preserved to posterity, to refer to some of those outstanding verities.

History is but the story of human behavior. Giving an account of the behavior involves a consideration at times of the motives back of it. In the interest of truth and correct history, therefore, I mention certain matters which I think ought to be stated in this presence, particularly in view of certain rude, unjust, and uncalled-for aspersions, which I dismiss without dignifying by further reference.

You aim to correct false representations, maintain the truth, and render what aid you can to those who suffered and sacrificed in defense of the homes and firesides of the Southland in times which tried human souls. You represent, in away, the devoted and consecrated women who supported the noble manhood of the South in the struggle for liberty and independence, driven to such struggle by the thunder of events, sustained by sublime faith in the righteousness of the cause and devotion to the principles for which they stood. No decent individuals should offer criticism for that attitude.

Your mothers and you, in your ideals and purposes, represent "the pure in spirit," for whom there is vouchsafed the blessings of heaven.

Suppose we say the cause was secession, and that was lost by the arbitrament of the sword.

The South was outnumbered in military strength four to one, and in resources greater than that.

The South, after four years of heroic defense, unparalled in all the world, was obliged to surrender.

But what was the cause of secession? We must go to the underlying conditions. Some say slavery was the cause. We will examine that briefly.

A recent writer, [Christopher] Hollis, in his *The American Heresy*, says slavery was not abolished in America by or as a result of the war, only slaveholders.

The truth is, the vital question involved, the real cause, was the South's insistence upon the Constitutional rights of the State.

When I say the Cause was not entirely lost, as claimed, I refer to the doctrine of States Rights.

Just exactly as Southern leaders contended, those rights have been declared by the Supreme Court of the United States, the highest authority in the land, as sound, constitutional, and valid then, and by later decisions since.

The Dred Scott decision, the [Lambdin P.] Milligan case, and numerous others of recent date have emphasized and construed the meaning of State Sovereignty and Rights of the States, in principle, as the South contended in and before 1861.

So, I say, the Cause was not entirely lost.

A modern, disinterested writer, Hollis, in his book on *The American Heresy*, says in 1816 the South was dominant in this country, and in 1828 the right of secession was taken for granted everywhere. "The old South," he asserts, "was not beaten and persuaded—she was beaten and murdered."

We shall see that there was a resurrection day—the spirit lives on!

In his life of [Daniel] Webster, Henry Cabot Lodge, historian and lately United States Senator from Massachusetts, says:

> "When the Constitution was adopted by the votes of States at Philadelphia and accepted by votes of States in popular conventions, it was safe to say there was not a man in the country, from [George] Washington and [Alexander] Hamilton on the one side to George Clinton and George Mason on the other, who regarded the new system as anything but an experiment entered upon by the States and from which each and every State had the right to peacefully withdraw—a right which was very likely to be exercised."

The contemporary opinion of Northern publicists and leading journals considered coercion out of the question. The New York *Tribune*, Horace Greeley [socialist] editor, said, November 9, 1860:

"If the cotton States shall decide they can do better out of the Union than in it, we insist on letting them go in peace. The right to secede may be a revolutionary one, but it exists nevertheless, and we do not see how one party can have a right to do what another party has a right to prevent. We must ever resist the asserted right of any State to remain in the Union and nullify or destroy the laws thereof; to withdraw from the Union is quite another matter."

This was precisely the position of Jefferson Davis. The South did not take a stand for nullification, but did exercise the right to withdraw when the North refused to be bound by the Constitution.

Similar statements appeared in the press, and, after Mr. Davis had been inaugurated as President at Montgomery, the *Tribune* published:

"We have repeatedly said, and we once more insist, that the great principle embodied by]Thomas] Jefferson in the Declaration of American Independence that governments derive their just powers from the consent of the governed is sound and just, and that if the slave States, the cotton States, or the Gulf States only choose to form an independent nation, they have a clear moral right to do so."

Secession had been preached and threatened in various sections, and the Northern stand for it and against extension of the Union was quite complete. In Congress and in conventions, when Jefferson was annexing Louisiana, they declared they were not bound. The same when Texas was annexed. The same when the Mexican War was being fought.

The truth is that, if we consider it an open question in 1861, it is equally true that

"it had never been denied until recent years. The right had been proclaimed upon the hustings, enunciated in political platforms, proclaimed in the Senate and House of Representatives, embodied in our literature, taught in schools and colleges, interwoven into the texts of jurisprudence, and maintained by scholars, statesmen, and constituencies of all States and sections of the country."

[St. George] Tucker, [William] Rawle, and Alexis de Tocqueville taught it.

The South had led in the establishment of the Union.

Southern leaders had never urged secession; they loved the Union. Such was the attitude of Jefferson Davis, Robert E. Lee,

Stonewall Jackson, [Alexander H.] Stephens, Ben [W.] Hill, and others.

Ben Hill, that great statesman, when usurpation was taking place, the Constitution being trampled upon, sought to rally his people "to save their civilization." He declared:

> "The Constitution is my client, and the preservation of its protection is the only fee I ask."

His was the last speech for the Union in Congress—but when the bugle called his people to the field he cast his lot with them, and in the Confederate Senate, the youngest member, he was the spokesman for the Administration and made the last speech for the continuance of the war. When the Constitution became effective again, he was in the Senate of the United States, and there, in that historic answer to [James G.] Blaine, in words "as sublime as those that fell from the lips of Paul on Mars' Hill," he declared, "We are in our Father's house and we have come to stay."

Pursuing the thought a moment concerning the leadership of the South and its accomplishments and its love for American institutions, reflect—

Who wrote the Declaration of Independence?
Who uttered the challenge, "Liberty or death"?
Who presided over the convention that framed the Constitution?
Who was the chief author of it?
Who became its great interpreter?
Who wrote the Bill of Rights?
Whose sword defended the young republic?

Every schoolboy must answer [Thomas] Jefferson, [Patrick] Henry, [James] Madison, [John] Marshall, [George] Mason, and [George] Washington—all men of the South!

We were then, at the close of the [American] Revolution, thirteen States straggling along the Atlantic Seaboard. How and by whom was this national domain extended?

Jefferson gave us the territory stretching from the Gulf of Mexico across the Rocky Mountains to Oregon.

President Madison, assisted by John C. Calhoun, Andrew Jackson sealing the victory, led us through the second war of independence in 1812.

Samuel Houston achieved Texas independence, admitted to the Union under James K. Polk.

The Northern Territory, north of the Ohio River, embracing

Ohio, Indiana, Illinois, Michigan, and Wisconsin, was conquered by George Rogers Clark, a soldier of Virginia. "By Virginia's gift and Southern votes this mighty land was made the dowry of the nation."

Then why should the South be driven from this Union she had done so much to create? That brings us to the principal cause for assailing by the North the foundation upon which the republic was built—a proper recognition, under the Constitution, of the Sovereign Rights of the States.

Slavery was that cause, and we must refer briefly to the salient truths in that connection. It became a very unpopular institution for sentimental reasons. The material interests of the North and East became antagonistic. Abolitionists [socialists and communists] aroused much feeling against it. Self-seeking politicians seized upon it to serve their ends. Jealous of the South's power, they sought to so direct affairs as to overcome the South and control the government, and particularly the offices. This finally led to a revolution against the Constitution by those agitators, selfish and party interests. This forced the South into a revolution to sustain and uphold the Constitution and laws of the country. We may call that secession.

An unbiased writer recently, looking over events, declares:

> "The Southern States had every legal right to retain slavery and to demand the return of fugitive slaves, and the Constitutional right to secede was incontestable."

I agree with Jay Hamilton. This is the absolute truth. It is unfair and unjust to blame the South for slavery. When [colonial] independence was declared, slavery was in existence in every State. When the Constitution was adopted in 1789, the institution still existed in every State except Massachusetts [the American birthplace of the institution]. Every State united in its recognition in the Federal compact. Three-fifths of the slaves were counted in the basis of representation in Congress; property in slaves was protected by rigid provisions regarding the rendition of slaves escaping from one State to another.

> "Thus embodied in the Constitution, thus interwoven in the very integrants of our political system, thus sustained by the oath to support the Constitution, executed by every public servant, and by the decisions of the Supreme tribunals, slavery was ratified by the unanimous voice of the nation and was recognized as an American institution and as a vested right by the most solemn pledge and sanction that man can

give."

It would be tedious to consider factors in the development and the changes in the institution, unsupported by any change in the Constitution or laws, and this probably states the case in the end:

> "But it was not hatred of the Union or love of slavery that inspired the South, nor love of the negro that inspired the North. Profounder thoughts and interests lay beneath these. The rivalry of cheap negro labor, aversion to the negro and to slavery alike, were the spurs of North action; that of the South was [political. That is, the] . . . question of slavery was one for the States."

It will be remembered that in the original draft of the Declaration of Independence, [Thomas] Jefferson included an indictment of King George [III] for his determination "to keep open a market where men could be bought and sold," and it was stricken out, because New England was then profitably operating slave ships and practically all the colonies owned slaves.

After the war was over, *after* the South had been subjugated, the Constitution was amended in a way to support the contention of the North *before* it was changed.

The Thirteenth Amendment, abolishing slavery, was adopted December 18, 1865.

The Fourteenth Amendment, containing Sections 3 and 4, prohibiting, in effect, secession, was adopted July 18, 1868.

The Fifteenth Amendment was adopted March 30, 1870, *after* all the plans and activities in connection with reconstruction had been by force put into effect.

The terms of surrender had been ignored; the South was treated by those in power as conquered provinces; and although they had waged war on the claim that the States could not leave the Union, they proceeded to deny the Southern States the status of States, and to impose on them the rule of Federal bayonets, supporting gross ignorance, incompetency, rascality, carpetbag corruption, and the rankest possible oppression; in fact, all the horrors, atrocities, crimes, and suffering of which human nature is capable.

Let the present-day historian speak: "This, then, was the combination against the peace of a fallen people—the soldiers inciting the blacks against their former masters, the Bureau agents preaching political and social equality, the white scum of the North fraternizing with the blacks in their shacks, and the thieves of the

Confederate Colonel Randall Lee Gibson of 13th Louisiana Infantry Regiment, circa 1862.

Treasury stealing cotton under the protection of Federal bayonets. And in the North, demagogic politicians and fanatics were demanding immediate negro suffrage and clamoring for the blood of Southern leaders. Why was not Jeff Davis hanged, and why was not Lee shot?" they said!

I am tempted to call some names of these South haters, usurpers, and oppressors. A few of them have statues about Washington [D.C.]. They ought not to be there. It is the only way posterity will know of them. Very few of them are in Statuary Hall, if any—the Parthenon of the Great of the United States. But there will be found today Jefferson Davis, James Z. George, Robert E. Lee, E. Kirby Smith, and others of their type.

You will not find [socialist] Thad [Thaddeus] Stevens there—that club-footed Caliban from Pennsylvania, who led in the Radical Republican [that is, socialist/communist] movement which brought about the conditions mentioned. Three days before the deplorable death of Lincoln, Stevens had denounced the terms of [Ulysses S.] Grant with Lee, said they were too easy, and that he would "dispossess those participating in the rebellion of every foot of ground they pretended to own." Supporting him were such delectable characters as Ben Wade, Ben [F.] Butler, Seward, Charles Sumner, [Edwin M.] Stanton, Grant (note particularly his use of Federal troops in Louisiana, South Carolina, and Florida), [Salmon P.] Chase (who favored negro suffrage), [socialist Carl] Schurz, Oliver P. Morton, Roscoe Conkling, and Zack [Zachariah] Chandler (the last three being Grant's "three musketeers"), [James] Don Cameron, W. E. Chandler, and Stanley Matthews (who did such dirty work in Florida), supported also by Robert G. Ingersoll, James G. Blaine, and [Philip H.] Sheridan.

It is worth while to observe that Jay Cooke and Henry Clews were close to the Grant Administration, and urged that if he and the Republican Party prevailed in the national election, it meant the country would continue prosperous and a bright future of increasing prosperity would follow.

This was in 1873.

In 1874 both of these failed, and Grant himself, who had acquired a desire for wealth, was financially involved in the crash.

Associated with these men were their agents and representatives in the Southern States, like [James W.] Hunnicutt in Virginia, [William W.] Holden in North Carolina, [Robert Kingston] Scott, [Franklin I.] Moses [Jr.], and [John James] Patterson in South Carolina, [Rufus] Bullock in Georgia, [Marcellus L.] Stearns and [Milton S.] Littlefield in Florida, [Adelbert] Ames in Mississippi, Powell Clayton in Arkansas, [Henry Clay] Warmoth in Louisiana, [William Gannaway] Brownlow in Tennessee, [Elisha M.] Pease in Texas, [Edward W.] Harrington and [George E.] Spencer in Alabama—all spokesmen and practically all carpetbaggers.

It may be mentioned that *Harper's Weekly*, the Chicago *Tribune*, and the Union League of Philadelphia did their best for the Radical Republican [socialist/communist] cause. They were joined by the Grand Army of the Republic [the U.S. army]—even then, in 1868, a political machine.

This disgraceful, outrageous work disgusted the decent people of the North, as well as all portions of the country. Public opinion revolted. This cruel, wicked, atrocious treatment of the South was about to come to an end.

It did when [Zebulon B.] Vance became Governor of North Carolina, [Wade] Hampton of South Carolina, [George Franklin] Drew of Florida, [Franklin T.] Nicholls of Louisiana, followed by other changes in the same direction—in 1876.

The States were free again, and each State began to rule itself—in 1876—after eleven years of humiliating, torturing, harrowing experience.

No country ever suffered as did the South except Poland—just one hundred years ago—and she did not survive.

She has at last risen again!

The [Conservative] South was no longer needed by the Republican Party [then Left-wing], and that may help to account for relaxing its grip.

There are some people and some events we cannot forget—while we harbor no grudges.

The South raised no question about the validity of the Amendments—accepted them, and it is today insisting upon standing by the Constitution.

Ben Hill's stirring declaration is sound today:

> "Tinkers may work, quacks may prescribe, and demagogues may deceive, but I declare to you that there is no remedy for us but in adhering to the Constitution."

[Hill is speaking of] the Constitution of the United States!

Slavery went by the board. Secession was determined against her. The South did not fight against amending the Constitution; she fought to uphold the Constitution as it was.

. . . The States are [still] in control of the people.

Local self-government, democratic government, [still] obtains. That was not lost.

The rights of the sovereign States, under the Constitution, are [still] recognized. We did not lose that.

See what a Republican [now a Conservative] Senator, the distinguished Senator and scholar from Connecticut, Senator Hiram Bingham, said in the Senate, January 17, 1928, to wit:

> "The Democratic Party [at this time Liberal] has no monopoly of a belief in State rights. Many of us who sit on this side of the aisle are earnest followers of the doctrine of local self-government and of State rights as laid down by Thomas Jefferson and the fathers."

And again:

> "Were I not so deeply interested in preserving to the States the rights guaranteed to them under the Constitution, rights which they never surrendered when they adopted the Constitution, I would not place myself in the unfortunate position of being one of those who are accused by the Senator from Missouri as being 'partners in crime.'"

Again he said in the Senate, December 12, 1926:

> "They say that State Rights disappeared sixty years ago. They seem to overlook the fact that the strength of our States and the responsibility have silenced the diverse wishes of self-respecting of our liberty and freedom. Otherwise, the great power of the Central Government would long ago have silenced the diverse wishes of self-respecting communities and crushed individual initiative and self-reliance."

James Bryce, the greatest authority on popular government in our generation, said:

> "The best school of democracy and the best guaranty for its success is the practice of local self-government."

In the Spring of 1926 [U.S.] President [Calvin] Coolidge said:

> "No method of procedure has ever been devised by which liberty could be divorced from local self-government. No plan of centralization has ever been adopted which did not result in bureaucracy, tyranny, inflexibility, reaction, and decline. . . . Unless bureaucracy is constantly resisted, it breaks down representative government and overwhelms democracy."

Mr. John H. Fahy, former President of the United States Chamber of Commerce, Publisher, of Worcester, Mass., in an address on the "Principles of Thomas Jefferson," April 13, 1931, said:

> "Jefferson demonstrated not only that sound and stable government must rest on the will of the people, but that real prosperity depended upon it. . . . He saw that too great centralization of power in the Federal Government would not only lead to inefficiency, waste, bureaucracy, and abuse of authority, but that the varied interests of the people of different sections were such that if concentration were carried too far, it would invite the breakdown of government."

He concluded by the statement:

> "But we cannot bring about, within a reasonable period, that more equitable distribution of the results of men's labor to which the people of the United States are entitled unless we insist uncompromisingly upon the application of those principles of government which Thomas Jefferson made the supporting pillars of the Temple of Democracy."

(Note: I am quoting from leading men of the North.)

A united and free government at Washington is assured for all time, but the rights and liberties of the people can be preserved only through the independent sovereignty of the States.

If you would remain assured as to the vital principles of our republic, the preservation of the States in all the completeness of their independence and power must continue with us for all time to come.

There is a strong appeal from all portions of the country to get back to the principles of Thomas Jefferson and to the Constitution, declaring,

"The powers not delegated to the United States by the Constitution, nor prohibited by it to the States, are reserved to the States, respectively, or to the people."

The issue of State rights was vital to the [Southern] Confederacy. It was the mountain peak. It still stands!

I submit that what is called "The Lost Cause" was not so much "lost" as is sometimes supposed.

The right of secession at that time under the Constitution, as they said, is [still] recognized by the best authorities.

The rights of the States, in principle, survive, although ignored, disregarded, and denounced as treason for a while, when it suited those in power.

The independent, unashamed spirit of the people survives.

. . . The vitality of the Constitution [still] exists.

Representation in Congress is now based, as it has always been based, upon the population, and not upon the voting or qualified electors. The suffrage is still with the States, unrestrained and uncontrolled by the Federal Government, except that, under the amendments to the Constitution, the States cannot make any discrimination on account of race, color, or previous condition of servitude, or sex. With those exceptions, the States have full power over suffrage.

The South, strengthened, rather than discouraged, by burdens borne and overcome, grew in patience as a result of long-suffering; made weak by great misfortune, increased in power by conquering difficulties and overcoming distress as great as ever afflicted a people; inherited and cherished the ideals and patriotism of her mighty men of her mighty past; pressed on in her self-reliance and faith in her resources and confidence in her strength, in the direction of industrial and economic progress, all of which combine to make her once again a wise leader of national thought and national achievement.

During the last thirty years the wealth of the South has increased from $10,000,000,000 to $80,970,000,000.

In population, in resources and industrial development, the South surpasses entire nations in other parts of the world.

The South leads the most of the country in population growth.

. . . Truth and honor are the pillars which sustain your organization. Justice to those who nobly sacrificed, comfort to those who survived, prompt you. May you find abundant happiness an everlasting reality. "Thine own wish, wish I thee in every place!"[341] — FLORIDA SENATOR DUNCAN U. FLETCHER,

ADDRESS BEFORE THE UNITED DAUGHTERS OF THE CONFEDERACY CONVENTION, JACKSONVILLE, FLORIDA, NOVEMBER 19, 1931

YANKEE ADMITS THE NORTH WAS IN THE WRONG
☛ I admit that my people and I were rebels. We were opposed to slavery, but the Constitution protected slavery, and we rebelled against the Constitution. We were Nationalists and opposed to State Rights. The Constitution protected State rights and we rebelled against the Constitution. The truth is that the defenders of the Constitution were in the Confederate Army, and the real rebels were in the Federal [Union] Army.[342] — DR. CHARLES EDWARD STOWE, SON OF LEFT-WING YANKEE AUTHORESS HARRIET BEECHER STOWE

WHY THE SOUTH FOUGHT
☛ A few years ago, a friend from the North said to me that he could not understand why we should have fought against the Northern States when, with their greater resources of all kinds, we should have known the inevitable result. To which I replied that we did not fight the North except to defend ourselves from invasion and subjugation. My friend said that view of the war had not occurred to him, and yet, as I endeavored to point out to him, this would appear to be the correct view of the conflict on the part of the Southern States. Had Lincoln not called out troops to invade the South, there would have been no war, for no man in the South had any thought of fighting except in self-defense. Virginia had, at the time, a commission endeavoring to negotiate terms upon which the questions in dispute might be settled. But upon Mr. Lincoln's call for 75,000 men to force the South to accede to his views, the peace commission automatically dissolved, the border States decided to aid in defending their Constitutional rights, and the war began with the Southern States on the defensive.[343] — DR. R. T. LAWRENCE, MARIETTA, GEORGIA

DEALING WITH A LEFT-WING DEMAGOGUE IN THE WHITE HOUSE
☛ [Concerning] "where Lincoln stood". . . I would add another instance of his "standing." It has been difficult to catch his poses, as he usually was on the "move" from one position to another.

It is rather notable that Mr. Lincoln did not stand very long on one position. He was quoted on both sides of about every issue which agitated the public mind from 1855 to 1865. He favored secession and then opposed it. He declared the negro was unfit for the ballot or citizenship, and yet he urged Andrew Johnson as his Military Governor of Tennessee to organize 50,000 negro troops—that with these along the Mississippi River the war would be ended in thirty days, but didn't say how, when 700,000 of the best white Northern men had failed to end it in over two years.

When declaring for "equal rights to all men," he wrote to Alexander H. Stephens after his election that he need have no fear that he would "ever offer to interfere" with their institutions, and yet he signed a proclamation in September, 1863, which purported to free the negroes of the Confederate States, while especially exempting those of the Northern and border States, admitting that there was no authority for it—but negro insurrection in the South might result.

Confederate Brigadier General Meriwether Jefferson Thompson, 3rd Missouri Infantry Regiment, Memphis, Tennessee, 1865.

Then, along this line, in 1859 he signed a pledge of $100 to John Brown's fund for arming the negroes of Virginia against the whites, who were to be persuaded to "rise up against the whites" and assert their liberty. But his friends claim for him "a kindly heart."

The Republican [then Left-wing] platform upon which he was elected declared it "the gravest of crimes to send an armed force into a State to coerce a State," and yet within a few weeks after his election, and before he was inaugurated, he sent word to General [Winfield] Scott to "be ready to retake the forts of the South" as soon as he was inaugurated, "and to the commandants of Forts Sumter and Pickens to "hold the forts" as he would send re-enforcements. While he was talking peace, he was organizing for war.

Let all the Truth come to the front. Future generations are entitled to it.[344] — C. E. GILBERT, HOUSTON, TEXAS

WARTIME NORTHERN CAPITALISTS FED OFF THE SUFFERING OF THE SOUTH

☞ . . . Secession finally became a reality. For years New England had attempted to coerce the South to this final drastic step. Lincoln's war finally started, and again throughout this period we find the perpetual Northern inconsistency whenever the "pocket-book" was touched. That this inconsistency was not the prerogative of the lower classes, but extended so far as the White House, has been often referred to.

. . . [During the war] while the South was suffering and bleeding and starving, the Jeffersonian "common man" was gradually losing his rightful place, and Hamiltonianism soon superseded what was once called a "Government of the People, for the People, and by the People." The power of the Northern oligarchy assumed ever increasing proportions. Fortunes were made not merely by army contractors, but investors in stocks, bonds, and securities. Fortunes were made in oil, discovered in Pennsylvania in 1859, and they increased to almost unbelievable proportions during the war. The famous "Comstock Lode" of Nevada poured her riches into Northern pockets, strengthening her credit tremendously. Immigration rapidly increased the population of the North, while war, waged pitilessly and inhumanly, decimated the South. Labor in the North, blinded by false propaganda, added its force in aiding the Northern unscrupulous capitalist to increase his wealth on the blood and suffering of all.

Among the most vindictive men, we find one Thaddeus Stevens, of whom James Truslow Adams (a Northern historian) expresses himself in these words:

> ". . . Unfortunately, on Lee's dash into Pennsylvania, the ironworks of a man whose one idea had been to get rich as quickly as possible were destroyed. They belonged to Thaddeus Stevens, perhaps the most despicable, malevolent, and morally deformed character who has ever risen to high power in America. . . ."

This [Yankee] vindictiveness was shown throughout the whole Reconstruction period, and well characterizes the whole manner of warfare, of destruction, and elevation of the Northern capital. Jefferson's "common man," North and South, Middle West and West, was sacrificed on the altar of rapacious greed and money-lust of the capitalist.[345] — WOLFE A. LEDERER, PHILADELPHIA, PENNSYLVANIA

THE TRUE CAUSE
☛ [Let us cast in stone] the true story of the cause for which our fathers fought and many of them died on the battle field—a cause that was not lost and one that will never die—one that is the most alive cause of the American people today—States Rights, home and Southern womanhood. . . .[346] — JAMES H. WHITE, COMMANDER MISSOURI DIVISION, SONS OF CONFEDERATE VETERANS

EXCERPT FROM OUR PRESIDENT'S LAST PUBLIC ADDRESS
☛ It behooves the Southern people to promote the welfare of the Union, to show to the world that hereafter, as heretofore, the patriotism of our people is not measured by lines of latitude and longitude, but is as broad as the obligations they have assumed, and embraces the whole of our ocean-bound domain.[347] — JEFFERSON DAVIS, MISSISSIPPI STATE CAPITOL, MARCH 10, 1884

The End

Confederate camp, Warrington Navy Yard, Pensacola, Florida, showing members of Company B, 9th Mississippi Infantry. Confederate soldiers identified: center standing, James Cunningham; holding newspaper, Thomas A. Falconer (of Holly Springs, Mississippi); the cook, Kinlock Falconer. Photographer: Jay Dearborn Edwards, 1861.

Confederate Captain Cuthbert Harrison Slocomb of Co. 5, Washington Artillery Battalion, circa 1862.

A Confederate Prayer

May Heaven's richest blessings ever be with you, protecting and supporting you in vindicating the Truth and the rights of the Confederate cause. God bless you!

Confederate Colonel John M. Simonton of Co. I, 1st Mississippi Infantry Regiment, St. Louis, Missouri, circa 1862.

NOTES

1. Seabrook, *Abraham Lincoln Was a Liberal, Jefferson Davis Was a Conservative*, p. 55.
2. Schlüter, p. 23.
3. Woods, p. 47.
4. On Lincoln's socialistic, Marxist, and communist thoughts, ideas, and tendencies, see my books: 1) *Lincoln's War: The Real Cause, The Real Winner, the Real Loser*; 2) *Abraham Lincoln Was a Liberal, Jefferson Davis Was a Conservative: The Missing Key to Understanding the American Civil War*; 3) *Abraham Lincoln: The Southern View*. Also see McCarty, passim; Browder, passim; Benson and Kennedy, passim.
5. See J. W. Jones, TDMV, pp. 144, 200-201, 273.
6. Schlüter, p. 23.
7. See Seabrook, *The Alexander H. Stephens Reader*, passim. See also, Pollard, LC, p. 178; J. H. Franklin, pp. 101, 111, 130, 149; Nicolay and Hay, ALCW, Vol. 1, p. 627.
8. *Confederate Veteran*, Vol. 12, 1904, p. 442.
9. Seabrook (ed.), *A Short History of the Confederate States of America* (J. Davis), p. 59.
10. Seabrook (ed.), *A Short History of the Confederate States of America* (J. Davis), pp. 55-56.
11. For more on this specific topic, see my book *Everything You Were Taught About the Civil War is Wrong, Ask a Southerner!*, pp. 34-39.
12. BISG (the "Book Industry Study Group"), for example—a Left-wing organization which describes itself as "the leading book trade association for standardized best practices, research and information, and events"—gives its BISAC ("Book Industry Standards and Communications") listing for works on the War for Southern Independence under the heading "Civil War Period, 1850-1877." Nearly all books published in the U.S.A. today are under the categorizational control of this progressive group located in New York City.
13. See e.g., Seabrook, *The Quotable Jefferson Davis*, pp. 30, 38, 76.
14. See e.g., Seabrook (ed.), *The Rise and Fall of the Confederate Government* (J. Davis), Vol. 1, pp. 55, 422; Vol. 2, pp. 4, 161, 454, 610. Besides using the term "Civil War" himself, President Davis cites numerous other individuals who use it as well.
15. See e.g., *Confederate Veteran*, Vol. 20, 1912, p. 122.
16. Minutes of the Eighth Annual Meeting, July 1898, p. 87.
17. For more on the nihilistic, atheistic, anti-life, anti-tradition, anti-American, anti-Constitution, anti-capitalism, anti-South agenda of the Victorian Republican Party (then the Liberal Party) and the modern Democrat Party (now the Liberal Party), otherwise known as "The Communist/Socialist Rules for Revolution," see Hasselberg, pp. 2350-2351; Lenin, passim; Marx and Engels, passim; B. Dodd, passim. Also see my book *What the Confederate Flag Means to Me: Americans Speak Out in Defense of Southern Honor, Heritage, and History*.
18. *Confederate Veteran*, Vol. 9, 1901, p. 318.
19. Due to my many writings on comparative religion and mythology, and more specifically thealogy (female spirituality), I am sometimes compared, justly or unjustly, with Graves.
20. *Confederate Veteran*, Vol. 25, 1917, p. 317.
21. *Confederate Veteran*, Vol. 1, 1893, p. 62.
22. *Confederate Veteran*, Vol. 25, 1917, p. 79.
23. *Confederate Veteran*, Vol. 25, 1917, p. 123.
24. *Confederate Veteran*, Vol. 13, 1905, p. 113.
25. *Confederate Veteran*, Vol. 25, 1917, p. 332.
26. *Confederate Veteran*, Vol. 25, 1917, p. 330.
27. *Confederate Veteran*, Vol. 25, 1917, p. 84.
28. *Confederate Veteran*, Vol. 25, 1917, p. 44.
29. *Confederate Veteran*, Vol. 1, 1893, p. 139.
30. *Confederate Veteran*, Vol. 25, 1917, p. 148.
31. *Confederate Veteran*, Vol. 25, 1917, p. 261.
32. *Confederate Veteran*, Vol. 5, 1897, p. 200.

33. *Confederate Veteran*, Vol. 25, 1917, p. 79.
34. *Confederate Veteran*, Vol. 1, 1893, p. 53.
35. *Confederate Veteran*, Vol. 25, 1917, p. 236.
36. *Confederate Veteran*, Vol. 25, 1917, p. 275.
37. *Confederate Veteran*, Vol. 25, 1917, p. 164.
38. *Confederate Veteran*, Vol. 25, 1917, p. 323.
39. *Confederate Veteran*, Vol. 1, 1893, p. 162.
40. *Confederate Veteran*, Vol. 25, 1917, p. 162.
41. *Confederate Veteran*, Vol. 1, 1893, p. 187.
42. *Confederate Veteran*, Vol. 25, 1917, p. 121.
43. *Confederate Veteran*, Vol. 20, 1912, p. 275.
44. *Confederate Veteran*, Vol. 1, 1893, p. 152.
45. *Confederate Veteran*, Vol. 26, 1918, p. 7.
46. *Confederate Veteran*, Vol. 38, 1930, p. 46.
47. *Confederate Veteran*, Vol. 8, 1900, p. 104.
48. *Confederate Veteran*, Vol. 7, 1899, p. 154.
49. *Confederate Veteran*, Vol. 25, 1917, p. 144.
50. *Confederate Veteran*, Vol. 6, 1898, p. 441.
51. *Confederate Veteran*, Vol. 39, 1931, p. 84.
52. *Confederate Veteran*, Vol. 30, 1922, p. 411.
53. *Confederate Veteran*, Vol. 25, 1917, p. 346.
54. *Confederate Veteran*, Vol. 20, 1912, p. 340.
55. *Confederate Veteran*, Vol. 17, 1909, p. 106.
56. Morse, "The Hon. James Brooks' Speech Before the Union Democratic Association," pp. 4-5; see also pp. 8, 9.
57. See my books *Everything You Were Taught About American Slavery is Wrong, Ask a Southerner!* and *Slavery 101: Amazing Facts You Never Knew About America's "Peculiar Institution."*
58. R. C. Minor, pp. 163-164. For more on this topic, see also Beman, pp. 122-158.
59. Seabrook, *Everything You Were Taught About the Civil War is Wrong, Ask a Southerner!*, pp. 122-123.
60. "The Great Gaslighter" is just one of the many nicknames I have bestowed on Lincoln, certainly one of the most skillful, double-dealing demagogues to have ever walked the earth.
61. See Heilbroner, pp. 40-41.
62. Carr, pp. 25, 67-68, 132.
63. Marx and Engels, p. 64.
64. Schlüter, p. 23.
65. Seabrook, *Lincoln's War*, p. 76.
66. See Wittke, p. 164.
67. Seabrook, *Lincoln's War*, pp. 76, 77.
68. For more of Page's address, vide infra, p. 58.
69. Washington, p. 20.
70. *Confederate Veteran*, Vol. 38, 1930, p. 46.
71. Seabrook (ed.), *The Rise and Fall of the Confederate Government* (J. Davis), Vol. 1, p. 85.
72. For an in-depth discussion of this and related topics, see my book *Everything You Were Taught About American Slavery is Wrong, Ask a Southerner!*
73. For a detailed study of the Articles, see my book *The Articles of Confederation Explained*.
74. Seabrook, *The Bittersweet Bond*, pp. 54-62.
75. *Confederate Veteran*, Vol. 1, 1893, p. 2. (Note: The title of this excerpt is mine. L.S.)
76. *Confederate Veteran*, Vol. 1, 1893, p. 15. (Note: The title of this excerpt is mine. L.S.)
77. For an in-depth discussion of this and related topics, see my book *Everything You Were Taught About American Slavery is Wrong, Ask a Southerner!*
78. *Confederate Veteran*, Vol. 1, 1893, pp. 210-211.
79. *Confederate Veteran*, Vol. 1, 1893, p. 214.
80. Communist sympathizing socialist Phillips is infamous for his statement: "There is no hope for France but in the Reds [that is, communists]." Seabrook, *The Bittersweet Bond*, p. 21.

81. *Confederate Veteran*, Vol. 1, 1893, pp. 214-215. (Note: The title of this excerpt is mine. L.S.)
82. The Confederate Cause was and is not a "lost cause." For a complete discussion of this topic, see my book *Lincoln's War: The Real Cause, the Real Winner, the Real Loser*.
83. *Confederate Veteran*, Vol. 1, 1893, p. 238. (Note: The title of this excerpt is mine. L.S.)
84. *Confederate Veteran*, Vol. 1, 1893, p. 279. (Note: The title of this excerpt is mine. L.S.)
85. *Confederate Veteran*, Vol. 1, 1893, p. 360. (Note: The title of this excerpt is mine. L.S.)
86. *Confederate Veteran*, Vol. 1, 1893, p. 368. (Note: The title of this excerpt is mine. L.S.)
87. *Confederate Veteran*, Vol. 1, 1893, p. 11. (Note: The title of this excerpt is mine. L.S.)
88. *Confederate Veteran*, Vol. 2, 1894, pp. 51-54. (Note: The title of this excerpt is mine. L.S.)
89. *Confederate Veteran*, Vol. 2, 1894, p. 57. (Note: The title of this excerpt is mine. L.S.)
90. *Confederate Veteran*, Vol. 2, 1894, p. 66. (Note: The title of this excerpt is mine. L.S.)
91. *Confederate Veteran*, Vol. 2, 1894, pp. 122-123. (Note: The title of this excerpt is mine. L.S.)
92. See this book in my bibliography.
93. *Confederate Veteran*, Vol. 2, 1894, pp. 126-127. (Note: The title of this excerpt is mine. L.S.)
94. *Confederate Veteran*, Vol. 2, 1894, pp. 144-145. (Note: The title of this excerpt is mine. L.S.)
95. *Confederate Veteran*, Vol. 2, 1894, p. 145. (Note: The title of this excerpt is mine. L.S.)
96. See my book, *The Articles of Confederation Explained*.
97. See my book, *The Articles of Confederation Explained*.
98. For an in-depth look at the history of our two-party system, see my book *Abraham Lincoln Was a Liberal, Jefferson Davis Was a Conservative*.
99. *Confederate Veteran*, Vol. 2, 1894, pp. 146-147.
100. *Confederate Veteran*, Vol. 2, 1894, pp. 162-163. (Note: The title of this excerpt is mine. L.S.)
101. *Confederate Veteran*, Vol. 3, 1895, p. 16. (Note: The title of this excerpt is mine. L.S.)
102. *Confederate Veteran*, Vol. 3, 1895, p. 309. (Note: The title of this excerpt is mine. L.S.)
103. *Confederate Veteran*, Vol. 4, 1896, p. 5. (Note: The title of this excerpt is mine. L.S.)
104. *Confederate Veteran*, Vol. 4, 1896, p. 25. (Note: The title of this excerpt is mine. L.S.)
105. *Confederate Veteran*, Vol. 4, 1896, p. 151. (Note: The title of this excerpt is mine. L.S.)
106. *Confederate Veteran*, Vol. 5, 1897, p. 69. (Note: The title of this excerpt is mine. L.S.)
107. *Confederate Veteran*, Vol. 5, 1897, p. 200. (Note: The title of this excerpt is mine. L.S.)
108. *Confederate Veteran*, Vol. 5, 1897, pp. 201-202. (Note: The title of this excerpt is mine. L.S.)
109. For more on this topic, see my book *Confederacy 101*.
110. *Confederate Veteran*, Vol. 5, 1897, p. 507. (Note: The title of this excerpt is mine. L.S.)
111. *Confederate Veteran*, Vol. 6, 1898, p. 33. (Note: The title of this excerpt is mine. L.S.)
112. *Confederate Veteran*, Vol. 6, 1898, pp. 467-468. (Note: The title of this excerpt is mine. L.S.)
113. *Confederate Veteran*, Vol. 7, 1899, p. 158. (Note: The title of this excerpt is mine. L.S.)
114. *Confederate Veteran*, Vol. 7, 1899, p. 457. (Note: The title of this excerpt is mine. L.S.)
115. *Confederate Veteran*, Vol. 8, 1900, pp. 5-6. (Note: The title of this excerpt is mine. L.S.)
116. *Confederate Veteran*, Vol. 8, 1900, pp. 60-61. (Note: The title of this excerpt is mine. L.S.)
117. *Confederate Veteran*, Vol. 8, 1900, p. 104. (Note: The title of this excerpt is mine. L.S.)
118. *Confederate Veteran*, Vol. 8, 1900, p. 248. (Note: The title of this excerpt is mine. L.S.)
119. For more on this topic, see my book *Abraham Lincoln Was a Liberal, Jefferson Davis Was a Conservative*.
120. *Confederate Veteran*, Vol. 8, 1900, pp. 248-249. (Note: The title of this excerpt is mine. L.S.)
121. *Confederate Veteran*, Vol. 8, 1900, p. 257. (Note: The title of this excerpt is mine. L.S.)
122. *Confederate Veteran*, Vol. 9, 1901, pp. 7-8. (Note: The title of this excerpt is mine. L.S.)
123. *Confederate Veteran*, Vol. 9, 1901, pp. 60-61. (Note: The title of this excerpt is mine. L.S.)
124. Alfriend, p. 79. (Note: The title of this excerpt is mine. L.S.)
125. *Confederate Veteran*, Vol. 9, 1901, p. 414. (Note: The title of this excerpt is mine. L.S.)
126. *Confederate Veteran*, Vol. 9, 1901, pp. 437-438. (Note: The title of this excerpt is mine. L.S.)
127. For more on this topic, see my introduction in my book *The Bittersweet Bond*.
128. See Steel, p. 53.
129. Note that at the start of his presidency neither Lincoln nor the Republican party, then the Liberal party, were antislavery. They desired merely to limit the growth of slavery outside the South. For a detailed discussion of this subject, see my book *Abraham Lincoln: The Southern View*.
130. *Confederate Veteran*, Vol. 10, 1902, pp. 17-20. (Note: The title of this excerpt is mine. L.S.)

131. *Confederate Veteran*, Vol. 10, 1902, pp. 28-29.
132. For a detailed examination of these topics, see my book *Everything You Were Taught About American Slavery is Wrong, Ask a Southerner!*
133. *Confederate Veteran*, Vol. 10, 1902, pp. 309-310. (Note: The title of this excerpt is mine. L.S.)
134. *Confederate Veteran*, Vol. 10, 1902, pp. 396-397.
135. See bibliography for my Sea Raven Press facsimile reprint edition of Davis' *The Rise and Fall of the Confederate Government*. It is the only reprint of its kind.
136. For a detailed study of the Articles, see my book *The Articles of Confederation Explained*.
137. *Confederate Veteran*, Vol. 10, 1902, p. 447. (Note: The title of this excerpt is mine. L.S.)
138. *Confederate Veteran*, Vol. 13, 1905, pp. 118-119. For a detailed examination of these topics, see my book *Everything You Were Taught About American Slavery is Wrong, Ask a Southerner!* (Note: The title of this excerpt is mine. L.S.)
139. *Confederate Veteran*, Vol. 11, 1903, p. 16. (Note: The title of this excerpt is mine. L.S.)
140. *Confederate Veteran*, Vol. 11, 1903, pp. 153, 154. (Note: The title of this excerpt is mine. L.S.)
141. *Confederate Veteran*, Vol. 11, 1903, pp. 216-217. (Note: The title of this excerpt is mine. L.S.)
142. *Confederate Veteran*, Vol. 11, 1903, pp. 253, 255. For more on the important topic of secession, see my book *All We Ask is to be Let Alone*. (Note: The title of this excerpt is mine. L.S.)
143. *Confederate Veteran*, Vol. 11, 1903, p. 273. (Note: The title of this excerpt is mine. L.S.)
144. *Confederate Veteran*, Vol. 11, 1903, pp. 313-314. (Note: The title of this excerpt is mine. L.S.)
145. *Confederate Veteran*, Vol. 12, 1904, p. 16. (Note: The title of this excerpt is mine. L.S.)
146. *Confederate Veteran*, Vol. 12, 1904, p. 285. (Note: The title of this excerpt is mine. L.S.)
147. *Confederate Veteran*, Vol. 12, 1904, p. 397. (Note: The title of this excerpt is mine. L.S.)
148. *Confederate Veteran*, Vol. 12, 1904, p. 402. (Note: The title of this excerpt is mine. L.S.)
149. *Confederate Veteran*, Vol. 12, 1904, pp. 517-518. (Note: The title of this excerpt is mine. L.S.)
150. *Confederate Veteran*, Vol. 12, 1904, p. 575. (Note: The title of this excerpt is mine. L.S.)
151. *Confederate Veteran*, Vol. 12, 1904, p. 9. (Note: The title of this excerpt is mine. L.S.)
152. *Confederate Veteran*, Vol. 13, 1905, p. 82. (Note: The title of this excerpt is mine. L.S.)
153. *Confederate Veteran*, Vol. 13, 1905, p. 86. (Note: The title of this excerpt is mine. L.S.)
154. *Confederate Veteran*, Vol. 13, 1905, pp. 115-116. (Note: The title of this excerpt is mine. L.S.)
155. *Confederate Veteran*, Vol. 13, 1905, p. 505. (Note: The title of this excerpt is mine. L.S.)
156. *Confederate Veteran*, Vol. 14, 1906, p. 5. (Note: The title of this excerpt is mine. L.S.)
157. *Confederate Veteran*, Vol. 14, 1906, p. 10. (Note: The title of this excerpt is mine. L.S.)
158. *Confederate Veteran*, Vol. 14, 1906, p. 11. (Note: The title of this excerpt is mine. L.S.)
159. *Confederate Veteran*, Vol. 14, 1906, p. 157. (Note: The title of this excerpt is mine. L.S.)
160. See this book in my bibliography.
161. See this book in my bibliography.
162. See this book in my bibliography.
163. See this book in my bibliography.
164. *Confederate Veteran*, Vol. 14, 1906, p. 166. (Note: The title of this excerpt is mine. L.S.)
165. *Confederate Veteran*, Vol. 14, 1906, p. 261. (Note: The title of this excerpt is mine. L.S.)
166. See this book in my bibliography.
167. *Confederate Veteran*, Vol. 14, 1906, p. 270. (Note: The title of this excerpt is mine. L.S.)
168. *Confederate Veteran*, Vol. 14, 1906, p. 343.
169. *Confederate Veteran*, Vol. 15, 1907, pp. 209-210. (Note: The title of this excerpt is mine. L.S.)
170. See ORA, Series 4, Vol. 2, p. 1193.
171. *Confederate Veteran*, Vol. 15, 1907, pp. 314-315. (Note: The title of this excerpt is mine. L.S.)
172. *Confederate Veteran*, Vol. 16, 1908, p. 112. (Note: The title of this excerpt is mine. L.S.)
173. *Confederate Veteran*, Vol. 17, 1909, p. 67. (Note: The title of this excerpt is mine. L.S.)
174. Morse, "The Hon. James Brooks' Speech Before the Union Democratic Association," pp. 4-5; see also pp. 8, 9.
175. Seabrook, *The Quotable Jefferson Davis*, p. 84.
176. *Confederate Veteran*, Vol. 17, 1909, p. 107. (Note: The title of this excerpt is mine. L.S.)
177. See this book in my bibliography.
178. Hutchins, pp. 13, 14. (Note: The title of this excerpt is mine. L.S.)

179. *Confederate Veteran*, Vol. 17, 1909, p. 313. (Note: The title of this excerpt is mine. L.S.)
180. *Confederate Veteran*, Vol. 17, 1909, p. 209. (Note: The title of this excerpt is mine. L.S.)
181. *Confederate Veteran*, Vol. 17, 1909, p. 378. (Note: The title of this excerpt is mine. L.S.)
182. *Confederate Veteran*, Vol. 17, 1909, p. 494. (Note: The title of this excerpt is mine. L.S.)
183. *Confederate Veteran*, Vol. 17, 1909, pp. 537-538. (Note: The title of this excerpt is mine. L.S.)
184. *Confederate Veteran*, Vol. 17, 1909, p. 536. (Note: The title of this excerpt is mine. L.S.)
185. *Confederate Veteran*, Vol. 18, 1910, p. 65. (Note: The title of this excerpt is mine. L.S.)
186. For a detailed discussion of this topic, see my book *The Articles of Confederation Explained*.
187. *Confederate Veteran*, Vol. 18, 1910, pp. 332, 333. (Note: The title of this excerpt is mine. L.S.)
188. *Confederate Veteran*, Vol. 18, 1910, p. 379. (Note: The title of this excerpt is mine. L.S.)
189. For a deep dive into this complex subject, see my book *Everything You Were Taught About American Slavery is Wrong, Ask a Southerner!*
190. *Confederate Veteran*, Vol. 18, 1910, p. 381. (Note: The title of this excerpt is mine. L.S.)
191. *Confederate Veteran*, Vol. 18, 1910, p. 395. (Note: The title of this excerpt is mine. L.S.)
192. *Confederate Veteran*, Vol. 19, 1911, p. 113. (Note: The title of this excerpt is mine. L.S.)
193. *Confederate Veteran*, Vol. 19, 1911, pp. 155-156. (Note: The title of this excerpt is mine. L.S.)
194. *Confederate Veteran*, Vol. 19, 1911, p. 196. (Note: The title of this excerpt is mine. L.S.)
195. *Confederate Veteran*, Vol. 19, 1911, p. 365. (Note: The title of this excerpt is mine. L.S.)
196. For a detailed discussion of this topic, see my book *Abraham Lincoln: The Southern View*.
197. For more on Lincoln's lifelong obsession with the A.C.S. and deporting blacks, see my book *Abraham Lincoln: The Southern View*.
198. *Confederate Veteran*, Vol. 19, 1911, pp. 326-327. (Note: The title of this excerpt is mine. L.S.)
199. *Confederate Veteran*, Vol. 19, 1911, p. 573. (Note: The title of this excerpt is mine. L.S.)
200. *Confederate Veteran*, Vol. 20, 1912, p. 71. (Note: The title of this excerpt is mine. L.S.)
201. *Confederate Veteran*, Vol. 20, 1912, pp. 341-342. (Note: The title of this excerpt is mine. L.S.)
202. *Confederate Veteran*, Vol. 20, 1912, pp. 429-430. (Note: The title of this excerpt is mine. L.S.)
203. *Confederate Veteran*, Vol. 20, 1912, p. 571. (Note: The title of this excerpt is mine. L.S.)
204. *Confederate Veteran*, Vol. 21, 1913, p. 31. (Note: The title of this excerpt is mine. L.S.)
205. *Confederate Veteran*, Vol. 21, 1913, p. 127. (Note: The title of this excerpt is mine. L.S.)
206. This last statement is highly debatable, and is, in my opinion, actually false. Why? See my book *All We Ask is to be Left Alone: The Southern Secession Fact Book*.
207. *Confederate Veteran*, Vol. 21, 1913, p. 427. (Note: The title of this excerpt is mine. L.S.)
208. *Confederate Veteran*, Vol. 22, 1914, p. 8. (Note: The title of this excerpt is mine. L.S.)
209. *Confederate Veteran*, Vol. 22, 1914, p. 17. (Note: The title of this excerpt is mine. L.S.)
210. *Confederate Veteran*, Vol. 22, 1914, pp. 253-254. (Note: The title of this excerpt is mine. L.S.)
211. For more on this topic, see my book *Lincoln's War*.
212. For more on this topic, see my book *All We Ask is to be Let Alone*.
213. *Confederate Veteran*, Vol. 23, 1915, p. 66. (Note: The title of this excerpt is mine. L.S.)
214. *Confederate Veteran*, Vol. 23, 1915, p. 531.
215. *Confederate Veteran*, Vol. 24, 1916, p. 66. (Note: The title of this excerpt is mine. L.S.)
216. For a detailed examination of these topics, see my book *Everything You Were Taught About American Slavery is Wrong, Ask a Southerner!*
217. *Confederate Veteran*, Vol. 24, 1916, pp. 566-567.
218. *Confederate Veteran*, Vol. 25, 1917, p. . (Note: The title of this excerpt is mine. L.S.)
219. *Confederate Veteran*, Vol. 25, 1917, p. 397. (Note: The title of this excerpt is mine. L.S.)
220. *Confederate Veteran*, January Vol. 25, 1917, p. 108. (Note: The title of this excerpt is mine. L.S.)
221. *Confederate Veteran*, Vol. 25, 1917, p. 234.
222. *Confederate Veteran*, Vol. 25, 1917, p. 344. (Note: The title of this excerpt is mine. L.S.)
223. *Confederate Veteran*, Vol. 25, 1917, p. 395.
224. For detailed historical discussions of the McGavocks, Carnton Plantation, and the Battle of Franklin II, see my numerous books on these subjects in my bibliography.
225. Rev. McNeilly incorrectly identifies the general as "W. H. Harding." He is referring to W. G. Harding, that is, General William Giles Harding. For those interested in Southern genealogy, I am a descendant of the Harding family of Belle Meade Plantation and a close cousin of General Harding.

226. See Schlüter, pp. 14-15.
227. Seabrook, *The Bittersweet Bond*, pp. 242-252. (Note: The title of this excerpt is mine. L.S.)
228. *Confederate Veteran*, Vol. 25, 1917, pp. 455-456.
229. For a detailed study of the Articles, see my book *The Articles of Confederation Explained*.
230. Seabrook, *The Bittersweet Bond*, pp. 73-74. (Note: The title of this excerpt is mine. L.S.)
231. *Confederate Veteran*, Vol. 25, 1917, p. 74. (Note: The title of this excerpt is mine. L.S.)
232. *Confederate Veteran*, Vol. 25, 1917, p. 81. (Note: The title of this excerpt is mine. L.S.)
233. *Confederate Veteran*, Vol. 25, 1917, p. 108. (Note: The title of this excerpt is mine. L.S.)
234. *Confederate Veteran*, Vol. 25, 1917, pp. 117-118.
235. For more on this topic, see my book: *Everything You Were Taught About American Slavery is Wrong, Ask a Southerner!*
236. *Confederate Veteran*, Vol. 25, 1917, pp. 254-257. (Note: The title of this excerpt is mine. L.S.)
237. *Confederate Veteran*, Vol. 25, 1917, p. 329. (Note: The title of this excerpt is mine. L.S.)
238. *Confederate Veteran*, Vol. 25, 1917, pp. 261-262.
239. *Confederate Veteran*, Vol. 25, 1917, pp. 270-271. (Note: The title of this excerpt is mine. L.S.)
240. *Confederate Veteran*, Vol. 25, 1917, pp. 296-297. (Note: The title of this excerpt is mine. L.S.)
241. *Confederate Veteran*, Vol. 25, 1917, p. 368. (Note: The title of this excerpt is mine. L.S.)
242. *Confederate Veteran*, Vol. 25, 1917, p. 392. (Note: The title of this excerpt is mine. L.S.)
243. *Confederate Veteran*, Vol. 25, 1917, pp. 398-399.
244. *Confederate Veteran*, Vol. 25, 1917, pp. 498-499. (Note: The title of this excerpt is mine. L.S.)
245. [Tyler's note:] In 1789 William Grayson, one of the first two Senators from Virginia, wrote to Patrick Henry: "The bill (to establish the seat of government) has been ultimately defeated in the Senate, but gentlemen now begin to feel the observation of the 'Antis' (i.e., the anti-Federalists in the Convention of 1787), when they informed them of the different interests of the Union and the probable consequences that would result therefrom to the Southern States, who would be the milch [milk] cow out of whom the substance would be extracted." (*Letters and Times of the Tylers*, I, p. 170.)
246. This statement is not historically accurate. For more on the Old South's white slave population, see my book, *Everything You Were Taught About American Slavery is Wrong, Ask a Southerner!*
247. [Tyler's note:] Wharton's *State Trials*.
248. [Tyler's note:] See correspondence between Moncure D. Conway, agent in London for the abolitionists [socialists and communists], and James M. Mason, the Confederate Commissioner (*William and Mary College Quarterly*, XXI, 221-224).
249. [Tyler's note:] Ibid., XXV., 9-12. "Kernel's Mission to Europe."
250. [Tyler's note:] In his work, *Some Information Respecting America*, published in 1794, Thomas Cooper, the celebrated philosopher, writes on page 53, referring to the United States: "The government is the government *of* the people and *for* the people." (Italics as in the book).
251. [Tyler's note:] *Complete Works of Abraham Lincoln*, Nicholay and Hay, Vol. VIII, 50.
252. [Tyler's note:] James Ford Rhodes, IV, p. 164.
253. [Tyler's note:] Arming the slaves by the British was particularly denounced by the Americans in the [American] Revolution as barbarous and savage.
254. [Tyler's note:] Lincoln's words were: "Abandon all the posts now garrisoned by black men, take 150,000 men from our side and put them in the battle field or cornfield against us, and we would be compelled to abandon the war in three weeks." (*Complete Works of Abraham Lincoln*, X, 190.) That the enlistment of the negroes was largely forced, see Charles L. C. Minor, *The Real Lincoln*, pp. 181-184.
255. [Tyler's note:] In his letter to the Russian government, setting forth the war aims of this government, [President] Wilson writes as follows: "No people must be forced under sovereignty under which it does not wish to live."
256. [Tyler's note:] *Complete Works of Abraham Lincoln*, X, 191.
257. [Tyler's note:] *Complete Works of Abraham Lincoln*, VIII, 30, 31.
258. [Tyler's note:] *Diary of Gideon Welles*, II, 237.
259. [Tyler's note:] See criticisms of Edmund Ruffin in *William and Mary Quarterly*, XXI, 224-228.
260. [Tyler's note:] For more than one hundred years there were practically no white servants in the South, and even now it is embarrassing to a Southern man to order white people around as they do in the North.

261. [Tyler's note:] In his message to the extra session of Congress, July 4, 1861, Lincoln, after rather tamely attempting to defend his unconstitutional action, falls back upon "necessity" for justification, as follows: "These measures, whether strictly legal or not, were ventured upon under what appeared to be a popular demand and a public necessity, trusting then as now that Congress would readily ratify them."
262. *Confederate Veteran*, Vol. 25, 1917, pp. 506-512. (Note: The title of this excerpt is mine. L.S.)
263. For a full discussion of this topic, see my book *Everything You Were Taught About the Civil War is Wrong, Ask a Southerner!*
264. *Confederate Veteran*, Vol. 25, 1917, pp. 542, 543. (Note: The title of this excerpt is mine. L.S.)
265. The writer, Col. Bingham, incorrectly refers to the Republican party of 1860 and the Republican party of 1903 as "the same Republican party," which they clearly were not, as the Republican party only swung Conservative (the party we know today) during the 1896 presidential election. For more on this fascinating and important topic, see my book *Abraham Lincoln Was a Liberal, Jefferson Davis Was a Conservative*.
266. *Confederate Veteran*, Vol. 25, 1917, p. 549. (Note: The title of this excerpt is mine. L.S.)
267. *Confederate Veteran*, Vol. 25, 1917, pp. 552-553. (Note: The title of this excerpt is mine. L.S.)
268. For more on the topic of confederation, see my book *Confederacy 101*.
269. For more on Lincoln's personal beliefs regarding blacks, see my book *Abraham Lincoln: The Southern View*.
270. *Confederate Veteran*, Vol. 25, 1917, pp. 453-454.
271. *Confederate Veteran*, Vol. 25, 1917, p. 554. (Note: The title of this excerpt is mine. L.S.)
272. *Confederate Veteran*, Vol. 25, 1917, p. 572. (Note: The title of this excerpt is mine. L.S.)
273. Seabrook, *The Bittersweet Bond*, p. 163. (Note: The title of this excerpt is mine. L.S.)
274. For a detailed study of the Articles, see my book *The Articles of Confederation Explained*.
275. For a thorough discussion of this topic, see my book *Confederacy 101*.
276. *Confederate Veteran*, Vol. 25, 1917, pp. 309-314. Note from *Confederate Veteran*: "This paper was awarded the U.D.C. prize offered students at Teachers' College, Columbia University, contest of 1915-1916. The author is now principal of Oakwood School, at Dayton, Ohio." (Note: The title of this excerpt is mine. L.S.)
277. [Everett's note:] "See the facts discussed at length, with verbatim communications to and from Secretary Seward, *Messages and Papers of the Confederacy*, Volume I, pages 82-98; also *Official Records of the War*, Series 4, Volume I, page 256, and Series I, Volume LIII, page 161, and A. H. Stephens's *History of the United States*, pages 607-609, and Appendix N.)"
278. For a detailed study of the Articles, see my book *The Articles of Confederation Explained*.
279. *Confederate Veteran*, Vol. 25, 1917, pp. 405-407. (Note: The title of this excerpt is mine. L.S.)
280. *Confederate Veteran*, Vol. 25, 1917, pp. 502, 503. (Note: The title of this excerpt is mine. L.S.)
281. *Confederate Veteran*, Vol. 26, 1918, p. 57. (Note: The title of this excerpt is mine. L.S.)
282. *Confederate Veteran*, Vol. 26, 1918, p. 7. (Note: The title of this excerpt is mine. L.S.)
283. See this book in my bibliography.
284. See this book in my bibliography.
285. *Confederate Veteran*, Vol. 27, 1919, pp. 89-91. (Note: The title of this excerpt is mine. L.S.)
286. *Confederate Veteran*, Vol. 28, 1920, pp. 49-50 . (Note: The title of this excerpt is mine. L.S.)
287. *Confederate Veteran*, Vol. 28, 1920, p. 284. (Note: The title of this excerpt is mind. L.S.)
288. *Confederate Veteran*, Vol. 28, 1920, p. 328. (Note: The title of this excerpt is mine. L.S.)
289. *Confederate Veteran*, Vol. 28, 1920, pp. 373-374. (Note: The title of this excerpt is mine. L.S.)
290. *Confederate Veteran*, Vol. 28, 1920, p. 404. (Note: The title of this excerpt is mine. L.S.)
291. *Confederate Veteran*, Vol. 29, 1921, p. 12. (Note: The title of this excerpt is mine. L.S.)
292. *Confederate Veteran*, Vol. 29, 1921, p. 47. (Note: The title of this excerpt is mine. L.S.)
293. *Confederate Veteran*, Vol. 29, 1921, p. 88. (Note: The title of this excerpt is mine. L.S.)
294. *Confederate Veteran*, Vol. 29, 1921, p. 404. (Note: The title of this excerpt is mine. L.S.)
295. *Confederate Veteran*, Vol. 29, 1921, p. 419. (Note: The title of this excerpt is mine. L.S.)
296. *Confederate Veteran*, Vol. 30, 1922, p. 8. (Note: The title of this excerpt is mine. L.S.)
297. Figgis and Laurence, pp. 302-305. For more on Gen. Lee and his life, beliefs, and views, see my books *The Old Rebel* and *The Quotable Robert E. Lee*. (Note: The title of this excerpt is mine. L.S.)
298. *Confederate Veteran*, Vol. 30, 1922, p. 416. (Note: The title of this excerpt is mine. L.S.)
299. *Confederate Veteran*, Vol. 31, 1923, p. 4. (Note: The title of this excerpt is mine. L.S.)
300. For more on this topic, see my book *Confederacy 101*.
301. *Confederate Veteran*, Vol. 31, 1923, p. 10. (Note: The title of this excerpt is mine. L.S.)

302. *Confederate Veteran*, Vol. 31, 1923, p. 404. According to the Confederate Congress, William Porcher Miles was the rightful designer of the Confederate First National Flag. For more on this topic, see my book *Confederate Flag Facts*. (Note: The title of this excerpt is mine. L.S.)
303. For more on this topic, see my book *Confederacy 101*.
304. For more on this topic, see my book *Everything You Were Taught About American Slavery is Wrong, Ask a Southerner!*
305. *Confederate Veteran*, Vol. 31, 1923, p. 422. (Note: The title of this excerpt is mine. L.S.)
306. *Confederate Veteran*, Vol. 32, 1924, pp. 9-10. (Note: The title of this excerpt is mine. L.S.)
307. *Confederate Veteran*, Vol. 32, 1924, p. 468. For more on Gen. Jackson's life, views, and beliefs, see my book *The Quotable Stonewall Jackson*. (Note: The title of this excerpt is mine. L.S.)
308. *Confederate Veteran*, Vol. 33, 1925, p. 50. (Note: The title of this excerpt is mine. L.S.)
309. For more on Lincoln's beliefs and views, see my books *Abraham Lincoln: The Southern View*; *The Unquotable Abraham Lincoln*; *The Great Impersonator*; and *Lincolnology*.
310. *Confederate Veteran*, Vol. 33, 1925, p. 316. (Note: The title of this excerpt is mine. L.S.)
311. *Confederate Veteran*, Vol. 33, 1925, p. 316. For more on Chase's comment, see my book *The Bittersweet Bond*, pp. 20-21. (Note: The title of this excerpt is mine. L.S.)
312. *Confederate Veteran*, Vol. 33, 1925, p. 316. (Note: The title of this excerpt is mine. L.S.)
313. *Confederate Veteran*, Vol. 34, 1926, p. 90. (Note: The title of this excerpt is mine. L.S.)
314. *Confederate Veteran*, Vol. 34, 1926, p. 324. (Note: The title of this excerpt is mine. L.S.)
315. *Confederate Veteran*, Vol. 34, 1926, p. 324. This missing words seem to be "if *we but* take hold." See my book *Abraham Lincoln: The Southern View*, p. 377. (Note: The title of this excerpt is mine. L.S.)
316. The Corwin Amendment would have allowed the seceded Southern states to continue practicing slavery in perpetuity if they would return to the Union. Lincoln fully supported the Corwin Amendment, declaring in his Inaugural Address that he "had no objection to its being made express and irrevocable." For more on this and related topics, see my book *Abraham Lincoln: The Southern View*.
317. *Confederate Veteran*, Vol. 35, 1927, p. 130. (Note: The title of this excerpt is mine. L.S.)
318. *Confederate Veteran*, Vol. 35, 1927, p. 204. (Note: The title of this excerpt is mine. L.S.)
319. *Confederate Veteran*, Vol. 35, 1927, p. 205. (Note: The title of this excerpt is mine. L.S.)
320. *Confederate Veteran*, Vol. 35, 1927, p. 208. (Note: The title of this excerpt is mine. L.S.)
321. *Confederate Veteran*, Vol. 35, 1927, p. 246. (Note: The title of this excerpt is mine. L.S.)
322. *Confederate Veteran*, Vol. 35, 1927, p. 317. (Note: The title of this excerpt is mine. L.S.)
323. *Confederate Veteran*, Vol. 36, 1928, p. 50. (Note: The title of this excerpt is mine. L.S.)
324. *Confederate Veteran*, Vol. 36, 1928, p. 127. (Note: The title of this excerpt is mine. L.S.)
325. *Confederate Veteran*, Vol. 36, 1928, p. 155. (Note: The title of this excerpt is mine. L.S.)
326. *Confederate Veteran*, Vol. 36, 1928, p. 209.
327. *Confederate Veteran*, Vol. 36, 1928, p. 333. (Note: The title of this excerpt is mine. L.S.)
328. *Confederate Veteran*, Vol. 36, 1928, p. 404.
329. *Confederate Veteran*, Vol. 36, 1928, p. 422. (Note: The title of this excerpt is mine. L.S.)
330. *Confederate Veteran*, Vol. 37, 1929, p. 15. (Note: The title of this excerpt is mine. L.S.)
331. *Confederate Veteran*, Vol. 37, 1929, p. 184. (Note: The title of this excerpt is mine. L.S.)
332. Unfortunately for modern Americans, when writing out the U.S. Constitution the Founding Fathers consciously chose not to make the inherent rights of the states explicit. Instead they tacitly insinuated their existence in the 9th and 10th Amendments. The main reason for this was that at the time, the late 1700s, the absolute sovereignty of the individual states (which included states' rights and secession) was well understood and accepted by every American, from school children to statesmen; therefore, it was not considered important to spell this well-known fact out in the Constitution. Thanks to big government Liberal Abraham Lincoln's cruel, illegal, and unnecessary war, the truth about states' rights and secession have virtually disappeared from mainstream history books (nearly all published by the states' rights-hating Left), and along with it nearly all knowledge and awareness of state sovereignty and the 9th and 10th Amendments. For more on this topic, see my books *All We Ask is to be Let Alone*, *Confederacy 101*, and *Lincoln's War*.
333. *Confederate Veteran*, Vol. 37, 1929, pp. 260-261. (Note: The title of this excerpt is mine. L.S.)
334. *Confederate Veteran*, Vol. 37, 1929, p. 435. (Note: The title of this excerpt is mine. L.S.)
335. *Confederate Veteran*, Vol. 38, 1930, p. 25. (Note: The title of this excerpt is mine. L.S.)
336. *Confederate Veteran*, Vol. 38, 1930, p. 205. (Note: The title of this excerpt is mine. L.S.)
337. *Confederate Veteran*, Vol. 38, 1930, p. 251. (Note: The title of this excerpt is mine. L.S.)

338. *Confederate Veteran*, Vol. 39, 1931, p. 84. (Note: The title of this excerpt is mine. L.S.)
339. For a detailed study of the Articles, see my book *The Articles of Confederation Explained*.
340. *Confederate Veteran*, Vol. 39, 1931, p. 131. (Note: The title of this excerpt is mine. L.S.)
341. *Confederate Veteran*, Vol. 40, 1932, pp. 8-13. (Note: The title of this excerpt is mine. L.S.)
342. *Confederate Veteran*, Vol. 40, 1932, p. 216. (Note: The title of this excerpt is mine. L.S.)
343. *Confederate Veteran*, Vol. 40, 1932, p. 238.
344. *Confederate Veteran*, Vol. 40, 1932, pp. 251-252. (Note: The title of this excerpt is mine. L.S.)
345. *Confederate Veteran*, Vol. 40, 1932, pp. 261, 262. (Note: The title of this excerpt is mine. L.S.)
346. *Confederate Veteran*, Vol. 40, 1932, p. 372. (Note: The title of this excerpt is mine. L.S.)
347. *Confederate Veteran*, Vol. 35, 1927, p. 204. (Note: The title of this excerpt is mine. L.S.)

"The aggressor in war—that is, he who begins it—is not the first who uses force, but the first who renders force necessary."

HENRY HALLAM
1855

Southern heroine, Confederate warrioress, Belle Boyd, circa 1860s.

BIBLIOGRAPHY
And Suggested Reading

Alexander, Edward Porter. *Military Memoirs of a Confederate*. New York: Charles Scribner's Sons, 1907.
Alfriend, Frank H. *The Life of Jefferson Davis*. Cincinnati, OH: Caxton Publishing House, 1868.
Anderson, Mabel Washbourne. *Life of General Stand Watie: The Only Indian Brigadier General of the Confederate Army and the Last General to Surrender*. Pryor, OK: self-published, 1915.
Armstrong, J. M. *The Biographical Encyclopedia of Kentucky of the Dead and Living Men of the Nineteenth Century*. Cincinnati, OH: J. M. Armstrong and Co., 1878.
Ashe, Samuel A'Court. *History of North Carolina*. 2 vols. Greensboro, NC: Charles L. Van Noppen, 1908.
Beck, James M. *The Constitution of the United States: Yesterday, Today, and Tomorrow?* New York: George H. Doran, 1922.
Beman, Lamar T. (ed.). *Selected Articles on States Rights*. New York: H. W. Wilson Co., 1926
Benson, Al, Jr., and Walter Donald Kennedy. *Lincoln's Marxists*. Gretna, LA: Pelican, 2011.
Bond, P. S. (ed.). *Military Science and Tactics: A Text and Reference for the Reserve Officers' Training Corps*. Washington, D.C.: P. S. Bond Publishing Co., 1938.
Boyd, James P. *Parties, Problems, and Leaders of 1896: An Impartial Presentation of Living National Questions*. Chicago, IL: Publishers' Union, 1896.
Brock, Robert Alonzo (ed.). *Southern Historical Society Papers*. 52 vols. Richmond, VA: Southern Historical Society, 1876-1943.
Browder, Earl. *Lincoln and the Communists*. New York, NY: Workers Library Publishers, Inc., 1936.
Bryan, William Jennings. *The First Battle: A Story of the Campaign of 1896*. Chicago, IL: W. B. Conkey Co., 1896.
Burns, James MacGregor. *The Vineyard of Liberty*. New York, NY: Alfred A. Knopf, 1982.
Carpenter, Stephen D. *Logic of History - Five Hundred Political Texts: Being Concentrated Extracts of Abolitionism; Also Results of Slavery Agitation and Emancipation; Together With Sundry Chapters on Despotism, Usurpations and Frauds*. Madison, WI: self-published, 1864.

Carr, Edward Hallett. *The Bolshevik Revolution: 1917-1923, Volume One*. 1950. Harmondsworth, UK: Penguin, 1971 ed.
Chesterton, Cecil. *A History of the United States*. London, UK: Chatto and Windus, 1919.
Christian, George Llewellyn. *Abraham Lincoln: An Address Delivered Before R. E. Lee Camp, No. 1 Confederate Veterans at Richmond, VA, October 29, 1909*. Richmond, VA: L. H. Jenkins, 1909.
——. *A Capitol Disaster: A Chapter of Reconstruction in Virginia*. Richmond, VA: self-published, 1915.
——. *Confederate Memories and Experiences*. Richmond, VA: self-published, 1915.
Committee on the Library (Massachusetts General Court). *State Papers on Nullification: Including the Public Acts of the Convention of the People of South Carolina, Assembled at Columbia, November 19, 1832 and March 11, 1833*. Boston, MA: self-published, 1834.
Confederate Veteran (Sumner Archibald Cunningham, ed., 1893-1913; Edith Drake Pope, ed., 1914-1932). 40 vols (original forty year run). Nashville, TN: Confederate Veteran, 1893-1932.
Curry, Jabez Lamar Monroe. *The Southern States of the American Union Considered in Their Relations to the Constitution of the United States and to the Resulting Union*. New York: G. P. Putnam's Sons, 1894.
Dean, Henry Clay. *Crimes of the Civil War, and Curse of the Funding System*. Baltimore, MD: self-published, 1869.
Dodd, Bella. *School of Darkness*. New York, NY: P. J. Kennedy and Sons, 1954.
Drayton, William, and Robert Young Hayne. *Proceedings of the State Rights Celebration at Charleston, S.C., July 1ˢᵗ, 1830*. Charleston, S.C.: self-published, 1830.
Early, Jubal Anderson. *A Memoir of the Last Year of the War for Independence, in the Confederate States of America*. Lynchburg, VA: Charles W. Button, 1867.
Edmonds, George. *Facts and Falsehoods Concerning the War on the South, 1861-1865*. Memphis, TN: self-published, 1904.
Evans, Clement Anselm (ed.). *Confederate Military History*. 12 vols. Atlanta, GA: Confederate Publishing Co., 1899.
Ewing, E. W. R. *Northern Rebellion, Southern Secession*. Philadelphia, PA: The John C. Winston Co., 1904.
Figgis, John Neville, and Reginald Vere Laurence (eds.). *Selections From the Correspondence of the First Lord Acton*. London, UK: Longmans, Green and Co., 1917.
Fitzhugh, George. *Cannibals All! Or, Slaves Without Masters*.

Richmond, VA: A. Morris, 1857.
Franklin, John Hope. *Reconstruction After the Civil War*. Chicago, IL: University of Chicago Press, 1961.
Gardiner, C. *Acts of the Republican Party as Seen by History*. Washington, D.C.: self-published, 1906.
Goodloe, Albert Theodore. *Some Rebel Relics From the Seat of the War*. Nashville, TN: Methodist Episcopal Church, South, 1893.
Greg, Percy. *History of the United States: From the Foundation of Virginia to the Reconstruction of the Union*. 2 vols. Richmond, VA: West, Johnston and Co., 1892.
Hallam, Henry. *The Constitutional History of England*. 3 vols. London, UK: John Murray, 1855.
Hasselberg, P. D. (ed.). *Parliamentary Debates: First Session, Fortieth Parliament, 1982, House of Representatives* (Vol. 445). Wellington, New Zealand: Government Printer, 1982.
Hazelton, John H. *The Declaration of Independence: Its History*. New York: Dodd, Mead, and Co., 1906.
Heilbroner, Robert L. *The Worldly Philosophers*. Lincoln, NE: Cliff Notes, 1965.
Hurd, John Codman. *The Union-State: A Letter to Our States Rights Friend*. New York: D. Van Nostrand Co., 1890.
Hutchings, Robert C. *The Usurpations of the Federal Government: The Dangers of Centralization*. Albany, NY: self-published, 1863.
Ingersoll, Lurton Dunham. *The Life of Horace Greeley*. Chicago, IL: Union Publishing Co., 1873.
Jackson, Andrew. *Proclamation of Andrew Jackson, President of the United States, to the People of South Carolina, December 10, 1832*. Harrisburg, PA: Singerly and Myers, 1864.
Jefferson, Thomas. *Notes on the State of Virginia*. Philadelphia, PA: H. C. Carey and I. Lea, 1825.
Johnson, Robert Underwood, and Clarence Clough Buel (eds.). *Battles and Leaders of the Civil War*. 4 vols. New York, NY: The Century Co., 1884-1888.
Johnstone, Huger William. *Truth of War Conspiracy, 1861*. Idylwild, GA: H. W. Johnstone, 1921.
Jones, John William. *The Davis Memorial Volume; Or Our Dead President, Jefferson Davis and the World's Tribute to His Memory*. Richmond, VA: B. F. Johnson, 1889.
Lamon, Ward Hill. *The Life of Abraham Lincoln: From His Birth to His Inauguration as President*. Boston, MA: James R. Osgood and Co., 1872.
——. *Recollections of Abraham Lincoln, 1847-1865*. Dorothy Lamon Teillard, ed. Washington, D.C.: self-published by the editor,

1911.
Leland, Charles Godfrey. *Centralization, or States Rights.* New York: C. T. Evans, 1863.
Lenin, Vladimir. *"Left Wing" Communism: An Infantile Disorder.* Detroit, MI: The Marxian Educational Society, 1921.
Lieber, Francis. *On Civil Liberty and Self-government.* Philadelphia, PA: J. B. Lippincott and Co., 1859.
Livermore, Thomas L. *Numbers and Losses in the Civil War in America, 1861-65.* 1900. Carlisle, PA: John Kallmann, 1996 ed.
Magliocca, Gerard N. *The Tragedy of William Jennings Bryan: Constitutional Law and the Politics of Backlash.* New Haven, CT: Yale University Press, 2011.
Marx, Karl, and Frederick Engels. *Manifesto of the Communist Party.* Chicago, IL: Charles H. Kerr and Co., 1906.
McCarty, Burke (ed.). *Little Sermons in Socialism by Abraham Lincoln.* Chicago, IL: The Chicago Daily Socialist, 1910.
McPherson, James M. *Abraham Lincoln and the Second American Revolution.* New York, NY: Oxford University Press, 1991.
Meriwether, Elizabeth Avery (pseudonym, "George Edmonds"). *Facts and Falsehoods Concerning the War on the South, 1861-1865.* Memphis, TN: A. R. Taylor and Co., 1904.
Messer-Kruse, Timothy. *The Yankee International: Marxism and the American Reform Tradition, 1848-1876.* Chapel Hill, NC: University of North Carolina Press, 1998.
Miller, Francis Trevelyan, and Robert S. Lanier (eds.). *The Photographic History of the Civil War.* 10 vols. New York, NY: The Review of Reviews Co., 1911.
Minor, Charles Landon Carter. *The Real Lincoln From the Testimony of His Contemporaries.* Richmond, VA: Everett Waddey Co., (second ed.) 1904.
Minor, Raleigh C. *Notes on the Science of Government and the Relations of the States to the United States.* Charlottesville, VA: Anderson Brothers (University of Virginia), 1913.
Minutes of the Eighth Annual Meeting and Reunion of the United Confederate Veterans, Atlanta, GA, July 20-23, 1898. New Orleans, LA: United Confederate Veterans, 1907.
Minutes of the Ninth Annual Meeting and Reunion of the United Confederate Veterans, Charleston, SC, May 10-13, 1899. New Orleans, LA: United Confederate Veterans, 1907.
Minutes of the Twelfth Annual Meeting and Reunion of the United Confederate Veterans, Dallas, TX, April 22-25, 1902. New Orleans, LA: United Confederate Veterans, 1907.
Morse, S. F. B. (pres.). *Hand-book of the Democracy for 1863 & '64.*

New York: Society for the Diffusion of Political Knowledge, 1864.
Muzzey, David Saville. *The United States of America: Vol. 1, To the Civil War*. Boston, MA: Ginn and Co., 1922.
——. *The American Adventure: Vol. 2, From the Civil War*. 1924. New York, NY: Harper and Brothers, 1927 ed.
Nicolay, John G., and John Hay (eds.). *Abraham Lincoln: A History*. 10 vols. New York, NY: The Century Co., 1890.
——. *Complete Works of Abraham Lincoln*. 12 vols. 1894. New York, NY: Francis D. Tandy Co., 1905 ed.
——. *Abraham Lincoln: Complete Works*. 12 vols. 1894. New York, NY: The Century Co., 1907 ed.
Oliver, Benjamin Lynde. *The Rights of an American Citizen: With a Commentary on States Rights, and on the Constitution and Policy of the United States*. Boston, MA: Marsh, Capen, and Lyon, 1832.
ORA (full title: *The War of the Rebellion: A Compilation of the Official Records of the Union and Confederate Armies*). 128 vols. Washington, DC: Government Printing Office, 1880.
ORN (full title: *Official Records of the Union and Confederate Navies in the War of the Rebellion*). 30 vols. Washington, DC: Government Printing Office, 1894.
Owsley, Frank Lawrence. *States' Rights in the Confederacy*. Chicago, IL: University of Chicago Press, 1931.
Parker, Theodore. *Historic Americans*. Boston, MA: Horace B. Fuller, 1878.
Pollard, Edward Alfred. *The Lost Cause*. New York, NY: E. B. Treat and Co., 1867.
Randall, James Garfield. *Constitutional Problems Under Lincoln*. New York: D. Appleton and Co., 1926.
Rawle, William. *A View of the Constitution of the United States of America*. Philadelphia, PA: self-published, 1825.
Richardson, John Anderson. *Richardson's Defense of the South*. Atlanta, GA: A. B. Caldwell, 1914.
Rogers, William P. *The Three Secession Movements in the United States: Samuel J. Tilden, the Democratic Candidate for Presidency; the Advisor, Aider and Abettor of the Great Secession Movement of 1860; and One of the Authors of the Infamous Resolution of 1864; His Claims as a Statesman and Reformer Considered*. Boston, MA: John Wilson and Son, 1876.
Root, Elihu. *How to Preserve the Local Self-Government of the States*. New York: Brentano's, 1907.
Rove, Karl. *The Triumph of William McKinley: Why the Election of 1896 Still Matters*. New York, NY: Simon and Schuster, 2015.

Rutherford, Mildred Lewis. *Truths of History: A Fair, Unbiased, Impartial, Unprejudiced and Conscientious Study of History*. Athens, GA: n.p., 1920.

Sage, Bernard Janin. *The Republic of Republics; or American Federal Liberty*. Boston, MA: Little, Brown, and Co., 1881.

Schlüter, Herman. *Lincoln, Labor and Slavery: A Chapter From the Social History of America*. New York: Socialist Literature Co., 1913.

Seabrook, Lochlainn. *Carnton Plantation Ghost Stories: True Tales of the Unexplained from Tennessee's Most Haunted Civil War House!* 2005. Franklin, TN, 2016 ed.

———. *Nathan Bedford Forrest: Southern Hero, American Patriot*. 2007. Franklin, TN, 2010 ed.

———. *Abraham Lincoln: The Southern View*. 2007. Franklin, TN: Sea Raven Press, 2013 ed.

———. *The McGavocks of Carnton Plantation: A Southern History - Celebrating One of Dixie's Most Noble Confederate Families and Their Tennessee Home*. 2008. Franklin, TN, 2011 ed.

———. *A Rebel Born: A Defense of Nathan Bedford Forrest*. 2010. Franklin, TN: Sea Raven Press, 2011 ed.

———. *Everything You Were Taught About the Civil War is Wrong, Ask a Southerner!* 2010. Franklin, TN: Sea Raven Press, revised 2019 ed.

———. *The Quotable Jefferson Davis: Selections From the Writings and Speeches of the Confederacy's First President*. Franklin, TN: Sea Raven Press, 2011.

———. *The Quotable Robert E. Lee: Selections From the Writings and Speeches of the South's Most Beloved Civil War General*. Franklin, TN: Sea Raven Press, 2011 Sesquicentennial Civil War Edition.

———. *Lincolnology: The Real Abraham Lincoln Revealed In His Own Words*. Franklin, TN: Sea Raven Press, 2011.

———. *The Unquotable Abraham Lincoln: The President's Quotes They Don't Want You To Know!* Franklin, TN: Sea Raven Press, 2011.

———. *Honest Jeff and Dishonest Abe: A Southern Children's Guide to the Civil War*. Franklin, TN: Sea Raven Press, 2012.

———. *Encyclopedia of the Battle of Franklin - A Comprehensive Guide to the Conflict that Changed the Civil War*. Franklin, TN: Sea Raven Press, 2012.

———. *The Quotable Nathan Bedford Forrest: Selections From the Writings and Speeches of the Confederacy's Most Brilliant Cavalryman*. Spring Hill, TN: Sea Raven Press, 2012.

———. *Forrest! 99 Reasons to Love Nathan Bedford Forrest*. Spring Hill, TN: Sea Raven Press, 2012.

——. *Give 'Em Hell Boys! The Complete Military Correspondence of Nathan Bedford Forrest*. Spring Hill, TN: Sea Raven Press, 2012.

——. *The Constitution of the Confederate States of America Explained: A Clause-by-Clause Study of the South's Magna Carta*. Spring Hill, TN: Sea Raven Press, 2012 Sesquicentennial Civil War Edition.

——. *The Great Impersonator: 99 Reasons to Dislike Abraham Lincoln*. Spring Hill, TN: Sea Raven Press, 2012.

——. *The Old Rebel: Robert E. Lee As He Was Seen By His Contemporaries*. Spring Hill, TN: Sea Raven Press, 2012 Sesquicentennial Civil War Edition.

——. *The Quotable Stonewall Jackson: Selections From the Writings and Speeches of the South's Most Famous General*. Spring Hill, TN: Sea Raven Press, 2012 Sesquicentennial Civil War Edition.

——. *Saddle, Sword, and Gun: A Biography of Nathan Bedford Forrest for Teens*. Spring Hill, TN: Sea Raven Press, 2013.

——. *The Alexander H. Stephens Reader: Excerpts From the Works of a Confederate Founding Father*. Spring Hill, TN: Sea Raven Press, 2013.

——. *The Quotable Alexander H. Stephens: Selections From the Writings and Speeches of the Confederacy's First Vice President*. Spring Hill, TN: Sea Raven Press, 2013 Sesquicentennial Civil War Edition.

——. *Give This Book to a Yankee! A Southern Guide to the Civil War for Northerners*. Spring Hill, TN: Sea Raven Press, 2014.

——. *The Articles of Confederation Explained: A Clause-by-Clause Study of America's First Constitution*. Spring Hill, TN: Sea Raven Press, 2014.

——. *Confederate Blood and Treasure: An Interview With Lochlainn Seabrook*. Spring Hill, TN: Sea Raven Press, 2015.

——. *Nathan Bedford Forrest and the Battle of Fort Pillow: Yankee Myth, Confederate Fact*. Spring Hill, TN: Sea Raven Press, 2015.

——. *Everything You Were Taught About American Slavery War is Wrong, Ask a Southerner!* Spring Hill, TN: Sea Raven Press, 2015.

——. *Confederacy 101: Amazing Facts You Never Knew About America's Oldest Political Tradition*. Spring Hill, TN: Sea Raven Press, 2015.

——. *The Great Yankee Coverup: What the North Doesn't Want You to Know About Lincoln's War!* Spring Hill, TN: Sea Raven Press, 2015.

——. *Slavery 101: Amazing Facts You Never Knew About America's "Peculiar Institution."* Spring Hill, TN: Sea Raven Press, 2015.

——. *Confederate Flag Facts: What Every American Should Know About Dixie's Southern Cross*. Spring Hill, TN: Sea Raven Press, 2016.

——. *Nathan Bedford Forrest and the Ku Klux Klan: Yankee Myth,*

Confederate Fact. Spring Hill, TN: Sea Raven Press, 2016.

——. *Seabrook's Bible Dictionary of Traditional and Mystical Christian Doctrines*. Spring Hill, TN: Sea Raven Press, 2016.

——. *Everything You Were Taught About African-Americans and the Civil War is Wrong, Ask a Southerner!* Spring Hill, TN: Sea Raven Press, 2016.

——. *Nathan Bedford Forrest and African-Americans: Yankee Myth, Confederate Fact*. Spring Hill, TN: Sea Raven Press, 2016.

——. *Women in Gray: A Tribute to the Ladies Who Supported the Southern Confederacy*. Spring Hill, TN: Sea Raven Press, 2016.

——. *Lincoln's War: The Real Cause, the Real Winner, the Real Loser*. Spring Hill, TN: Sea Raven Press, 2016.

——. *The Unholy Crusade: Lincoln's Legacy of Destruction in the American South*. Spring Hill, TN: Sea Raven Press, 2017.

——. *Abraham Lincoln Was a Liberal, Jefferson Davis Was a Conservative: The Missing Key to Understanding the American Civil War*. Spring Hill, TN: Sea Raven Press, 2017.

——. *All We Ask is to be Let Alone: The Southern Secession Fact Book*. Spring Hill, TN: Sea Raven Press, 2017.

——. *The Ultimate Civil War Quiz Book: How Much Do You Really Know About America's Most Misunderstood Conflict?* Spring Hill, TN: Sea Raven Press, 2017.

——. *Rise Up and Call Them Blessed: Victorian Tributes to the Confederate Soldier, 1861-1901*. Spring Hill, TN: Sea Raven Press, 2017.

——. *Victorian Confederate Poetry: The Southern Cause in Verse, 1861-1901*. Spring Hill, TN: Sea Raven Press, 2018.

——. *Confederate Monuments: Why Every American Should Honor Confederate Soldiers and Their Memorials*. Spring Hill, TN: Sea Raven Press, 2018.

——. *The God of War: Nathan Bedford Forrest as He Was Seen by His Contemporaries*. Spring Hill, TN: Sea Raven Press, 2018.

——. *The Battle of Spring Hill: Recollections of Confederate and Union Soldiers*. Spring Hill, TN: Sea Raven Press, 2018.

——. *I Rode With Forrest! Confederate Soldiers Who Served With the World's Greatest Cavalry Leader*. Spring Hill, TN: Sea Raven Press, 2018.

——. *The Battle of Nashville: Recollections of Confederate and Union Soldiers*. Spring Hill, TN: Sea Raven Press, 2018.

——. *The Battle of Franklin: Recollections of Confederate and Union Soldiers*. Spring Hill, TN: Sea Raven Press, 2018.

——. *A Rebel Born: The Screenplay* (for the film). Written 2011. Franklin, TN: Sea Raven Press, 2020.

——. (ed.) *A Short History of the Confederate States of America*

(Jefferson Davis, Belford Company, NY, 1890). A Sea Raven Press Reprint. Spring Hill, TN: Sea Raven Press, 2020.

———. (ed.) *Prison Life of Jefferson Davis: Embracing Details and Incidents in his Captivity, With Conversations on Topics of Public Interest* (John J. Craven, Sampson, Low, Son, and Marston, London, UK, 1866). A Sea Raven Press Reprint. Spring Hill, TN: Sea Raven Press, 2020.

———. *What the Confederate Flag Means to Me: Americans Speak Out in Defense of Southern Honor, Heritage, and History*. Spring Hill, TN: Sea Raven Press, 2021.

———. *Heroes of the Southern Confederacy: The Illustrated Book of Confederate Officials, Soldiers, and Civilians*. Spring Hill, TN: Sea Raven Press, 2021.

———. *Support Your Local Confederate: Wit and Humor in the Southern Confederacy*. Spring Hill, TN: Sea Raven Press, 2021.

———. *America's Three Constitutions: Complete Texts of the Articles of Confederation, Constitution of the United States of America, and Constitution of the Confederate States of America*. Spring Hill, TN: Sea Raven Press, 2021.

———. *Vintage Southern Cookbook: 2,000 Delicious Dishes From Dixie*. Spring Hill, TN: Sea Raven Press, 2021.

———. *The Bittersweet Bond: Race Relations in the Old South as Described by White and Black Southerners*. Spring Hill, TN: Sea Raven Press, 2022.

———. (ed.) *The Rise and Fall of the Confederate Government* (Jefferson Davis, D. Appleton, New York, 1881). 2 vols. A Sea Raven Press Facsimile Reprint. Spring Hill, TN: Sea Raven Press, 2022.

Solger, Reinhold. *The States-System of Europe: Being a Course of Lectures Exposing Modern Functionary-ism and Diplomacy*. London, UK: Robert Theobold, 1854.

Steel, Samuel Augustus. *The South Was Right*. Columbia, SC: R. L. Bryan Co., 1914.

Stephens, Alexander Hamilton. *Speech of Mr. Stephens, of Georgia, on the War and Taxation*. Washington, D.C.: J & G. Gideon, 1848.

———. *A Constitutional View of the Late War Between the States; Its Causes, Character, Conduct and Results*. 2 vols. Philadelphia, PA: National Publishing, Co., 1870.

———. *Recollections of Alexander H. Stephens: His Diary Kept When a Prisoner at Fort Warren, Boston Harbour, 1865*. New York, NY: Doubleday, Page, and Co., 1910.

Thompson, Holland. *The New South: A Chronicle of Social and Industrial Evolution*. New Haven, CT: Yale University Press,

1920.

Thorpe, Francis Newton. *The Civil War From a Northern Standpoint.* Philadelphia, PA: George Barrie and Sons, 1906.

Warner, Ezra J. *Generals in Gray: Lives of the Confederate Commanders.* 1959. Baton Rouge, LA: Louisiana State University Press, 1989 ed.

——. *Generals in Blue: Lives of the Union Commanders.* 1964. Baton Rouge, LA: Louisiana State University Press, 2006 ed.

Washington, H. A. (ed.). *The Writings of Thomas Jefferson.* Washington, D.C.: Taylor and Maury, 1853.

Wilson, Henry. *History of the Rise and Fall of the Slave Power in America.* 3 vols. Boston, MA: James R. Osgood and Co., 1875.

Wittke, Carl. *Refugees of Revolution: The German Forty-Eighters in America.* Philadelphia, PA: University of Pennsylvania, 1952.

Woods, Thomas E., Jr. *The Politically Incorrect Guide to American History.* Washington, D.C.: Regnery, 2004.

Sumter Light Guards, Company K, 4th Regiment Georgia Volunteer Infantry, Confederate States of America, April 1861.

INDEX

Abraham (Bible), 190
Acton, John D. (Lord), 299
Adams, Charles F., 117, 156, 242, 280, 281
Adams, Henry, 236
Adams, James T., 339
Adams, John, 46, 66, 133, 181, 236, 246
Adams, John Q., 133, 254, 305
Adams, Samuel, 133
Alston, R. A., 45
Ames, Adelbert, 333
Ames, Fisher, 133
Andrews, Matthew P., 22
Arnold, Benedict, 161
Arnot, William, 195, 196
Ashby, Turner, 40
Ashe, Samuel A., 312
Asquith, Henry H., 291
Atticus, 172
Attila the Hun, 211
Austin, Mrs. Valerie E., 136
Bacon, L. W., 142
Bacon, Nathaniel, 132
Baird, E. T., 194, 196
Baldwin, Abraham, 267
Baldwin, Henry, 141
Baldwin, John B., 38
Bancroft, George, 56
Barrell, Harry F., 313
Bass, E. D., 295
Baxter, Ed, 63
Bayard, Chevalier de, 111
Bear, Alexander, 82
Beard, John S., 171
Beauregard, Pierre G. T., 63, 142, 184, 206, 374
Beckham, John C. W., 122
Beecher, Henry W., 180
Belville, J. B., 95
Bennett, James G., 206
Benton, Thomas H., 170, 189
Beveridge, Albert J., 302
Bingham, Hiram, 334
Bingham, Robert, 253
Bismarck, Otto von, 237, 242

Black Dog, 321
Black, Jeremiah S., 145
Blacknall, O. W., 211
Blacknall, T. H., 179
Blaine, James G., 329, 332
Blake, Harold R., 276
Bob (black servant), 189
Boisseau, Sterling, 306
Bonaparte, Napoleon, 37, 181
Bond, Daniel, 73
Bowdoin, James, 133
Boyd, Belle, 352
Bragg, Braxton, 63
Breckinridge, John C., 63, 171, 303
Breese, W. E., 78
Brooks, James, 22, 147
Brown, Albert G., 212
Brown, John, 65, 107, 145, 206, 208, 226, 281, 306, 338
Brown, Joseph E., 208
Browne, William M., 372
Brownlow, William G., 333
Bryce, James, 334
Buchanan, James, 171
Buchanan, John A., 152
Buckner, Montgomery G., 152
Buell, Don C., 86
Bullock, Rufus, 333
Burlingame, Anson P., 107
Burnley, W. Sam, 155
Burnside, Ambrose E., 310
Butler, Benjamin F., 282, 332
Butler, Pierce, 268, 273
Buttre, John C., 73
Cabell, William L., 63, 137
Cabot, George, 254
Cadwalader, John, 124
Caesar, Julius, 293
Caldwell, Joshua W., 56
Calhoun, John C., 42, 65, 189, 232, 237, 319, 329
Callaway, W. A., 292
Cameron, James D., 332
Campbell, John A., 278
Campbell, Mrs. A. A., 293, 304

Canby, Edward R. S., 84
Cave, R. C., 69
Cawein, Madison J., 184
Chandler, A. M., 206
Chandler, Silas, 206
Chandler, W. E., 332
Chandler, Zachariah, 332
Charles I, King, 284
Chase, Salmon P., 134, 141, 206, 243, 288, 298, 308, 332
Chase, Samuel, 160
Chatham, Lord, 148
Cheatham, Benjamin F., 292, 293
Chesterton, Cecil, 290
Christian, George L., 145
Churchill, John, 90
Cicero, Marcus T., 172, 326
Clark, Frank, 178
Clark, George R., 330
Clark, T. H., 208
Clay, Henry, 98, 121, 168, 189, 267
Clayton, Henry D., 158
Clayton, Powell, 333
Clayton, W. W., 45
Cleburne, Patrick R., 63
Clews, Henry, 332
Clifford, Nathan, 287
Clinton, George, 327
Cobb, Howell, 158
Conkling, Roscoe, 332
Cooke, George A., 323
Cooke, Jay, 332
Coolidge, Calvin, 313, 335
Corwin, Thomas, 310
Courtney, W. J., 316
Cowherd, Edwin F., 229
Crittenden, John J., 298
Cromwell, Oliver, 131, 188, 219, 284
Crouch, Walter V., 151
Cunningham, James, 340
Cunningham, R. H., 100
Cunningham, Sumner A., 42, 44, 57, 70, 86, 87, 130, 150, 154, 160
Curry, Jabez L. M., 107
Curtis, George T., 262, 268, 269, 273
Dana, Charles A., 25
Daniel, Miss Cary, 129

Davies, William W., 6
Davis, Jefferson, 11, 14, 22, 31, 41, 42, 50, 51, 68, 77, 78, 95, 110, 119, 121, 126, 141, 142, 147, 152, 153, 155, 158, 161, 163, 166, 171, 174, 185, 206-209, 211, 216, 217, 237, 240, 245, 252, 255, 259, 277, 286-288, 294, 296, 298, 302, 304, 308, 313, 318, 319, 324, 328, 332, 340, 372-374
Davis, Mrs. W. L., 112
Davis, Sam, 152
Davis, Varina A. "Winnie", 81
Davis, Varina H., 118
Denny, Collins, 231
Dickinson, Jacob M., 153
Dinkins, James, 310
Disney, Walt, 369
Dodson, E. M., 129
Douglas, Stephen A., 106, 289, 298, 303
Downing, Lewis, 215
Dozier, Mrs. N. B., 165
Drew, George F., 333
Echols, S. A., 45
Ector, Matthew D., 63
Edgar, Dr., 192
Edwards, Jay D., 340
Edwards, Joab, 208
Elgin, Thomas A., 145
Ellsworth, Oliver, 264, 266, 272
Elson, Henry W., 164, 165
Evans, Clement A., 150
Evarts, William M., 287
Everett, Lloyd T., 282
Ewell, Richard S., 73
Fahy, John H., 335
Fairbairn, Patrick, 195
Falconer, Kinlock, 340
Falconer, Thomas A., 340
Farabaugh, W. W., 99
Farrand, Max, 268-270, 275
Faulkner, Charles J., 34
Fauntleroy, Cornelius H., 284
Fields, Mrs. S. M., 320
Fiske, John, 56, 251, 262, 268, 271, 276
Fitzgerald, O. P., 143
Fletcher, Duncan U., 336

Foot, Samuel A., 69
Foote, Shelby, 373
Forrest, Nathan B., 14, 56, 63, 77, 175, 194, 373
Franklin, Benjamin, 266, 267
Fredricks, Charles D., 118
Freeman, W. B., 316
French, Samuel G., 45, 76
Gahagan, Andrew J., 297
Gaines, Sam A., 184
Galleher, John N., 76
Garrison, William L., 106, 146, 253
George III, King, 12, 211, 331
George, J. Z., 219
George, James Z., 332
Gerry, Elbridge, 261, 267-269, 271, 272, 275
Gibson, Randall L., 331
Gilbert, C. E., 338
Gist, States Rights, 54
Gladstone, William E., 207, 302
Gochenour, Jacob, 161
God, 32, 40, 41, 44, 46, 47, 50, 58, 63, 70, 82, 83, 94, 100, 128, 143, 145, 158, 180, 183, 185, 187, 190, 196, 197, 203, 217, 218, 220-222, 239, 257, 282, 302, 306, 315, 316
Gordon, John B., 14, 54, 63
Gorham, Nathaniel, 265, 269
Granbury, Hiram B., 63
Grant, Frederick D., 153
Grant, Ulysses S., 42, 71, 98, 153, 157, 207, 209, 242, 332
Graves, Robert, 19, 373
Greeley, Horace, 327
Green, Thomas, 63
Greg, Percy, 139
Gregg, John, 63
Hale, John P., 134
Hall, L. P., 73
Hallam, Henry, 351
Halleck, Henry W., 243, 282
Hambleton, J. P., 45
Hamilton, Alexander, 66, 99, 103, 112, 123, 134, 135, 156, 236, 246, 251, 270, 327, 339
Hamilton, Jay, 330

Hamlin, Hannibal, 240
Hampden, John, 219, 284
Hampton, Wade, 163, 175, 333
Hancock, F. W., 144
Hancock, John, 133
Hansell, George, 52
Harding, William G., 189, 193, 373
Harper, Henry W., 317
Harrington, Edward W., 333
Harrison, Benjamin, 161
Harrison, William H., 215, 251
Hartman, J. C., 159
Hatton, Robert H., 41
Hawthorne, Nathaniel, 190
Hayne, Robert Y., 372
Hecker, Friedrich K. F., 25
Henry, Patrick, 36, 37, 69, 97, 99, 132, 135, 156, 173, 182, 213, 214, 216, 219, 329
Henry, Patrick (Confederate soldier), 288
Herman, Miss Maud V., 136
Herndon, William H., 139
Hewitt, John, 128
Hickman, Mrs. John P., 117
Hill, Ambrose P., 40, 73, 305, 374
Hill, Benjamin W., 45, 329, 333
Hitler, Adolf, 24
Hitner, John K., 307
Hobby, William P., 293
Hogan, N. B., 50
Hoge, Moses, 195, 196
Hogg, John B., 293
Hoke, Robert F., 173
Holden, William W., 209, 333
Holland, T. C., 305
Hollis, Christopher, 327
Hood, John B., 56, 63, 158, 175, 374
Houston, Samuel, 329
Howard, C. B., 45, 47
Howard, David R., 49
Howard, James M., 49
Howard, T. C., 45
Howe, Samuel G., 324
Howell, Varina, 212
Hulsey, Eli, 45
Hunneberger, Mrs. Maude B., 319
Hunnicutt, James W., 333

Hunter, David, 243
Hutchings, Robert C., 149
Ingalls, John J., 110
Ingersoll, Robert G., 332
Isaiah (Bible), 37
Jackson, Andrew, 49, 65, 70, 92, 189, 200, 253, 329
Jackson, Stonewall, 40, 49, 63, 73, 97, 153, 155, 166, 174, 175, 184, 186, 250, 305, 306, 313, 319, 329, 372, 374
Jackson, William H., 321
Janney, John, 38
Jefferson, Thomas, 26, 36, 37, 42, 56, 66, 67, 99, 103, 114, 121, 124, 131, 132, 134, 171, 181, 182, 199, 200, 213-216, 224, 236, 239, 242, 246, 251, 252, 279, 290, 297, 302, 305, 325, 328, 329, 331, 334, 335, 339
Jehovah, 302
Jennings, Arthur H., 182, 307-309
Jeremiah (Bible), 303
Jesus, 47
Job (Bible), 304
Johnson, Andrew, 207, 252, 310, 315, 338
Johnson, Bradley T., 79
Johnston, Albert S., 50, 56, 63, 163, 174, 175, 255, 372
Johnston, Joseph E., 14, 22, 50, 56, 63, 157, 174, 175, 250, 255, 305, 374
Jones, Charles C., 294
Jones, Cicero, 223
Keitt, Lawrence M., 312
Kellam, Mrs. W. L., 302
Kellogg, Frances L., 176
Kelsey, Jasper, 202
Kenner, Duncan F., 240
Ketcham, William A., 161
Keyes, Erasmus D., 176
Kincheloe, David H., 218
King, Rufus, 264, 269, 274
Knox, Robert T., 303
Kramer, Peter, 73
Lamar, Lucius Q. C., 172
Lamar, Mrs. W. D., 174
Lamon, Ward H., 139
Lawrence, R. T., 337

Lederer, Wolfe A., 339
Lee, Fitzhugh, 63, 305
Lee, Harry "Light Horse", 319
Lee, Henry, III, 248
Lee, Richard H., 37, 41, 132
Lee, Robert E., 30, 40, 42, 43, 49, 54, 63, 70, 72, 77, 89, 98, 117, 122, 153, 155, 157, 158, 161-164, 166, 170-172, 174, 175, 179, 183, 184, 216, 226, 238, 245, 247, 248, 250, 255, 279, 282, 293, 296-299, 305, 306, 313, 316, 317, 319, 322, 328, 332, 339, 372, 374
Lee, Stephen D., 62, 162
Lee, William H. F., 63
Leigh, Watkins, 146
Letcher, John, 38
Lieber, Francis, 148
Lincoln, Abraham, 11, 13, 15, 17, 25, 35, 39, 40, 44, 92, 94, 106, 128, 130, 137, 139, 141, 143, 148, 153, 159, 164, 166, 167, 171, 178, 182, 185, 202, 207, 216, 219, 224-226, 233, 239-246, 248, 255, 257-259, 277-279, 282, 286-289, 302, 305, 307-312, 320, 332, 337, 371
Lincoln, Robert T., 153
Littlefield, Milton S., 333
Livingston, Henry W., 275
Lodge, Henry C., 132, 254, 255, 327
Longfellow, Henry W., 190
Longstreet, James, 14, 63, 175, 374
Love, W. A., 307
Lovett, Howard M., 200
Lucas, Daniel B., 186
Lucullus, Lucius L., 172
Lunt, George, 121, 144, 145
Lyne, Mrs. William, 319
Macaulay, Thomas B., 284
MacLachlan, H. D. C., 219
Madison, James, 36, 56, 67, 121, 131, 132, 135, 198, 199, 213, 214, 216, 224, 236, 246, 248, 251, 259, 265, 267, 269-271, 273, 302, 325,

329
Maltby, Frances G., 309
Marion, Francis, 173
Marlborough, Duke of, 90
Marshall, John, 56, 132, 182, 251, 302, 305, 329
Martin, Luther, 266-268, 271, 272
Marx, Karl, 15, 24, 25
Mason, George, 36, 37, 132, 267-269, 274, 327, 329
Mather, Cotton, 180
Matthews, Stanley, 332
Maury, Dabney H., 79
Maury, Matthew F., 305
McBlair, William, Jr., 62, 95
McCabe, W. Gordon, 176
McCausland, John A., 246
McClellan, George B., 158, 159, 246
McCord, Miss Annie, 325
McCosh, James, 195, 196
McCulloch, Ben, 63
McDowell, James, 34
McFarland, L. B., 173
McGavock, John W., 189
McGehee, Harney M., 302
McGowan, Samuel, 250
McGuire, Hunter, 306
McKellar, Kenneth D., 173
McKim, R. H., 22, 121, 135
McKinley, William, 90, 92
McNeill, John H., 165
McNeilly, James H., 22, 60, 81, 84, 179, 197, 227, 258, 283, 285, 296
Milligan, Lambdin P., 327
Minor, Berkeley, 309
Minor, Charles L. C., 138, 139
Minor, Raleigh C., 23
Mitchell, William L., 172
Moltke, Helmuth von, 237
Monroe, James, 67, 160, 211, 305
Moore, T. E., 151
Moore, Thomas V., 194
Morgan, John H., 175
Morris, Gouverneur, 268, 273, 275
Morton, Oliver P., 332
Mosby, John S., 6, 32, 373
Moses (Bible), 40

Moses, Franklin I., Jr., 333
Nelson, Hugh M., 38
Nelson, Thomas, Jr., 37
Ney, Michel, 289
Nicholls, Franklin T., 333
Nickerson, Miss Edmonda A., 120
Niles, Hezekiah, 200
O'Neal, Emmet, 164
Obenchain, William A., 115
Overton, John, 193
Owen, William M., 72
Page, Frank, 25, 59
Palmer, B. M., 89
Parsons, Theophilus, 133, 254
Patterson, John J., 333
Patterson, William, 260, 262, 264, 267
Paul, Saint, 329
Pearce, James A., 255
Pease, Elisha M., 333
Pelham, John C., 226
Pendleton, Louis, 258
Pendleton, William N., 223
Perkins, J. R., 128
Perrin, Achilles, 277
Peters, James A., 95
Phillips, Wendell, 46, 106
Pickering, Timothy, 133, 213, 254
Pierce, Franklin, 190, 212
Pinckney, Charles C., 56, 261, 265, 272, 273
Pitt, William, 148
Polk, James K., 37, 49, 252, 329, 371
Polk, Leonidas, 49, 63, 292
Pope, Edith D., 325
Pope, John, 45, 46
Porter, James D., 94
Powell, Miss Ida P., 324
Preston, William B., 39
Price, Sterling, 63, 128, 220, 315
Pym, John, 219
Quincey, Edward, 106
Quincy, Josiah, 133, 174, 181, 252, 254, 290
Quintard, Charles T., 57
Raguet, Condy, 198
Randal, Horace, 63
Randolph, Edmund, 36, 260, 262, 271
Randolph, George W., 39

Rawle, William, 142, 174, 255, 286, 328
Read, C. A., 41
Reagan, John H., 68, 109, 126, 259
Reed, William B., 141
Rhodes, James F., 241
Richard, the Lionheart, 129
Richardson, John A., 290, 372
Rives, William C., 39
Rodgers, R. H., 82
Rodgers, Samuel D., 318
Rogers, J. H., 127
Roosevelt, Theodore, 90, 170
Ross, Lawrence S., 63
Rowland, Miss Kate M., 139
Roy, Thomas B., 261
Rucker, Edmund W., 373
Ruffin, Edmund, 300
Rutherford, Mildred L., 181
Rutledge, John, 56, 271
Ryan, Abram J., 157
Safford, A. P., 274
Sage, Bernard J., 287
Schofield, John M., 117
Schurman, Janet, 129
Schurz, Carl, 332
Scott, Dred, 98, 288, 327
Scott, Robert E., 38
Scott, Robert K., 333
Scott, Winfield, 37, 247, 319, 338
Scurry, William R., 63
Sea, Andrew M., 130
Seabrook, Lochlainn, 6, 11-17, 19, 21-27, 369, 373, 375
Seddon, James A., 39
Semmes, Raphael, 238, 245, 282, 315
Semmes, Samuel M., 315
Seward, William H., 61, 106, 134, 211, 241, 278, 308, 332
Shanks, David, 315
Shelby, Joseph O., 315
Sheridan, Philip H., 238, 242, 282, 332
Sherman, Roger, 267, 271, 272, 274
Sherman, William T., 46, 84, 93, 157, 207, 209, 211, 238, 242, 282, 308, 310
Shishmanian, John A., 185

Shorter, John G., 208
Simonton, John M., 342
Slocomb, Cuthbert H., 341
Smith, Adam, 200
Smith, Edmund K., 63, 332
Smith, Miss Nannie D., 316
Smith, Orren R., 304
Smith, William C., 74
Solger, Reinhold, 25
Speed, James, 287
Speight, Jesse, 212
Spencer, George E., 333
Stanton, Edwin M., 241, 332
Stearns, Marcellus L., 333
Stephens, Alexander H., 11, 14, 45, 91, 141, 142, 258, 329, 338, 373
Stevens, Thaddeus, 332, 339
Stewart, Alexander P., 88
Stewart, W. H., 158
Stiles, John C., 203
Stone, J. B., 318
Stone, Joshua, 318
Stone, Mrs. C. B., 158
Storey, L. J., 110
Story, Joseph, 132, 141
Stowe, Charles E., 169, 287, 290, 337
Stowe, Harriet B., 170, 190, 207, 287, 337
Strahl, Otho F., 292
Strong, Caleb, 268
Stuart, Alexander H. H., 38, 39, 306
Stuart, James E. B. "Jeb", 40, 63, 175, 305, 374
Stubbs, William, 11
Summers, George W., 39
Summers, George Y., 38
Sumner, Charles, 332
Tacitus, 55
Taft, William H., 153, 154
Taylor, Richard, 14, 247
Taylor, Sarah K., 212
Taylor, Zachary, 212
Teillard, Dorothy L., 139
Terrail, Pierre, 111
Thomas, Frank M., 175
Thomas, George H., 122, 161, 176
Thompson, John, 191-193

Thompson, Joseph H., 191
Thompson, Mary, 191, 192, 194
Thompson, Meriwether J., 337
Thorpe, Francis N., 288
Tituba (Indian servant girl), 180
Tocqueville, Alexis de, 328
Toombs, Robert A., 278, 298, 371
Travis, W. F., 50
Trescott, Austin A., 228
Truman, William, 127
Tucker, John R., 50
Tucker, St. George, 255, 328
Turner, Edward R., 171
Turner, Smith S., 185
Turney, Mr., 42
Tyler, John, 37, 39
Tyler, Lyon G., 247
Tyson, L. D., 250
Underwood, John C., 208
Van Pelt, S. D., 149
Vance, Zebulon B., 208, 333
Von Der Au, Miss Mary L., 178
Ward, William W., 320
Warmoth, Henry C., 333
Washington, Booker T., 170
Washington, George, 12, 36, 37, 46, 49, 54, 56, 66, 70, 77, 113, 126, 131-133, 135, 156, 163, 172, 173, 182, 213, 219, 224, 245, 251, 255, 256, 279, 297, 319, 327, 329
Waul, Thomas N., 63
Webster, Daniel, 42, 72, 105, 131, 132, 135, 189, 224, 282, 288, 305, 319, 321, 327, 372
Wellesley, Arthur, 90
Wellington, Duke of, 90
Wheeler, Joseph, 56, 63, 174, 175
Whistler, William M., 143
Whitcomb, Paul S., 321
White, James H., 340
Whitney, Eli, 166
Wilhelm II, King, 258
Williams, John S., 130
Williamson, Hugh, 268, 269
Willich, August von, 15, 25
Wilson, Henry, 60
Wilson, James, 264, 269, 271, 273
Wilson, Woodrow, 113, 218, 220, 221, 223, 233, 241, 242, 246, 372
Winder, Mrs. Florence T., 131
Woodard, J. H., 92
Woodward, Thomas G. Y., 84
Wright, Arnold, 183
Wright, Daniel G., 94
Wright, William M., 239
Yates, H. K., 176
Yates, Robert, 267
Yerger, Mrs. Lucy G., 148
Young Black Dog, 321
Young, Bennett H., 17, 176, 183
Young, Mrs. L. G., 137

"There is more treasure in books than in all the pirates' loot on Treasure Island. Best of all, you can enjoy these riches every day of your life." — WALT DISNEY

Confederate soldier, identity unknown, circa 1863.

QUOTABLE QUOTES
Related to the Southern Cause

AN EARLY WARNING
☞ "It becomes the duty of all States, and especially of those whose constitutions recognize the existence of domestic slavery, to look with watchfulness to the attempts which have been recently made to disturb the rights secured to them by the Constitution of the United States. The agitation of the abolitionists [that is, socialists and communists] can by no possibility produce good to any portion of the Union and must, if persisted in, lead to incalculable mischief." — JAMES KNOX POLK, NASHVILLE TENNESSEE, OCTOBER 14, 1839

BEFORE HE BECAME LIBERALIZED
☞ "Any people, anywhere, being inclined and having the power, have the right to rise up and shake off the existing government, and to form a new one that suits them better. This is a most valuable right, a sacred right, which we hope and believe is to liberate the world. Nor is this right confined to cases in which the whole of any existing government may choose to exercise it. Any portion of Such people that can may revolutionize and make their own of so much of the territory as they inhabit." — ABRAHAM LINCOLN, U.S. CONGRESS, JANUARY 12, 1848

COERCION OR CONCILIATION
☞ "You [Liberal Yankees] say we shall submit to your construction. We shall do it if you can make us, but not otherwise or in any other manner. That is settled. You may call it secession, or you may call it revolution; but there is a big fact standing before you ready to oppose you. That fact is freemen with arms in their hands. The cry of the Union will not disperse them; we have passed that point. They demand equal rights; you had better heed the demand." — ROBERT A. TOOMBS OF GEORGIA, LAST ADDRESS IN U.S. SENATE, 1861

THE SOUTH FOLLOWED THE FOUNDING FATHERS

☛ "Statesmanlike wisdom spoke in the contention of [Daniel] Webster that the Constitution had created . . . a single Federal State, complete in itself, enacting legislation which was the supreme law of the land. It may, nevertheless, be doubted whether this was the doctrine upon which the Union was founded. It seems impossible to deny that the argument of [South Carolina Senator Robert Y.] Hayne contains much more nearly the sentiment of 1787-89. In seceding in 1860-61 the South resumed most naturally the methods of 1788. . . . As the whole country acted then, so did South Carolina and her companion States act now in the momentous winter of 1860-61.

. . . It is impossible to believe that what was done lacked the substantial support of the people. That secession was the project of the leading classes in the South is not to be doubted; but the voting population of the Southern States was in a sense the most political in the world, the least likely to follow blindly because most deeply interested in politics. It could be managed by its leaders only because it was so thoroughly homogeneous, only because it so entirely understood and sympathized with their point of view. If some were moved against their judgment, very few were moved against their principles." — WOODROW WILSON, 1893

MORE PROOF THAT THE SOUTH DID NOT FIGHT OVER SLAVERY

☛ "Learn . . . a lesson from the rank and file of the Confederate army. Commence with the peerless Lee, commander in chief. Did he not free all his slaves before the war began? Is it not known that Gen. Albert Sidney Johnston never owned a slave? Yet he sacrificed his life in the battle of Shiloh for the cause of the South and the Constitution. (Yes, I mean the cause of the one was that of the other.) General [William M.] Browne, a member of the staff of Jefferson Davis, never owned a slave. Stonewall Jackson also opposed slavery, yet fighting in behalf of the constitutional South he received his death wound at Chancellorsville. Other leaders could be named, but what is the use? May I not also inform you that eighty per cent of the Confederate army owned no slaves? Do these facts teach that the South fought to enslave a race?" — JOHN ANDERSON RICHARDSON, 1919

MEET THE AUTHOR-EDITOR

NEO-VICTORIAN SCHOLAR LOCHLAINN SEABROOK, a descendant of the families of Alexander Hamilton Stephens, John Singleton Mosby, Edmund Winchester Rucker, and William Giles Harding, is a 7th generation Kentuckian and one of the most prolific and widely read writers in the world today. Known by literary critics as the "new Shelby Foote" and the "American Robert Graves," and by his fans as the "Voice of the Traditional South," he is a recipient of the United Daughters of the Confederacy's prestigious Jefferson Davis Historical Gold Medal. A lifelong writer, the Sons of Confederate Veterans member has authored and edited books ranging in topics from history, politics, science, religion, astronomy, military, and biography, to nature, music, humor, gastronomy, alternative health, genealogy, and the paranormal; books that his readers describe as "game changers," "transformative," and "life altering."

One of the world's most popular and esteemed living historians, he is a 17th generation Southerner of Appalachian heritage who descends from dozens of patriotic Revolutionary War soldiers and Confederate soldiers from Kentucky, Tennessee, North Carolina, and Virginia. Also a history, wildlife, and nature preservationist, he began life as a child prodigy, later transforming into an archetypal Renaissance Man. Besides being an accomplished and well respected author-historian and Bible authority, he is also a Kentucky Colonel, eagle scout, screenwriter, nature, wildlife, and landscape photographer, videographer, artist, graphic designer, songwriter (3,000 songs), film composer, multi-instrument musician, vocalist, session player, music producer, genealogist, former history museum docent, and a former ranch hand, zookeeper, and wrangler.

Currently Seabrook is the author and editor of nearly 100 adult and children's books (a total of 27,000 pages and 13,000,000 words) that have earned him accolades from around the globe. He holds the world record for writing the most books on Southern icon Nathan Bedford Forrest: 12. His works, which have sold on every continent except Antarctica, have introduced hundreds of thousands to vital facts that have been left out of our mainstream books. He has been endorsed internationally by leading experts, museum curators, award-winning historians, bestselling authors, celebrities, filmmakers, noted scientists, well regarded educators, TV show hosts and producers, renowned military artists, esteemed heritage organizations, and distinguished academicians of all races, creeds, and colors.

Of northern, western, and central European ancestry, he is the 6th great-grandson of the Earl of Oxford and a descendant of European royalty through his Kentucky father and West Virginia mother. His modern day cousins include: Johnny Cash, Elvis Presley, Lisa Marie Presley, Billy Ray and Miley Cyrus, Patty Loveless, Tim McGraw, Lee Ann Womack, Dolly Parton, Pat Boone, Naomi, Wynonna, and Ashley Judd, Ricky Skaggs, the Sunshine Sisters, Martha Carson, Chet Atkins, Patrick J. Buchanan, Cindy Crawford, Bertram Thomas Combs (Kentucky's 50th governor), Edith Bolling (second wife of President Woodrow Wilson), Andy Griffith, Riley Keough, George C. Scott, Robert Duvall, Reese Witherspoon, Lee Marvin, Rebecca Gayheart, and Tom Cruise.

A constitutionalist and avid outdoorsman and gun rights advocate, Seabrook is the author of the international blockbuster, *Everything You Were Taught About the Civil War is Wrong, Ask a Southerner!* He lives with his wife and family in beautiful historic Middle Tennessee, the heart of the Old South.

For more information on author Mr. Seabrook visit
LochlainnSeabrook.com

Our Heroes

This montage recreates an imaginary meeting of nine of the South's most famous and influential commanders. President Jefferson Davis, seated at lower left, is surrounded by, from left to right: General Ambrose Powell Hill, General John Bell Hood, Major General Jeb Stuart, General Stonewall Jackson, General Robert E. Lee, General James Longstreet, General Joseph Eggleston Johnston and General Pierre Gustave Toutant Beauregard. This respectful Yankee artwork was published in Albany, New York, in 1885.

If you enjoyed this book you will be interested in Colonel Seabrook's popular related titles:

- Abraham Lincoln Was a Liberal, Jefferson Davis Was a Conservative
- Everything You Were Taught About the Civil War is Wrong, Ask a Southerner!
- All We Ask is to be Let Alone: The Southern Secession Fact Book
- Everything You Were Taught About American Slavery is Wrong, Ask a Southerner!
- Confederate Flag Facts: What Every American Should Know About Dixie's Southern Cross
- Lincoln's War: The Real Cause, the Real Winner, the Real Loser

Available from Sea Raven Press and wherever fine books are sold

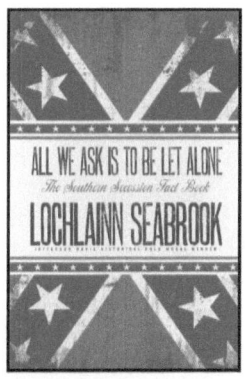
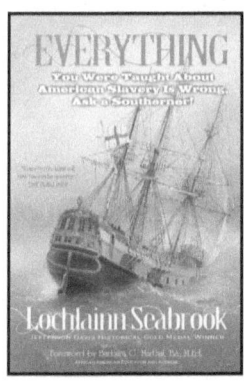

ALL OF OUR BOOK COVERS ARE AVAILABLE AS 11" X 17" COLOR POSTERS, SUITABLE FOR FRAMING

SeaRavenPress.com